Politics in
Britain

POLITICS IN BRITAIN

Bruce F. Norton

CQ PRESS

A Division of
Congressional Quarterly Inc.
Washington, D.C.

CQ Press
1255 22nd Street, NW, Suite 400
Washington, DC 20037

Phone: 202-729-1900; toll-free, 1-866-4CQ-PRESS (1-866-427-7737)

Web: www.cqpress.com

Cover design: Kimberly Glyder Design

♾ The paper used in this publication exceeds the requirements of the American National Standard for Information Sciences—Permanence of Paper for Printed Library Materials, ANSI Z39.48-1992.

Printed and bound in the United States of America

11   10   09   08   07   1   2   3   4   5

Library of Congress Cataloging-in-Publication Data

Norton, Bruce F.
  Politics in Britain / Bruce F. Norton.
      p. cm.
  Includes bibliographical references and index.
  ISBN-13: 978-0-87187-924-0 (alk. paper)
  ISBN-10: 0-87187-924-7 (alk. paper)
  1. Great Britain—Politics and government—Textbooks.   I. Title.

  JN175.N67 2006
  320.441—dc22

                                                     2006035967

To
Elizabeth

and
Professor Robert Rienow
(1907–1989)

Contents

Tables, Figures, and Text Boxes

Figures

Speaking of . . . Britain

Acronyms and Abbreviations

ACE	agency chief executive
AMS	additional member system
ASH	Action on Smoking and Health
BBC	British Broadcasting Corporation
BENELUX	Belgium, the Netherlands, and Luxembourg
BMA	British Medical Association
BSE	bovine spongiform encephalopathy, or mad cow disease
C&AG	comptroller and auditor general
CAP	Common Agricultural Policy
CASE	Campaign for the Advancement of State Education
CBI	Confederation of British Industry
CCA	Conservative constituency association
CCT	compulsory competitive tendering
CLP	constituency Labour Party
COREPER	Committee of Permanent Representatives
CPA	comprehensive performance assessment
CPRS	Central Policy Review Staff
CRD	Conservative Research Department
CRE	Commission for Racial Equality
DfEE	Department for Education and Employment
DGs	directorates general
DUP	Democratic Unionist Party
EC	European Community
ECHR	European Court of Human Rights
ECJ	European Court of Justice
ECSC	European Coal and Steel Community
EDM	early day motion
EEC	European Economic Community
EFTA	European Free Trade Association
EM	explanation memorandum
EMU	Economic and Monetary Union
EOC	Equal Opportunities Commission
EU	European Union
EURATOM	European Atomic Energy Community
FCO	Foreign and Commonwealth Office
FMI	Financial Management Initiative

FoE	Friends of the Earth
FPTP	first-past-the-post
GMT	Greenwich Mean Time
HRA	Human Rights Act of 1998
IRA	Irish Republican Army
JAC	Judicial Appointments Commission
JPC	Joint Policy Committee
LPSA	local public service agreement
MAFF	Ministry of Agriculture, Fisheries and Food
MEP	member of the European Parliament
MMSP	multimember, simple-plurality system
MP	member of Parliament
MSP	member of the Scottish parliament
NAO	National Audit Office
NatCen	National Centre for Social Research
NATO	North Atlantic Treaty Organization
NEC	National Executive Committee
NEDC	National Economic Development Council
NFU	National Farmers Union
NPF	National Policy Forum
OFFA	Office for Fair Access
OMOV	One Man One Vote
PEB	party election broadcast
PLP	Parliamentary Labour Party
PMB	private member bill
PMQs	Prime Minister's Questions
PPERA	Political Parties, Elections and Referendums Act
PPS	parliamentary private secretary
PR	proportional representation
QBD	Queen's Bench Division
QMV	qualified majority voting
quagos	quasi-autonomous government organizations
qualgos	quasi-autonomous local government organizations
quangos	quasi-autonomous non-governmental organizations
RDA	regional development agency
RSPB	Royal Society for the Protection of Birds
SEA	Single European Act
SI	statutory instrument
SMSP	single-member, simple-plurality system
SNP	Scottish National Party
STV	single transferable vote
TUC	Trades Union Congress
UK	United Kingdom
UKREP	United Kingdom Permanent Representation

UNITED KINGDOM

Shetland Islands

ATLANTIC OCEAN

Orkney Islands

Hebrides

SCOTLAND

● Aberdeen

North Sea

● Edinburgh

● Glasgow

NORTHERN IRELAND

● Belfast

● Newcastle upon Tyne

ENGLAND

Irish Sea

● Manchester
Liverpool ●

● Leeds
● Sheffield
Nottingham ●

IRELAND

● Leicester

● Birmingham

WALES

● Cardiff

★ **London**

● Bristol

● Brighton

Isle of Wight

English Channel

BELGIUM

● Plymouth

Isles of Scilly

Channel Islands

FRANCE

50   100 Mi

50   100 Km

Preface

Prefaces are alcoves found at the entrance of books where authors position themselves to say something about what they have written, throw modesty to the wind as they explain why everyone should read their works, and acknowledge the debts they have accumulated while writing them. They are also places where authors may free themselves from the sometimes leaden constraints of formal writing by using the "I" word and possibly even embracing the occasional contraction—all of which are liberties I've joyously taken here.

This is a book about contemporary British politics, which means it's also a book about historic transitions and dynamic changes in the institutions, character, and conduct of British politics and in the behavior of Britain's political leaders and the electorate. Political junkies who have visited Britain frequently over the past twenty to thirty years, or anyone who has lived and taught there as I have over the past two decades, can't help but be struck by the enormity of these changes. Who would have thought thirty years ago that Britons today would have enshrined in their law something equivalent to a bill of rights? Or who would have thought that as recently as 2006 the Government's chief lawyer, the attorney general, would argue, as he did that autumn, that Britain should seriously consider adopting a codified constitution?

The changes, especially those introduced from the early 1980s onward, have been substantial: from the ideology-driven changes of the Thatcher years through the relatively ideology-free changes of the Blair years, from the institutional changes of the 1980s and much of the 1990s through the constitutional changes of the late 1990s and early years of the twenty-first century. Only by dropping back occasionally to explore briefly Britain's political past can the reader acquire a fuller understanding of Britain's political present.

With that thought in mind, chapter 1 of *Politics in Britain* takes the reader back in time to the building of the British nation by examining political, historical, economic, cultural, and geographic factors that contributed to making Britain British—all factors that help explain how it was possible for the English, Welsh, Scots, and Northern Irish to be joined together and coexist as one nation and become a viable political union. We then shift to the present in a chapter about the body politic. This chapter offers glimpses into various aspects of Britain and British life—in particular, ethnic Britain, religious Britain, and social Britain—in an effort to provide some insight into the lives of the nation's sixty million subjects, and later in this chapter, into how the governed feel about the monarchy, their form of government, and those who represent them.

A chapter on the constitution is next. One might well ask: what constitution? Unlike the U.S. Constitution, the UK's constitution is not actually codified and can't be found in the local library, but that doesn't mean it doesn't exist. Britain does indeed have a constitution, and we explore its chief features and provisions. However, what do we make of it when we learn that the Queen herself admits to finding it "puzzling"? Would she, and others, find it less puzzling were the constitution codified, and if they did, shouldn't Britain start the process of codifying it?

Two chapters on political parties follow. Chapter 4 explains why British politics is party politics, guides the reader through various forms of party government, and explores three successive periods in the politics of party governance: consensus politics, politics as usual, and convergence politics. Chapter 5 explores the ways political parties organize and operate in Parliament and how they function beyond it.

Parties purport to represent the interests of the people, but the three largest parties in combination have fewer paid-up members than the Royal Society for the Protection of Birds, a pressure group. What does that say about political parties—and pressure groups? It's tempting to conclude from this that the public has more faith in the latter than the former in representing their interests. But political parties represent more than single issues. Moreover, they do more than represent. Pressure groups nevertheless play vital roles in public policy making, and to discover what those roles are, in chapter 6 we explore the three Ts of pressure groups—their types, targets, and tactics. What's more, as we trace their targets and tactics, we discover telltale signs about where political power lies in Britain.

One of many things that parties do that pressure groups almost never do is contest elections, a subject which, along with campaigns for elections, is taken up in chapter 7. Voters today are expected to turn out to elect politicians to an expanded array of newly created positions. But ironically, expanding the number of elective positions has not expanded the number of voters who have participated in this democratic exercise. Of particular concern is the dramatic drop in the number who voted in the 2001 and 2005 general elections. There are several plausible reasons for this drop, and they are explored in chapter 7. Those who do go to the polls use one or more of six electoral systems in different elections; however, not all of them produce results that are consistent with standards of equity and proportionality. The system most vulnerable to criticism is the one used to elect members of Parliament. What are the reasons for this criticism, and why, soon after Labour came to power with a resolve to reform this system, did it decide to abandon its pledge? The answers to these questions become clear by the end of this chapter.

Chapter 8 is devoted to Parliament. We explore three functions of Parliament that are generic to many Western legislatures: representation, lawmaking, and oversight of the executive. The party of Government in the House of Commons, the elected chamber, has staged several rebellions since the early part of the twenty-first century, and its select committees have become much more energetic in overseeing the work of the executive. In addition, the unelected chamber, the House of Lords, plays an enormously important role as a revising chamber, in recent years especially, much to the consternation and frustration of Conservative and Labour Governments alike. Despite this surge of activity, the reader is reminded that government is "not government *by* Parliament, but government *through* Parliament," and Parliament can't be anything more than that in Britain's parliamentary form of government.

Drawn from Parliament are the prime minister and the cabinet, subjects that are dealt with in chapter 9. What has prompted prime ministers to adopt a less prime ministerial and more presidential style of leadership in recent years? Moreover, what impact does such a presidential style of leadership have on the cabinet and its work? Is cabinet government no longer viable in British politics, and if not, why not? Before answering that question, the reader is encouraged to explore in this chapter what role the cabinet played in the Blair Government's decision to go to war in Iraq in 2003.

Administering the programs and policies of government is the subject of the two chapters that follow. Chapter 10 focuses on the departments and executive agencies that are commissioned to deliver the promises the party in power made in the election campaign. One key part of this chapter deals with ministerial responsibility, a convention of the constitution that, for a variety of reasons, has become so weakened that it is questionable whether it can any longer be regarded as a bedrock of the constitution. The next chapter examines devolved governments—local governments in the four nations and devolved assemblies and executives in Scotland, Wales, and Northern Ireland. Why is it that, as one scholar put it, local government is "close to being no longer local, and to being no longer government"? Apart from local government, why is there such asymmetry in the powers and functions devolved to Scotland and Wales? Why has there been on-again/off-again devolution for Northern Ireland since the late 1990s? And why is England the only one of the four nations that has no devolved government? These issues are addressed and answers provided in chapter 11.

Until recently, the subject "Law, Courts, and Judges," the title for chapter 12, was given little attention in treatments of British politics. The most likely reason for this inattention was that courts and judges made few decisions that could be considered political. But that all changed when judges were legally required to nullify British law whenever it contravened European Community law and to use the newly enacted Human Rights Act as a reference point for any decision involving a human rights issue. As a result of these and other developments, which are described in this chapter, in no previous period have judges been more involved in shaping the policies of the nation.

The probable loss of British sovereignty concerned many when Britain contemplated becoming a member of the European Union, and it concerns even more today, years after the country became a member in 1973. British membership also has raised questions about other issues central to democratic decision making. These issues are addressed in chapter 13. First, however, the reader is introduced to some background on Britain's relations with the rest of Europe and to the ways in which Britain works alongside other member nations in the governance of the European Union.

Politics in Britain is written for anyone having a curiosity and interest in the subject. To that end—and seeing as I've had a foot on either side of the Atlantic for the past two decades—I've written the book with both British and non-British readers in mind, making no assumptions that my readers have any prior knowledge of the British political system. I hope the reader will find it clearly written, free of the impenetrable jargon that is invariably introduced in academic writing, and easy to understand. The questions raised by American students studying in London in my British Politics and the European Union seminar helped me clarify the central issues in this book, as did a steady stream of guest speakers drawn from all corners of the British political community in approximately eight hundred seminars over eleven years. Many years of university teaching convinced me of the value of using examples to make a point, to clarify it, or to enhance it, and it is that thought that prompted me to deploy the examples I have used in this work. Other features, including nearly fifty tables and figures, similarly help present information and ideas effectively and efficiently, and should also help convey what's most interesting and vital about British politics to Brits and non-Britons alike. "Speaking of . . . Britain" boxes feature the best in British journalism and scholarship on the UK and focus on contemporary issues, giving students a sense of the nature and flavor of the most pressing debates. The conclusions found at the end of each chapter are comprehensive and yet to the point, and I hope they will stimulate readers to think further about what has been written. Finally, I hope I have spared the reader from having to wade through massive numbers of pages. I've kept my eye on the page numbers as I have proceeded with the thought that a tome too heavy is often a tome too heavy to read.

Acknowledgments

Having said something about what this book is about, I move on to acknowledge my debts to others. I first thank friends who have been a source of encouragement throughout this project—especially Alan and Sheila Thompson, Deip and Joan Guha, Rosemary Williams, John and Fenella Davis, B. J. Rahn, Donald and Sheila Anderson, Tim Kidd, Barry Clarke, Roger and Mary Cooke, Alan and Hazel Jacobs, Julie Short, Michael Norton, Catherine Gentle, Daniel Stephenson, Ingun Borg, Eugenie and Bernard Lambert, and Janice and Brian Capstick. Second, I'm deeply grateful to two friends and former colleagues, Daniel Snowman and Richard Tames, for the thoroughness with which they reviewed and commented on rough drafts of some of the early chapters. Third, I'm beholden to Mathias Albert, Bielefeld University; Gavin Drewry, Royal Holloway, University of London; and Anthony M. Messina, University of Notre Dame, as well as a handful of anonymous reviewers, every one of whom made suggestions and comments I found helpful. Fourth, I offer my long-lasting thanks to Elise Frasier and Charisse Kiino—cracking good editors with CQ Press who must have been born with smiles on their faces. I'm indebted to them not only for their smiles (which they have kept), but also for their advice, encouragement, and patience. My heartfelt thanks, too, to Dwain Smith and Allison McKay for their editorial assistance and to Lorna Notsch for her tireless work as this book's project editor.

And now, saving the best for last, I'm grateful to my wife Elizabeth, who represents the Anglo part of the Anglo-American special relationship we formed some years ago. She was present at the book's creation—and long before that—and, although she never told me this, there were times when I suspect she wondered whether I would ever emerge from my study. It is to Elizabeth that I affectionately dedicate this book. There is a second dedication as well—to Professor Robert Rienow, who sparked my interest in European politics when I was an undergraduate student all those many years ago.

Bruce F. Norton
Grange-in-Borrowdale
15 December 2006

1

Nation Building: Making Britain British

It took nearly four hundred years for the United Kingdom (UK) to form in the way that it is known today. The first step in its formation was taken when Wales was joined to England in the sixteenth century. Scotland was added in the eighteenth century, and Ireland in the nineteenth. In 1922, the boundaries were drawn a final time when Ireland—with the exception of six counties in the north called Ulster—left the UK and became the Irish Free State and later the Republic of Ireland. From 1922 to the present, England, Wales, and Scotland have made up what is called Great Britain (or Britain) and when the reference includes Ulster, the formal name is the United Kingdom of Great Britain and Northern Ireland. Less formally, the four nations are called the British Isles.

The instruments that joined Wales, Scotland, and Ireland to England were acts of union. In each case, however, "union" was a euphemism for an event that inspired few celebrations among the Welsh, Scots, and Irish. As each act was signed, some saw them as marriages of convenience, among them the English journalist Daniel Defoe who, when Scotland was joined to England, observed: "A firmer union of policy with less union of affection has hardly been known in the whole world."[1]

Before Wales, Scotland, and Northern Ireland signed their respective acts of union, each had territory with reasonably stable boundaries, a people who dwelled in the territory, the rudiments of a political system along with a corps of leaders, and a system of laws. In other words, each had already begun to acquire the classic trappings of a state. In addition, new shoots of nationhood were starting to break through the soil. Although each nation was far from culturally homogeneous when it came into the union, most who lived within the nations' respective boundaries communicated in the same language, were expected to obey the same laws, shared the same

1

historical memories, often worshipped at the same altar, and feared the same invaders (who were sometimes English). What chance was there, then, that three relatively disparate nations, each having its own historical roots and experiences—and each its own animus against England—could be molded into one nation, a British nation, and that its people could be made to feel British? If such were possible, would the English lose their English-ness, the Welsh their Welsh-ness, the Scots their Scottish-ness, and the Irish their Irish-ness? And if they did not, how could they be any one of these and also British?

In time, it became clear to the people of the four nations that they had more to gain economically, politically, and socially by acting in common cause than acting separately. Protestantism, the predominant religion of England, Wales, and much of Scotland, gave the people of three of the four nations a common cultural base. Going to war with Catholic France, their enemy of many generations, generated fear of invasion and, later, pride of military victory. In the meantime, the expansion of markets at home and throughout the empire beyond produced economic growth, material goods, profits, and jobs. No sooner had the Napoleonic Wars ended than Britain was linked increasingly by advances in transportation and communication. Monarchs became personal symbols of the new nation-state, and political reforms brought people directly into the mainstream of political life. All of these contributed enormously to nation building—to making Britain British.

The Protestant Ascendancy

Midway through the sixteenth century, most in England and Wales and many in Scotland developed an unswerving allegiance to Protestantism and harbored a deep-seated aversion to Catholicism. These feelings had their origins in the Protestant Reformation, after Henry VIII (reign: 1509–1547) quarrelled with the pontiff of Rome in the 1530s over his matrimonial status. When Pope Clement VII refused to annul Henry's marriage to Catherine of Aragon to free him to marry Anne Boleyn, Henry renounced the pope's authority, established the Church of England with himself as its head, appointed Thomas Cranmer as the Archbishop of Canterbury, sought and received from Cranmer an annulment of his marriage to Catherine, and then married Anne. Later, Henry's daughter Elizabeth I (reign: 1558–1603) agreed to the Church of England's Thirty-nine Articles of Religion, and she became Supreme Governor of the Church, making her (and every monarch since) *fidei defensor,* or defender of the faith. In 1570 Pope Pius VI excommunicated Elizabeth, an act that prompted Parliament to approve laws that imposed the death penalty on Catholic priests who said mass and on priests who returned to England from their travels abroad.

It was this allegiance to Protestantism that so emphatically shaped a British identity from the sixteenth through the eighteenth centuries and set the English, Welsh, and Scots apart from the Catholic powers of Europe.

Although doctrinal disputes led to the rise of different sects of Protestantism, a rabid fear of Catholicism persuaded the people of these three nations to close ranks by minimizing their sectarian differences and embracing a broadly Protestant culture. After all, the British were told, it was a Protestant God who watched over them, and this was what they felt they earnestly needed, especially at a time when Catholics were reportedly committing atrocities in nearby lands. From Sunday sermons, churchgoers learned about Catholic France's expulsion of Protestant Huguenots in 1685, Catholic Spain's longstanding persecution of Protestants at the hand of its Inquisition, and the Catholic German states' relentless discrimination against Protestants. It was only a matter of time, some feared, before such acts would spread to their own shores.

Adding to this fear were Protestant publicists, chief among them John Foxe and John Bunyan. Foxe wrote the *Book of Martyrs,* a work replete with grisly tales and graphic illustrations of the alleged suffering of Protestant martyrs during the brief reign of Henry VIII's eldest daughter, the Catholic Queen Mary (1553–1558). Foxe's book first appeared in 1563 and was distributed widely as late as the eighteenth century. John Bunyan's allegory, *The Pilgrim's Progress,* celebrated the efforts of stout-hearted Protestants who persevered against Catholics, among others, as they made their pilgrimages to heaven. Published originally in two parts, in 1678 and 1684, this book was still sought after in England one hundred years later, when its fifty-seventh edition rolled off the presses in 1789. Scottish and Welsh presses, meanwhile, published their own editions, with Welsh-language editions appearing as early as 1688 and as late as 1790.[2]

Reinforcing the anti-Catholic prejudice unleashed by the works of Protestant polemicists were widespread reports of disaffected Catholics plotting to assassinate Protestant monarchs. The most celebrated of these were the Gunpowder Plot of 1605 and the Popish Plot of 1678. Distressed that yet another Protestant, James I (reign: 1603–1625), had come to the throne, a band of Catholic militants devised a plan to kill the King by blowing up the House of Lords when he appeared to open a new session of parliament. The plot, however, was foiled when thirty-six barrels of gunpowder and Guy Fawkes, one of the conspirators, were discovered the night before the planned event. Whereas the Gunpowder Plot was verified, the Popish Plot was apocryphal. Jesuit priests, it was claimed, were scheming to burn London, kill Protestants, and assassinate the Protestant monarch Charles II (reign: 1660–1685) so that his younger brother James, a Catholic, could succeed him as king. Or so went the rumor spread by Titus Oates, a failed Anglican clergyman. Today this tale is known to have been nothing more than a rumor. But in that day, the rumor was thought to be true, Titus Oates was hailed a national hero, and thirty-five alleged conspirators were executed.

Unfazed by these events and other rumoured plots, Charles was determined to uphold his brother's right to succeed him. This he did by dissolving an angry Parliament after it passed a bill to exclude James from the throne.

3

When Parliament passed the same bill again in two successive sessions, the King resorted to the same tactic twice more. As these skirmishes between the palace and Parliament intensified, the prospect of a Catholic assuming the throne appeared all but certain. And then it happened. In 1685, Charles died, and his brother succeeded him as James II.

At first, James (reign: 1685–1688) received widespread support from his subjects. Despite his Catholicism, they felt they could count on him to uphold laws enacted to sustain the primacy of Protestantism. Uphold these laws he did—until he demanded that the English and Scottish parliaments repeal some of them and then ruled by royal edict when they refused. Midway through 1688, news spread that James had sired a son. At that point, popular support for the King, which by then had all but disappeared, transformed into popular outrage as the public awakened to the idea that Protestant Britain would be governed by a Catholic king well into the next century. So infuriated was the public by the autumn of 1688 that even the military refused to support James. As anti-Catholic riots erupted in London and elsewhere in England, and the Protestant William of Orange and his forces from the Netherlands approached London to seize the throne, James "dethroned himself," as one historian put it,[3] fleeing with his family to France. A few months later, Parliament offered the throne to James's eldest daughter Mary, a Protestant, but in reality, to her Dutch husband William of Orange, the grandson of Charles I.

Mid-eighteenth century commentators were fond of calling the events of 1688 the "Glorious Revolution," although it was not a revolution in the ordinary sense. There was no denying, however, that it was glorious. It was certainly glorious for William III (reign: 1688–1702) and Mary II (reign: 1688–1694), but for William especially, for he was a staunch defender of Protestantism in his native Netherlands and indeed in all of Europe. And with a Protestant presence on the throne, it was glorious for most of their new subjects as well.

Yet as events would soon demonstrate, the threat of the return of a Catholic monarch could not be discounted. To prevent this from happening, a provision of the Bill of Rights passed in 1689 that barred Catholics from the throne. That is why William and Mary became the first monarchs ever to swear at their coronation that they would rule in accord with the "true profession of the gospel, and the Protestant reformed religion established by law."[4] Several years later, with William widowed and childless, concern mounted that the Stuart dynasty would run its course with the death of his successor, his sister-in-law Anne, who was also childless. With support growing in the Scottish Highlands for the return to the throne of the deposed Stuart king James II, Parliament lost no time in passing the Act of Settlement in 1701. This law stipulated that a Catholic or one married to a Catholic was "forever uncapable to inherit, possess, or enjoy the crown and government of this realm."[5] Moreover, it established that upon Anne's death the Protestant House of Hanover would be the successor dynasty and that Anne's distant cousin from Hanover would follow her to the throne.

The Protestant ascendancy made a long-lasting contribution to nation building. It gave a common identity to most who lived in England and Wales and to many who lived in Scotland. One historian went so far as to say that Protestantism was "the foundation that made the invention of Great Britain possible."[6] By 1702, however, William, who had valiantly restored Protestantism to the throne fourteen years before, was in poor health; relations between England and Scotland had sunk to a low point; and having just finished fighting France for nine long years, England feared it would soon have to do so again. Given these events, could nation building be sustained?

Fear, Relief, and Pride

If the Protestant ascendancy cultivated nation building, it was more than fifty years of grueling wars with France that fortified it. In the period from 1689 to 1815, the English, Welsh, and Scots fought the French in six wars, and as they did so, they saw themselves as Protestants locked in a struggle for survival against a Catholic power of colossal proportions. Living on an island with six thousand miles of mostly unguarded coastline, the populace knew how vulnerable to attack they were. People also realized that were the enemy to advance on them, they might not know it until it was too late, for if word about war spread at all, it was patchy and traveled slowly. Many lived in fear. Indeed, fear became part of the emotional make-up of the peoples of the three nations. In time, so did relief and pride—relief as one war and then another spared them from defeat, and pride as news spread of their country's victories over France on land and sea. Fear, relief, and pride helped bond the people of the three nations together emotionally. One of these emotions—fear—bonded them together physically as well, for Scotland during one war and Ireland during another were joined to England and Wales out of fear that France would use either as a staging area to attack England and Wales.

The Nine Years' War (1689–1697), the War of the Spanish Succession (1702–1713), and the War of the Austrian Succession (1743–1748) were the first three wars waged against the French by a united Britain. These three were in a class of their own because they were fought not only to maintain the balance of power on the continent but also to stop France from insisting that the deposed James II (or one of his heirs) had a legitimate claim to the English throne. In time, however, it became clear that Louis XIV (reign: 1643–1715) had more in mind than sympathizing with a deposed monarch. Siding with James was part of a master plan to bring Britain under French control—and James's flight to France in 1688 played right into Louis's hands. James was welcomed with open arms; Louis gave him asylum and encouraged him to recruit troops to help him take back the throne by force, if necessary. He even promised him men and materiel, because if all went according to plan, Louis could rule England and Wales through James.

Fortified with French troops and Louis's money, James ventured to Catholic Ireland to recruit troops there. He planned to travel next to the British mainland to enlist additional troops in the Scottish Highlands, where many of his Catholic supporters lived, and then to sweep through England and on to London. But James never got beyond Ireland, for William and his thirty-six thousand men met him and his recruits on the field of battle there in 1690 and gave them a severe thrashing. Louis in the meantime was having more success than James, for while James's forces were losing to William's, Louis's navy won control of the English Channel after inflicting heavy losses on a combined English-Dutch force. It took two years for the English to regain control of the channel. This meant that for two years fear gripped the land. The populace never knew when French troops would be put ashore to plunder and pillage. "The whole nation," wrote a contemporary public records diarist, is "now exceedingly alarmed by the French fleet braving our coast even to the very Thames mouth." [7]

The duration of this war gave it its name—the Nine Years' War—although the English thought it more appropriately named the War of English Succession. When the Treaty of Ryswick was drawn up in 1697, Louis's attention was drawn to a provision dealing with succession. It required him to recognize William as king and to abandon his support of James or his descendants. He agreed. But would he keep his word?

Louis reneged four years later, long before age could discolor the parchment on which the treaty was written. The year was 1701. James had just died, and Louis lost no time in insisting that James's Catholic son, James Edward Stuart, be accepted as the rightful heir to the throne. Moreover, Louis did this a mere three months after Parliament passed the Act of Settlement barring Catholics from the throne. Infuriated by Louis's claim, William declared war on France in 1702. He was determined to settle the dynastic quarrel he had with his old nemesis once and for all, but also to stop Louis from fusing the Spanish and French crowns and forging a vast new empire that could threaten Britain's security.

This new war, called the War of the Spanish Succession (1702–1713), provoked as much fear of invasion as the last one. Before long, however, reports from the fields of battle had a calming effect. Word quickly spread of the victories of the English, Welsh, and Scots over the French, in particular their victories at Blenheim in 1704 and Ramillies in 1706, and later of England's growing reputation as a naval power. Such reports gave rise to a growing sense of security and surging national pride.

That was the good news. There was some disturbing news as well, news that reached Anne shortly after she became queen following William's death in 1702. Unrest was brewing in Scotland. Its origin can be found in events that occurred at opposite ends of the seventeenth century—in 1603 and 1689. In 1603, King James VI of Scotland became James I of England following the death of his cousin, Elizabeth I, and called himself "King of Great Britain." Yet such a dynastic union, that is, a one-sovereign-for-two-countries arrangement, did not mean that the two countries functioned as one. Indeed, they remained separate and independent.

Matters became somewhat more complicated in 1689, when William and Mary agreed to abide by the Bill of Rights. Their agreement meant that they were legally accountable to the English parliament. But being accountable to the English parliament when there was no comparable legal arrangement with Scotland's caused some Scottish leaders to fear that England's affairs would take precedence over Scotland's and that Scotland's independence would eventually be sapped.

The relationship between the two countries really started to sour in 1703, when the Scottish parliament passed two measures. The first put England on notice that all foreign policy decisions affecting Scotland after Anne's death required the Scottish parliament's approval. The second asserted Scotland's right to choose its own sovereign, which meant that the one-hundred-year-old dynastic union between Scotland and England might well dissolve. In the meantime, the Scottish Highlanders had not lost their enthusiasm for James II's son James Edward, and France continued to insist that he, not Anne, should be regarded as the rightful sovereign of England and Scotland. Anne's fear was that Scotland's differences with England—exacerbated by France's meddling to boost the Highlanders' support for James Edward—could lead to Scotland's withdrawing its troops from the struggle with France. Worse still, France might persuade the Scots to allow France to station troops on Scottish soil, thus giving the French a significant staging area from which to attack England.

In an attempt to allay her fears, Anne persuaded Scottish leaders to agree to a treaty joining Scotland to England. This of course meant that Scotland would lose its independence, and many Scots recoiled from the idea. Eventually, however, the sweeteners that England wrote into the treaty were too appetizing for most members of the Scottish parliament to pass up, and in 1707 the Act of Union of "one united kingdom of Great Britain" was agreed to. Scotland retained its legal system, its education system, and its state Presbyterian Church; achieved representation in the English parliament; and acquired access to the markets of England and Wales and England's growing colonies—eighteenth-century Europe's largest free-trade area. Scotland gained economically; but Anne was convinced that England gained more, for now that Scotland was part of Britain, it would not sell out to France.

France did little before the war ended in 1713 to exploit sentiment for James Edward, especially after British ships gave chase off Scotland's east coast to a French fleet equipped with troops and arms destined for his supporters. The relief felt by the populace at the cessation of hostilities was probably not exaggerated by one member of Parliament when he wrote: "In the churches the bells, in the streets the bonfires, and in the windows the illuminations, proclaimed the joy of the people."[8] With the Treaty of Utrecht, the French and Spanish thrones remained separate, and France once again was forced to renounce its support of James II's descendants and to acknowledge the legitimacy of England's sitting monarch.

Thirty years of peace followed, only to be interrupted in 1743 when Britain declared war on France for a third time—this time to stop France from seizing the German states. Called the War of the Austrian Succession (1743–1748), this conflict struck more fear into the hearts of the populace than the previous two because James Edward's son, Charles Edward, and his Highland supporters carried the fight to the heart of England. It started soon after Louis XV (reign: 1715–1774) put a frigate at Charles's disposal. Charles (or Bonnie Prince Charlie, as he was called) landed on Scotland's west coast, recruited a fighting force of between five thousand and ten thousand men, and went on to capture Edinburgh and drive English defenders into the English midlands, terrorizing the populace as his forces proceeded. It was months before the British were able to drive the rebels back into Scotland; after they had done so they humiliated them at the battle of Culloden in 1746. With Culloden, the British destroyed Charles's plans of pressing on to London to claim the throne for his father and dashed Louis's hopes of ruling Britain through a subaltern.

When the Treaty of Aix-la-Chapelle was signed in 1748, France for the third time in as many treaties agreed to recognize the current and future occupants of the throne and to deny support to any who might challenge them. The treaty silenced once and for all France's sixty-year dynastic quarrel with England, and in a brutal campaign British forces stormed through the Highlands of Scotland to silence those known to have sided with Bonnie Prince Charlie.

Eight years later, Britain was drawn into the Seven Years' War (1756–1763) with its archrival. The conflict's precipitating cause was France's capture of Minorca, a British possession in the Mediterranean. Following news of France's conquest, rumors that the French were planning a major invasion of England and Scotland unleashed waves of fear throughout the British mainland. An invasion never materialized, however, and before long, fear gave way to relief and then pride as word spread of Britain's victories over France at sea and on land, in India especially. To dispel the public's fear that France would attack the mainland while Britain was defending its overseas interests, the British navy launched an assault on the port of LeHavre, devastating French transport ships and those under construction.

Thirty years after the conclusion of the Seven Years' War, Britain declared war on France yet again. This was in fact one long twenty-one-year war divided by a thirteen-month interlude that was little more than an armed truce. The first part was the French Revolutionary War (1793–1802); the second, the Napoleonic War (1803–1815). So long were these wars that many men fighting Napoleon Bonaparte at Waterloo in 1815 had not yet been born when their fathers fought the French in that same region two decades before.

In the French Revolutionary War, a fighting force far greater than any that France previously had assembled spread fear among the British populace. Although Britain's naval superiority was an effective deterrent to invasion, its navy could not be ubiquitous, and starting at the end of 1797 the French attempted to invade Ireland three times and Wales once. None of these attempts succeeded, however. On one occasion an invasion force of fourteen thousand carried by thirty-five ships were kept from reaching Ireland's shores by inclement weather. Two other attempts were short lived and inflicted little damage. As for Wales, two thousand French forces were put ashore on its west coast, but vast numbers of Welsh volunteers brought about their surrender after only three days. For weeks after this, any unidentified vessels sighted off the Welsh coast raised the alarm bells.

These four invasions, plus intermittent skirmishes off the coast of Ireland, all occurred in just eight months. Like Scotland years before, this time Ireland was Britain's Achilles heel. England had attempted to impose control over Ireland since the early thirteenth century, but it had had little success until Elizabeth I's reign in the sixteenth century. By the mid-1600s, England exercised even greater control, but certainly not enough to quell the animosities that had grown between the Irish Protestant and Irish Catholic communities or to put an end to the hostilities these animosities sometimes precipitated.

By the end of the 1600s, ill feelings had come to a head. The all-Protestant Irish parliament unleashed a series of laws that stripped Catholics of their religious, economic, and political rights. It was only when Wolfe Tone, a Presbyterian radical, organized the Society of United Irishmen in 1791 to restore these rights that the British parliament persuaded the Irish parliament to repeal the most punitive of these laws. Highest on the society's agenda, however, was making Ireland a republic—something Wolfe Tone knew the British would never agree to. He therefore called upon France to help liberate Ireland—a call that France was more than happy to take.

It was at this point that the Government of William Pitt (the Younger) suspected that a quid pro quo was in the making. The *quid* was France's helping Ireland to cut its ties with Britain; the *quo* was France's reward for doing so—using Ireland as a staging area from which to attack Britain. Acting on its suspicions, the Government quickly proposed to the Irish parliament that Ireland be joined to Britain. At first, this proposal met with howls of derision, but in 1801 most Irish parliamentarians were won over to the Government's side by a combination of cajolery and bribery. Soon after, the Irish parliament was dissolved, and in 1801 an Act of Union made Ireland part of Britain, which in effect put Napoleon on notice that he would have to think twice if he ever considered occupying Ireland and using it to launch attacks against the British mainland.

As it happened, France's attack on the Welsh coast in 1798 was the only time Napoleon succeeded in invading the British mainland, and even then it had limited impact. Four years later, in 1802, the war ended. A peace treaty followed, but it ushered in not a period of reconciliation, but rather a break in hostilities during which France engaged in frenzied preparations for another war. Anticipating the inevitable, Britain too began to mobilize. In 1803, the Napoleonic War began.

The war raged from 1803 to 1815, but it was in the first three years that Britain faced the greatest threat of invasion. The nation had no allies, and

France's efforts were directed toward preparing a massive cross-Channel invasion of Britain. "Let us be masters of the Channel for six hours and we are masters of the world," Napoleon declared two months after he was crowned emperor in 1804.[9] As the months passed, however, Napoleon realized that the Royal Navy's defense of the mainland along the Channel was impregnable. His hopes for invasion faded and then disappeared altogether after he suffered two monumental defeats—the first in 1805, when Admiral Nelson took on a French fleet at Trafalgar; the second ten years later, when the Duke of Wellington brought the war to a conclusion at Waterloo.

Fear, relief, and pride had brought the people of England, Wales, and Scotland closer. War, and a union that now included Ireland, had encouraged them to start thinking of themselves as Britons, something that became increasingly evident when the homeland called them to arms, especially during the French Revolutionary and Napoleonic Wars.

The Call to Arms

Nothing galvanizes people to unite more than a common threat. When British government authorities sounded the call to arms to defend the nation against the threat from France the response was overwhelming. Britain had only twenty-nine thousand individuals in military service at the start of the French Revolutionary and Napoleonic Wars in 1793; when the conflict ended in 1815, the number of military personnel had swollen more than seventeen fold to five hundred thousand. Another four hundred thousand came to serve as volunteers on the home front. All told, this represented between one fifth and one fourth of the adult male population of the British Isles. One half were English, one third were Irish, and one sixth were Scottish.[10]

Recruiting men from all parts of the British Isles presented London with an opportunity to involve the four nations in common cause. Ireland, however, posed a challenge of massive proportions. In the 1790s the island was seething with ferment. On the wrong side of the sectarian divide, its Catholic majority chafed under a system of laws that denied them rights their Protestant countrymen had been granted years before. With Wolfe Tone and his Society of United Irishmen pressing for equal treatment and war with France under way, the Government of William Pitt (the Younger) thought it time to persuade the Irish parliament to change course in its treatment of Catholics.

Ultimately, the Irish parliament repealed the most punitive of the laws when it passed the Catholic Relief Act of 1793. Its timing was unfortunate, however, for soon after, the Irish parliament enacted a compulsory military conscription law. Catholics concluded that being sent off to war was the price they had to pay for winning back their rights. In 1795, Catholic and Protestant radicals, under Wolfe Tone's leadership, organized for insurrection and sought assurances from France to back them in their struggle for an independent Ireland. Three years later, Irish radicals staged a series of insurrections in various parts of Ireland that, with a death toll of an estimated thirty thousand, was "probably the most concentrated episode of violence in Irish history."[11] Resolved now to seal off Ireland from France and restore order to the island, London prepared the formal instruments joining Ireland to Britain in an Act of Union.

It was against this backdrop that the British grappled with the challenge of recruiting the Irish to help them fight the French. A vast majority of propertied Catholics supported the Act of Union of 1800 with the expectation that membership in the United Kingdom would soon lead to a full emancipation of their rights. Ultimately, Irish on all social and economic levels responded to the call to arms, and during the second grueling war in this period, as many as one third of Britain's army was Irish, the vast majority of whom were Catholic.

Recruiting in Scotland, by contrast, posed little challenge. Support for Bonnie Prince Charlie in the Scottish Highlands had all but disappeared following the War of the Austrian Succession (1743–1748). In the Seven Years' War (1756–1763), Britain for the first time recruited massive numbers of Highlanders to fight the French, prompting Prime Minister William Pitt (the Elder) to boast later that he had found "a hardy and intrepid race of men" from "the mountains of the North" who "served with fidelity as they fought with valour."[12] The War of American Independence (1775–1783) that followed provided a further opportunity for Scots to pledge their loyalty, and many did so by flooding into the regular army. Between 1715 and 1739, long before the Seven Years' War, 20 percent of new appointments to the rank of colonel in the British army were Scots (principally from the Lowlands), and so too were 24 percent of new appointments between 1739 and 1763—this despite English prejudice against the Scots.[13] For most Scots, the army offered a clear path to a career and advancement when other options were limited. Toward the close of the Napoleonic War, Scottish and Irish officers outnumbered English officers. The regular army thus had become a vehicle to demonstrate patriotism and even profit from the economic and social advantages that military service offered.

Profiting economically and socially also was among the incentives of those who volunteered to defend their communities. Not all agreed to serve, of course, and not all who served did so out of patriotic fervor. Some sought to escape conscription, others to earn pocket money while receiving training, and still others to avoid reprimands from their employers. Whatever their motives, greater numbers volunteered than had been expected, especially when the threat of invasion increased in the years between 1798 and 1805. The more vulnerable to invasion an area was, the more likely its male inhabitants would volunteer to defend it. Thus, in 1803, an average of 50 percent of men between the ages of seventeen and fifty-five in the seven vulnerable western and southern coast counties of England volunteered, and not out of camaraderie or greed or coercion, but out of fear.

By 1804 fear had penetrated even the rural backwaters of Britain, and greater-than-anticipated numbers came forward to serve in the Home Guard.

Government authorities did not coerce men to serve. Rather, they asked them to serve. They sweetened their requests with promises that the men could serve with friends and relatives from their own village and county. The wartime propaganda of the day encouraged volunteers to see themselves as guardians "of British freedom and to think in terms of Britain as a whole." [14] They were fitted out in impressive uniforms and asked to swear their allegiance to the King and, until 1802, to the Protestant religion. In addition, every volunteer corps was presented with a pennant emblazoned with an emblem of the community or county it defended alongside the emblem of the British nation as a way of linking local loyalty to loyalty to Britain as a whole.

Men from all over Britain, from most walks of life, and from every social class responded to the call to arms. By one historian's account, they "were drawn into military service not just by apprehension but by the excitement of it all, by a pleasurable sense of risk and imminent drama, by the lure of a free, brightly coloured uniform and by the powerful seduction exerted by martial music." [15] And after the wars ended, it was a sense of triumph that contributed more than anything else to making Britons feel British.

Markets and Profits

Although Britain was drawn into war repeatedly between 1756 and 1815, trade and commerce flourished—in spite of war but also because of it, for there were profits to be made from servicing the war machine. All parts of the British Isles were involved in profit making. With the Industrial Revolution in full swing from the second half of the eighteenth century into the nineteenth, the English and Scots built ships of war, the Welsh produced iron, and the English and Welsh mined coal to fire iron foundries for the manufacture of cannons, swords, and muskets. As they assembled the weapons of war, others produced creature comforts for the soldiers: English and Irish wool made up their heavy coats, English looms spun their uniforms, Scottish tanners made their boots, and Irish grain and milk products and Scottish porridge fed them. Not only war, but commerce as well, was a four-nation enterprise.

Wartime was not the only time profits were made. When the guns fell silent, traders and merchants from all parts of the British Isles continued to prosper, unencumbered by customs duties and other trade barriers in the largest free-trade area in Europe. As the boundaries of this free-trade area stretched well beyond Britain to include its fast-growing empire, traders became infatuated with the lure of the even greater prosperity certain to be theirs from tapping the markets that emerged with Britain's acquisition of new lands. "Let's learn to think Imperially/'Twill smooth our path materially." [16] So goes a tongue-in-cheek couplet written by a latter-day critic of the empire. It sums up well the spirit of the age.

Traders, of course, were not the only ones to "think Imperially"; explorers, missionaries, and scientists responded to the siren calls of the empire as well. Still others left Britain altogether to seek fulfillment in various parts of

Britain's vast realm. But above all, it was commerce that attracted the greatest attention, and with fortunes to be made abroad as well as at home, "a cult of commerce," as one scholar put it, "became an increasingly important part of being British." [17]

A broadened sense of patriotism was the inevitable outcome of Britain's expanding empire. After all, it was not the English Empire, but rather the *British* Empire, for those who participated in winning much of it and then fighting to protect it were not just English; they were also Scottish, Welsh, and Irish. All participated in the imperial dream as partners of the English, whether they were Welsh farmers and missionaries, Scottish engineers and doctors, or Irish soldiers and merchants. After Canada and parts of the West Indies, Africa, and India were absorbed into the empire in 1763 as the spoils of the Seven Years' War, the people of the British Isles exulted in Britain's becoming the largest imperial power in Europe and a world power of the first order. Probably none exulted more than Britain's traders, who were eager to exploit the raw materials and markets for their manufactured goods that the enlarged empire yielded. Britain in the second half of the eighteenth century came to be known as "the warehouse and shop window of the world." [18]

The heyday of the British Empire was the nineteenth century, after the British had accumulated even more spoils after struggling with Napoleon for twenty-one years. The empire swelled to unimaginable proportions. Britain now claimed dominion over a quarter of the world's population and huge swathes of territory in Canada, New Zealand, Australia, Africa, Asia, India, and the Caribbean. It was, literally, an empire on which the sun never set.

As early as the eighteenth century, one out of every five families was making its living from trade and the distribution of goods. Britain's traders, its international traders in particular, began to realize how much the government contributed to their undertakings. They looked to it to help create a climate conducive to commercial activity by maintaining civil order and defending the populace against external aggression. Traders and merchants depended on the government to establish at least rudimentary rules and regulations to facilitate commercial and credit transactions within Britain and beyond. When they sought new laws to strengthen their mercantile position, they petitioned members of Parliament and employed lobbyists to put their case before government ministers on a multitude of issues ranging from standardizing weights and measures to improving port facilities to relaxing tariff restrictions. Beyond Britain's shores, they depended on the government to maintain the empire and even extend its imperial reach as their ships plied the seas in search of new possessions to acquire and fresh markets to exploit. Just as important, once they had established their markets, they received the protection of the Royal Navy to fend off foreign predators and provide their merchant ships safe passage on dangerous trade routes as they shipped goods to and from distant parts.

Conversely, the British government appreciated the extent to which British entrepreneurs contributed to the national treasury. From all parts of

Britain, investors did their part to keep the government solvent by extending it credit. In addition, they paid taxes, some of which were enormous. Until the end of the eighteenth century, international traders alone contributed between 60 percent and 70 percent of government receipts.[19]

As the empire's expanding markets provided even greater profits for its traders, and as customs and excise taxes produced a steady stream of revenue for the public treasury, the fruits of the empire became increasingly apparent to the people of the British Isles. As imperial trade expanded and standards of living rose and such exotic imports as tea, sugar, coffee, tobacco, rice, and silk arrived in village shops, the centrality of the empire became ever greater. The empire promoted not only a sense of economic wellbeing, but also pride in being British. Britons started to see themselves as one people, distinct and even unique. "The Empire penetrated the emotions of millions," asserted one historian. He then went on to say:

> It gave Britain its position among the nations and confirmed a national, not to say racial superiority. Taken together with Britain's insularity, the Empire marked out an "island race" as a people set apart, with connections across the globe matched by no other state.[20]

Britain's Protestant heritage, repeated wars against France, and the emergence of its enormous empire each made a significant contribution to making Britons feel British in the eighteenth century. As influential as these factors were, however, the effects of their influence probably would not have been sustained for long had they not been reinforced by other forces at work in the century that followed.

Linking the Nation

As the nineteenth century dawned, Britain was still a nation of remote areas and unconnected parts. It was not until a network of transportation and communication linked Britain's backwaters with its urban centers that a British identity became more sharply delineated. Roads were constructed, canals dug, and railroads built, which allowed goods and materials to be shipped faster, farther, and more cheaply. The postal service extended its reach, helping relatives and friends to stay in touch; leisure travel grew, making it possible for Britons to explore other parts of their homeland; and a telegraph system was inaugurated and newspapers published, informing their readers of events, places, and people all across the empire. Linking the nation in these ways profoundly contributed to reinforcing what it meant to be British.

"In 1832," as one scholar expressed it, "Britain was still essentially horse drawn and sail driven."[21] The pace of public road construction surged in the second half of the eighteenth century, however, and by the late 1830s, nearly 127,000 miles of road had been built. In 1783, thirty stagecoaches a week traveled between London and Birmingham; by 1829, there were up to thirty-four a day. The number of stagecoach services increased eightfold in Britain's ten leading urban centers between 1790 and 1836; by the end of the same period an estimated three thousand coaches transported fifteen times as many passengers.[22] Traders benefited as much as travelers. In the mid-eighteenth century, for example, a businessman in London had to wait more than a week to receive confirmation from a supplier in Birmingham that his order had been received; after the Royal Mail initiated postal service by stagecoach in the English Midlands in 1785, he could expect a reply in two days.[23]

Stagecoaches, however, were not suited for hauling freight. A team of horses could pull at most two tons of goods on the best of roads, but one horse alone could draw as many as fifty tons on a river barge. So crucial was long-distance hauling to the Industrial Revolution that the Government of William Pitt (the Younger) authorized fifty-one new canal companies between 1791 and 1796 alone. By 1830, heavy goods were transported on 3,000 miles of canal and improved rivers; by 1858 that number had risen to 4,250 miles. By the middle of the nineteenth century, every year more than twenty-five thousand barges hauled an estimated thirty to thirty-five million tons of coal and iron and other heavy manufactured freight, and they did so much less expensively than by coach and covered greater distances.[24]

With the appearance of steam locomotives in the early 1800s and the construction in northern England of a rail link between the coal mines of South Durham and the river port of Stockton in 1825, it was not long before railroads replaced barges. Railroad companies, which multiplied in number in the 1830s, had built 1,860 miles of track by 1840; by 1855 they had laid as many as 8,000 miles. By then, rail service had become accessible to traders in nearly every major town, and freight was shipped with speed. This same combination of accessibility and speed also made it possible to haul perishable goods from various parts of Britain to markets in urban areas. Soon, products grown locally were consumed nationally, as motley groups of sellers converged on city centers to set up their stalls. So struck by the diversity of vendors at London's busy Smithfield market was one commentator of the day that he was moved to write: [H]ere are all the country costumes that a man might find between South Wales and Northumberland or further north. The stubby, round-faced Welshman, the huge North Briton, the breeder from the fens, the London drover."[25]

Accessibility and speed made the journey from London to far-off Edinburgh much less daunting for travelers, for a trip that had taken ten to twelve days to complete by stagecoach in 1750 was trimmed to less than eighteen hours by rail in 1850. This was a dramatic contrast to the first few decades following Scotland's union with England in 1707, when these two cities were so distant in place and time from each other that they were in effect the capitals of two largely self-governing nations.

Although leisure travel in the second half of the eighteenth century was a pastime ordinarily restricted to those with means, by the mid-nineteenth century it came within the grasp of the middle class. They could experience for themselves the fullness of the beauty of the Lake District in the northwest of England, Snowdonia in North Wales, and the Isle of Skye in western Scotland. Maps and atlases became increasingly available. Up and down the country, tourists took in not only the natural wonders of their land, but also local customs, diets, and accents—in short, ways of life different from their own. More important, they came to see Britain as a nation of sizable proportions and rich diversity. When "local time," which varied in different parts of the country, gave way to Greenwich Mean Time (GMT) in 1840 to allow railroad companies to develop uniform timetables throughout Britain, GMT became "an ever-present reminder, from John O'Groat's [in the far north of Scotland] to Land's End [in the far southwest of England], that all communities belonged to Britain."[26]

The age of communication followed naturally from the age of transportation. With the invention of the telegraph in the 1830s, telegraph offices, which increasingly were found at railroad stations, transmitted news all across Britain, including weather forecasts and shipping news. And just as telegraphic communication went hand in hand with the railroads, so too did the delivery of mail. The General Post Office, established as a state monopoly in 1660, played a crucial role in linking the nation, for as one scholar observed, without a postal service, "The moulders of the British mind in the nineteenth century would have had little impact."[27] Stagecoaches did an admirable job in providing that link; by 1830 they were able to deliver mail 120 miles away within 24 hours after it was collected. As letter writing developed into something of a national pastime, by the end of the century letters were sorted en route on the train as they speeded to their destinations as far as four hundred miles away for delivery the day after they were posted.

Trains delivered newspapers as well and, together with the telegraph, became accessories in the press "revolution" of the nineteenth century. Newspapers, however, had made their appearance long before the invention of the steam locomotive and the telegraph. In England, the first paper came off the presses in London in 1702. By the 1730s Londoners were reading a half dozen dailies, and in the 1780s, as many as fifty different newspapers were published in various parts of England. *The Times,* a daily, first appeared in 1785, and *The Observer,* a Sunday newspaper, in 1791. *The Guardian,* once *The Manchester Guardian* until it dropped *Manchester* from its masthead in 1959 and became a national newspaper, had its beginnings in 1821. *The Daily Telegraph* first rolled off the presses in 1855. Scotland, too, published newspapers in the eighteenth century—nine by the 1780s and at least thirteen by 1800. A few years later, Wales followed suit when in 1804 one newspaper was published in South Wales and another in 1807 in North Wales. By 1820, as many as three hundred different newspapers were available throughout all of Britain.[28]

With the spread of the telegraph, news items became less expensive to acquire and less difficult to gather. As a result, press coverage became more extensive and more varied. The rapid shipment of newspapers by rail meant that the news was fresh, and the economies of scale that publishers realized by using the telegraph to collect news and rail to dispatch newspapers persuaded them to drop the price of newspapers, thus putting these publications within the reach of more people. Whether readers purchased their own newspapers or devoured those freely available to read in taverns, one historian has suggested that the press, the national press in particular, "must have made it easier to imagine Great Britain as a whole." Their readers, she continued,

> would be constantly reminded that their private lives were bounded by a wider context, that whether they liked it or not they were caught up in decisions taken by men in London, or in battles fought out on the other side of the world.[29]

Looking back, Protestantism, war, and empire helped forge a British identity in the eighteenth century that was fortified in the nineteenth by dramatic technological strides in transportation and communication. Not to be overlooked, however, was the influence of the monarchy on nation building. Although in the first half of the eighteenth century its contribution was weak, its influence grew steadily later in that century and even more perceptibly in the one that followed.

The Magic of Monarchy

It was not until the second half of the eighteenth century, during the sixty-year reign of George III (1760–1820), that the Crown acquired what one scholar called the "secular magic of monarchy."[30] Key to the rise in prominence of the monarchy were mass-circulation newspapers, many of which relied on the royal court for copy. Although the few newspapers that had emerged earlier in that century carried accounts of the monarchy, their coverage was scant and invariably the news was neither very cheerful nor very flattering. Readers learned, for example, when Queen Anne (reign: 1702–1714) was in mourning following the deaths of all four of her babies and her eleven-year-old son. They also learned that the two kings who followed Queen Anne to the throne—George I (reign: 1714–1727) and George II (reign: 1727–1760)—came from Hanover, Germany, spoke little English, made regular sojourns back to Hanover, and evinced little interest in their subjects. George I visited Hanover four times during his thirteen years as king and George II a dozen times during his thirty-three-year reign; however, neither visited Wales, Scotland, or Ireland or even the north of England. So distant from their subjects were they that after George I died, no monument was erected in his memory; and after George II died, few of his former servants even attended his funeral.

After the death of George II, monarchs became more visible, thanks to the rise of mass-circulation newspapers, and with George III and, later, Queen Victoria on the throne, much more popular. They cultivated and won the affection of their subjects not only because they understood the value of royal rituals and symbols in British life but also because they manipulated them in ways not used before to generate cohesiveness among their subjects. In fact, so successful were they in using the pageantry of monarchy that to many Britons, they personified the nation-state.

Even though a rare disorder affected George III's nervous system and occasionally fueled speculation that he was mad, during the French Revolutionary and Napoleonic Wars he became a symbol of national unity, skillfully using royal displays to rally his subjects. For example, on one occasion when, at his instigation, he processed through the streets of London to St. Paul's Cathedral for a service to give thanks for Britain's naval victories over the French, two hundred thousand of his subjects thronged the streets as he passed. Apart from the trappings of monarchy attached to his position, he projected a persona that was far less inscrutable and more down-to-earth than that of either of his two predecessors. He would often walk, in plain garb and unattended, in the streets of Windsor and strike up conversations with townspeople. His amiable personality and simple tastes touched his subjects most. As one major political thinker of the day, Walter Bagehot, wrote, he was "a family man, and a man of business, and sincerely preferred a leg of mutton and turnips after a good day's work, to the best fashion and the most exciting talk."[31]

Unlike the two Georges who preceded him, George III traveled to all parts of Britain. Whether staged in England, Wales, Scotland, or Ireland, these visits were meticulously choreographed and attracted people from all classes and walks of life. His travels must have had an impact on his subjects, for in his Golden Jubilee year in 1810, he was feted in as many as 666 locations in England alone, as well as in numerous places in Wales, Scotland, and Ireland and throughout the empire.[32] In preparation for these visits, newspapers published notices of jubilee meetings, carried advertisements on jubilee souvenirs, and identified procession routes. His subjects bought commemorative pictures, books, medals, and mugs, and reveled in endless numbers of celebratory poems, many of which were written by his Scottish and Irish subjects.[33] When he died, more than three hundred thousand mourners converged on the outskirts of Windsor Castle to pay their respects at his funeral, although this was one royal event that was to have been strictly private.

George III's granddaughter, Victoria, was the next monarch to touch the lives of the British. She occupied the throne from 1837 to 1901, longer than any other sovereign before her. Her subjects soon took to her, despite the unpopularity of her two uncles, George IV (reign: 1820–1830) and William IV (reign: 1830–1837), who preceded her on the throne. Britons were drawn to her because, as a wife and mother, she embodied the ideal notion of family life, an image popularized in newspapers and the expanding number of women's magazines that regularly relied on the royal family for news. Moreover, like George III, she traveled to the distant parts of mainland Britain to demonstrate her interest in her subjects and their circumstances, and wherever she visited, whether in England, Wales, or Scotland, people received her warmly. So fond of Scotland and its inhabitants was she that in 1847 she acquired Balmoral Castle so that she could spend more time there.

Also like George III, Victoria became a link in the minds of her subjects with the nation-state. But there was a dark period in her life, in the middle years of her rule, that threatened to weaken that link. In 1861, twenty-four years into her reign, her consort Prince Albert died from typhoid, prompting her to remove herself from the public stage and settle into a period of reclusion that lasted more than twenty-five years. As time passed, her subjects' compassion turned to criticism. Even staunch defenders of monarchy were critical, among them Bagehot, who in the 1870s wrote admonishingly: "To be a symbol, and an effective symbol, you must be vividly and often seen."[34] Despite her reclusion, she never backed away from performing her royal duties and carried on working with six prime ministers during her protracted period of mourning.

When Victoria returned to public life in 1887 to be feted on the occasion of her Golden Jubilee, she was deeply touched by the enthusiastic outpouring of affection from her subjects. No less enthusiastic was the public affection displayed ten years later when she celebrated her sixtieth year on the throne. Crowds pressed into the streets to greet her as she passed along a six-mile procession route. The intervening decade had marked the end of her dark period and of the criticism.

Contributing to the restoration of Victoria's popularity was the development of new techniques of printing and photography. Now "the great royal ceremonies were described with unprecedented immediacy and vividness in a sentimental, emotional, admiring way, which appealed to a greater cross section of the public than ever before."[35] News of Victoria's death in 1901 was reported with particular poignancy. Her death was the end of a reign; it was also the end of an era. Only the very elderly could claim a faint recollection of the sovereign who had preceded her. So admired was she that within a month of her death, three thousand eulogies were published in the UK extolling her as the "most excellent of sovereigns," one who "bequeathed a name eternally to be revered."[36]

The magic of monarchy persisted through much of the second half of the eighteenth century and most of the nineteenth, thanks to George III and Victoria. Never before had monarchs been held in such high esteem by their subjects, and the combined length of their reigns—nearly 125 years— produced a continuity and stability in British rule unrivaled by any other European state. Moreover, the skill with which they embellished the rituals, spectacles, and symbols of monarchy inspired the loyalty of their subjects, generated social cohesion, and cultivated all the more a sense of what it meant to be British. All that remained to make the people feel even more genuinely British was to bring them more forthrightly into the political life of the nation.

Speaking of ...

E PLURIBUS UNUM?

In his book, *Nationhood and Identity: The British State since 1800,* David Powell makes the point that those living in Britain in the nineteenth century were largely "content" to see themselves as "citizens of a British state," but not "solely as part of a British 'nation'." The distinction Powell draws is pivotal to understanding the British polity not only in the nineteenth century but in the twentieth and twenty-first as well. While the state has held itself intact, has it succeeded in instilling a sense of "nation" among Britain's diverse people? That is how Powell frames the question. But his answer is guarded:

> Ethnic or racial definitions of Britishness ... are limiting and divisive in the multi-cultural Britain of the twenty-first century.

"For each country [of the UK], questions of nationhood and identity have presented their own problems. Britain's difficulty has been to reconcile the institutions of what for much of the modern period was a centralized unitary state with the multi-national realities of the political communities of the British Isles. For a time in the nineteenth century it seemed as if the solution might be to concentrate on building a British identity to match the British state, but while the peoples of Britain were for the most part content to be citizens of a British state they did not see themselves solely as part of a British 'nation'. Accordingly rather than try to create a nation to match the state, from the late nineteenth century the attempt was made to reform the state in ways that could more accurately reflect national diversities. The process has continued to the present day, with the result that a British state has been preserved intact. Whether, as a consequence, 'Britishness' remains a meaningful badge of identity has been the subject of much debate. Certainly the artificial, eighteenth-century Britishness based around loyalty to an exclusively Protestant state has become less and less relevant in a more religiously tolerant and increasingly secular society. Ethnic or racial definitions of Britishness ... are limiting and divisive in the multi-cultural Britain of the twenty-first century. If Britishness is to survive, therefore, it can only be in a form of symbiotic relationship with the state with which its history has been intertwined—an umbrella identity reflecting a mingling of other identities in a common marketplace, a cultural community with shared values and traditions and a common relationship to a body of historical and political experience and the institutions in which they are embodied. The question of whether this will be enough to sustain the British as a people, or ever again to bring them close to being a nation, remains to be seen."

Source: David Powell, *Nationhood and Identity: The British State since 1800* (London: I. B. Tauris, 2002), pp. 255–256.

Political Reform

Long before Victoria came to the throne in 1837, many legislative institutions in Europe were in decline, but not the British parliament. It enjoyed a reputation as a relatively assertive lawmaking body, meeting as it did every year for several months at a time and receiving new members following elections held every three years and sometimes more frequently. There was one major flaw it had in common with most other legislative bodies. However, the right to elect politicians was severely restricted. Only well-born and wealthy males were eligible, and that meant that entire parts of Britain went unrepresented, large industrial towns in particular. Those denied the right to vote nevertheless felt that they had a right to present their views and to be represented—a point dramatized by the numerous petitions directed to parliamentarians in the 1730s and in the decades that followed. By the 1780s and 1790s, increasing numbers were convinced that the right to be represented, although long thought to be a given, could be conveniently ignored unless enshrined in law. It was this thought that prompted the birth of a reform movement of tradesmen, trade union members, and professionals, many inspired by Thomas Paine's *The Rights of Man,* and all intent on persuading Parliament to enact universal manhood suffrage legislation.

With wars against the French consuming the nation from 1793 to 1815, the reform movement all but dissolved, only to reemerge in the 1820s, when it attracted more adherents than ever. By 1829, reform groups had stepped up their campaigns. They intensified their efforts through the general election of 1831, when they helped elect candidates who had pledged their support to extending the franchise. Reformers continued to press for change through the summer of 1832, when Parliament enacted the first of three franchise reform bills. A second was enacted in 1867 and a third in 1884, and although each increased the number of voters only fractionally, the cumulative effect was to expand the electorate by an estimated sixfold.[37] Reformers championed several other proposals as well, one to create constituencies in parts of Britain previously unrepresented and another to reduce the disparities that existed in the number of electors from constituency to constituency. As the reforms took hold and political parties began to recruit vast numbers of the newly enfranchised to their ranks, ever-increasing numbers of Britons were gradually incorporated into the political life of the nation.

The most intense demands for franchise reform occurred in the three years before the 1832 reform bill was enacted. Fearing that reform might favor one section of society or one part of Britain over others, reform leaders argued that voting rights should not be confined to one social class, or just to England or Wales or Scotland or Ireland—but should instead apply to the whole of Britain. Men and women from all sections of society and all parts of Britain rallied behind the reform banner. Indeed, as one historian pointed out, "The sheer numbers ... who took part in marches, in demonstrations and in petitions during these years were astonishing."[38]

As debate on the measure dragged on in Parliament, however, and as the prospects for reform appeared to be increasingly remote, the disaffected took to the streets. Public protests erupted and then exploded into riots in Derby, Nottingham, and Bristol when word spread that the House of Lords had rejected the measure. Reformers tried to convince antireform elements in the House of Lords that riots would not lead to mob rule if the legislation were enacted. Their arguments fell on deaf ears. Reform legislation appeared to be dead, until William IV—alarmed by the magnitude of the public outcry—threatened to pack the House of Lords with peers who supported the bill. The King's intervention averted a full-scale revolution, and after fifteen months of debate, Parliament agreed to the legislation.

The reformers got their legislation, but not all that they wanted from it. Although it boosted the number of first-time male voters throughout the whole of Britain, the margin of the increase was a huge disappointment to reformers. The Scots were an exception. There was rejoicing in the streets of Edinburgh when, following the enactment of separate legislation for Scotland, the number of new Scottish voters soared from one out of every 125 adult males to one out of every 8—a dramatic 1300 percent increase.

The Reform Act still required voters either to own or to occupy property that was quite expensive, so essentially all but upper-middle class males were still denied the right to vote. Moreover, those who gained the most lived where property values were the highest—in London, in counties near London, and in the southeast of England generally. The overall result was that the number of English and Welsh who qualified to vote jumped from one out of eight adult males to one out of five. The proportion was somewhat less favorable in Scotland, where it was one out of eight males, and considerably less so in Ireland, where it was one of twenty males. Frustrated and embittered, the working class would have to wait until another day.

"Another day" came thirty-five years later when Parliament enacted the Representation of the People Act of 1867. Those who had drafted the first reform bill in 1831 had been instructed to satisfy public opinion in limited measure, but "to afford sure ground of resistance to further innovation."[39] More than thirty years later, however, "further innovation" could be resisted no longer. By then, population increases and rising real estate values had boosted the number qualified to vote by 70 percent.[40] By then, too, the Conservatives, who had lost five general elections in a row to the Liberals, were convinced that they should cease their age-old opposition to franchise reform, for they had little to lose and possibly much to gain by agreeing to give the right to vote to the working class in cities and towns and then winning them over to their side.

And winning elections *was* a priority. The argument used by opponents of the 1832 act that the working class lacked the capacity for political judgment was no longer compelling; Liberals and Conservatives vied to champion reform. After both parties agreed to a series of compromises, the Representation of the People Act of 1867 gave the vote for the first time to the better-paid working class living in cities and towns all across England and Wales, and to Scots and the Irish in separate legislation that followed. The number of electors increased from 1.3 million to 2.4 million, giving more than a million males a more direct role to play in the political life of the nation.[41]

The working class who lived in rural areas were left out of the 1867 act, however, and had to wait nearly two decades before they were included in the Representation of the People Act of 1884. When that happened, as shown in Table 1.1, more than half of all adult males in England, Wales, and Scotland were allowed to vote. more than 2.5 million new voters joined 3.1 million existing electors, with the most dramatic increases recorded in Ireland.[42] Despite these gains, an estimated one third of adult males were still denied the vote. These were the poor and uneducated—the poor because the franchise was still based on the value of property occupied, and the uneducated because the registration process was so complex. They—and women—were required to wait until the first part of the next century before they could claim the right to vote.

Broadening the franchise was a crucial plank in the platform of nineteenth-century reformers. But it was not the only one. Representation in Britain could not be made rational and fair, they argued, unless two other inequities in the system also were addressed. One was the gross disparities in the size of constituencies, an inequity that would persist as long as a vote cast for a parliamentarian in a small seat was worth many times more than a vote cast for a parliamentarian in a large seat. Worse still, the people in some parts of Britain were apportioned no seats at all.

The reform acts of 1832 and 1867 addressed both of these inequities, albeit imperfectly. The 1832 act in particular eliminated most "rotten boroughs" by joining them to larger constituencies. So small were these boroughs that a member of Parliament was elected by only a few electors. The most notorious of these was Old Sarum, in which just seven qualified voters elected not one, but two, members of Parliament. The 1832 act also increased the

Table 1.1	Estimated Increases in Number of Adult Males Entitled to Vote in Nineteenth-Century Britain		
	England and Wales	Scotland	Ireland
1832	49%	1300%	21%
Reform Act 1867	(1 of 5 males) 88%	(1 of 8 males) 119%	(1 of 20 males) 8%
Reform Act 1884	(1 of 3 males) 67%	(1 of 3 males) 77%	(1 of 6 males) 229%
Reform Act	(2 of 3 males)	(3 of 5 males)	(1 of 3 males)

Source: W. D. Rubinstein, *Britain's Century: A Political and Social History, 1815–1905* (London: Arnold Publishers, 1998), pp. 43–44 (1832 act), p. 111 (1867 act), and p.198 (1884 act).

number of parliamentary seats for counties, rural ones in particular, and provided seats to some new urban areas that had never been represented before.

As significant as these strides were, deficiencies remained, and reformers pressed on with their campaigns. Dozens of small boroughs only slightly larger than the rotten boroughs of the past had been unaffected by the 1832 reform act, and only a few new urban industrial seats were created. Several cities remained underrepresented, London in particular.

One reason the 1867 reform bill was introduced was to redress these imbalances. The legislation eliminated a number of small boroughs untouched by the 1832 act by joining them to larger constituencies; reduced from two to one the number of members of Parliament who represented several larger boroughs; and assigned seats to a few previously underrepresented large boroughs. It also increased the number of seats apportioned to cities, but not by much, and Manchester and Birmingham were among the cities still underrepresented. London in particular was still materially underrepresented. As a result, what one part of the 1867 legislation gave, another took away, for the vastly enlarged urban electorate that one provision created was in another provision assigned far fewer parliamentary seats than its numbers warranted.

This anomaly persisted until the House of Lords insisted that it be addressed in legislation following passage of the Reform Act of 1884. In 1885, the House got its way when Parliament approved the Redistribution of Seats bill. Having extended the franchise, the Lords had argued that the next step had to be a radical reordering of Britain's constituencies. The intent was to reduce the gross disparities in the population of constituencies, the largest of which was forty times the size of the smallest. Moreover, constituencies all across Britain were a hodgepodge of single- and multi-member constituencies, with the smaller constituencies electing one parliamentarian and the larger ones more than one. To correct these disparities, Parliament in the 1885 act required that all of the UK be divided for the first time into single-member constituencies with each having roughly the same number of electors.

The reforms of the nineteenth century made it possible for several million more Britons to be drawn into the political life of the nation. To many, being given the right to vote was tantamount to receiving a badge of honor, a badge that assumed even greater meaning as agents of the two major political parties of the day sought to recruit them to their ranks. No longer could the parties in Parliament rely on the landed gentry in the rotten boroughs and the sprawling rural counties to mobilize support for their candidates. They now had to select candidates who would appeal to the newly enfranchised in constituencies that were sometimes much larger and often more heterogeneous than before, and almost always more unpredictable. In the meantime, British political parties—and indeed they were British, for there were no significant or successful English, Welsh, or Scottish political parties—became increasingly national in their reach and functions. For the first time, they built an organizational infrastructure outside Parliament to register new voters and wage election campaigns across the whole of Britain.

They also became more national in their perspective and more competitive in their approach. They focused increasingly on the broad national issues of the day, and they sponsored candidates to campaign for seats that had not been subjected to two-party contests before and called greater attention to those policies that set each apart from the other. The parties had thus set the stage for the rise of mass parties, and as they did so, the British electorate was drawn more emphatically into the body politic.

Conclusion

When the separate nations of Britain became the United Kingdom of Great Britain and Ireland (later, Northern Ireland), did the people of these four nations forsake their national identities and allegiances to embrace a new, overarching British identity? This question has two parts, and each requires a separate answer. The answer to the first part is "no." Although they were incorporated into what would become known as the United Kingdom, the English, Welsh, Scots, and Irish did not forsake their national identities. They were not required to do so and there is no evidence to suggest that they did. As a result, with few exceptions, they retained their respective cultures, including their own languages. But they were connected nevertheless to a larger, invented union, one that provided them with certain tangible benefits.

These benefits help answer the second part of the question, that is, did the people of the four nations embrace a new, overarching British identity? The answer is a qualified "yes." In the case of Wales, the embrace was hesitant at first, initially grudging in Scotland, and given with little affection in Ireland. In time, however, it became clear that these nations had more to gain economically, politically, and socially by acting in common cause than acting separately. Protestantism, the predominant religion of England, Wales, and much of Scotland, gave them a common cultural base. Going to war with Catholic France gave them a sense of kinship and a pride in their military victories, as countless numbers took up arms to defend their homeland. The expansion of markets at home and throughout the empire produced economic growth, material goods, profits, and jobs. No sooner had the Napoleonic Wars ended than Britain was linked increasingly by advances in transportation and communication. Monarchs became personal symbols of the new nation-state, and political reforms brought people directly into the mainstream of political life. Each of these contributed unambiguously to nation building—to making Britain British—over the eighteenth and nineteenth centuries.

Britain is a relatively new nation and the sum of its older parts. When Britain emerged, it did so as a coalition of four nations whose interrelationships have rarely been smooth. Its history has been complex. For example, when the historian and diplomat James Bryce wrote in 1887 that the Welsh and Scots cherished a "distinct national feeling," he found that it was "happily not incompatible with attachment to the greater nationality of the United Kingdom."[43] Were Bryce writing about Wales and Scotland today, however, he would probably shy away from such generalizations. The allegiance of Irish living in the south of Ireland—"marginal Britons," as they've been called[44]—was not the same as those living in Ulster, the vast majority of whom treasured their ties to the British mainland. Today, even the people of Ulster are divided in their allegiance, with Catholics claiming they are Irish and Protestants that they are British. The English, on the other hand, have never appeared to be divided in their identity or allegiance. To many English, England is interchangeable with Britain, no doubt because England—which has had the largest population, the richest economy, and wielded the most political control—has always been the dominant partner in the union.

Those factors that contributed so enormously to the forging of Britain in the eighteenth and nineteenth centuries no longer exist in the twenty-first. No longer do Britons share a dominantly Protestant culture. As Britain has become increasingly multiethnic since the 1950s, new religions, particularly from the East, have been woven into the cultural fabric of the nation. Gone too is the threat of external aggression, although acts of terrorism have touched the nation. Instead, over the last quarter of the twentieth century, the threat came from within—from the Irish Republican Army (IRA) and loyalist groups. Moreover, the empire is no longer. In its place is the fifty-three-member Commonwealth of Nations, most of whose members were once British colonies, and which together have drawn up rules governing their trading practices. Even the monarchy, for a time seen as the personification of the British nation-state, has come in for sharp criticism from time to time.

In the absence of new forces to take the place of those that helped to make Britain British, the country has been made vulnerable by the same centrifugal forces that have contributed to the demise of many multinational states. There is perhaps some truth to the notion that small states derive strength in their bid for independence by asserting their national distinctiveness. That appears to be the case in Scotland and Northern Ireland, and to a lesser degree in Wales. Sentiment among some Scots that they should be governed only by themselves led to a referendum that resulted in the devolution of legislative and executive powers to Scotland in 1999. Northern Ireland also was granted its own assembly in 1999, although devolution there has been suspended several times since. As for Wales, it is the least likely to break away from the union. Some Welsh nationalists have long argued for an independent Wales; some regard the Welsh assembly that was organized in 1999, after Welsh voters approved its creation in a referendum held in 1997, as a half-way measure.

The decision of the Labour Government in 1997 to give the voters of Scotland and Wales the right to decide whether they wished some authority to be devolved from London met with a torrent of criticism from the Conservative Party. John Major, prime minister from 1990 to 1997, warned that it would "destroy 1,000 years of British history."[45] However great the risk, it probably would have been far more risky had no action been taken. At the very least, devolution satisfied those who interpreted it as a significant shift in the relationship between Britain and its four older parts. No signs appeared warning that devolution was a "motorway without exits" to separation, as one member of Parliament put it.[46] But no longer would the United Kingdom be quite the same, for it was becoming less one nation which represented four different peoples and more a union of nations. Yet for the time being at least, it appeared that Britain will remain British.

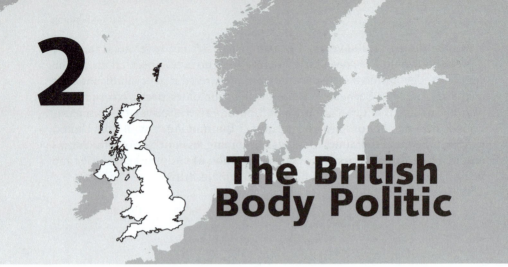

2

The British Body Politic

It took nearly four hundred years before the English, Welsh, Scots, and Northern Irish became the UK that we know today, and nearly as long as that before they developed a sense of being British. And although they were British, the individuating characteristics of the people of the four nations have made the British not only demonstrably multinational but also decidedly multicultural. However, there are other factors as well that have contributed to the heterogeneity of the British body politic.

The first part of this chapter deals with where the people of the UK live, what their ethnic roots are, what their religious orientations are, and what their social structure, or class system, is. The second part examines what Britons think of their system of government. Are they satisfied with the way government ministers and other politicians do their jobs? Do they trust political parties to look after the interests of the nation? How much influence do they feel they have over what government does? The answers to these and similar questions will suggest just how "united" members of the United Kingdom's body politic are in their attitudes toward their political system.

Island Britain

Britain is a nation of nearly sixty million people who live in what one writer called the "kingdom by the sea."[1] It is a long, thin, densely populated island off the northwest corner of the continent of Europe that is embraced by six thousand miles of zigzagging coastline and stretches approximately six hundred miles from Dunnet Head in the far north of Scotland to Lizard Point in the far southwest of England and no more than three hundred miles from east to west at its widest point. Britain is the largest island in Europe and the eighth largest in the world.

Literally, however, it is not one island but several, and thus it is aptly called the British *Isles*. The largest island is mainland Britain, which encompasses England, Scotland, and Wales. Separated from the British mainland by the Irish Sea is Northern Ireland, which occupies the northeastern part of another island, the Republic of Ireland. Northern Ireland is made up of six counties called Ulster, which has a common border with the republic. In addition, there are several other, smaller islands. Among them are the Isle of Wight off the south coast of England, the Isles of Scilly off the southwest coast of England, and the island groups off the northwest and north coasts of Scotland—the Hebrides, the Orkneys, and the Shetlands.

Britain is the short version for United Kingdom of Great Britain, the name first used when Scotland was joined to England and Wales in 1707. Because the northwest provinces of France are close to mainland Britain, the "Great" in Great Britain was used to distinguish Britain from the French province of Brittany, or Bretagne. Grande Bretagne, or Great Britain, was "grande" simply because it was larger than Brittany, which lay one hundred miles to the south of it, separated by that narrow stretch of water between the North Sea and the Atlantic Ocean called the English Channel.

Although larger than Brittany, the UK is smaller than all of France. It is also smaller than six of its other Western European neighbors—Spain, Germany, Italy, Sweden, Finland, and Norway. If it were one of the states of the United States, it would rank tenth in square miles but first in population. It is nearly the size of the state of Oregon; its population, however, is nearly seventeen times greater. Put another way, based on the decennial censuses taken in the United States in 2000 and in the UK in 2001, the UK's population of nearly sixty million is close to that of Oregon combined with the populations of nine additional western states: California, Washington, Montana, Idaho, Wyoming, Utah, Arizona, New Mexico, and Nevada.

It is not enough to say that the UK is densely populated. It also must be said that it is one of the most densely populated countries in the world, with an average of 625 people per square mile, eight times greater than that of the United States. Within the UK, England is by far the most densely populated, with 976 people per square mile; it is also the most populated, with nearly 84 percent of the population. It is comparable in size to the state of New York, but its population of nearly 49.2 million is roughly equal to the combined populations of three Mid-Atlantic states—New York, New Jersey, and Pennsylvania plus four New England states—Massachusetts, Maine, Rhode Island, and Vermont. Less densely populated are Wales and Northern Ireland. Wales is comparable in size to the state of Massachusetts, although its population of three million is less than half that of the state. As for Northern Ireland, its 1.7 million people live on a landmass approaching the size of the state of Connecticut, the population of which is roughly twice that of Northern Ireland's. Last—but least in population density only—is Scotland. It is roughly equal in size to the state of South Carolina, although its population of five million exceeds South Carolina's by nearly a million.

Pride of Place

Where did the people who originally inhabited this island come from? "Each of the peoples of the British Isles is a mongrel," as one historian put it,[2] born of Celtic, Roman, Anglo-Saxon, Danish, Norwegian, and Norman French stock. Later, a different form of mongrel emerged, one defined and imposed by the British state as Wales, Scotland, and Northern Ireland were joined to England. Through intermarriage, many today have overlapping national identities. Among them is Prime Minister Tony Blair, who, although he has lived most of his life in England, was born in Scotland and raised there by an Irish mother and an English father. Blair refers to himself as British. Others, however, prefer to use "British" as a secondary form of identification, suggesting that other allegiances take precedence. Among the latter are Scots, even many who live in England, who generally consider themselves Scottish first and British second. The permutations become even more curious, if not more confusing, among the people of Northern Ireland. Whereas most Catholics there feel a kinship with the Republic of Ireland and are loath to call themselves anything but Irish, most Protestants regard themselves as British or Northern Irish, but not at all Irish.

Pride of nation within the UK extends to pride of region and even pride of locality. People identify themselves as coming from the north of England, from the home counties (the counties around London), from the south of Wales, or from a specific county, such as Cornwall (in England), County Down (in Northern Ireland), Powys (in Wales), or Dumfries and Galloway (in Scotland). If they are from a certain city or area nearby, they might refer to themselves as Mancunians (Manchester), Brummies (Birmingham), Liverpudlians (Liverpool), Geordies (Tyneside), Glaswegians (Glasgow), or Londoners.

If the British fail to identify where they live, their accents could do it for them. Few speak with what is commonly referred to as a "posh" accent, or what is formally called the "received pronunciation" associated with the English upper class. Accents vary enormously, sometimes even within a small area. For example, those living in Berwick-upon-Tweed, tucked away in the far northeastern corner of England, speak with a Scottish burr not heard twenty-five miles to the south in Alnwick, and the accent of those from Alnwick is notably different from that heard in Amble, a mere eight miles away. One accent, cockney, heard in London's east end, is known to many beyond Britain, thanks to Alan Jay Lerner and Frederick Loewe. It was spoken by Eliza Doolittle, the flower girl in *My Fair Lady* who thought she spoke properly until Professor Henry Higgins assured her that she did not and gave her elocution lessons so that she could "speak like the rest of us." Different slang and dialects abound—cockney rhyming slang in particular, which is rarely understood by those living beyond east London. The same is true of the dialect of many who live deep in the rural valley of Borrowdale in England's Lake District; it often needs to be translated before it can be understood by most of those living in the nearby town of Keswick. There are, in fact, as many as twenty-eight words in England and Scotland for "left handed," among them "keggy," "scoochy," "skiffy," "quippy," and "watty." [3]

Ethnic Britain

It is hardly surprising that, having established its presence in so many places around the globe in the days of its empire, Britain would become something of a magnet years later for many from its erstwhile colonies seeking to improve their lot. As a result, one difference that stands out among the British today, particularly in the cities, is their ethnic mix. According to one account, in London alone, there are more than fifty ethnic communities of ten thousand or more. As many as three hundred languages are spoken, and London ethnic restaurants offer in excess of seventy national dishes. [4] Ethnic differences of an even more overt nature are in evidence in London's Notting Hill at the end of summer, when Trinidadians and Barbadians stage a colorful carnival, and in London's Soho, when the Chinese celebrate their new year. One can stroll through the streets of Bradford in North Yorkshire and pass any number of people whose grandparents or parents, or they themselves, came from Pakistan. If one is spending some time in Leicester in Leicestershire, one is likely to hear Gujarati, the language of northwest India, spoken in the corner grocer's shop. A large number of Jews also emigrated from Eastern Europe and settled in Britain in the late nineteenth and early twentieth centuries and again just before and after the Second World War.

In the 1950s and 1960s, labor shortages became so acute that Britain actively promoted emigration from its former colonies. In the 1950s, most came from the Caribbean, and in the 1960s, from India, all lured by the prospect of employment with the National Health Service, in factories, or with London's public transportation system. Since then, however, a series of laws have limited the entry of immigrants, including British passport holders from Hong Kong who wished to immigrate to Britain prior to the UK's returning this Dependent Territory to China in 1997 after having annexed it more than 150 years before.

Limiting the entry of immigrants does not mean that the UK has sealed off its shores. New immigrants from third world Commonwealth nations, India and Pakistan in particular, continue to settle there. Moreover, the European Union's policy of allowing the relatively free movement of people among the member states has meant that citizens from twenty-six other European Union (EU) member nations are allowed to settle and work in the UK. Added to these has been a steady stream of refugees who have made their way to Britain in recent years. All three forms of entry help explain why figures from the decennial census taken in 2001 reveal that one in every twelve people living in the United Kingdom was born in a country other than the UK. [5]

It used to be difficult to ascertain how many people could be described as members of ethnic minorities. To overcome this problem, beginning with the 1991 census, respondents were asked to identify which "ethnic or racial group" they belonged to. The answers, per the census form, would help government "assess the extent and nature of racial disadvantage and what needs to be done to overcome it." The same question was asked in the 2001 census, and after computers spewed out the results, more than 4.6 million—nearly 8 percent of the total population—were found to belong to minority ethnic groups. (See Table 2.1.)

What did those who devised the census form mean by "racial disadvantage"? For that matter, what did they mean by "racial"? The latter was answered in 1983 by the highest court in the land, the House of Lords, or more accurately, the Appellate Committee of the House of Lords, when its judges, the Law Lords, ruled that the headmaster of a private school had discriminated against a Sikh pupil when he forbade him from wearing his headgear in school.[6] The Law Lords' reference was the Race Relations Act of 1976, in which race was defined as meaning color, nationality, or ethnic or national origin. The term "race" was therefore lumped together with "ethnicity," and it mattered little whether discrimination was based on one or the other. When the census form used the term racial disadvantage, it was referring to both.

Substandard public housing, dead-end jobs, and inferior schools were presumably among the disadvantages that British policymakers felt had to be overcome. More difficult to overcome, however, was the prejudice that nourishes discrimination, especially in certain urban areas whose residents became alarmed by what they perceived as an endless flow of black and Asian immigrants settling in their neighborhoods. Tolerance, fair-mindedness,

Table 2.1	Ethnic Group Population of the United Kingdom, 2001 Census	
Group	Number	% of Total Population
White	54,153,898	92.1
Mixed	677,117	1.2
Indian	1,053,411	1.8
Pakistani	747,285	1.3
Bangladeshi	283,063	0.5
Other Asian	247,664	0.4
Total Asian or Asian British	2,331,423	4.0
Black Caribbean	565,876	1.0
Black African	485,277	0.8
Black Other	97,585	0.2
Total Black or Black British	1,148,738	2.0
Chinese	247,403	0.4
Other Ethnic Groups	230,615	0.4
All Minority Ethnic Population	4,635,296	7.9
Total Population	58,789,194	100.0

Source: 2001 Census, Office for National Statistics (www.ons.gov.uk).

and self-restraint—qualities for which the British are well known—were stretched to the limit, and racial tensions soon flared into encounters in the London boroughs of Southall and Brixton, in the St. Paul's area of Bristol, Moss Side in Manchester, Toxteth in Liverpool, and Handsworth in Birmingham. Gangs of young whites clashed with ethnic minorities, hurled abuse, inflicted injury, and destroyed property. Chants of "Go back where you came from!" echoed through the streets as they directed their wrath at second- and third-generation Britons.

The National Centre for Social Research (NatCen) has reported on British opinion over the years, and among the many questions it asks in its British Social Attitudes surveys are questions about racial prejudice. Responses to one question in particular reveal the extent to which the public has admitted to feelings of prejudice. As Figure 2.1 shows, there has been a discernible (but by no means dramatic) decrease in the percentage of respondents who admit to having harbored prejudice against other races, with the combined percentage of those feeling "very prejudiced" and "a little prejudiced" down slightly from 1998 compared to earlier years. More to the point, however, when respondents were asked whether they are prejudiced against people of other races living in Britain, roughly one third admitted to an attitude that runs counter to the storied British sense of tolerance.

Apart from their own prejudices, how have these same respondents perceived the prejudice of others? As they see it, others are more prejudiced than they. This was the case when they were asked about blacks (individuals originally from the West Indies and Africa) and Asians (individuals originally from India and Pakistan) living in Britain. Figures 2.2a and 2.2b show that approximately one half thought that both ethnic minorities were the target of "a lot of" prejudice, but Asian ethnic minorities perceptibly more than black ethnic minorities. Combining "a little" with "a lot" of prejudice suggests how widespread prejudice against blacks and Asians is thought to

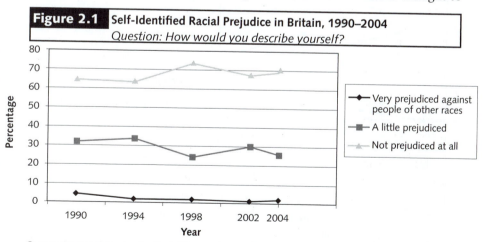

Figure 2.1 Self-Identified Racial Prejudice in Britain, 1990–2004
Question: How would you describe yourself?

Source: National Centre for Social Research, British Social Attitudes (www.britsocat.com).

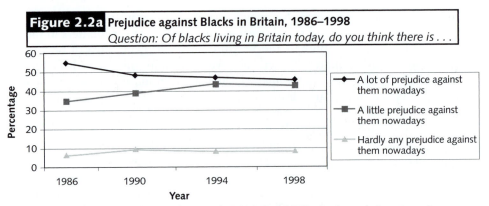

Figure 2.2a Prejudice against Blacks in Britain, 1986–1998

Question: Of blacks living in Britain today, do you think there is . . .

Source: National Centre for Social Research, British Social Attitudes (www.britsocat.com).

be, with as many as nine out of ten respondents assigning such attitudes to others.

Despite these responses, evidence that came to light at the end of the twentieth century suggests that the Race Relations Act of 1976 and the Commission for Racial Equality's efforts to promote harmonious relations among ethnic groups have had positive effects. Nearly 16 percent of those entering the law profession were black. Twenty-three percent of those enrolling in medical school were nonwhite, and 7 percent of secondary school teachers were of minority ethnic origin. More than 7 percent on the staff of the British Broadcasting Corporation (BBC) were black or Asian, and 12 percent of those registered as British at British universities were black or

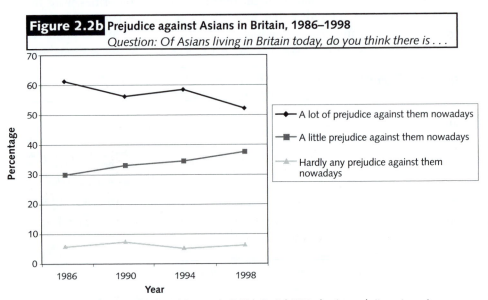

Figure 2.2b Prejudice against Asians in Britain, 1986–1998

Question: Of Asians living in Britain today, do you think there is . . .

Source: National Centre for Social Research, British Social Attitudes (www.britsocat.com).

Asian. In addition, black women were earning slightly more than white women, and Indian men a little more than white men.[7]

However, not all the news in that period was good. Unemployment rates were higher among blacks and Asians (24 percent) than among whites (13 percent), although they were dropping faster among the former than the latter.[8] Less than 2 percent of police officers in England and Wales were black or Asian,[9] and less than 2 percent of ethnic minorities held the most senior posts in the civil service.[10] Moreover, by 2004, it was found that although 8.3 percent of judges were Asian, only 2.5 percent were black, and only 4 percent were from other ethnic minority groups.[11] In the world of business, only 1 percent of senior managers from one hundred major firms were from an ethnic minority in 2002—as were 2.3 percent of board members of Britain's largest companies listed on the London Stock Exchange in 2005.[12] The percentages were better in the world of Parliament than in the world of business, but not by much. Although 109 minority candidates ran for Parliament in the 2005 general election, only 15 won seats, but this was twice the number than who had won in 1992.[13]

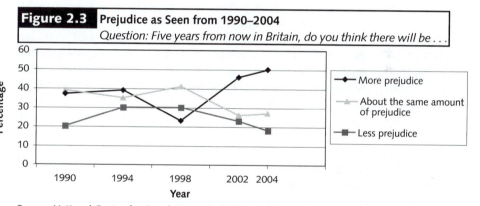

Figure 2.3 Prejudice as Seen from 1990–2004

Question: Five years from now in Britain, do you think there will be . . .

- More prejudice
- About the same amount of prejudice
- Less prejudice

Source: National Centre for Social Research, British Social Attitudes (www.britsocat.com).

These findings suggest that, overall, strides are being made to stamp out discrimination, although the pace is slow. But data from NatCen's British Social Attitudes surveys have produced some disquieting news as well. When respondents were asked to reflect on how much prejudice there would likely be in five years' time, between two thirds and three fourths thought it would continue unabated or become even more pervasive. (See Figure 2.3.) If such projections prove to be a self-fulfilling prophecy, then eliminating prejudice will remain high on the agenda of those working for racial harmony in Britain for some years to come.

Religious Britain

One factor more than any other steeled Britons' resolve to defend their homeland when they went to war with France in the eighteenth century:

their unshakable allegiance to Protestantism. They were convinced that God was a Protestant, and perhaps even British, and if they had to rise to the occasion and fight, God was sure to protect them from Catholic militancy. The Church of England, established two centuries before by Henry VIII, had set Britain apart from the Catholic powers on the European continent and given the British a common identity and a common cause: to defend the realm against French invaders.

Time and tide have moved on since then, and so too has the salience of the Anglican faith to many Britons. In 2004, a little more than one third called themselves Protestants, and less than one third identified themselves as Church of England communicants, or Anglicans. When the Irish and other Catholics from Western Europe immigrated to Britain in the nineteenth and twentieth centuries, their numbers boosted the small minority of Catholics on the island. By then, members of other Christian denominations—Presbyterians; Methodists; and Baptists, or Nonconformists, as they were called—had broken with Anglicanism and settled in England, Scotland, and Wales. In the twentieth century, when immigrants from the Commonwealth nations settled in Britain they, like the Irish before them, brought their religions with them. Thus it is not at all uncommon today to find synagogues, temples, mosques, and other places of worship alongside churches. And although Queen Elizabeth II, as Supreme Governor of the Church of England, is Defender of the (Anglican) Faith, her words and actions demonstrate her commitment to good relations among all faiths and ethnic groups. For example, during her Golden Jubilee in 2002 she visited a variety of centers and places of worship, among them a Hindu temple in London, Manchester's Jewish Museum, a Sikh temple in Leicester, and an Islamic center in Scunthorpe.

For some years, NatCen has asked respondents to identify which religion, if any, they belong to. What stands out in its findings, set forth in Figure 2.4, is that people have become decidedly less Protestant, decidedly less Anglican, and decidedly less affiliated with an institutionalized religion. Whereas in 1983 slightly more than 50 percent belonged to one of the major Protestant churches (Church of England, Baptist, Methodist, or Presbyterian), in 2004 only 34 percent did so. Between 1983 and 2004 the number who identified with the Church of England dropped from nearly 40 percent to less than 30 percent. Those belonging to "no religion" jumped from 31 percent in 1983 to 43 percent in 2004, and by 2004 they had overtaken and passed those affiliated with the major Protestant churches by eight percentage points and those affiliated with the Church of England by 14 percentage points.

Those who claim affiliation with a religion do not necessarily practice it in the sense that they attend religious services often and regularly. NatCen's British Social Attitudes surveys provide some evidence of church attendance in Figure 2.5 on page 38. The population samples include only those affiliated with an institutionalized religion. As the figure shows, the number who say they attend once a week, once a month, twice a year, and once a year has

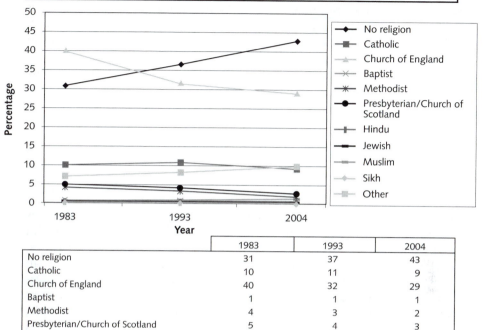

Figure 2.4 Religious Affiliation in the United Kingdom, 1983–2004
Question: Do you regard yourself as belonging to any particular religion? If yes, which?

	1983	1993	2004
No religion	31	37	43
Catholic	10	11	9
Church of England	40	32	29
Baptist	1	1	1
Methodist	4	3	2
Presbyterian/Church of Scotland	5	4	3
Hindu	0.4	0.9	0.8
Jewish	0.6	0.6	0.3
Muslim	0.6	1.4	1.5
Sikh	0.2	0.2	0.1
Other	7	8	10

Source: National Centre for Social Research, British Social Attitudes (www.britsocat.com).

remained relatively stable over the three intervals. So too has the number who indicate that they never attend. What may surprise some is the high percentage—the 50 percent to 54 percent—who say they are affiliated with a religion but never attend religious services or meetings.

It is clear that, starting before the close of the twentieth century, citizens of the UK have increasingly turned away from organized religion and organized religious practices. Fewer have chosen to affiliate with an institutionalized religion, and of those who do affiliate, more than half never attend religious services or meetings. Perhaps these trends explain why there have been more churches closing than opening. Between 1989 and 1998, a total of 2,800 churches closed and 1,900 opened.[14] Today some cathedrals and churches are visited more regularly by tourists than worshippers; vicarages and rectories are dwelled in less by clerics than by the laity. The figures are not going in the right direction for the leaders of Protestant religions in the UK. That includes the Archbishop of Canterbury and the rest of the Anglican hierarchy. Although

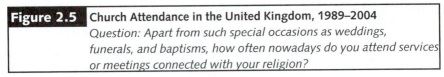

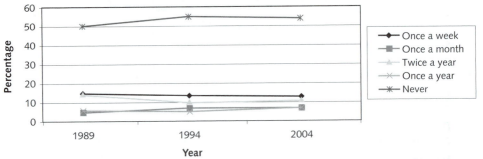

Figure 2.5 Church Attendance in the United Kingdom, 1989–2004

Question: Apart from such special occasions as weddings, funerals, and baptisms, how often nowadays do you attend services or meetings connected with your religion?

Source: National Centre for Social Research, British Social Attitudes (www.britsocat.com).

Anglicans still attend church in greater numbers than Methodists, Baptists, Presbyterians, and Congregationalists, there are fewer Anglicans in attendance than Catholics. This fact will not escape the notice of those looking for history's ironies, for the Church of Rome was once the object of untold fear and loathing. Clearly, the state-established Church of England—and God—no longer appear to be as British as they once were.

Class-Conscious Britain

Three men stood in a line—a tall one, one of average height, and a short one. Casting his eyes at the man of average height, the tall one said, "I look down on him because I am upper class." Pointing to the tall man, the one of average height said, "I look up to him because he's upper class," and then, glancing at the short one, he added, "but down on him because he's working class"—whereupon the short man whispered, "I know my place." [15] This sketch, first used in a 1950s television program, epitomized the sharp class divisions that ran through British society in the post–Second World War years. Indeed, class was seen as the major factor that shaped the behavior, values, and outlook of many in this period, including how the electorate voted. For example, as late as the mid-1970s, whenever students of politics were asked how the British voted, the answer they invariably gave was the one so compendiously expressed by one scholar: "Class is the basis of British party politics; all else is embellishment and detail." [16] His assertion did not arise from idle speculation; it was supported by numerous investigations conducted from 1945 through the 1960s that pointed to one unassailable finding: the Labour Party attracted the vast majority of the working class, and the Conservative Party attracted the middle and upper classes.

Life in Britain was seen through the lens of class in the first three decades or so following the Second World War; it still is, although the lens has had to be adjusted somewhat to accommodate changes that have taken place in recent decades. But first, what exactly is class? One social historian defined classes as "groupings across society, broadly recognized by members of that society, involving inequalities, or, certainly, *differences,* in such areas as power, authority, wealth, income, prestige, working conditions, lifestyles and culture." [17]

As comprehensive as this definition is, devising categories of class is not a simple exercise, for some placements can be highly subjective. One can find any number of indicators of class, such as type of employment, income, level of education, reading material, leisure activities, type and location of accommodation, vacation venues, social contacts and friendships, and even accent and slang. For example, if one were to take just one indicator, employment, the chief executive of British Airways is not in the same class as a coal miner. That would not be in dispute. But it would be difficult to decide whether to assign a self-employed electrician to the same class as the chief electrician on the permanent staff of a large factory. And what about the London taxi driver who has a passion for Mozart, holds an Oxford Ph.D. in history, and spends some of his weekends hunting pheasants in Buckinghamshire's Chiltern Hills? One could puzzle endlessly over where to assign him on the class pecking order.

Moving from employment to income, what about the vicar and his next-door neighbor, the high-powered lawyer? The vicar's salary is low in comparison to the lawyer's earnings, perhaps one twentieth of the latter's, yet both could be indisputably placed in the upper middle class because they work in prestigious professions. What one does for a living, in other words, is regarded as more important than how much one earns.

As difficult as it is to devise categories of class, assigning people to classes is even more difficult. Any number of methods have been tested and used, but the preference is to classify people by occupation, the rationale for which is that different kinds of occupations offer various clues about people's educational qualifications, incomes, living standards, and lifestyles. These clues do not produce definitive profiles of class, but social scientists, market researchers, and pollsters see them as contributing to such an effort and have been using them for several decades. They break the data down into five categories (with a sixth called "residual") and correlate these by class, as seen in Table 2.2.

Turning now to Figure 2.6, one can see the structural shifts in class that occurred between 1966 and 2005. At the top end of the scale, the A and B categories, which have been combined, show a marked increase in the percentage of those in middle- and upper middle-class occupations. When lower middle-class workers, the C1s, are added to the A and B categories, the growth in British middle-class occupations becomes all the more evident, rising as it did from 31 percent in 1966 to 55 percent in 2005. Also noteworthy over this period is the drop in the percentage of those in skilled working-class occupations (the C2s)—from 37 percent in 1966 to 21 percent

Table 2.2   Occupations and Class

Category	Class	Description	Examples
A	Upper middle class	high professional and managerial	lawyers, physicians, top-level civil servants
B	Middle class	intermediate professional and managerial	small business owners, teachers
C1	Lower middle class	junior managers, clerical, and other non-manual workers	secretaries, bank tellers, salesmen
C2	Skilled working class	manual workers	electricians, machinists
D	Semi-skilled and unskilled working class	manual workers	factory fitters, bus conductors, postmen
E	Residual	casual workers and those receiving state benefits	apple pickers, state pensioners (with no other earnings), the long-term unemployed

Source: National Readership Surveys, Ltd.

in 2005—many of whom, it is thought, moved up a notch and joined the C1s in the lower middle class.

What factors account for these changes in the labor market? One is that big government got bigger. As government services multiplied in the years following the Second World War, so too did the need for government to recruit many thousands of additional employees to staff positions at the national and local levels. By 1961, nearly one in every four in the labor force—24 percent—worked in the public sector; by 1982 that number had climbed to 31

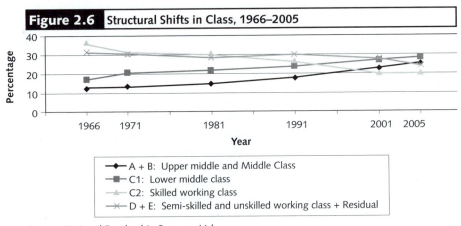

Figure 2.6   Structural Shifts in Class, 1966–2005

◆ A + B: Upper middle and Middle Class
■ C1: Lower middle class
▲ C2: Skilled working class
✕ D + E: Semi-skilled and unskilled working class + Residual

Source: National Readership Surveys, Ltd.

percent. A good number of these new recruits—National Health Service managers, teachers, doctors, and others—took on middle-class jobs after rising from working-class backgrounds largely through the benefits of tuition-free higher education and state-provided student living allowances.

A second factor can be traced to the spurt of growth in the high-tech and service industries, some of which operate in the public sector and others in the private sector. Communications, transportation, health services, information processing, food catering, and many other types of services play an increasingly vital role in the economy. As they do so, the need for many new nonmanual and manual workers grows accordingly. In 1961, 47 percent of the labor force was working in these industries; by 1981 this number had swollen to 62 percent.

A third factor that accounts for the changes in the labor force was the relentless downturn in the manufacturing sector. Output dropped as British industries failed to introduce state-of-the-art technology in their operations to compete efficiently and effectively in the world market. As a result, layoffs became a way of life in the traditional manufacturing regions in the north of England, Wales, and Scotland in the 1970s and 1980s as decisions were made to downsize or close such age-old industries as coal mining, steel manufacturing, and shipbuilding. The number working in manufacturing dropped from 38 percent in 1961 to 28 percent in 1981. Some found work in C1 and C2 jobs, but others lacked the skills to compete for them.

As the numbers working in middle-class jobs grew, so too did their incomes and their acquisitiveness. As two observers put it, they became "a new breed of well-dressed, home-owning, car-driving, holiday-taking middle class folk."[18] Two indices lent credence to this point: the number of homeowners rose from 31 percent in 1951 to 66 percent in 1990, and the number of individuals who purchased stocks soared from one million in 1979 to nine million in 1989. Clearly, the middle class had become better off. So, too, had the working class. Contributing to this economic betterment were two major policies of government in the 1980s. One encouraged tenants in public housing to buy their homes by offering them cut-rate prices, with the result that by 1988, 65 percent of the working class owned their own homes. The other policy, which followed the transfer of several major publicly owned industries to the private sector, provided opportunities to the public to purchase stocks in these industries, at special introductory prices. As a result, by 1987, 20 percent of manual workers owned stock, compared with 6 percent in 1979.

Today, there is much less evidence of a homogeneous working class than in the past. Rather, there is what one political scientist called a "new" working class and a "traditional" working class.[19] Put another way: there are the well off and the not so well off. The well off are the manual workers, many of whom are C2s and the Ds, but especially the former. These are the ones who took jobs in the high-tech and service industries. Fewer of them work on assembly lines and join trade unions.

Speaking of . . .

The British Class System as Seen by a Former American Ambassador

There is something rather permanent-sounding about the second word in the term "class system." "System" implies structure and order, perhaps even something that one cannot break out of. It is not uncommon to hear the phrase "the British class system" referred to in Britain, but it is rare to hear "the American class

> "Americans ... seemed to resent the suggestion that in Britain they would be called 'working class'."

system" spoken of in the United States. Perhaps that is because vast numbers of Americans consider themselves "middle class" or because the "lower classes" tend to be hidden from view.

Whether Americans leave home for work with a lunch box or a briefcase, they know that their ticket to middle-class status or to moving up further in the middle-class world is a job that pays enough to buy a second car or send their youngsters to college or install the latest plasma screen television in the family room—or all three. In Britain, however, it is not just what job one has or how much it pays. There is more to it than that, as a former American ambassador to the Court of St. James's points out in this comparison of class in the two cultures:

"The American distinction between 'blue collar' and 'white collar' never caught on in Britain. I think this is because in America a job describes the kind of work you happen to do at the time and not necessarily your assigned rung on the social ladder. Job mobility, at least for your offspring if not for yourself, is part of the American legend. So most American workers identify themselves socially and even economically as 'middle class'. With their own houses and their own cars and their own lawn mowers, American workers, even if union members, usually place themselves on this wide, middle ground in the social landscape of the country.

"The reverse still seems to be the case in Britain. The material circumstances of the working class have changed dramatically in the last few decades, but the spiritual attitudes persist. Two-thirds of the British workforce describe themselves as 'working class'. A union friend of mine recalled his first visit to the United States, perhaps twenty years ago or so [about 1978], where he encountered many people who performed the same kind of unionized factory work as workers in Britain. But the Americans called themselves 'middle class', and they seemed to resent the suggestion that in Britain they would be called 'working class'. The distinction is that a British worker isn't defined merely by his job or even by his mortgage. In Britain, he is defined by his accent, his education, his newspaper and his memory. And it is loyalty to all of these that makes the British working class as conservative as the upper class...."

Source: Raymond Seitz, *Over Here* (London: Phoenix, 1998), p. 129.

The middle class today is also less homogeneous. At first, as a "new" middle class emerged alongside the established middle class, some of the new arrivals became uncomfortable with what one sociologist called a "contradictory class location," or, as he explained it, those who were "in more than one class simultaneously."[20] By 1987, as many as four out of five were in more than one class at the same time; for example, there were middle-class trade unionists, working-class homeowners, and blue-collar workers married to white-collar employees.

The spread of affluence, starting especially in the 1980s, had a remarkable leveling effect on the middle and working classes, whether "old" or "new." As inequalities in income became less pronounced and more people were able to buy consumer goods, take vacations abroad, and go to concerts and sporting events, the more superficial differences between the two classes began to fade. It became harder to know whether the man in faded jeans shopping in Harrods was the managing director of a dot-com company or an off-duty policeman, or whether a London cyclist was a judge on the way to chambers or a bank teller summoned to appear before that court as a juror.

Many who are lower on the social ladder today no longer accept the assumption widely held in the post–Second World War years that they, like the short man in the sketch, know their place and that life's chances are limited. The numbers who have moved from the working class to the middle class in recent years demonstrate that this assumption is no longer valid. Yet many newcomers to the middle class eschew the middle-class label, insisting that they are really working class, and they speak proudly of the proletarian world they inhabit. This has puzzled social scientists. One explanation is that the new middle class have "preferred to claim that they had resisted the charms of embourgeoisement and still stood shoulder to shoulder with the fellow toilers from whom they or their parents had sprung."[21] For them, perhaps, being working class is fashionable. Another theory suggests that many of the new middle class feel this way because of the "growing class of super-rich individuals who make everybody else feel poor by comparison."[22]

However people label themselves, the fact that many have risen on the economic ladder is not in dispute. One study found that nearly one half of those with professional and managerial positions in the 1980s came from homes in which the fathers had held jobs in a lower occupational class.[23] The paving stones to such intergenerational mobility, it became clear, took the form of post-secondary education. As the number of young people going on to study at Britain's one hundred universities increased from one in seven in 1987 to more than four in ten in 2005, more paving stones were laid in place.

With greater numbers going to university, the barriers between the classes were not quite as high as they once were. But barriers, even lowered ones, are still barriers. The admissions committees of Britain's elite universities have been criticized for favoring the scions of the socially and economically advantaged and in particular those completing their secondary education at such prestigious fee-paying schools as Eton and Harrow. "Not much has changed since [1955]," reflected the authors of a 1998 book on class in Britain. They were reacting to an article written by a sociologist in 1955 who observed that if an educated stranger asked a student whether he was at Oxford or Cambridge and the student "says Aberystwyth or Nottingham, there is disappointment on the one side and embarrassment on the other."[24] In 2004, the Labour Government created the Office for Fair Access (OFFA) to ensure that university applicants were considered on their academic merits and not on their socioeconomic background. Whether OFFA will succeed in lowering the barriers is yet to be seen. One impediment is the cost of going to university. Tuition fees were introduced for the first time in 2003 and raised dramatically in 2006. And even though a student loan program was organized and funds have been set aside to award to students in financial need, OFFA's job will be far from easy.

When it became official in the 1990s that for the first time a majority of Britons were middle class, the enormous gap that existed between two other groups in society remained unchanged. One group was the 1 percent who are the very wealthy, the other the 25 percent who are very poor. The latter are those living on the edge—single people and families whose incomes fall below the poverty line. In 1999, 20 percent of the population lived in households in which no one worked; many did not even qualify to be officially unemployed either because they had been out of work too long to qualify to be counted or because they were unemployable.[25]

That same year, a quarter of all children in the UK—3.1 million—were classified as poor. This percentage dropped to 2.4 million six years later, in 2005, after the Blair Government embarked on a series of policies designed to cut this number. However, it appeared that the Government was fighting a losing battle, as no further sizable outlays from the Treasury were forthcoming, and findings on the number of poor who were parenting continued to make grim reading.[26] Few analysts were inclined to bet their pensions on sizable percentages of these children breaking out of the poverty cycle in the foreseeable future. As one commentator put it, "Intergenerational poverty is solidifying, so poor children are more firmly anchored to the floor than for decades, their social mobility frozen."[27] From all of this it can be concluded that it is fatuous for politicians and others to claim that "Britain is on the road to a classless society."[28] As things stand, Britain is far from even finding the road, let alone attempting to travel on it. And if it ever does find it, the journey may be impossible to complete.

The foregoing is a sketch, not a comprehensive treatment, of the people of Britain. Although only a sketch, it hopefully conveys at least a rudimentary understanding of those who live in this "kingdom by the sea." Yet there is one more aspect of the British body politic so central that it deserves separate treatment. It is central because it reveals what the British think about certain major aspects of their political system.

Attitudes toward the Political System

How easy or difficult it is for a governing authority to exercise power depends in no small measure on the extent to which the governed accept the authority's legitimacy to govern. In a democracy, legitimacy derives first from elections—as long as they are regular and genuinely competitive, attract a substantial turnout of voters whose eligibility to participate is fairly and equitably provided for, and produce outcomes that reasonably reflect the overall choice of the electorate. Whether a regime is capable of sustaining its legitimacy between elections, however, depends on a host of factors. How satisfied is the public with its system of government and with the ways in which government ministers and other politicians do their jobs? In a related vein, to what extent does the public trust politicians to tell the truth and to place the nation's needs over their parties' interests? And to what extent does the public feel that it has any influence over what governments do? The answers to these and other questions provide some insight into the context within which political decision makers operate and into the kind of relationship the governed perceive they have with the governors.

Importance of the Monarchy

A useful starting point in exploring Britons' attitudes toward their political system is the British monarchy. Britain is a constitutional monarchy, and the Queen (or King) is Britain's head of state. Although she does not govern, she performs four roles that allow government to function. First, she confirms the choice of the voters after an election by naming the leader of the winning party as prime minister. Second, she has the right to be consulted by the prime minister on issues of the day and to offer advice. Third, she gives the Royal Assent to all bills approved by Parliament. And fourth, at the prime minister's request, she dissolves Parliament prior to a general election campaign. No evidence exists to suggest that the public is troubled by the Queen's performing these roles, probably because of long-standing conventions that dictate that she not ignore or overturn the decisions of the electorate, the prime minister, or the government, or interfere with the way government is run. Were she to do so, she would seriously compromise the political neutrality she is obliged to uphold. The monarchy is a powerful symbol of the British nation, and the present monarch, Elizabeth II, like those who preceded her, gives expression to that symbol by the ceremonial functions she performs and the care that she and members of the royal family exhibit through their many acts of charity.

With all of this in mind, how important is it to the public that the monarchy continue? According to the NatCen survey data presented in Figure 2.7, two thirds of respondents think it "very important" or "quite important" that it continue (except in 2003, when the percentage dropped below 60 percent). However, between 21 and 30 percent say that the monarchy is "not very important" or "not at all important," and between 8 and 10 percent take the

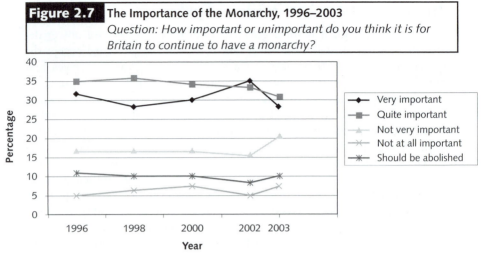

Figure 2.7 The Importance of the Monarchy, 1996–2003

Question: How important or unimportant do you think it is for Britain to continue to have a monarchy?

Source: National Centre for Social Research, British Social Attitudes (www.britsocat.com).

position that it "should be abolished." Presumably, most of those who call for abolishing the monarchy support a republican form of government, which normally includes the election of a head of state. But their numbers and the numbers of others unenthusiastic about the monarchy are vastly short of the robust majority who feel it is important to keep it.

Satisfaction with the System of Government

A substantial majority of Britons think it is important to carry on having a monarchy, which presumably means that they are satisfied with it. But are they satisfied with their system of government? NatCen's British Social Attitudes survey data, reflected in Figure 2.8, indicate that opinion is mixed. Roughly one third of respondents say that they think the present system of governing

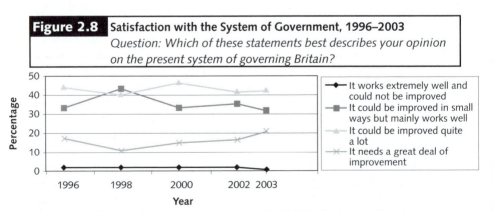

Figure 2.8 Satisfaction with the System of Government, 1996–2003

Question: Which of these statements best describes your opinion on the present system of governing Britain?

Source: National Centre for Social Research, British Social Attitudes (www.britsocat.com).

the country works "extremely well" or "mainly well." Almost all who plumped for these two choices, however, held that the present system "could be improved in small ways." On the other hand, in each of the five years depicted, a majority of respondents—and, aside from 1998, significant majorities—had a less-than-positive view of the way their system of government works, saying either that it "could be improved quite a lot" or that it "needs a great deal of improvement."

Satisfaction with the Way Politicians Are Doing Their Jobs

How well or how poorly a system of government seems to be working in the minds of the public is no doubt ultimately tied to its perceptions of how well decision makers in government are performing their jobs. The assumption here is that the system of government is seen as working well if those who have a major hand in running it are judged to be performing their jobs satisfactorily. But that assumption is moot. Whether or not it is correct, responses to a poll question on the public's satisfaction with the way government ministers and other politicians work reflect a low level of regard for the way they do their jobs compared with the way those in other professions perform theirs. As Table 2.3 shows, ministers and politicians are the only professions to which respondents have consistently assigned a higher level of dissatisfaction than satisfaction. Moreover, when it comes to level of satisfaction, nurses and doctors score far higher than government ministers and other politicians by a margin of three to one.

Trust in Politicians

One should tread carefully when interpreting poll data, but if one were searching for reasons why the public is dissatisfied with the way ministers

Table 2.3	Satisfaction with the Jobs of Politicians and Others, 2000–2004

Question: How satisfied or dissatisfied are you with the way the following types of people do their jobs?

Profession	2000 Sat.	2000 Dissat.	2002 Sat.	2002 Dissat.	2004 Sat.	2004 Dissat.
Nurses	95%	1%	94%	2%	96%	1%
Doctors	90%	6%	91%	4%	92%	4%
Teachers	83%	6%	84%	6%	86%	5%
Police	65%	19%	68%	18%	67%	18%
Judges	59%	14%	60%	15%	58%	18%
Lawyers	56%	13%	56%	15%	54%	15%
Government ministers	28%	42%	30%	45%	27%	47%
Politicians generally	27%	44%	31%	44%	27%	48%

Source: MORI public opinion polls (www.mori.com).

and other politicians perform their jobs, some explanation may be found in another set of poll findings. A reason might be that the public feels that politicians cannot be trusted. Whether that also explains the public's comparative dissatisfaction with Britain's system of government is debatable. Beyond dispute is the public's lack of trust in politicians when it comes to their telling the truth and placing the needs of the nation ahead of party interests. Specifically, data from NatCen's British Social Attitudes surveys reveal (in Figure 2.9) that the public thinks politicians are not always truthful and (in Figure 2.10) that the political party in power puts its interests ahead of the needs of the nation.

What stands out in Figure 2.9 is that in the five survey years shown, anywhere from 87 percent to 92 percent of the public felt that when politicians are in a tight corner, they tell the truth only "some of the time" or "almost never." Less than 10 percent maintain that politicians tell the truth "most of the time." In the eyes of a majority of the public, politicians have failed the "trust test" not only when it comes to their telling the truth, but also when it comes to the party in power placing the nation's needs over party interests. Figure 2.10 reveals that in the five survey years, between 16 percent and 28 percent of respondents said that the party in power places the nation's needs ahead of its interests "almost always" or "most of the time"; by contrast, roughly three quarters (anywhere from 69 percent to 82 percent) said that the party did so only "some of the time" or "almost never."

Popular Influence on Government

In a representative democracy, it is an age-old assumption that the people have an influence on the policies of the government they elected. But how much influence does the public think it has? Figures 2.11 and 2.12 reveal a widespread view that suggests that people think they have little influence. The data for the two figures are drawn once again from NatCen's British

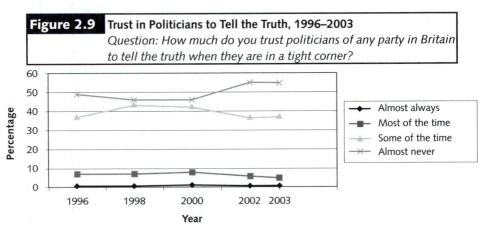

Figure 2.9 Trust in Politicians to Tell the Truth, 1996–2003

Question: How much do you trust politicians of any party in Britain to tell the truth when they are in a tight corner?

Legend:
- Almost always
- Most of the time
- Some of the time
- Almost never

Source: National Centre for Social Research, British Social Attitudes (www.britsocat.com).

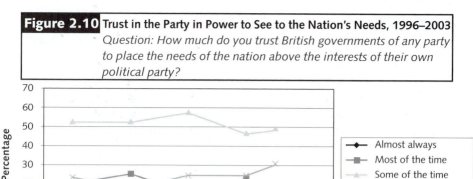

Figure 2.10 Trust in the Party in Power to See to the Nation's Needs, 1996–2003

Question: How much do you trust British governments of any party to place the needs of the nation above the interests of their own political party?

Source: National Centre for Social Research, British Social Attitudes (www.britsocat.com).

Social Attitudes surveys. Figure 2.11 indicates that a clear majority of the public—roughly two thirds—thinks that it has "no say" in what the government does. Moreover, in four of the five years found in the figure, as many as one fourth of respondents indicated that they felt "strongly" that this was the case.

Perhaps the reasons why so many feel that they have "no say" in what government does can be found in the responses reported in Figure 2.12, which re-

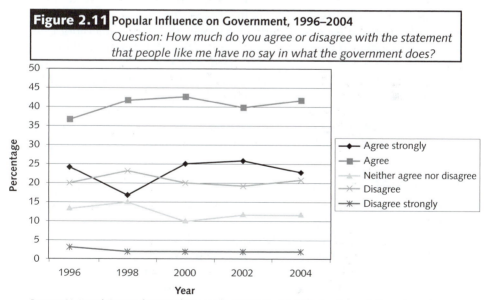

Figure 2.11 Popular Influence on Government, 1996–2004

Question: How much do you agree or disagree with the statement that people like me have no say in what the government does?

Source: National Centre for Social Research, British Social Attitudes (www.britsocat.com).

49

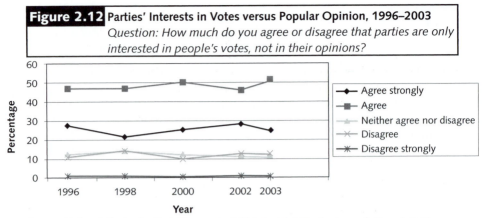

Figure 2.12 Parties' Interests in Votes versus Popular Opinion, 1996–2003

Question: How much do you agree or disagree that parties are only interested in people's votes, not in their opinions?

Source: National Centre for Social Research, British Social Attitudes (www.britsocat.com).

veals what respondents think political parties' relative interests are in regard to winning votes and soliciting voters' opinion. Over the seven years depicted in Figure 2.12, between 68 percent and 76 percent "agreed" or "agreed strongly" that political parties are interested in their votes rather than their opinions. Less than 1 percent disagreed "strongly" with that position.

More than half of the British public thinks that their system of government needs either "quite a lot" or "a great deal" of improvement; more are dissatisfied than satisfied with the way government ministers and politicians generally perform their jobs. Public trust in politicians is at a low ebb, and most feel that they are estranged from their members of Parliament and have no say in what the government does. No doubt these survey findings make for sobering reading for political leaders. Rightly or wrongly, they reflect a level of cynicism, even anomie, in the body politic that is reflected in near-record lows in voter turnout, starting with the general election of 1997. Is low voter turnout a function of the public's diminished confidence in the political system? One can only speculate. No doubt there is some relationship between the two. On another matter there can be little doubt: if public confidence erodes further, political leaders will need to brace themselves for what is likely to follow—the slow but inevitable decline in their ability to inspire and convince.

Conclusion

There were two objectives in this chapter. The first was to develop a sketch of the British, a people living on a cramped island off the northwest coast of continental Europe whose ancestors incubated and nourished what some claim is the world's oldest surviving representative democracy. The second was to probe what their attitudes are toward their political system.

Cultures have sprung from two forms of migration. The first is internal as the English, Welsh, Scots, and Northern Irish crisscrossed their respective borders to settle in other parts of the larger British nation, a pattern that continues to some extent today. The second form is from lands beyond Britain, when Indians, Pakistanis, Bangladeshis, Chinese, Jamaicans, Trinidadians, and others made their way to Britain's shores. With them they bring their skills, their customs, their music, their languages, their literature, and their religions. Not all are made to feel welcome in their new homeland. Once settled, they are forced to cope with racial, ethnic, and religious prejudice and discrimination. In fact, discrimination continues—in particular discrimination against Asian and black Britons. Combating racism and dealing with its root causes has been high on the agendas of Conservative and Labour Governments since the 1970s, and there is evidence to suggest that campaigns to eliminate it have had some beneficial effects.

Class also was discussed. Many Britons have moved up from one class to the next—from the working class to the middle class especially—and from within a class, for example, from middle class to upper middle class. The differences between and sometimes within classes are still detectable, but with the general spread of affluence and acquisitiveness, the distinctions have become much less stark and sometimes quite subtle. Certainly not at all subtle, however, are the differences that exist between the very wealthy and the very poor.

Turning now to the second objective of this chapter, that of probing the attitudes of the British people toward their political system, the less-than-positive responses the public has given pollsters should serve as alarm bells for Britain's political leaders. Governing is never an easy thing. It is an enormous job, particularly in a representative democracy, in which it is expected that political leadership is nourished by at least a modicum of acceptance and public trust. The poll data reported earlier, plus the low voter turnout in recent general elections, are disquieting enough to suggest that Britain is on the way to becoming a "disaffected" democracy.[29] However, some will not be too troubled by that, for, as they argue, governments, wherever they are found, are rarely popular anyway. Perhaps they see a silver lining, for their lack of popularity could well prompt those in power to try all the harder to meet the public's demands and expectations. Whether or not they try harder is one of the tests of democratic governance, and whether they will succeed or not will ultimately shape the form of democratic governance that future generations will inherit.

3

The Constitution

The British historian Peter Hennessy once told the story of a visit the Queen made to a seminar he was conducting at one of the colleges of the University of London in the early 1990s. The subject of the seminar was one on which she had been well tutored—the British constitution. After contributing to the discussion, the Queen departed, but not before making what amounted to a rather remarkable admission. "The British Constitution," she said, "has always been puzzling and always will be."[1] After taking in the Queen's comment, Hennessy confessed to feeling a sense of relief, for, as he put it, "If she does not know quite what her Constitution amounts to, one can feel in the very best of company at moments of personal confusion about its workings."[2]

At the risk of distorting the Queen's use of the word "puzzling," the British constitution is indeed a vast and complicated puzzle. Finding the correct slot for each piece in the sprawling jigsaw is difficult enough. Even more difficult is the task of collecting all the pieces, for the various parts of the constitution are drawn from many different sources. Once slotted in, the puzzle may have to be reconfigured and some of the pieces replaced with others, for change is an all-important feature of this constitution. And as one nears the end of this daunting exercise, one finds occasional gaps for which there are no pieces, an indication that constitutional questions arise from time to time for which there are no tidy answers.

From this, one could assume that the British constitution is no more puzzling than any other. After all, constitutions undergo change, and they do not always provide the answer to every constitutional question that arises. But how much less puzzling would the British constitution be if one could actually put one's hands on a copy of it? That cannot be done, however, for none exists—at least in the form of a single, systematically laid out, codified document. The constitution will thus frustrate those with minds craving order and completeness, for it does not come in the form of a tidy volume available for purchase at a bookshop to pore over at a coffee bar.

It would be incorrect to conclude from this that Britain has no constitution. It would be equally incorrect to conclude that Britain's constitution is unwritten, for even though some parts are unwritten, most are set down in writing. But even these parts are not collected together and codified in one document. Major statutes enacted by Parliament, which are a primary source of the constitution, are available to read. So, too, are judge-made laws, which constitute another source. These are judicial decisions based on precedent-making findings handed down by courts over the years after judges have concluded that the statutes are silent about what legal remedies should be applied.

Conventions—which are another major constitutional source—are not set down in writing, although some become the subject of rather esoteric commentary by constitutional authorities and political scientists. Conventions are rules of practice that regulate political behavior and the ways government operates. Most are not altered, but they can be modified to suit the needs of the day, and brand new ones can emerge at any point. All three of these—statutes, judge-made laws, and conventions—form major sources of the British constitution. They, together with other sources, will be discussed later in this chapter.

Why Constitutions?

Before continuing with this examination of the British constitution, it would be helpful to reflect briefly on why constitutions occupy such a prominent, if not sacrosanct, position in the constellation of laws, political institutions, and cultural values of so many societies. Much of the answer is found in the definition of constitution itself, as well as in the meaning of two other terms that derive from the same root—constitutionality and constitutionalism.

A constitution often is referred to as the fundamental law of the nation-state. It is fundamental in that it enshrines in law the rules about the most important institutions of government, the authority they are assigned, the relationships between these institutions, and their relationships with the governed. Fundamental law is almost always found in a written, codified form. A constitution also is referred to as organic law. This means that it will undergo change—but change that usually evolves gradually, not abruptly. Almost all constitutions are subject to change, although some are more difficult to amend than others. So open-ended and flexible are the provisions of some that constitutional authorities will disagree, sometimes vigorously, about how they should be interpreted. However flexible or inflexible they are, constitutions serve as the ultimate reference for determining whether the actions of a government comply with the fundamental law.

If a statute or other decision of government is seen by an aggrieved party as contravening a precept of the fundamental law, then that party may challenge the constitutionality of the government's action in an appropriate court of law. If the court agrees to a hearing, it will determine either that the government's action did indeed run counter to a constitutional principle or that it acted in conformity with it. Such a determination might be made even before a government enacts a law, as in Germany, if its parliament chooses to submit a proposed bill to the Constitutional Court for its opinion. Or a determination might have to wait until after a bill has been enacted and put into effect, as happens in the United States when a party decides to challenge the constitutionality of the law in a federal court.

Constitutionalism, a principle that springs from a belief that government should be limited, is the sum total of the restraints a constitution imposes on government and the rights it confers on citizens to protect them from government should it threaten to exceed its constitutional authority or otherwise act in a constitutionally arbitrary manner. The rights of individuals often are safeguarded in the form of a bill of rights. These rights are enumerated in a document that either stands alone or is incorporated into the body of the constitution itself.

The British Constitution Is Different

Britain has no codified constitution. This is a striking difference from other nations because, apart from Israel and New Zealand, Britain is the only liberal democracy with no written constitution. Because it is unwritten, some argue that it is unknowable. Even constitutional experts disagree on what is in it and what is not. To correct this and other shortcomings of an unwritten constitution, the pressure group Charter 88 and the think tank Institute for Public Policy Research have over the years marshaled compelling arguments for a codified British constitution. In 1991 each even published their version of what a written constitution should include. Despite the arguments of these and other campaigners, however, those in power have countered that Britain has no need for a written document. Their reasons are twofold: there is no evidence that Britain's unwritten constitution has ever posed a problem to governing democratically, and because a written constitution would presumably be difficult to amend, codifying it would deny government the flexibility necessary to discharge its responsibilities fairly and efficiently.

The single most important contributor to the constitution is Parliament. It alone makes or changes the law—whether it is a law of great significance or one of lesser stature. Every time Parliament enacts a law, the constitution grows. It also changes in other ways, for example, when Parliament either amends or repeals a statute, or on those rare occasions when it passes legislation to override judge-made laws and conventions.

So closely does Parliament guard its role as constitution maker that should a party challenge a decision of government in the courts, the only constitutional authority the judges may invoke in the case is the act of Parliament on which that decision is based. Judges may not make a pronouncement on the constitutionality of an act of Parliament, for the act itself is part of the constitution, but they may nevertheless be asked to determine whether government ministers and civil servants allegedly at fault acted within the permissible limits of the act. Judges determine this after accepting an application from an aggrieved party to undertake a process called judicial review.

From the review judges conclude either that the law allowed government ministers and civil servants to take the action they did or that they violated the principle of *ultra vires,* that is, they went beyond the scope of what the law permitted. In other words, judges cannot be asked to question or overturn the constitutionality of the law. The exception would be if the government acted not in violation of a British law, but rather in violation of a law of the European Union (EU)—European Community (EC) law, as it is called. One of the conditions of entry into the EU that Parliament accepted when it enacted the European Communities Bill in 1972 was that Britain agree to all existing and future EC laws when it joined a year later. That means that when British judges find that a law of the UK conflicts with an EC law, the EC law trumps the British law.

The absence of a written, codified constitution has not appeared to absolve British governments from adhering to the principle of constitutionalism, for despite the absence of such a constitution, a series of laws has made it incumbent upon government to safeguard the rights of individuals. Nor have Britons had a separate catalogue of rights to consult—that is, not until 1998, when Parliament incorporated the European Convention for the Protection of Human Rights and Fundamental Freedoms into a British law called the Human Rights Act. The European Convention, as it is called for short, originated in 1953. That was the year the British government and the governments of several other nations agreed to abide by a comprehensive codification of individual rights to serve as a bulwark against such atrocities as those committed against the innocent in Europe just before and during the Second World War. The European Court of Human Rights, in Strasbourg, France, hears cases that deal with convention rights issues. Citizens of the signatory nations may appeal to this court if a law or practice in their home country denies them rights guaranteed by the convention. Britons have been allowed access to this court since 1966—so long as they exhaust all judicial remedies in Britain first.

Five Hallmarks of the British Constitution

The British constitution is the product of laws and conventions that have evolved over several centuries. The most important features, or hallmarks, of the constitution that have endured are (1) constitutional monarchy, (2) unitarism, (3) parliamentary sovereignty, (4) cabinet government, and (5) the judiciary. Each of these will be discussed in turn.

Constitutional Monarchy

Britain is a constitutional monarchy. Another way of putting it is that it has a constitution plus a monarch who reigns but does not rule. Rule is undertaken by the government of the day, that is, the prime minister and those who make up his or her cabinet. Although formed by the prime minister, the government is formally referred to as "Her Majesty's Government," for it acts in the Queen's name. The term is a throwback to an era when the monarch appointed and dismissed all ministers, determined what policies they should pursue, and summoned Parliament to approve legislation or, if necessary, dismissed it on those rare occasions when Parliament refused to do the monarch's bidding.

Monarchs today perform four constitutional functions. They appoint prime ministers, advise prime ministers, give their assent to legislation, and dissolve Parliament. All four are profoundly shaped by constitutional conventions.

The first function of the monarch is appointing the prime minister. Once the election results are known, the monarch summons the leader of the winning party to Buckingham Palace and asks him or her to form a government, or if the leader is already in office, to carry on serving as prime minister. Whether the person the Queen invites is her personal choice is irrelevant (indeed, her personal choice is not known), for the invitation she extends is undertaken in her capacity as sovereign and is strictly constrained by two conventions. The first requires the monarch to remain above party politics. The second flows from the first: the sovereign can do no more than confirm the electorate's choice by appointing the leader of the party that won a majority of seats in the House of Commons. In the unlikely event that no party wins a majority, this second convention is backed up by two others. First, the incumbent prime minister is at liberty to try to persuade a minor parliamentary party to work with his or her party in Parliament and thus forge a governing majority. However, if no party comes to the prime minister's aid, a second course of action occurs. The prime minister resigns, and the monarch asks the leader of the other parliamentary party having a sizable number of seats to form a government—even a minority government, if the leader is unable to convince a minor party to rule with it in coalition. In these ways, others sort out the mechanics of governing, and the sovereign keeps a safe distance from party politics.

Advising the prime minister is a second function of the monarch. It takes the form of what Walter Bagehot in the nineteenth century referred to as "the right to be consulted, the right to encourage, the right to warn."[3] These rights the monarch fulfills in meetings with the prime minister every Tuesday evening at Buckingham Palace or nearby Windsor Castle. The sovereign and the prime minister are the only ones present. No notes are taken, and no press conferences follow. Their exchanges are undertaken in complete confidence, and politicians and journalists may do no more than speculate about their substance. What could well result is "a kind of catharsis by Royal appointment," as one scholar wrote.[4] Or, as Queen Elizabeth II herself put it, prime ministers

> unburden themselves or they tell me what's going on or if they've got any problems and sometimes one can help in that way too. They know

that one can be impartial.... I think it's rather nice to feel that one's a sort of sponge and everybody can come and tell one things. And some things stay there and some things go out of the other ear and some things never come out at all. And occasionally you can be able to put one's point of view which perhaps they hadn't seen ... from that angle.[5]

It is from this free exchange of information and views that the monarch can be seen as taking an interest in the affairs of the realm without becoming involved in its politics.

A third function of the monarch is assenting to legislation. When the monarch gives what is called the Royal Assent, it means that she acknowledges that a bill has been agreed to in identical form by the House of Commons and the House of Lords. Queen Anne (reign: 1702–1714) was the last monarch to veto a bill. That was in 1707. Ever since then, convention has required that the monarch not substitute his or her personal preference for the collective decision of the two houses of Parliament. The most common way by which the Queen registers her assent is by addressing letters of patent to the speakers of the two houses that ask them to announce that the monarch has agreed to a bill. Before a bill has gotten to that stage, it is thought that if a monarch had qualms about a piece of legislation, she would have aired her concerns about it with the prime minister during one of their Tuesday evening meetings as the bill was making its way through Parliament. Whether or not the legislation is to the monarch's liking is immaterial, for convention dictates that she has no choice but to acknowledge its passage.

Dissolving Parliament is the fourth constitutional function of the monarch. This she does at the request of the prime minister, after the prime minister has presumably consulted the cabinet. Parliament is then prorogued, that is, it ceases to function until after a new general election is held and a new government is formed. Parliament is dissolved for one of three reasons: (1) the life of a parliament is about to reach its statutory limit of five years, (2) the party in power is unable to muster support in the House of Commons for key bills because, although it is the largest party, it does not have an overall majority of seats, or (3) the governing party wishes to capitalize on its popularity in the country by scheduling an election well in advance of the five-year limit so that it can increase the number of seats it holds in the House of Commons and remain in power for a longer period. Whatever the basis for the prime minister's request, not once in modern times has a monarch turned down a prime minister's request to dissolve Parliament.

These four constitutional functions had their origins in the eighteenth century and had two very practical effects as they became entrenched in the nineteenth. First, they diluted the monarch's authority, and second, they insulated the sovereign from partisan controversy at a time when the electoral franchise was being extended, and thus they helped legitimize the monarch's role as a politically neutral head of state. So crucial has it been since the beginning of the twentieth century that the monarch remain faithful to these conventions that prime ministers and other political leaders have scrupulously avoided taking any action that might be interpreted as pushing the monarch beyond the constraints that these conventions impose and by so doing provoke a constitutional crisis. In that respect, these conventions cut both ways for they check prime ministers and other politicians as much as they check the monarch.

Unitarism

The constitutions of most states provide for either a unitary or a federal form of government. The majority are unitary, and Britain's is among them. A classic definition of the unitary model is a state "built up around one unambiguous centre which enjoys economic dominance and pursues a more or less undeviating policy of administrative standardisation. All areas of the state are treated alike, and all institutions are directly under the control of the centre."[6] The "institutions" referred to are any regional or local units of government that government at the center may choose to create and empower. Should it decide to create such units, it will transfer certain executive and legislative powers to them through a process called devolution. These governments are at all times subordinate to the central government. "Subordinate" is a key word found in the legislative language effecting the transfer. It is key because it implies that, even though these governments have a legal right to function, they have no constitutional right to do so. The central government, if it succeeds in marshalling a majority in Parliament, is at liberty to dismantle them or alter their powers as it sees fit. In other words, what central government gives it can also take away. Therein lies the essential difference between unitarism and federalism, for only in a federal form will a constitution prohibit either level of government from dismantling the other or repealing the other's powers.

Not all forms of government operate in perfect conformity with the unitary model just described—or with the federal model, for that matter—for each model allows for some variation. Just as the federal form found in the United States is not the same as that found in Canada or Germany, so too Britain's unitary form is different from that of France or Sweden. Indeed, Britain's form of unitarism conforms only partially to the definition referred to above, for not all policies and institutions of the four nations fall directly under the control of the central government. For example, Scotland's legal and judicial systems have always been separate and different from those of Northern Ireland, and each of these is separate and different yet again from those of England and Wales, where they are uniform. If it chose, the central government through Parliament could establish precise uniformity among the four nations. However, that is not at all likely to happen, for certain historical forces that have shaped these differences over the years would surely pose insurmountable obstacles to any attempts made to sweep them away.

The most recent historical forces are the strains of nationalism that have gained momentum since the 1970s in Scotland and Wales, particularly in

Scotland. So virulent were these strains in the 1990s that the Government of Tony Blair was persuaded to give the voters of these two nations an opportunity to decide whether they wished the central government to form legislatures and executive bodies in Edinburgh and Cardiff and devolve certain powers to them. In 1998, two referendums were held, one in Scotland and the other in Wales, and a majority of voters in both nations supported the devolution of powers. Elections were held a year later, and shortly after them the winners took their seats in the newly created Scottish parliament and Welsh National Assembly.

Different forces shaped conditions in Northern Ireland. The greatest amount of autonomy the central government ever devolved on any one of the nations was conferred there in 1921 after Northern Ireland, or Ulster, was partitioned from southern Ireland, and southern Ireland became an independent republic. Parliament gave Northern Ireland its own parliament in Belfast, an executive body headed by a governor, and a civil service. An understanding was struck that London would not interfere in Ulster's day-to-day affairs. But prolonged sectarian strife, instigated by the Irish Republican Army (IRA), erupted in the 1960s, and in 1972 Britain brought an end to its first experiment in devolution.

By the late 1990s, however, there were signs that peace was at hand. In 1996, the IRA announced a cease-fire. Representatives of Sinn Fein, the political party with ties to the IRA that for many years had insisted that Northern Ireland be incorporated into the Republic of Ireland, participated in talks to bring a permanent end to the strife. From these talks came an agreement in 1998 to allow the voters of Ulster and the Republic of Ireland to decide in a referendum whether Northern Ireland should be incorporated into the Irish Republic or remain with Britain. Until such a referendum is held, however, the agreement provides for devolving considerable powers to a government in Belfast. Elections to an assembly followed, and a power-sharing executive body was created in 1999. Devolution in this part of the United Kingdom has had a checkered history, however. Devolution was authorized in 1999, suspended and then reauthorized in 2000, and suspended again in 2002. As of this writing, it remains suspended.

When the Blair Government drafted its devolution bills in the late 1990s, it apportioned powers to the three nations, but different powers to each. Greater power was granted to Scotland than Wales and Northern Ireland, largely to still the voices of those Scots who had been so strident in their demands for independence. As a result, the Scottish parliament was given legislative power over a broad range of domestic policies, plus authority to raise or lower in limited measure the basic rate of income tax levied in Scotland.

Without a doubt, Britain's unitary form of government has undergone a major transformation since the late 1990s. Moreover, it could be argued that, for three reasons, central government is locked into the transformed arrangement that it organized with the Scottish parliament. First, the British parliament is unlikely to repeal the law devolving power to Scotland when more than 74 percent of the Scottish electorate who turned out to vote supported a Scottish parliament. Second, Parliament would be reluctant to bring an end to devolved government for Scotland for fear that doing so would encourage disaffected Scots to resume their agitation for Scotland's independence.

A third reason is that the Judicial Committee of the Privy Council could rule in favor of any one of the three devolved legislatures if a dispute arose between one of them and Parliament. This committee is not a new creation; for some years it has been the court of final appeal for Britain's dependent territories and those Commonwealth nations that agreed to its jurisdiction when they became independent. However, extending its jurisdiction to include the resolution of disputes between Parliament and the devolved legislatures is new. If it rules in favor of one of the devolved legislatures, it could be politically awkward for Parliament to overturn its decision. It would presumably have to rewrite the laws pertaining to devolution, and if that were to happen, it would be seen as an attempt to subvert the principle of devolution and alter the rules on devolution in a self-serving way.

Thus, although Parliament retains the constitutional right to repeal the laws on devolution or amend them in a significant way, it is highly doubtful that it would have the political will to do so. A full account of devolution is found in chapter 11. For now, it can be concluded that the relationship between the central government and the Scottish parliament in particular represents a serious departure from the classic model of the unitary form of government—so much of a departure that one leading scholar on the subject was persuaded to describe the relationship as "quasi-federal."[7]

Parliamentary Sovereignty

Parliamentary sovereignty is a third hallmark of the British constitution. The origin of this term is not known, but it was probably coined more than three hundred years ago when Parliament was locked in a struggle with the Crown as each sought to gain the upper hand in governing the nation. Curious though the term is, however, what does it mean? A leading contemporary authority came close to defining it when he called it "the one fundamental law of the British Constitution."[8] For a comprehensive definition, one is advised to turn to A. V. Dicey's *An Introduction to the Study of the Law of the Constitution*, a work that, although first published in 1885, is consulted even today by those who choose to pick their way through the rather arcane details of the British constitution. In Dicey's words, parliamentary sovereignty means that "Parliament ... has ... the right to make or unmake any law whatever; and, further, that no person or body is recognized by the law ... as having a right to override or set aside the legislation of Parliament."[9] In short, there are no limits imposed on Parliament's authority to legislate. Or so Dicey would have had one believe.

Parliament's sovereignty (or supremacy, as some prefer it) is not found in a statute. It exists in common law, which is law derived not from statute but from precedents established by the decisions of judges over the years. One example as it pertains to Parliament is *Bradlaugh v. Gossett,* a case from the nineteenth century in which the court held that it had no power to interfere with the internal affairs of the House of Commons. Common law provides that which statute law cannot, a point that, in effect, is reduced to something of a riddle: "No statute can confer the power of parliamentary sovereignty, for that would be to confer the very power which is being acted upon."[10]

By implication, parliamentary sovereignty also means that no parliament is bound by any previous parliament, and it follows that no parliament may bind any of its successors. But here one must exercise caution in couching one's words. Parliament, simply put, is free to amend or repeal any existing statute it wishes. In reality, however, Parliament cannot help but bind a successor parliament, for, as one commentator, Ferdinand Mount, put it, binding a successor parliament "is what defines its successor as a true parliament and endows its decisions with proper authority."[11] Mount went on to say, "parliamentary sovereignty is a jealous god."[12]

Are there no bounds to Parliament's sovereignty? Mount lays bare the absurdity of the notion that Parliament is absolutely sovereign with the hypothetical example that if it chose to pass a law making a man a woman, "then *for the purposes of the law* a man is a woman."[13] One does not have to go to such lengths to understand that there are certain practical limits imposed on what Parliament can legislate. For example, as seen in the previous section on unitarism, there are practical political limits imposed on Parliament's repeal of the Government of Scotland Act of 1998. Another example is European Community (EC) law.

With respect to EC law, critics of the UK's membership in the European Union (EU) echo the claim once made by Lord Radcliffe that Parliament is not even "the instrument of power," let alone "its holder."[14] The crux of their argument is that when Parliament joined the EU in 1973, it sacrificed its sovereignty at the altar of the EU by ceding authority to this supranational organization to make laws for Britain. Thus, whenever a particularly controversial EC law is agreed to, critics of the EU are quick to assert (as they often have) that Parliament paid too high a price for entering what in 2007 had expanded into a union of twenty-seven nation-states by agreeing to accept not only all EC laws that existed when Britain joined, but to forfeit to the EU the authority to enact all future laws in designated policy realms as well.

In those areas of policy spelled out in various treaties, EC legislation for all twenty-seven member states of the EU is agreed to by two bodies in Brussels, Belgium, the host city of most of the institutions of the EU. The two bodies are the European Parliament and the Council of Ministers. Both are involved in making laws, and Britain is represented on each. Seventy-eight British members of the European Parliament (MEPs) sit in the 786-member European Parliament, and one minister from the British government acts on behalf of Britain's interests in the 27-member Council of Ministers.

A fuller account of Britain's involvement in these two bodies and in the EU overall is provided in chapter 13. For now the focus is on the claim that EC law represents an assault on the sovereignty of Parliament. Those who make this claim base their arguments on three major points. First, because British MEPs make up only 10 percent of the total membership of the European Parliament, they easily can be outvoted by a majority of MEPs from the other twenty-six national delegations. Second, the minister who defends Britain's position on an issue before the Council of Ministers, the EU's other legislative body, can be left in the minority when the final vote is cast. And third, if the British parliament is dissatisfied with the outcome of the vote, it has no unilateral authority to overturn it. The government may lodge an appeal with the European Court of Justice, the EU's supreme court, but such an appeal would be considered frivolous, for this court may reverse a law only if it runs counter to what various EU treaties provide for. From this, critics of Britain's membership in the EU argue that not only did Parliament cede lawmaking authority to the EU; it also gave the EU power to make laws that Parliament might oppose.

One could say, then, that since 1973 Britain has been endowed with two constitutions. In addition to its own, it is governed by the Treaty of Rome of 1958, the EU's founding constitution, along with subsequent treaties that amended this original treaty. Some who lament what they dub the "surrender" of parliamentary sovereignty see only one way to resolve this constitutional dilemma—Parliament's repeal of the legislation that took Britain into the EU in the first place. No one would deny that Parliament possesses this right. But so drastic a move would this be that even many who decry Britain's membership in the EU agree that the resulting fallout would be unthinkable. Sovereign though Parliament is in the field of law, certain major practical political considerations make its sovereignty far from absolute. Were A. V. Dicey still living, he might well agree.

Cabinet Government

It is not uncommon for those who compare constitutions to single out Britain's as one that fuses the legislative and executive powers of its government. Walter Bagehot did so when in the nineteenth century he contrasted the separation of powers in the United States with what he called the "fusion" of legislative and executive powers in the United Kingdom.[15] A close inspection of the British form of government casts doubt on the appropriateness of the concept of fusion, however. To fuse is to "mix," "blend," or "make as one." None of these definitions applies. For example, although civil servants and military personnel occupy positions in the executive, they are prohibited from serving as members of Parliament. Ministers are the exception. They hold the most senior posts in the executive and sit in Parliament as well.

The executive in Bagehot's day was far different from what it is today. Those unaware of the differences therefore can be easily confused. In Bagehot's world of the nineteenth century, "executive" was the prime minister and the cabinet. Today, however, it means not only the prime minister and the cabinet, but also the departments of government and numerous executive agencies, regulatory bodies, and advisory bodies—all of which are at the central level of government. The executive has grown hugely since Bagehot's day, and so too have its functions. It is important to bear in mind this broader, twenty-first-century meaning of "executive," as it is used in these pages and in the chapters that follow.

It also is important to keep in mind that Parliament and the executive perform exclusively different functions. Just as Parliament has no authority to implement the policies it provides for in law, so too the executive has no power to enact the legislation that produces these polices. The executive and Parliament are two separate and independent entities, charged with what one authority argued are "two distinct functions of leadership, direction and command on the one hand, and of critical discussion and examination on the other." Parliament and the executive, he continued, "start from separate historical origins, and each is perpetuated in accordance with its own methods and its own continuity." [16]

Bagehot was on much firmer ground with his fusion analogy when he referred not to the whole of the executive but to the cabinet only, that select circle of ministers who hold the most senior positions in the executive and sit as members of Parliament as well. The cabinet was, in his words, the "connecting link" between Parliament and the executive,[17] a characterization that describes the cabinet of today as accurately as it did in his day. One major difference between the cabinet then and now is its size. Today's cabinet is larger. Most of its twenty-two or twenty-three ministers are drawn from the House of Commons; the remaining few come from the House of Lords. It is at the apex of the executive hierarchy, which also includes a number of departments, all of which are headed by more than half the members of the cabinet. The cabinet is the Government—capital G—or the government of the day, as it is also called. Its members constitute a body of equals, called "colleagues," headed by the prime minister, who is first among equals. This nucleus of senior ministers forms what is called cabinet government. Its powers, which are not spelled out in any statute, are limited primarily by a combination of conventions, political common sense, and what the majority party in Parliament is willing to tolerate.

Although the cabinet is formed *from* Parliament, it is not formed *by* Parliament, for Parliament has no hand in selecting its members. That task is left to the prime minister, who is free to choose from the ranks of his or her party in Parliament, although the prime minister must carefully weigh the political ramifications of choosing certain members over others. After the prime minister has announced his or her choice of cabinet members, Parliament is not even called upon to confirm or veto the appointments. Once they take their places in the cabinet, ministers continue to serve in Parliament. Indeed, convention requires them to do so, and thus they perform two functions, one legislative and the other executive.

More will be said about the cabinet and its functions in chapter 9. For the moment, it can be said that cabinet government, the fourth hallmark of the British constitution, is the most distinguishing characteristic of a parliamentary form of government. It is in fact the British model that many other nation-states have sought to copy in varying ways over the years.

The Judiciary

A fifth hallmark of the British constitution is the judiciary. It is made up of an autonomous yet subordinate body of judges entrusted to act in a politically neutral manner when called upon to adjudicate disputes between private individuals or between private individuals and the state. This characterization, however, sounds like constitutional doublethink, for one is left to wonder how it is that the judiciary can be both autonomous and subordinate and subordinate yet neutral. These apparent contradictions can be reconciled, but only by understanding how the pivotal word "subordinate" is used. To whom or to what is the judiciary subordinate and in what way?

The judiciary is subordinate only to Parliament, but here one must be precise. Because there is no higher law than the laws of Parliament, judges must confine their assessment of the facts in a case to the provisions of the law. In that sense only is the judiciary subordinate to Parliament, and it has been ever since the Bill of Rights established the doctrine of parliamentary sovereignty in 1689. Judges are not a law unto themselves, nor may they be, for they have no constitutional right to substitute their judgment for the judgment of Parliament. However, when no statute applies to the facts in a case, judges are at liberty to search for a judicial remedy in the common law, or when a statute does apply but its provisions are unclear, judges are allowed the discretion to interpret its meaning.

In these two ways, judges can be seen as shaping the law. There are three other ways as well. First, when they feel strongly about certain issues of law and order and the administration of justice, they speak out publicly with the hope of influencing the future course of legislation. Second, if they determine that a provision in an act of Parliament runs counter to the Convention on Human Rights, which was incorporated into British law in the Human Rights Act of 1998, they are bound by that act to alert Parliament that the provision is incompatible with the Human Rights Act. And third, the Judicial Committee of the Privy Council may rule in favor of any one of the three devolved legislatures if a dispute arises between one of them and Parliament.

Not only is the judiciary not subordinate to Parliament—only to its laws—so, too, is it not subordinate to the executive. However, it is dependent on the executive for appointments, for funding, and for enforcement. In the first realm, when a senior judge has to be appointed, it is the prime minister who does so, albeit appointing one recommended by the lord chancellor. But, in fact, the individual has been recommended to the lord chancellor by an independent body called the Judicial Appointments Commission. Second, the courts are supported with funds provided by the Treasury, and third, judges rely on the various departments and agencies of the executive to carry out their decisions. Court and judges, then, are dependent upon the executive, but not subordinate to it. Indeed, they cannot be if the judiciary is obliged to uphold the doctrine of parliamentary sovereignty, which it will do when, among other things, it decides whether a minister has complied with the law or broken it, either by neglecting to perform a statutory duty or by straying beyond the limits of the statute.

Those who sit on the bench have been chosen not only because of their experience in the practice of law, but also because they can be trusted to render decisions free of partisan or personal bias. Although their decisions are subordinate to the laws of Parliament and they depend on funds from the executive, they are allowed to function without interference from Parliament and the executive, thanks to a string of laws and conventions, some of which stretch back more than three hundred years. To attract and retain the best judicial minds possible, the compensation is generous. Salaries are never at issue when the budget is debated every year, for they are permanently fixed in law, and judges receive salary increases just like civil servants. Moreover, judges enjoy security of tenure and may serve on the bench for the remainder of their professional lives, although once they reach age seventy they must retire. If they serve until age sixty-five, they are assured of receiving a full pension when they retire. All these safeguards not only help to foster respect for the courts, they also bolster the independence of the judiciary, enhance the doctrine of parliamentary sovereignty, and give legitimacy to the authority of the executive side of government as long as ministers correct their actions in the event judges find they have strayed from the law.

The subject of the judiciary is taken up in greater depth in chapter 12. Before proceeding, however, it is important to emphasize that the many statutes and conventions that have been added to the constitution over the years, including the landmark Constitutional Reform Act of 2005, have fortified the position of the judiciary by giving it the means to resist possible assaults on its independence. Just as important, these safeguards are seen as so sacrosanct that they are not at all likely to be revoked or diminished in any way in the decades ahead.

The Sources of the British Constitution

Britain's leaders did not have to assemble, as delegates did in Philadelphia in 1787, to devise theories for a constitution, debate them, and ultimately codify them into a constitution from scratch. The closest Britain came to having a written constitution was in 1653, when Oliver Cromwell penned the *Instrument of Government,* a framework he formulated four years after Charles I was executed, in a twelve-year period when there was no monarch and England was governed as a republic. However, Britain's first and only written constitution was scrapped several years later, along with the republican form of government for which it was intended, when the son of Charles I returned from exile in 1660 and the monarchy was restored. Despite the social unrest in the interregnum, it never reached a point at which Britain's leaders had to turn their backs on an *ancien regime* and devise a constitutional document befitting a new order. As a result, Britain's constitution was left to grow piecemeal over the centuries, quite impervious to any efforts to reproduce it in a codified form. Because it is not set down in one document, it is difficult to comprehend. But knowing the sources upon which it rests helps one achieve a greater understanding of one of the world's oldest surviving blueprints for governance.

The British constitution has seven sources. The laws of Parliament and conventions have figured prominently in shaping the modern British nation-state. Britain's membership in the European Union gave rise to the introduction of another source—EC law. The four sources that remain are human rights law, case law, the rules and practices of Parliament, and scholarly treatises. All seven can be grouped under two categories of constitutional sources—legal and nonlegal sources.

Legal Sources of the Constitution

The four legal sources of the constitution are the laws of Parliament, European Community law, human rights law, and case law. The laws of Parliament are the most important because of the doctrine of parliamentary sovereignty. However, some acts of Parliament are more important than others. So strikingly important are some that there is little doubt they form major building blocks of the constitution. Among them are laws that some years ago profoundly altered the relationship between the monarchy and Parliament. The most important are the Magna Carta of 1215 (enacted in 1225), the Petition of Right Act of 1628, the Bill of Rights of 1689, and the Act of Settlement of 1701.

Other statutes of constitutional significance also have affected the rights and responsibilities of the British people. Examples are several laws that expanded the franchise from 1832 to 1969, the Race Relations Act of 1976, and the Human Rights Act of 1998. Still others have fundamentally reordered the relationships between the central government in London and governments beyond, such as a series of local government acts, the Scotland Act of 1998, the Government of Wales Act of 1998, and the European Communities Act of 1972. Two of these laws, the Human Rights Act and the European Communities Act, produced two further categories of legal sources of the constitution.

EC law is a second legal source of the constitution. When Parliament enacted the European Communities Bill in 1972 and thereby agreed to join the European Economic Community (now called the European Union) some fifteen years after it had been founded, it accepted as British law all EC law, both past and future. This meant that if a British law were inconsistent with an EC law, the former would have to yield to the latter even if the British statute contained significant constitutional provisions. As a consequence, a considerable amount of social and economic legislation—some containing provisions of far-reaching constitutional importance—has been incorporated into British law. For example, most tariff and nontariff barriers affecting trade with the other member states have been eliminated, citizens of the other EU states are allowed (with some exceptions) to live in Britain and work there without a work permit, the rights of women in the workforce have been strengthened by requiring their salaries to be equal to those of men for work of equal value, and the differential age requirement that women must be sixty and men sixty-five before qualifying for a state pension has given way to a uniform age requirement.

A third legal source of the constitution is the Human Rights Act, which took effect in 2000. When Parliament agreed to this act in 1998, it incorporated into British law the sixty-six articles of the European Convention for the Protection of Human Rights and Fundamental Freedoms. This convention, which the Churchill Government and the governments of fourteen other nations ratified in 1953, systematically enumerates individual civil and political rights that the fifteen governments agreed to honor. They include, among others, the right to a fair trial, freedom of expression, freedom of peaceful assembly and association, freedom of religion, and freedom of the press, plus the all-important right to petition the European Court of Human Rights, in Strasbourg, France.

When the Human Rights Act of 1998 went into effect, almost all the signatory nations—now forty-six of them—already had incorporated the European Convention into their laws. It was not until 1998 that the British government chose to do so, even though Britons had been allowed since 1966 to lodge an appeal with the Strasbourg court if they had first exhausted all judicial remedies in Britain. Once the European Convention was incorporated into British law, complainants were spared the time, expense, and general inconvenience of appealing to yet another court to seek redress of their grievances, although they still may petition the court in Strasbourg as long as they have exhausted all judicial remedies on their own soil.

Case law is the fourth legal source of the constitution. It is also known as judge-made law. There are two variants of case law, common law and law based on statutory interpretation. Common law is law made by judges based not on a law of Parliament, but rather on what they determine is custom, fortified by what one judge called "common sense under a judge's wig."[18] A considerable body of common law decisions and principles has been created over the centuries and survives as precedents that judges rely on when they are called upon to render a decision based on similar facts in a new case.

Two very different decisions serve as examples. In the first decision, the Law Lords in the House of Lords drew from a principle of common law that the government must compensate a private party for property it damages. This was the principle that led to its decision in *Burmah Oil Company v. Lord Advocate* (1965) that the company was due compensation for the destruction of its oil installations during the Second World War by British

Speaking of . . .

Two Constitutional Principles in Conflict

Two constitutional principles appear to be in conflict. On the one hand, the Human Rights Act of 1998 empowered judges to identify any parts of a statute that are incompatible with the European Convention on Human Rights. On the other hand, it is Parliament, not judges, that decides the contents of the law. Parliament's granting this authority to judges has triggered clashes between judges and those who think that the sovereignty of Parliament is under threat.

> "The British Constitution is coming to mean . . . something different to the judges from what it means to government."

Professor Vernon Bogdanor spoke of these clashes in a public lecture he delivered at Gresham College in 2006. He was concerned that, in his words, they "could easily lead to a constitutional crisis." After sketching out the problem, Professor Bogdanor suggested how it could be resolved:

"The European Convention of Human Rights [incorporated into British law as the Human Rights Act] is coming to take on the status of ... a written or codified constitution. Yet, the traditional view is that there can be no such higher law in our system of government. The great 19th century constitutional lawyer, A. V. Dicey, declared that 'There is no law which Parliament cannot change. There is no fundamental or so-called constitutional law....' Formally, of course, these propositions remain true. Judges can do no more than issue a declaration of incompatibility if they believe that a particular statute or part of a statute cannot be reconciled with the European Convention. They cannot declare it void, and Parliament can still refrain from amending or repealing the offending statute or part of a statute, although it has not yet done so....

"Government and Parliament say that judges are usurping power and seeking to thwart the will of Parliament. Judges say that the government is abandoning basic civil liberties and then attacking the judiciary for doing its job in implementing the provisions of the Human Rights Act. The British Constitution is coming to mean ... something different to the judges from what it means to government.... There will therefore be a conflict and a struggle. How will it be resolved?

"There are two possible outcomes. The first is that Parliament succeeds in defeating the challenge of the judges, and that parliamentary sovereignty is preserved. The second is that, like almost every other democracy, we come to develop a codified constitution, in which judges, as in the United States, have the right to strike down laws which offend against human rights. We would then become what Lord Steyn ... has called a true constitutional state."

Source: Vernon Bogdanor, "The Judges and the Constitution," a lecture delivered at Gresham College, London, May 30, 2006.

troops in Rangoon to prevent them from falling into enemy hands. In the second example, a court in 1736 ruled that a husband could not be charged for raping his wife.

The vast majority of common law decisions have remained unchanged through the years. Parliament and the superior courts may choose to set them aside, however, as one of them did in each of these two examples. In the first example, Parliament nullified the Burmah Oil Company ruling by enacting a statute that forbade compensation. In the second example, the Court of Appeal and then the Law Lords unanimously reversed a lower court's decision in *Regina v. R* (1991) and overturned the 1736 common law ruling upon which it had been based. The common law, said the presiding Law Lord, was "capable of evolving in the light of changing social, economic and cultural developments" and a wife could no longer be considered "the subservient chattel of the husband." [19]

The second variant of case law is law based on statutory interpretation. This law is also called judge-made law because, even though a statute exists in this instance, judges are expected to provide an interpretation of the meaning of its relevant provisions if they are unclear or they appear to contradict the provisions of one or more other statutes. Often it is difficult to draft legislation that is unambiguous, and it is impossible to devise laws that foresee events and circumstances that are not foreseeable. This explains why some of the language of a statute is couched in general terms and why Parliament accepts that judges will apply a reasonable interpretation of what Parliament intended the statute to mean, as reflected primarily in ministers' statements in debate. That was what happened, for example, in *Fox v. Stirk*, a Court of Appeal decision handed down in 1970. Judges in this case declared that Parliament had intended students to register to vote in the constituency in which they were residing while at university and not necessarily in the constituency in which they had lived before going off to university. This decision introduced clarity into the law by stipulating that which they believed Parliament had intended.

At other times, the provisions of one law may contradict the provisions contained in one or more other laws. For example, in *Gillick v. West Norfolk Health Authority*, the Court of Appeal ruled in 1984 on whether a doctor acted lawfully in offering contraceptive advice to a girl younger than sixteen years of age. No law prohibited the doctor from doing so. The judges had to strike a balance between one law and several others—one that stipulated that it was a criminal offense to have sexual intercourse with a girl younger than the age of sixteen and other laws that required that the interests of children be safeguarded. One judge held that the doctor could be criminally liable for offering such advice because it "might encourage girls under 16 to have sexual intercourse." The other judges disagreed, arguing that they had a duty to adhere to "a bigger principle," that of protecting the interests of girls younger than sixteen years of age by allowing doctors "to advise them in such a way that they won't become pregnant." Judges in this case, as Justice Leonard Hoffman explained, were "making law in that there was no specific rule before. But they were not making it up. They were deriving it from the existing law."[20]

Nonlegal Sources of the Constitution

The remaining three sources of the constitution are nonlegal in that they are not derived from statutes or other legal instruments. The sources are conventions, the laws and customs of Parliament, and scholarly treatises. A convention has been described by one scholar as "a generally accepted political practice, usually with a record of successful applications or precedents."[21] Moreover, as two other scholars note, conventions are "considered binding by and upon those who operate the Constitution."[22] As pivotal as they are to the workings of the constitution, however, they are not collected together and codified in one document. Nor are they enforceable in courts of law. Yet so regularly accepted are they that only on the rarest of occasions has Parliament found it necessary to override them with legislation.

Indeed, Parliament may choose to underscore their importance by taking action in one of two ways. First, it could dignify the existence of a convention by acknowledging it in a statute, as it did in the Ministers of the Crown Act of 1937, when Parliament set the salary of the prime minister, whose position and functions had been created not by law but by convention more than two hundred years before. Or second, it could give a convention legal force by incorporating it into statute, as it did in the Parliament Act of 1911, after the House of Lords rejected the annual budget in 1910, defying the convention that it defer to the House of Commons on matters of finance. The preponderant number of conventions that have evolved over the years have shaped the ways in which government is organized and the rules under which it operates. For example, conventions dictate that the monarch appoint as prime minister the leader of the political party that won a majority of seats in the House of Commons and that a Government must resign if it is defeated on a vote of no confidence. Indeed, the prime minister and cabinet are creatures of conventions.

A second nonlegal source of the constitution is the rules and practices of Parliament, many of which are regarded as having constitutional authority.[23] Although some are unwritten norms, most are set down in *Erskine May's Treatise on the Law, Privileges, Proceedings and Usage of Parliament*, a set of volumes containing the rules of procedure, rulings by the Speaker of the House of Commons, and precedents of both houses of Parliament, first edited by Sir Thomas Erskine May, clerk of the House of Commons in the 1870s and 1880s, and updated over the years by his successors. Those norms not found in this rule book of Parliament (or *Erskine May*, as it usually is called) are informal, many of which are conventions of the constitution. These are practices that, for example, guide the majority party's relations with the Opposition party and the major parties' relations with minor parties. Because the houses of Parliament have an inherent right to control their own practices, the courts have chosen not to rule on them.

The third and final nonlegal source of the constitution is a genre of literature that has evolved over the years—scholarly treatises penned by those well recognized for their insights into the workings of the constitution. A poll, were it to be conducted among constitutional scholars, would yield the names of dozens who have contributed seminal works on the constitution, some of whom have been referred to in this chapter and undoubtedly would be among the top on the list. One certain to be there is A. V. Dicey, whose works in the nineteenth century inspired two contemporary scholars to remark that for some years his "word was just about the only written constitution we had." [24] Another sure to be among those at the top of the list is the nineteenth-century political thinker, Walter Bagehot, about whom one scholar remarked: "before Bagehot wrote [*The English Constitution*], there was no English constitution that people could recognise." [25] Others likely to be found on the list reflect the distilled wisdom of scholars from a much earlier era and undoubtedly would include Edward Coke (*Institutes of the Laws of England* [1628]), Matthew Hale (*History of the Common Law of England* [1713]), William Blackstone (*Commentaries on the Laws of England* [1765]), and John James Park (*The Dogmas of the Constitution* [1832]). In the twentieth century, Sir Ivor Jennings and John P. Mackintosh left their mark, with, among other works, *The Law and the Constitution* (1959) and *The British Cabinet* (1977), respectively.

Scholarly treatises do not carry the force of law; however, judges invariably benefit from the insights they provide as they ponder obscure points of the constitution or search for ways to reconcile two seemingly contradictory constitutional principles—especially when "a statute has not yet been judicially interpreted, or where no court has pronounced authoritatively on a matter of common law." [26] The names of Dicey, Blackstone, Jennings, and others may not be invoked in the decisions of judges, but the legacies these legal scholars have left provide yet one more source of the constitution.

Conclusion

The British constitution is not codified. As a result, it contains a certain degree of flexibility that codified constitutions do not possess. There is, however, a possible price to pay for this flexibility, for as one authority observed, "[p]olitics is the final arbiter under an unwritten constitution." [27] That is why political leaders are advised to be mindful of Prime Minister William Gladstone's admonition, written in his memoirs in 1879, that the British constitution "presumes more boldly than any other the good sense and the good faith of those who work it." [28] This friendly reminder, which has echoed down through the years, is especially compelling today because of the number of dramatic changes produced by several pieces of legislation—in particular the European Communities Act of 1972, the Human Rights Act of 1998, the Scotland Act of 1998, and the Government of Wales Act of 1998.

When Dicey wrote in 1885 that "no person or body is recognized by the law … as having a right to override or set aside the legislation of Parliament," [29] he could hardly have envisioned the extent to which parliamentary sovereignty would be modified, if not eroded, by the changes wrought by EC law, human rights law, and devolution. In particular, he could not have foreseen the new role British judges would play in interpreting the law.

The British constitution has always been in flux, but especially so in recent decades. Constitutional reforms have modified the doctrine of parliamentary sovereignty and thrust a new role on judges, and the unitary form of government that for so long was a hallmark of the British political system has been transformed. In addition, the first steps were taken to reform the House of Lords, a freedom of information act was put into effect, and a constitutional reform act introduced landmark reforms of the judiciary. Perhaps one day Britain will overturn centuries of tradition and adopt a codified constitution. Remote though that possibility may be, given the nature and pace of recent constitutional change, it is one that cannot be discounted.

4

Political Parties and Party Government

British politics is quintessentially party politics. Nothing better describes it or better explains it. Political parties suffuse nearly every aspect of political life, and most decidedly so if one is speaking of the decisions of government, of votes cast in Parliament, or of the choices voters make on election day. Little wonder, then, that British government is party government. It starts to take form immediately after the collective choice of the voters is known on election day and the Queen has discharged her constitutional duty of receiving the leader of the winning party at Buckingham Palace to name him or her prime minister.

The prime minister assumes office without the benefit of the ten to eleven weeks of transition afforded a newly elected president in the United States between the election and the inauguration. In fact, there is barely a pause between the prime minister being named and his or her move into (or remaining at) No. 10 Downing Street, which doubles as the prime minister's official residence and place of work. In other words, the prime minister has little time to ponder whom to appoint from his or her party in Parliament to fill the more than one hundred ministerial posts that will constitute the government of the day. However, those worthy of appointment have not been far from the prime minister's thoughts before the campaign, and normally within a day or two after the election the names of the first twenty or so are announced. These are the most senior ministers of government. They will sit in the cabinet, the collective decision-making body at the apex of the executive, which the prime minister chairs. About fifteen of these are appointed to head the departments of government. Rounding out the government of the day are an additional eighty to ninety junior ministers, almost all of whom are assigned to the various departments to assist their respective senior minister heads by taking charge of major areas of responsibility.

The leader of the runner-up party becomes leader of the official Opposition and appoints parliamentarians from his or her party to the shadow cabinet. They are mirror opposites of cabinet ministers and, as the government-in-waiting, are poised to assume the reins should the electorate return their party to power at the next election. The pledges the winning party made to the electorate, which are outlined in a campaign document called a manifesto and cited often on the hustings, are normally translated into legislative proposals the Government seeks to enact. The Opposition is ever on guard to find fault with these proposals and often counters them with its own. But because the ruling party usually commands an overall majority and party discipline in the House of Commons is robustly enforced, the government of the day almost always has its way while the Opposition merely has its say.

Political parties in Britain perform ten functions, identified in Table 4.1. The first five of these are common to most political systems that hold free elections and are fulfilled even before elections are held and governments are formed. The remaining five, which are specific to Britain, are performed after the results of an election are known.

Political parties in Britain have not always performed these functions. Some did not evolve until the latter part of the nineteenth century and the beginning of the twentieth. Parties first had to take root, and they did so in two stages and in two realms. They first developed in Parliament over a period of more than 150 years, from the 1670s to the 1830s, as the House of Commons began to acquire more powers. They then organized beyond Parliament, following a succession of reforms starting in the 1830s that gave increasing numbers of people the right to vote.

Parliament as Incubator of Parties

The first political parties emerged in Parliament, but under what circumstances? Parties in their embryonic form appeared during the reign of Elizabeth I (1558–1603), but at this stage they were nothing more than factions. They had no formal names, and their membership shifted from issue to issue. Moreover, because monarchs, who had the exclusive right to summon and dissolve Parliament, seldom summoned it, parliamentarians had little opportunity to organize into parties even if they had wanted to.[1]

On those occasions when the monarch did summon Parliament, however, relations between the two invariably became acrimonious when the latter refused to do the bidding of the former. In 1642 relations between the monarchy and Parliament dropped to a new low. After being denied funds by Parliament to pay for his unsuccessful military campaigns to quash rebellions in Scotland and Ireland, Charles I (reign: 1625–1649) ordered four hundred of his troops to take up positions outside of Parliament as he stormed into the House of Commons chamber to arrest five of his most vocal critics. When the King approached Speaker of the House William

Table 4.1	Ten Functions of British Political Parties

• Before Elections:

Parties represent the public by placing issues of concern on their political agendas.	Parties identify and assess the demands, preferences, expectations, and hopes of the public and express these in their manifestos.
Parties communicate and inform.	They call attention to issues of concern, outline proposed solutions, and develop priorities for action.
Parties involve the public in politics.	Parties encourage the electorate to join their ranks, contribute their time and money to promote them, and support them on election day.
Parties recruit candidates from within their ranks to stand for election.	They assess the qualifications of potential candidates and select those they think will best achieve the party's objectives.
Parties organize elections.	Parties have the competence and organizational infrastructure to campaign for electoral support.

• After Elections:

Parties function to win elections.	The party that wins becomes the Government.
The winning party organizes the Government and controls Parliament's work.	The prime minister, the cabinet and all other ministers are drawn from the ranks of Parliament, and the Government manages the scheduling of legislation.
The party of government pursues its legislative program.	The party in power sets out to put its manifesto pledges into effect.
The runner-up party serves as the official Opposition party.	As the government-in-waiting, the Opposition party is prepared to assume power if it wins the next election.
The Opposition party holds the Government accountable for its actions.	The Opposition checks the Government by calling attention to instances when it strays from its manifesto pledges or makes other decisions with which it disagrees.

Lenthal and demanded that he point them out, the Speaker responded, "I have neither eye to see, nor tongue to speak here, but as the House is pleased to direct me." Because the House directed him to do neither, Charles reluctantly withdrew from the chamber and ever since, convention has dictated that monarchs not set foot in the Commons chamber.

It was primarily because of Parliament's skirmishes with the monarchy that groups in Parliament became more clearly identifiable. The Earl of Danby, principal adviser to Charles II (reign: 1660–1685), urged members of Parliament to pledge their loyalty to the monarch and the Anglican Church. Those who did so became members of the Court Party, later called the Tory Party. Opposing the Court Party was the Country Party, led by the

Earl of Shaftesbury. Its members, who championed Parliament as a check on the monarch's claim to absolute power, later changed the name of the Country Party to the Whig Party. The general election held in 1679 was the first to be fought largely along party lines, and by then the names "Whigs" and "Tories" had come into common usage.[2]

Although born in opposition to each other, the Tories and Whigs buried their differences just before and during the Glorious Revolution of 1688. This bloodless "revolution" unfolded when James II abandoned the throne in 1688 and Parliament invited William and Mary to take his place. William and Mary first had to agree to abide by the Declaration of Rights, and soon after they assumed the throne in 1689, both the Tories and the Whigs were united in giving their support to the declaration, which then became the Bill of Rights of 1689. A milestone in the political development of the nation, the Bill of Rights enshrined the principle of parliamentary sovereignty. No longer required to answer to the monarch at every turn, Parliament started to meet every year, and for longer sessions.

The differences that had divided the Tories and Whigs before the Glorious Revolution surfaced again by the end of the seventeenth century. By then, the two parties could be differentiated by their causes more than ever, even though the rhetoric they used to describe what they stood for clouded precise meaning. The Whigs emphasized "reform, Parliament and the people"; the Tories, "King, Church and Constitution."[3] By 1715, however, the distinctions between the two were becoming more sharply drawn, especially on issues dealing with taxation and foreign policy.[4] The Whigs dominated Parliament in the eighteenth century, but it was not until after they went into opposition in 1784 that they assigned a party manager to raise funds for election campaigns, select candidates to stand for election, and commandeer members of Parliament (MPs) to support the party on important votes.[5] Some years later, under Tory Lord Liverpool's premiership (1812–1827), the Tories adopted similar practices.[6]

The custom of the runner-up party in an election functioning as the official Opposition to the governing party became institutionalized in the eighteenth century. As Whigs and Tories competed to win votes in Parliament, members from each party took up positions on opposite sides of the chamber during debates,[7] an arrangement formalized in the 1830s. Two sets of benches were constructed, each running the length of the chamber and each facing the other with a central aisle between them, at the rear of which the Speaker of the House of Commons presided on a raised platform. Benches to the Speaker's right were reserved for the party of government; those to his left for the Opposition party. It is probably not just coincidental that in this same decade evidence started to emerge that suggested that parliamentarians were becoming increasingly cohesive in supporting the positions taken by their respective party leaders.

By the midpoint of the nineteenth century, it became clear to politicians and the public alike that British politics had become party politics and, increasingly, two-party politics. During what remained of the century, parties became even more deeply entrenched in Parliament. Meanwhile, they started to take root and spread beyond the Commons chamber as well.

Parties beyond Parliament

As the electorate expanded following Parliament's enactment of franchise legislation in 1832, 1867, and 1884, political parties were determined to win over new voters. The 1832 Reform Act raised the number of voters from 5 percent to 7 percent of the adult population. Although not much of an increase and although women were denied the vote, the increase was enough to convince political party leaders that they should lose no time in organizing themselves throughout the country. Political clubs, many of which had formed in London in the eighteenth century as centers of political debate, took on part of this responsibility by registering voters and canvassing for their support in election campaigns. So prominent were the Carlton Club, founded by the Tories in 1832, and the Reform Club, founded by the Whigs in 1836, that they are regarded as precursors of extraparliamentary party organizations.

In 1834, two years after the Reform Act, the Tory Robert Peel wrote the first party manifesto. Because Parliament was not in session when he became prime minister, he was unable to announce his policies there, so he chose to deliver his manifesto as an address to the electors of his constituency of Tamworth. Issuing manifestos, documents containing pledges that a party would make good on if elected, did not become a standard party practice until the 1880s, but the Tamworth Manifesto, as it came to be called, was still another milestone in the development of parties, for it demonstrated for the first time a party's commitment to inform voters of its plans for legislation.

In 1867, Parliament passed a second landmark reform that more than doubled the size of the electorate from 7 percent to 16 percent of all adults twenty-one years of age or older. In that same year, the Conservatives, as the Tories came to be known, founded the National Union of Conservative and Constitutional Associations (National Union, for short) to recruit the newly enfranchised to the party's ranks. They also sought to inform and enthuse party activists throughout the country by holding party conferences every year. In 1874, the Conservatives won an overall majority of seats for the first time since 1841. Their success was largely attributable to campaigns managed by the National Union along with the help of Conservative Central Office, a second extraparliamentary party organization that Conservative Party leader Benjamin Disraeli had established in 1870 to support the party in Parliament. In that same year, the Whig Party, which by then had become known as the Liberal Party, also founded a national headquarters, the National Liberal Federation, to attract new members and win more seats.

The third and final enlargement of the electorate in the nineteenth century was achieved with passage of the Representation of the People Act of 1884, which boosted the numbers of all adults twenty-one years of age and older entitled to vote from 16 percent to 28 percent. With the passage of each successive franchise law, candidates for elective office realized it was foolish to continue to court the favor of the aristocracy and landed gentry, for no longer were they the nation's only electors. Instead, candidates had to set their sights on middle-class and working-class voters and rally them to their side.

As the century wore on, political parties took root by founding national headquarters and creating organizations at the constituency level, writing election manifestos, and initiating publicity campaigns. They persuaded voters to register to vote, undertook membership drives, canvassed voters, and directed the work of legions of volunteers. Two additional reform acts in the first third of the twentieth century enlarged the electorate even further by giving all men—and, by then, all women—the right to vote. But by 1900, even before these two reforms were enacted, mass political parties had come of age.

Parties and Party Government since 1900: An Overview

Britain has a two-party system. Or does it? Between them, two parties captured a majority of seats in Parliament in every one of the twenty-eight general elections held from 1900 through 2005. But other, minor parties won seats in these elections as well. For that reason, ought not Britain's party system be described as multiparty? On the other hand, how can it be called a two-party system, let alone a multiparty system, if the same party is in power for long stretches of time without interruption, as the Conservatives were from 1979 to 1997? The answers to these questions lie in the definitions for terms used to classify party systems generally, but which are tailored here somewhat to apply specifically to Britain.

Single-Party System. One party wins every parliamentary seat either because the constitution bans the existence of other parties or political leaders prevent other parties from putting the names of their candidates on the ballot.

Two-Party System. Almost all parliamentary seats are held by two large parties and a few—usually no more than 5 percent—by minor parties. One of the two large parties wins an overall majority of seats and forms a government.

Two-Party Dominant System. Five percent to ten percent of the seats in Parliament are won by minor parties, but the two largest parties are dominant. Because one of these dominant parties normally has an overall majority of seats, it has no need to consider appealing to one or more of the minor parties to form a coalition government.

Two-and-a-Half Party System. This is a party system in which there are two large parties, neither of which has won an overall majority of seats, plus one or more smaller, or minor, parties. The party in power may try to form a coalition with one or more of the minor parties, solicit the support of a minor party (or parties) agreeable to supporting it as the need arises, or attempt to govern unaided by one or more of the minor parties.

Multiparty System. Three and more parties hold seats in Parliament, and because there are sizeable numbers of parliamentarians in at least three parties, no single party can claim a majority. The major parties govern in coalition.

Britain at various times since 1900 has had three of these five party systems: a two-party system, a two-party dominant system, and a two-and-a-half party system. In answer to the first question raised on the previous page—"Does the presence of minor parties along with major parties not make Britain's party system multiparty?"—only rarely do minor parties have enough parliamentarians to control legislative outcomes. (Chapter 7 discusses how Britain's voting system is heavily biased in favor of the two largest parties, Labour and the Conservatives.) One member of Parliament is elected to each constituency; the seat goes to the candidate who wins by a plurality, that is, the one who attracts more votes than any other single candidate on the ballot. Britain's single-member constituency/plurality voting system is dramatically different from the multimember constituency/proportional voting system used on the Continent, which allocates seats to candidates based on the proportion of the popular vote they win. Proportional voting systems contribute to multiparty systems, such as those found in France, Germany, and Italy, and predictably, multiparty systems lead to coalition governments, as they have in these three countries.

As for the second question raised on the previous page—"How could Britain's party system be described as two-party if one party governs for long periods?"—the question implies that there is only one party in Parliament. But an Opposition party operates there as well. As for the number of consecutive years that the same party can govern, there are no rules: which party governs is the electorate's choice.

The first half of the twentieth century is associated with a two-and-a-half party system in Britain. Then for nearly three decades following the end of the Second World War (1945–1973), the country had a two-party system, which in turn gave way to the two-party dominant system that exists today. The British political system has accommodated each one of these party systems, and because any one of them could come into being following an election, it is worth examining the circumstances under which they have come about and operated.

Two-and-a-Half Party System (1900–1945)

The years between 1900 and 1945 were years of disruption in Britain. Particularly disruptive were Britain's fighting in two devastating world wars and its having to cope with the staggering effects of a protracted depression between the wars. There was disruption even on the political front in the interwar years, as voters turned their backs on one long-standing major party, the Liberals, to make way for its rival, the Labour Party.

Eleven general elections were held between 1900 and 1935, the last year that elections were held before the conclusion of the Second World War in 1945. They produced a variety of governing arrangements—majority governments, minority governments, and coalition governments. Table 4.2 outlines the eleven electoral events and the kinds of governments that resulted.

There were five majority governments. Of the five, the one elected in 1935 was the only majority government to become a coalition government; it did so in 1940 to demonstrate cross-party unity after the start of the Second World War. Four more governments were minority governments, two of which became coalition governments some while after they were elected because of the onset of national emergencies. The first of these was elected in December 1910; it became a coalition government in 1915 after the First World War began. The second was elected in 1929; it became a coalition government in August 1931 to cope with problems precipitated by a worldwide economic depression.

The two remaining governments were elected on coalition tickets, that is, they were coalition governments from the outset. They included those Conservative, Labour, and Liberal parliamentarians who had agreed to run on a coalition ticket (most did). One coalition was elected in 1918 to deal with the country's recovery from the First World War. The other was elected in October 1931 to continue the work of the coalition that had formed two months earlier.

Of the eleven governments formed from 1900 to 1945, four were governments in which a two-and-a-half party system was embedded. When they were elected, all four were minority governments. These were the two elections held in 1910 and the elections of 1923 and 1929.

Table 4.2	Majority, Minority, and Coalition Governments, 1900–1935
Election	Result
1900	majority government
1906	majority government
1910 (January)	minority government
1910 (December)	minority government, but became a coalition government in 1915
1918	coalition government
1922	majority government
1923	minority government
1924	majority government
1929	minority government, but became a coalition government in August 1931
1931 (October)	coalition government
1935	majority government, but became a coalition government in 1940

The Two Elections of 1910

The Liberals had advanced from second place in the 1900 election to a victory of landslide proportions in the 1906 election, only to see many of their gains wiped away in the next election, which was held in January 1910. They were still the largest party in Parliament, but with only two seats more than the Conservatives, not by much. More discomfiting to the Liberals was that they were more than sixty seats shy of an overall majority. The result was a hung parliament—a parliament in which no party has more seats than all the other parties combined. Despite this handicap, the Liberals limped along as a minority government until Prime Minister Herbert Asquith announced toward the end of 1910 that another general election would be held just before Christmas. His objective, of course, was to emerge from that contest with enough seats to give his party the overall majority it lacked.

Unfortunately for him and his party, this election also produced a hung parliament. At this stage, the Irish Nationalists, a minor party that held more than 12 percent of the seats, threw the Liberals a lifeline by offering them their support, figuring they could broker a better deal with them than with the Conservatives to advance their cause of home rule for Ireland. The Liberals chose not to go into coalition following each election; nevertheless, the Nationalists provided them with what effectively became a forty-two-seat majority (356 to 314), which allowed them to remain in power as a minority government until 1915. It was in that year, not long after the outbreak of hostilities in the First World War, that the Liberals formed a coalition with Conservative and Labour parliamentarians to demonstrate a united cross-party front during the war years.

The Election of 1923

The next general election that produced a hung parliament was in 1923, when the largest party, the Conservatives, took only 42 percent of the seats. Unfortunately for them, they could not contemplate going into coalition with the Irish Nationalists even if they had wanted to, for Ireland (apart from Ulster) had achieved its independence from Britain in 1921, and the Irish Nationalists had dissolved as a party. And the Conservatives did not feel comfortable forming a coalition with the Liberals or with Labour. The Liberal Party since 1916 had been less one party than two warring factions, and the Labour Party was emerging as a formidable Opposition party in the electoral sweepstakes, winning 9 percent of the seats in 1918, 23 percent in 1922, and 31 percent in 1923.

Like the Liberals after the 1910 elections, the Conservatives in 1923 struggled to sustain themselves in office. Their efforts proved fruitless. Several weeks after election day, Labour and Liberal members of Parliament combined to defeat the Government on a key vote. However, it was much too soon to hold another election, and for that reason Conservative Stanley Baldwin resigned as prime minister to make way for the leader of Parliament's second largest party, Labour. Ramsay MacDonald became Labour's first prime minister, although his tenure also was short-lived. His party held fewer than one third of the seats in Parliament, but he refused to go into coalition with the Liberals, the third largest party. That meant that he had to depend on the good will of the Liberals and the Conservatives. But as Mac-Donald learned, there were limits to their good will; eight months into his premiership they combined forces to defeat the Government on a motion of censure, and MacDonald felt obliged to call a general election. It was held in the autumn of 1924, a little more than ten months after the previous one, and the voters returned the Conservatives to power with a thumping majority.

The Election of 1929

Another general election was held in 1929. Labour won more seats than ever, capturing five times as many seats as the Liberals to become the largest party in Parliament. That was the good news for Labour. The bad news was that it was twenty-one seats shy of an overall majority. Ramsay MacDonald, prime minister once more, again refused to go into coalition with another party and again found himself clinging to power and reluctant to promote radical measures to deal with the effects of the Great Depression for fear any one of them could trigger a vote of no confidence against his Government. By 1931, with his cabinet seriously divided on how to come to grips with the economic emergencies created by the global depression, MacDonald met with King George V to inform him that his Government was at an impasse and that he was prepared to resign. But the King persuaded him to stay on as leader of a coalition that included Conservatives and Liberals.

Britain had had coalition governments before, one during the First World War and one just after it in a period of post-war recovery. Indeed, Britain again would be governed by a coalition from 1940 through mid-1945, when the country was once more at war. Nineteen thirty-one, however, was the second (and last) time in the twentieth century that a coalition government was formed following the election of a hung parliament, just two years after one election and two months before the next one. It is debatable whether it would have formed had problems inflicted by the depression not been so intractable.

Two-Party System (1945–1973)

The years from 1945 to 1973 stand in stark contrast to the previous four-and-a-half decades. Although there were the old stand-by minor parties—the Liberals and the Communists—plus the new Welsh and Scottish national parties, there were no minority governments, and in the absence of national emergencies, no coalition governments. The Conservatives and Labour clashed in eight general elections in this period, each winning four. On each occasion the victorious party secured an overall majority of seats. Moreover, between them they received anywhere from 87 percent to 97 percent of the popular vote and captured 95 percent to 99 percent of the seats. Never before in the twentieth century or since have two major parties received such overwhelming support for such a long period.

In the first quarter of the century, the Irish Nationalists and then Labour performed so well at the polls—in the two elections of 1910 and in 1923, respectively—that they effectively prevented any party from capturing an overall majority of seats. But the "spoiler" role of minor parties was not in evidence from 1945 to 1973. Minor parties existed, but they won only 1 percent to 5 percent of the seats and posed no threat to the robust two-party system of that period.

Two-Party Dominant System (1974–Present)

In the nine elections held from 1974 through 2005, the Conservative and Labour Parties continued to take the lion's share of seats in Parliament. Minor parties, in the 1970s and 1980s the Liberal Party, and from the early 1990s the Liberal Democrat Party, made impressive gains in the popular vote, however. In each of the two general elections held in 1974, minor party candidates, most of whom were Liberals, won the support of one out of every four voters. In the first of these elections, neither the Conservatives nor Labour achieved victory in the category that counted—seats in the Commons. Harold Wilson, whose Labour Party had won the most seats, became prime minister of the first hung parliament since 1929. He made no overtures to the third largest party—the Liberals—to join him in a coalition, however, and after repeated setbacks in the Commons, called another election later in 1974 to shore up his governing position. But his party did not fare much better than it had ten months before, winding up with an overall majority of only three seats.

In every one of the nine elections from 1974 through 2005, the combined support for both major parties fell dramatically below the 87-to-97-percent level of 1945–1973. Only in 1979 did party support come remotely close to the bottom of that range when the major parties attracted 81 percent of the vote. In the six elections that followed, their average combined return hovered around 73 percent; in the last of these six, in 2005, it dropped to 69 percent, the lowest since the elections of 1922 and 1923.

The Liberals staged a comeback in the two general elections of 1974, winning a higher percentage of the vote than in any election since 1929. They did less well in the 1979 election, but their fortunes increased following the 1983 and 1987 campaigns after they negotiated an electoral alliance with the Social Democrats, a small party founded by several MPs who had left the Labour Party after becoming disenchanted with its left-wing policies. In 1988 the vast majority of Liberals and Social Democrats combined forces to become the Liberal Democrats. As the strongest minor party, it captured between 17 percent and 22 percent of the popular vote in the four elections held after its founding. Keeping in mind that Britain's voting system does not award seats in proportion to the popular vote, this translated into only 4 percent to 12 percent of the seats in Parliament.

Parties and Party Government since 1945: A Closer Look

Dividing the period from 1900 to 2005 into nearly equal halves reveals some striking contrasts in party government. From 1945 to 2005, party government was far less erratic in nature than in the first half of the twentieth century. Neither of the two major parties displaced the other, only one election out of seventeen produced a hung parliament, and the absence of national emergencies made coalition governments unnecessary. The only major similarity between these two periods was that the Conservatives were the dominant party, although Labour won a dramatic victory at the polls in 1945 and even more dramatic ones in 1997 and 2001.

A closer look at the behavior of political parties when in power and when in opposition reveals that there have been three distinctive phases of party politics since 1945. First, there was a nearly thirty-year phase of consensus politics. From the end of the Second World War in 1945 until the mid-1970s, Labour and the Conservatives pursued essentially the same core policies when one and then the other was in power. There were differences between them; however, these were "less about absolutes than questions of '*more*' or '*less*'."[8]

After a brief interlude, consensus politics gave way to politics as usual. During this phase, Margaret Thatcher (1979–1990) and then John Major (1990–1997) served as prime minister. With the Conservatives in power and Labour in opposition, the two parties scrapped unremittingly, especially during Thatcher's premiership. Not until after Labour returned to power in 1997 did the gulf between the two parties narrow—so much so that Labour, or "New Labour," as Prime Minister Tony Blair preferred to call it, embraced many policies that the Conservatives had implemented in the previous eighteen years. To be sure, there still were differences between the two parties, but despite these, 1997 marked the beginning of the third phase of party politics, that of convergence politics.

Consensus Politics (1945–mid-1970s)

There was nothing particularly mystifying about Britain's two major parties finding common ground to solve the country's problems at war's end in 1945 or about their continuing to do so for the following thirty years. They realized they had to work together, and did so relatively harmoniously when the Conservatives, Labour, and the Liberals governed in coalition. The coalition was led by Prime Minister Winston Churchill, whose Conservative Party held two thirds of the seats. He took primary responsibility for the war effort. The deputy prime minister, Labour leader Clement Attlee, whose party held the second highest number of seats, had principal responsibility for domestic policy. (The Liberal Party, which held only twenty seats, was awarded less than a handful of ministerial posts.) The parties agreed to suspend general elections to avoid diverting attention from mobilizing for war or dividing the country during a national emergency. Suspended, too, was the familiar cut and thrust of debate across the center aisle of the Commons chamber, for the parties thought it best to hold their fire for the duration of the hostilities. However, the truce they called would not last indefinitely; once the Allies achieved victory in Europe and a general election was held, it would be only a matter of time before there was a return to a period of politics as usual. Or so it was thought.

Victory in the European theater of war was finally achieved in the spring of 1945, and a general election was held that summer. Labour won by a landslide, which allowed the party to govern under Clement Attlee's stewardship with an overall majority of seats for the first time in its history. But a return to politics as usual was far from imminent, for so devastated were Britain's economy and its people that the Conservative and Labour Parties put aside many of their differences as they searched for ways to speed the nation's recovery. Urgently required were programs that addressed the most pressing needs of the people—housing for families who had been bombed out of their homes, assistance to war widows, help for children whose mothers worked in vital industries—plus solutions to the problems of poor health care, high unemployment, and food shortages.

The election manifestos the two parties issued at the outset of the campaign in 1945 were broadly similar. Each was committed to adopting an interventionist role in managing the economy and maintaining a mixed economy, that is, one in which there was a combination of public and private ownership. Each supported the implementation of cradle-to-grave benefits, including a comprehensive national health service that would provide free medical treatment; the initiation of a massive housing program; and a comprehensive rise in education standards. The parties also pledged to consult with the trade unions and business interests before embarking on new policies, just as they had during the war. On foreign policy, they were in general agreement about making plans to grant independence to several of Britain's colonies, fostering closer ties with the United States, and maintaining a nuclear deterrent. The parties disagreed on some of the means to these ends, but on only one major issue did they part company on the means *and* the ends—the nationalization of certain industries, a program to which Labour was firmly committed.

The extent to which the two parties were committed to achieving consensus became apparent after the Conservatives wrested power from Labour in the 1951 election. Instead of overturning what Labour had accomplished in the previous six years, the Conservatives upheld most of the post-war settlement, as it came to be called. For example, so consistent were the Conservative Government's economic policies with those of the previous Labour

Government that the policies pursued by Conservative chancellor of the exchequer Rab Butler from 1951 to 1955 departed only fractionally from those adopted by his Labour predecessor Hugh Gaitskell in 1950–1951. For example, each party was committed to funding welfare programs. Levels of funding rose at a steady clip between 1951 and 1976, and from the early 1960s at a rate far faster than public spending overall, at a time when the Conservatives and Labour rotated in power. This consistency prompted *The Economist* in 1954 to coin a new term—*Butskellism*—by playfully cobbling together the first syllable from the last name of one with the second syllable from the last name of the other.

It should be emphasized at this point that, overall, the post-war settlement was more the product of a fragile compromise than a deep-down agreement. When they were in opposition, the parties took positions that were far from identical. It was when they won power that their differences dissolved, despite the extreme positions taken at times by clutches of backbench MPs on the left and right wings of their parties. Leaders took more centrist positions, and theirs were the positions that really mattered, along with the continuity of policies their parties pursued while in office. But the spirit of compromise that nourished the politics of consensus would not last indefinitely.

Politics as Usual (1979–1997)

There was a sharp contrast between the era of the post-war settlement and the period that followed, one which was marked by a return to politics as usual as the parties clashed over just about every major domestic issue of the day. The beginning of the end of the post-war political consensus came just days after the February 1974 election. No party had won a majority of seats, and because Conservative prime minister Edward Heath failed to persuade Liberal MPs to help him form a government, he had no choice but to resign. As one political historian put it, when Heath went to the palace to inform the Queen of his decision, "the postwar consensus, too, went with him to resign."[9]

A steady downturn in the economy was the underlying cause of the breakdown in consensus. Serious problems had started to surface during Heath's time in office, and Labour—namely, prime ministers Harold Wilson (1974–1976) and James Callaghan (1976–1979)—was left to preside over much of the downturn. It was brought about by rampant stagflation—a combination of rising unemployment, accelerating inflation, and low economic growth. By the end of 1974, retail price increases were averaging 19 percent a year; in 1975 interest on loans soared to 15 percent; and in 1977 unemployment climbed to a post-war high of nearly 1.5 million.

To make matters worse for Labour, the public became convinced that the welfare state and nationalized industries had become too costly and the unions too powerful as they called one strike after another and demanded ever-higher wages for their members. This meant that some of the key elements of the post-war settlement—welfare, nationalized industries, and government's consulting the unions on the wages of their members—were under siege. Also under attack was the economic consensus, occasioned by Labour's dramatic break with the past when it abandoned the Keynesian fiscal pump-priming strategy of increasing government spending to reduce unemployment. The party instead chose to reduce government spending to lower the growing deficit and to adopt a monetary strategy of setting limits on the growth of the money supply to check inflation.

The Callaghan Government scored a partial victory over rising prices in 1978 when the rate of increase in inflation dropped to 8 percent. Nevertheless, inflation continued to sap economic growth. High levels of unemployment persisted, and the economy continued to languish. In the meantime, increasing numbers of members of Parliament on Labour's left became restive and called for the nationalization of even more private industries and a return to Keynesian orthodoxy. Members of the public became restive as well. In their mind, the post-war settlement that had brought prosperity in the 1950s had become the underlying cause of Britain's economic malaise. Public opinion polls detected that a disillusioned and frustrated body politic was starting to shift to the right on the political spectrum.

Margaret Thatcher administered the coup de grâce to consensus politics soon after the Conservative Party returned to power in 1979 and she became prime minister. An insight into what it would be like during her premiership was revealed in a speech she made during the campaign. Thatcher likened herself (in her words) to the "Old Testament Prophets, who did not say, 'Brothers, I want a consensus.' They said: 'This is my faith. This is what I passionately believe. If you believe it too, then come with me.'"[10] She left little doubt from the start that she was a conviction politician, but few anticipated that her convictions would divide the parties more than at any time since the end of the Second World War.

Resuscitating the economy was Thatcher's most immediate, overriding objective. When the Callaghan Government adopted a monetary strategy, it did so half-heartedly. On the other hand, when Thatcher took office, she embraced monetarism with enthusiasm, convinced that it was the only effective weapon to check inflation, lower interest rates, and rejuvenate the competitiveness of British goods and services in the world market. She also was convinced that government could be scaled down and public spending reduced, and that the resultant savings could be more efficiently invested in the private sector. In her view, the continued funding of massive industries nationalized in the post-war period was part of the problem, and she set about selling many of them to the private sector. Privatizing them, in turn, boosted government revenue and paved the way for tax cuts. She also ended the formal tripartite arrangements established by governments in the 1970s that put the unions and employer organizations on an equal footing with the government as unions bargained for higher salaries for their members. In the meantime, her Government deliberately chose not to intervene in wage negotiations. Later, she piloted tough reforms through Parliament that made it difficult for unions to call strikes. To stem the rising costs of the welfare state, Thatcher sought to end what she called the "culture of dependency" by reducing some benefits and holding the line on others. She was determined to "roll back the frontiers of the state," and, as she shifted her party to the right, Labour MPs moved to the left.

The first sign of Labour's move to the left became apparent in 1980 when James Callaghan, who was on the center-right of the party, resigned as leader and was replaced by Michael Foot, an ardent advocate of policies emanating from the party's left. Foot's election split the party into center-right and far-left factions and precipitated the departure from the party of fourteen leading MPs, all from the center-right. These individuals went on to form the Social Democratic Party, a moderate alternative to Labour. All the while, Labour clashed with the Conservatives in Parliament as Thatcher continued her mission.

There was no mistaking Labour's continued drift to the left when, in the general election of 1983, the party issued a manifesto that shocked many in the party, including one former Labour cabinet minister who dubbed it "the longest suicide note in history." It called for withdrawing Britain from the European Union (then called the European Economic Community) and pursuing a policy of unilateral nuclear disarmament. Both policy commitments, but unilateralism in particular, went against the grain of public opinion at a time when the nation was still basking in the patriotic afterglow of its victory over Argentina in 1982 following that country's seizure of the Falkland Islands, a British crown colony. And as fresh evidence emerged that the economy was on the rebound, many in the public, including many long-term Labour supporters, wanted little to do with the party's manifesto pledges to increase public spending, restore the powers of the trade unions, and renationalize privatized industries. On polling day, there were massive defections among Labour's traditional working-class supporters, including trade unionists and skilled workers, to the Liberal Party and the Social Democratic Party that had formed an alliance for the campaign. The effects were devastating. Labour managed to attract only 28 percent of the popular vote, the lowest share since 1918, and only 209 out of 650 seats. The electorate had delivered a stern rebuke to Labour and its policies, and many began to wonder whether the party was up to the job of mounting credible assaults against the Conservative Government both in the Commons and beyond it.

Reversing Labour's fortunes required that the party do something more than put more firepower into its debates in the Commons. So divided and demoralized had the party become that Michael Foot stepped down after the election to make way for a new leader, Neil Kinnock. Because Kinnock had at one time been a firebrand on the party's left, many were convinced he had the credibility to isolate the far left, which he did when he began expelling supporters of Militant Tendency, a group on the hard-left wing of the party whose members had become active in a number of local party organizations and had won office in several local governments. As Kinnock reached out to heal the rift between the factions on the soft-left and the right, Thatcher called another election in 1987. By then, Labour had distanced itself from its 1983 manifesto and moved towards the political center. It still stood by its position that Britain should disarm its nuclear weapons unilaterally, but now the party endorsed lower rates of income tax, no longer insisted on re-nationalizing privatized industries, and agreed that Britain should remain in the European Union (EU).

Despite these U-turns—or perhaps because of them—the voters were skeptical. They still perceived Labour as being committed to high taxes and spending, ill-prepared to deal with inflation, and beholden to the trade unions. Standards of living had risen, and Britons were becoming increasingly middle class as they found jobs in emerging service industries, bought their first homes, and profited from stocks they had purchased in the newly privatized industries. Many who were reluctant to turn their backs on a government that had contributed to their economic well-being helped to elect the Conservatives to a third consecutive term with an overall majority of 102 seats.

Little changed between the parties from 1987 to 1997. Still highly polarized, they continued to scrap savagely in the Commons. But there was change *within* the parties, for the Conservatives starting in 1990, when Margaret Thatcher resigned as prime minister, and for Labour starting in 1994, when Tony Blair was elected leader. In 1990, because of a bitter controversy that erupted over a radical new local tax policy that Thatcher championed and because of her increasingly combative style of leadership, one of Thatcher's former ministers challenged her in a leadership contest. After she consulted her cabinet ministers one by one and learned that support for her continuing as leader was rapidly slipping away, she pulled out of the contest and resigned. Soon after, John Major was elected to take her place.

There was also a change at the top of the Labour Party after it failed for yet a fourth time to wrest power from the Conservatives in 1992. The party had come within striking distance of winning, but Neil Kinnock nevertheless resigned as leader and was replaced by John Smith, who pledged to carry on the reforms Kinnock had initiated. Not long after the election, public opinion polls showed Labour pulling ahead of the Conservatives. The economy was in the doldrums and division within the Conservative ranks appeared as John Major, who had an overall majority of only twenty-one seats, clashed with those in his party who opposed the terms of the EU's new Maastricht Treaty, which he had had a hand in negotiating.

The spring of 1994 was bittersweet for Labour. Sweet because, with the Conservatives increasingly divided over Britain's role in the EU and the economy still in the doldrums, Labour made sweeping gains in elections to local government held that May and in the election of British members to the European Parliament in June. Bitter because the party lost its leader, John Smith, after he suffered a fatal heart attack. Smith's legacy was new party rules that marginalized the influence of the unions in leadership elections, and the first to benefit from them was Tony Blair, who won the leadership contest that summer by a decisive margin.

Blair, who had been elected to Parliament only eleven years before, was from a generation far less tied to the party's past thinking. No sooner was he elected leader than he signaled his commitment to transform the party with even greater resolve than his two predecessors. The conditions for change were ripe. With union influence in decline, the left largely isolated, and the party hungry for power, Blair drove one last nail into the party's ideological coffin—Clause 4 of Labour's 1918 constitution. For more than seventy-five years, Clause 4 had served as a rallying point for Labour to introduce socialism by providing for "the common ownership of the means of production, distribution and exchange." However, when it was in power, Labour did nothing to implement this clause other than nationalize selected key industries, which some socialist critics dismissed as nothing more than a form of state capitalism. Conservative polemicists, in an attempt to arouse suspicion about Labour's true intentions, had nevertheless taken delight over the years in tagging Labour as the party of socialism, despite the fact that in its 1987 and 1992 campaigns the party had turned its back on nationalizing private industries.

Tony Blair redrafted Clause 4 to silence once and for all those who remained unconvinced that Labour had repudiated socialism. For six months, he campaigned up and down the country to win the party's support for the new Clause 4, and at a special conference of the party's rank and file in 1995 delegates endorsed it by a margin of three to one. Out went the old language and in came the new, ringing with passages extolling the virtues of "enterprise," "competition," and "a thriving private sector." Transforming the party was Blair's master plan, and gutting the old Clause 4 was key to realizing that plan. No longer would Labour be just "Labour," but "New Labour," a phrase used no fewer than 107 times in a first draft of the manifesto that the party's rank and file, in an unprecedented move, was called upon to approve several months before the next election was called.

As the 1997 election campaign drew near, Labour was better placed than ever to wrest power from the Conservatives. John Major had held out as long as he could to still the voices of dissent within his party over Britain's role in the EU and reverse Labour's overwhelming lead in the public opinion polls. He succeeded in doing neither; with parliament nearing the end of its five-year statutory limit, his hand was forced. He had to call an election.

With the turbulent years of in-fighting in the 1980s behind it, Labour was prepared to present itself to the voters as *New* Labour. As the campaign got under way, opinion polls recorded a massive lead by Labour that held through the campaign. On election day, a record 418 Labour candidates were swept into Parliament; the Conservatives were sidelined with 165, their lowest number since 1906. After Labour had waged a campaign aimed at seizing the center ground of British politics, twenty years of "politics as usual" drew to a close.

Convergence Politics (1997–?)

Following the 1997 election, Labour seized the center ground in British politics. The Conservatives, in an effort to demonstrate that they were different,
went in search of new issues and ideas that some in the party feared could
move them too far to the right on the political spectrum. Labour in the meantime courted the business community, refused to restore the power of the
unions, held down public spending, pursued policies to reduce inflation, and
reduced the tax bite on lower-income taxpayers. The party also embarked on
a series of welfare reforms and even partially privatized the National Air
Traffic Services (the air traffic control agency) and part of London's transportation system, the London Underground, under what it called public-
private partnerships. Significantly, Labour chose to continue many of the policies the Conservatives had initiated, and before long political observers began
to wonder whether any real differences existed between the two parties.

To be sure, there were differences. During the campaign, Blair had trum-
peted the need for a swathe of constitutional reforms that included devolving power to Scotland and Wales, incorporating the Convention on
Human Rights into British law, reforming the House of Lords, and introducing a Freedom of Information Act. On an issue that had deeply divided
the public—replacing British sterling with the European Union's single currency, or euro—he promised that his government would not make that decision on its own. If his Government determined that economic conditions
were ripe for adopting the euro, the final decision would rest with the electorate in a referendum.

Apart from Labour's plans for a referendum on the euro and constitutional reform, however, the parties had indeed converged in their thinking
about many policies that had previously brought them into contention. But
convergence politics was not a replication of the consensus politics that had
prevailed in the first thirty years or so following the war. Whereas consensus
politics had been marked by the Conservatives' often grudging agreement to
compromise their differences with Labour on selected major policies, convergence politics resulted from New Labour's genuine acceptance of certain
Conservative policies consistent with its own objectives, economic policies
in particular.

Predictably, this approach generated controversy among some within the
party who claimed that Labour had foolishly abandoned certain cherished
core beliefs. To show their displeasure, these individuals even staged a few
minor back-bench rebellions in Labour's first Government (1997–2001) and
several major ones in the two Labour Governments that followed
(2001–2005 and 2005–?). Moreover, as they and others argued, New
Labour offered no ideological pegs on which to hang its policies. Eclecticism
had replaced ideology—or as one veteran Labour member of Parliament put
it, there were "No poles. No fixed positions. No Right. No Left. Just multi-
hued blancmange." [11] Blair's response was that his party would be guided by

Speaking of . . .

Where Have All the Party Faithful Gone?

At one time, political parties in the UK were mass membership organizations. Members would gather to debate issues, select candidates for election, distribute literature identifying what their party stood for, and get out the vote on election day. For many, volunteering time to advance their party's causes was a fulfilling activity. But times have changed. Floating voters are on the rise. Voter turnout is in decline. And between the mid-1980s and 2005, parties lost an estimated 80–90 percent of their card-carrying members. Where have all the party faithful gone? *The Economist* offers some answers and reflects on one of the adverse consequences of diminished membership subscriptions—but then ends on a positive note:

> "Weak parties . . . reflect a welcome decline in class conflict in British politics. . . ."

"For a start, British politics has become less controversial. All three main parties now contain people at the top who believe in breaking up state monopolies in public services and giving power to consumers. All the parties are nervous about raising taxes, while none of them is in a rush to shrink the state.

"In the absence of a big political or cultural rift, there are few reasons for people to join parties. Fifteen years ago [1990], Labour conferences were unpredictable affairs, where members would gleefully pass resolutions designed to embarrass the party leadership. Since then, [annual] conferences have become more like stage-managed rallies, choreographed around the set-piece of the leader's speech, at the expense of members' scope to influence policy.

"Another reason . . . is the feeble state of local politics. Although Scotland and Wales now have their own assemblies, Britain is still the most centralised state in western Europe. Local government has little discretionary power to raise taxes and spends most of its time managing services that central government tells it to provide. The system has the advantage of making reform easier to pursue nationally, but the cost is to make local politics anaemic and unrewarding.

"[A decline in] membership subscriptions . . . has left the parties more reliant on the largesse of a few big donors. The problem with these is not so much that they leave the parties in thrall to a few wealthy individuals. . . . It is rather that the cheques tend to come in only when there is an election on. The parties then spend the money on urgent advertising campaigns, leaving no funds for rebuilding party organisations in places where they have declined. . . .

"Weak parties . . . reflect a welcome decline in class conflict in British politics: at the last election [2005] the Tories, once recognised as the party of the establishment, made their biggest gains among poorer voters while suffering among the more affluent and educated, who used to be their main supporters. . . .

"When voters really need them, parties can be reinvigorated. And when they don't, most voters are content to let them go and play beside the sea [at their annual conferences]."

Source: © 2005 The Economist Newspaper Ltd. All rights reserved. Reprinted with permission. Further reproduction prohibited. www.economist.com.

the principle of "what matters is what works." [12] He was determined not to run everything through the government, which was what the old Clause 4 had called for. Nor would he rely too heavily on the market, as Thatcher and Major had. No longer was there any relevance to a left or a right approach to economic management, he continued, for "the battle between the market and the public sector was over." [13] Neither of these two ways was appropriate. Rather, there was a better approach, one called "the Third Way." [14]

Blair outlined his thoughts about the Third Way in a 1998 pamphlet published by the Fabian Society, a small Labour think tank that had contributed intellectual grist to the party's thinking through the century. Blair the prime minister became Blair the political philosopher when he argued that the Third Way demanded that policies flow from values and not the other way around. The values he cited were derived from social justice, among them "equal worth" and "opportunity for all," and the means taken to achieve them had to be "flexible, innovative and forward looking." This required what he called a "permanent revisionism"—a nonstop "search for better means to meet our goals, based on a clear view of the changes taking place in advanced industrial societies." [15]

As Blair spoke of revisionism in his speeches, the Conservatives found themselves in disarray. They had been defeated by a party that essentially had purloined many of their policies. Desperate to portray themselves as different from and more competent than Labour, their options were limited. They could neither denounce the core policies that Labour had chosen to take from them nor risk defeat at the next election by embracing extremist policies. As a result, William Hague, who became Opposition leader after John Major, "let policy bob around like a buoy in a choppy sea." [16]

Bob around Conservative policies did. For example, when Hague attempted to present his party as "caring" and "compassionate" (qualities on which the Conservatives had scored low in opinion polls), his efforts were effectively negated by his opposition to such "caring" Labour Government initiatives as establishing a minimum wage and increasing spending for education. Hague also sought to champion what he called the "British Way," a concept that enshrined individualism, enterprise, and social mobility. And although it gave him the potential leverage to distinguish his party's thinking from Labour's by moving beyond economic policies, it was too abstract to generate much excitement. He then shifted his party in a populist direction, declaiming what he called "bogus" asylum seekers and rising crime. His stance on both issues attracted attention, and his determination to "save the pound" by rejecting proposals that Britain adopt the euro struck a responsive chord with the public and became the centerpiece of the Conservative campaign when Blair called an election in 2001.

Despite the Conservative Party's efforts to stage a comeback, the 2001 election was a near perfect replay of the 1997 election. Throughout the four intervening years, Labour had sustained a comfortable lead in the public opinion polls—an historic first for any government since 1945. The polls also revealed that the public judged Labour to be the more competent of the two major parties in managing the economy. That too was an historic first, and it confirmed Labour's beliefs that the economic policies on which it had embarked were seen as having the impact it had hoped for. After all the ballots were counted following the election on June 7, 2001, the nation learned that Labour candidates had won a total of 412 seats out of 659, only six fewer than in 1997. Only twice before—in 1945 and 1997—had Labour won by such an impressive margin, but never had it won by an impressive margin twice in a row. That was still another first. Meanwhile, the 166 Conservative candidates elected had to content themselves with sitting on the Opposition benches for another parliament.

Every prime minister enjoys a political honeymoon. So too did Tony Blair. His probably lasted longer than that of any of his predecessors. Then, in his second term, five years after his Government was first elected in 1997, it all came to a halt. Signs that it would not last forever appeared when increasing numbers of Labour backbenchers refused to toe the party line on whipped votes—votes on which the party whips try to enforce discipline by insisting that members not deviate from the party's position. In the first two sessions of the 2001–2005 parliament, backbenchers defied the instructions of their party whips on 141 occasions. Not once in the post–Second World War period had backbenchers from the governing party ignored the whips as often in the first two sessions of a parliament.[17] The most dramatic instances of defiance occurred in 2003 when backbenchers staged two rebellions against Britain's joining the United States in invading Iraq without a second United Nations resolution. On one of the two votes, as many as 139 Labour MPs ignored the whips. Not since the middle of the nineteenth century had backbench members of the governing party participated in rebellions as large as these.[18]

The rebels were responsible for a few more close votes as well in the four-year parliament that ended in 2005. Fortunately for the Government, however, most were not close. Some on the backbenchs felt free to defy the whips from time to time, although it is not known whether they figured that on most votes, with Labour's majority of 166, Government bills were certain to pass despite their opposition. Others became members of the "awkward squad," as they came to be called, with several rebelling many times over. Among them were those who resented the short shrift the leadership was giving to many of Labour's traditional values, especially those supporting the trade unions, levying higher rates of tax on the wealthy, and expanding welfare benefits. Despite the awkward squad's growing membership roster, the Blair Government, after eight years in office, succeeded in overcoming every rebellion on whipped votes staged against it in the House of Commons and became the first government to do so since 1966.[19]

However, this was a record that Labour could not repeat in its third term. In the first year of that term, 2005–2006, Labour MPs rebelled on more than one of every four whipped votes cast. More significantly, the Government lost four whipped votes, won another by just one vote, and was forced by Labour backbenchers to modify several key bills.

The Conservatives reveled in the divisions in Labour's ranks, for they calculated that Labour's supporters and the electorate in general soon would become irritated by the bickering mounting within the party. But the Conservatives had their own problems. Members of the parliamentary party gradually tired of what they regarded as the lackluster leadership of Iain Duncan Smith, who had replaced William Hague after he resigned following the 2001 election. For nearly two and a half years under Duncan Smith the party had failed to improve its standing in the polls and consistently trailed Labour by a wide margin. After months of speculation about the Conservative leader's future, some within the party mounted a leadership challenge that led to his dismissal. It was better to make a change then, they figured, than to wait until closer to (or after) the next general election, for a new leader would need time to focus on ways of making the party more electable.

Duncan Smith's successor, Michael Howard, became the Conservative Party's third leader in six years. His tenure was to be even shorter than that of either of his predecessors. On May 6, 2005, the day after the general election and eighteen months to the day after he had been elected leader, he announced that he would resign as leader as soon as the party could find a replacement. His decision came as no surprise, for the Conservatives had just suffered another electoral defeat, their third in a row. Although many credited Howard with reducing Labour's overall majority by more than 90 seats and increasing the number of Conservative seats by 32, with just 198 seats, the party was still a dozen seats shy of the 209 that Labour had won at its nadir in 1983.

From 1979 to 1987, Labour was in the political wilderness; in 1997 some within the Conservative ranks feared their party was destined to spend time there as well. In 2005, after three general election defeats, their fears were confirmed. But they found themselves there for not quite the same reason as Labour had in the 1980s. In Labour's case, the party had insisted on promoting ideas that had gone out of favor years before. Only when it advanced ideas that attracted the support of the political center was it able to come out of the wilderness.

The politics of convergence goes a long way in explaining why the Conservatives found themselves in the political wilderness. The 1997 election had been a watershed as much for them as for Labour. Leading up to it was a series of sex scandals, bitterly fought rows over Britain's role in the EU, and impressions that the leadership was dithering—all of which brought the Conservative Party in Parliament into disfavor. Labour in the meantime had succeeded in shedding its socialist image and, as New Labour, had moved confidently into the political center and embraced several key policies of the Conservative Party it thought consistent with its objectives. That left the Conservatives struggling for ideas that they hoped to claim were genuinely theirs but ones also that would set them apart from their rivals and attract the support of the electorate—and all that without moving to the extreme right.

At the end of 2005, the Conservatives elected David Cameron to succeed Michael Howard. Soon after, the party's standing in the polls started to rise. By the late spring of 2006, the Conservatives had moved ahead of Labour on the key question of which party voters would support. That summer, they continued to move ahead; on one occasion, they achieved a fourteen-year high in the rankings. There were no clear-cut explanations for this about-face. It is not that the party had announced a raft of major new policy positions that attracted enthusiastic public support, for the party was not scheduled to unveil its thinking about policies until 2007–2008—after it had finished consulting the party at the grassroots level in 2007.

Ironically, three factors that helped Labour win power in 1997 appeared to benefit the Conservatives in 2006. First, not only were David Cameron's presentational skills as Opposition leader more effective than those of his three predecessors, they were also every bit as effective as Tony Blair's when he was Opposition leader. Second, allegations of improper behavior directed at certain ministers and backbenchers who had helped bring down the Conservative Government in 1997 were beginning to be leveled against some in the cabinet, among them the deputy prime minister, and against Labour's chief fund-raiser. Third, like John Major's parliamentary Conservatives, Blair's Labour Party in Parliament was riven by differences between old Labour values and new Labour values and between the so-called Blairites and Brownites, that is, those loyal to Blair and his ideas and those who thought it time for Blair to step down as prime minister to make way for Gordon Brown to have a turn at No. 10 Downing Street.

Conclusion

Political parties had their beginnings in Parliament in the seventeenth century, entrenched themselves there in the eighteenth, and then spread beyond Parliament in the nineteenth as local party organizations sprang up around the country in the aftermath of reforms that gave increasing numbers of people the right to vote. It was then that party government took root and became a dominant feature of British politics. Awakening to the need to attract new voters to their side, the parties spelled out their positions in election manifestos and then acted on them when they came to power. Party leaders in Parliament exerted greater discipline over their party colleagues to support the pledges they had made in their manifestos. If a government was defeated on key votes in Parliament, it was expected to resign so that the electorate could choose which party it preferred in a fresh round of elections. All the while, the party in opposition organized to hold the party of government to account if it strayed from its manifesto pledges, and it staked out positions to convince the public that it was more competent to govern than the party in power. By the beginning of the twentieth century, these practices had become the hallmarks of party government in Britain and they remain so today.

Party government has not always been neat and tidy in the sense that one party captures an overall majority of seats and governs for four or five years before another election is called. That is perhaps the beau ideal of parliamentary government in Britain and satisfies those who crave order and predictability. However, there have been times when British voters—whether because of the idiosyncrasies of the voting system or the spread of popular minor parties, or both—have turned this model on its head by preventing any party from winning a majority of seats. The result is a minority government, or hung parliament, with the largest party normally becoming the party of government. But governing without a majority usually means governing by fits and starts. Herbert Asquith found this to be the case after the first of the two elections held in 1910, as did Ramsay MacDonald in 1923 and 1929, and Harold Wilson after the first of the two elections held in 1974.

There is an alternative to governing with a minority, and that is governing by coalition. With, say, a second party joining the dominant party in a coalition, the leader of the dominant party can count on Parliament's support of legislation and look forward to sustaining his or her tenure as prime minister for more than just a brief period. Yet the parties in coalition could pay a heavy price at the next election. Each could antagonize its supporters if it had to jettison some of its major manifesto pledges as a condition for participating in the coalition. In addition, it is highly likely that the second party would be treated as a subaltern, working in the shadow of the dominant party and being held responsible for the dominant party's mistakes on election day. For these reasons, second parties prefer the freedom of pursuing their own agendas, including taking on the dominant party in the next election. All this is not to suggest that British political parties are loath to form coalitions; there were four coalition governments in the twentieth century and they lasted for a total of twenty years. It is important to cite the reasons for their having formed. All four formed in response to national emergencies—during and after the First World War, during the Second World War, and during a worldwide depression—and each time to demonstrate that the major parties had abandoned partisanship in favor of standing as one to cope with the emergency at hand.

Coalitions are not the only occasions when the parties have stood as one. They also did so—up to a point at least—in the years following the end of the Second World War. Consensus dominated the politics of that period, and it was the first of two stages through which the parties have passed since 1945. By 1979, consensus politics gave way to adversarial politics. The two dominant parties found little on which to base a consensus and scrapped more than they had in decades. It was a period reminiscent of the scraps of the interwar years and the years before the First World War—a period of politics as usual. That was the second stage through which the parties have passed. The third stage, the current stage as of this writing, began in 1997 with the election of the first Blair Government and has been a period of convergence, thus called because Labour embraced some of its rival's basic policies. The Conservatives were left to accomplish three goals: devise a body of policies that conveys a clear picture of what they stand for, make what they stand for appealing to the electorate, and talk up its policies to convince the electorate that they are superior to Labour's.

Despite the difficult times, the minority governments, the coalition governments, the periods when both agreed on the basic needs of the nation and the periods when they disagreed, the Conservative and Labour Parties made it through the twentieth century and into the twenty-first. That they succeeded in doing so is attributable to four factors. First, they demonstrated that the values and policies they espoused were different from those of their rivals. Second, they capitalized on these differences when they appealed for electoral support. Third, they adjusted their policies as events warranted and new issues emerged. And fourth, they remained relatively united in the positions they took. Doing anything less than any one of these could have led to their demise. The Liberal Party's demise and the near demise of the Labour Party illustrate this point. During and just after the First World War, the Liberals failed to respond to the needs of the emerging working class. The Labour Party did so instead, and the Liberal Party's leaders fell out and became so deeply divided over what policies their party should pursue that the electorate drove it into the political wilderness. Later, the Labour Party nearly met its demise when, out of power in the 1980s, deep fissures materialized within the party and the policies it adopted alienated even many of its traditional supporters. It was only after Labour made a series of major policy U-turns that it was able to recoup its position as a viable contender for office and succeed in its bid to return to power. The Conservatives, in the meantime, were relegated to the wilderness, from which, as of this writing, only now are they making their exodus. Most analysts are convinced that it is only a matter of time before they emerge from it completely intact and, like Labour before them, one day stage a return to power.

5

Parties in Parliament and Beyond

"Diplomacy is about surviving till the next century—politics is about surviving till Friday afternoon."[1] So murmured the prime minister's principal adviser to his boss as he was reflecting on a foreign policy issue in BBC Television's *Yes, Prime Minister,* a series of political parodies that had Britons in stitches in the 1980s. This was a throwaway line, but most politicians would agree with the spirit of his remark. They are confident about surviving until Friday afternoon but confess to not knowing whether they can count on keeping their seat past the Friday following the next election. Whether they do depends primarily on the voter. The other factor is the political party.

The extraparliamentary party recruits members, raises funds, organizes national conferences, selects candidates, and helps elect them—all activities that could make the difference between a politician's winning or losing the next election. Perhaps it is more the leadership of the party in power than the individual politician who frets about "surviving till Friday afternoon." Here, the party in Parliament could make a difference. It helps shape policy, marshals arguments extolling its merits, and ensures that backbenchers toe the party line when the bells summon them to the House of Commons chamber to vote. Survival, in other words, is as much the aspiration of the party leadership as it is of the individual politician.

Because political parties dominate British politics, they deserve closer examination. In chapter 4, the focus was on Britain's different party systems and three stages of party politics since 1945. This chapter investigates what kind of work the parties perform in Parliament and beyond. Which wields greater power—the parliamentary party or the extraparliamentary party?

Does power flow from the top of the party down or from the bottom of the party up? The answers to these questions differ depending on whether one is referring to the Conservative Party or the Labour Party. In view of that, what are the differences?

The Parties in Parliament

Parliament is the arena in which the winning party transforms its pledges into public policy. Parliament itself is dealt with in chapter 8. The first part of this chapter examines the ways the two major parties operate in Parliament.

Electing Party Leaders

Party leaders in all cases are members of Parliament, and the leader of the party that wins a majority of seats in the general election becomes the prime minister. The leaders speak for their parties, shape their parties' policies, and oversee the work of their parties both inside and outside Parliament. How does a member of Parliament become leader of a party? That depends on the party to which he or she belongs.

Labour Party

Delegates who gather at the Labour Party conference every autumn make the rules governing the election of the party leader. According to these rules, when Labour is out of power, delegates are entitled to elect a leader at every conference, but they regularly pass up this opportunity unless they are determined to back someone they think is superior to the incumbent and who has a better-than-even chance of winning. They have taken this opportunity at only three conferences since 1945, and on each occasion the incumbent emerged unscathed.

The rules are different when Labour is in power. An election is then out of order unless a majority of the delegates decide otherwise. However, most would not even consider mounting a challenge, for the incumbent is also the prime minister and it would make little sense to conspire to unseat the head of your party if he or she is also the head of government. Almost all leadership elections have taken place either after the incumbent has resigned, as Neil Kinnock did following Labour's fourth consecutive general election defeat in 1992, or after the leader has died, as John Smith did in 1994.

When the election of a new leader is in the offing, the election wheels start to turn almost immediately. The party's electorate, called the electoral college, is made up of three constituencies: (1) Labour members of Parliament (MPs) and Labour members of the European Parliament (MEPs), (2) members of the Labour party at the constituency level, and (3) members of party-affiliated trade unions, which have been the party's *raison d'être* for most of its life. Since 1993, the rules agreed to by conference delegates have apportioned voting strength to each of these three in equal measure—33.3 percent apiece. Also agreed to by conference delegates in 1993 was a procedure that governs the balloting of union members and members of the party at the constituency level. Called One Man, One Vote (OMOV), a party-affiliated union distributes a postal ballot to each member who has paid a political levy to the union, signified support for the Labour Party, and declared that he or she is not a member of another party. Under OMOV, those at the constituency level who have been paid-up party members for at least a year also are balloted. After the ballots from these two constituencies are added to those cast by the MPs and MEPs, the ballots are counted and the results announced at the autumn party conference. To win, the candidate must receive more than 50 percent of the vote.

The party elects a deputy leader as well as a leader, usually with the intention of balancing the representation of interests at the top of the party. Balance is what Tony Blair had in mind when he let it be known that he supported John Prescott in the election of deputy leader in 1994. Prescott was from the left of the party and had a strong union connection and thus would serve as a bridge between "old" Labour and what Blair was calling "new" Labour. A deputy serves another purpose as well, but certainly not one the party anticipated the deputy would serve so soon after it elected John Smith and Margaret Beckett as leader and deputy leader in 1992. In the spring of 1994, Smith suffered a fatal heart attack and Beckett stepped into the leadership role until the party could hold an election to replace him. Blair became leader in the subsequent election held that summer; when he became prime minister in 1997 he appointed Prescott, the deputy leader, to serve as deputy prime minister and did so again after the elections of 2001 and 2005. Although there is no constitutional convention that requires a prime minister to appoint a deputy, were a Labour prime minister to die, it is assumed that the deputy prime minister would serve as prime minister until the party elected a new leader.

Conservative Party

Until the close of the last century, electing the Conservative leader had been the exclusive prerogative of the party's MPs. So too was approval of the rules by which the leader was chosen. All that changed, however, following the party's defeat in the 1997 general election. John Major promptly announced that he would resign, and the parliamentary party held an election for a new leader. Two rounds of voting later, William Hague emerged victorious. One of the first tasks he set for himself was to draw up new rules pertaining to the election of the party leader. What he proposed was a bold departure from past procedures. First, not only would the parliamentary party be asked to approve the new rules (as before), but for the first time ever, all members of the party throughout the country who had paid their membership subscription would be called upon to approve them as well. Before these rules could take effect, a majority of the party in Parliament and a majority of the party throughout the country had to agree. A second departure from past procedures was even more dramatic: no longer would the parliamentary party have a monopoly on deciding who should be leader. Conservative MPs would nominate two from their ranks, and these names would be placed on a ballot and mailed to active party members at the grassroots level. Those at the grassroots level would then decide between the two. Hague's rules were adopted by both constituencies—by 60 percent of the parliamentary party and 80 percent of the rank and file who voted.

These rules were activated for the first time in 2001 when Hague resigned as leader in the wake of his party's defeat at the polls. Balloting the rank and file proved to be time-consuming, so much so that the new election rules became a concern of the parliamentary party. What came to be of even greater concern to many was the rank and file's choice of leader—Iain Duncan Smith. By the autumn of 2003, after Duncan Smith had served more than two years, the party in Parliament and beyond had become disillusioned with his leadership and, frustrated that it was no closer to wresting power from Labour than in 2001, many were prepared to replace him.

The 1922 Committee, a committee of Conservative backbenchers, supervises not only the nomination and election of the party leader, but also the removal of the leader should the party wish to replace the incumbent. This is exactly what some Conservative MPs had in mind when they took the first step to remove Duncan Smith in the autumn of 2003. The rules of removal differ from the rules of appointment in that only Conservative MPs—not the party in the country—may vote to remove someone. The discontented MPs proceeded in two stages. The first involved satisfying the requirement that a minimum of 15 percent of all Conservative MPs write the chair of the 1922 Committee to ask that a meeting of the full 1922 Committee be held so that a vote can be taken on whether the incumbent should remain as leader. After the requisite number of MPs had written their requests, a meeting was called. Secret ballots were cast, and Duncan Smith was removed from his post by a vote of 90–75. (Had he received the support of a simple majority, the rules would have prevented any in the parliamentary party from challenging him again for another twelve months.)

Duncan Smith's successor was Michael Howard, but his tenure was even shorter than Duncan Smith's. The day after the Conservatives were defeated in the 2005 election, he announced he would step down as leader—but not before the election of his replacement. The Hague rules were invoked for the third time in four years, and toward the end of 2005, the party elected David Cameron as its new leader.

Conservative prime minister Winston Churchill inaugurated the custom of appointing a deputy prime minister during the Second World War, and most of his Conservative successors followed suit. Margaret Thatcher and John Major both did so, but each for a different reason. Willie Whitelaw was Thatcher's deputy in all but name for most of her premiership, working diligently as a Mr. Fix-it when problems arose. When poor health forced Whitelaw to give up his duties, Thatcher appointed Sir Geoffrey Howe as deputy. Whitelaw had been given the job but not the title; Howe was given the title but not much of a job. He and Thatcher did not get on well, especially after she dismissed him as Foreign Secretary. It was only because he was so well liked by members of the parliamentary party that she felt constrained to give him the consolation prize of deputy prime minister.

When John Major became prime minister in 1990, he chose not to have a deputy prime minister but changed his mind five years later and appointed Michael Heseltine. Heseltine had come in second to Major in the race to replace Thatcher after she resigned in 1990, and in what appeared to be a maneuver to prevent a possible challenge from a rival by conferring an entitlement of substance, Major named Heseltine First Secretary of State and Deputy Prime Minister. Already a member of the cabinet, Heseltine was given greater authority and visibility. Not only did Major ask him to chair four cabinet committees, he also called upon him to shoulder some of the burdens of the office of prime minister that had started to take a personal toll on its incumbent.

Not every prime minister chooses a deputy. It appears that appointing one has not yet been elevated to the status of a constitutional convention. One day it could become one. If it does, should a prime minister decide to appoint a deputy, the job description is likely to vary from one party to another—if not from one prime minister to another.

The Roles of Party Leaders

The party leader fulfills several roles in Parliament, the most important of which are party spokesperson, party disciplinarian, and party troubleshooter. How the leader carries out these roles will very likely depend on his or her personality and style of leadership. Just as likely is it that the leader's roles will be shaped by the party the incumbent leads and the position he or she holds—prime minister or leader of the official Opposition.

Party Spokesperson

Prime Minister

Although the prime minister is a member of Parliament and maintains an office in the House of Commons, the prime ministerial office is a few blocks away, at No. 10 Downing Street. When the prime minister appears at Westminster, he or she is probably heading for the chamber of the House of Commons to make an important announcement or, much more likely, to participate in a ritual called Prime Minister's Questions (PMQs). Questioning prime ministers in the chamber has been a common practice for MPs since 1961. The prime minister responds to questions at the dispatch box, which is stationed just a few feet from the Government front bench, and since 1997, has done so every Wednesday at midday for thirty minutes. The questions touch on any number of subjects. The prime minister is called on to explain, elaborate, and clarify Government policy, and in most cases, defend it. PMQs can be an ordeal for the most seasoned prime minister, especially when a particularly skillful leader of an opposition party fires off questions from across the aisle. The pressure is on to turn in a winning performance, for, with television cameras trained on each move and facial expression and legions of journalists scrutinizing the proceedings from the press galleries above, words and even demeanor are likely to become grist for that evening's news broadcasts and the next morning's newspapers. PMQs have been described many ways, but probably most memorably by Margaret Thatcher, who once called them her "hotline" to the British people.[2]

Opposition Leader

PMQs are as much a hotline for Opposition leaders as for prime ministers. Questions Opposition leaders put to prime ministers provide an opportunity to advance their party's cause by trying to discredit the party in power while raising the credibility of their own, demonstrate their skills in rhetorical combat, and project a persona more attractive than that of the prime minister. Prime ministers can be put at a disadvantage in the process, for they can only speculate about what issues Opposition leaders will raise as they hammer away with their allotted six questions to draw attention to their party's concerns.

Opposition Days give Opposition leaders a further opportunity to draw attention to their party's concerns. These are days when opposition parties are given parliamentary time to take up issues of their own choosing. There are twenty such days every parliamentary session, seventeen of which normally are allocated to the official Opposition and three to the Liberal Democrats, the second-largest opposition party. Opposition leaders usually consult members of their shadow cabinet when selecting topics for debate and sometimes join those in the shadow cabinet who have responsibility for the topics selected when they present the party's position and lead the assault on the Government's policies. Because only the Government may introduce public bills, Opposition Days present opposition parties and their leaders with the chance to pound away at what they allege are the shortcomings of the Government's policies and emphasize what their parties would do were they in power.

Party Disciplinarian

Prime Minister

Being loyal to the prime minister, which essentially means supporting the Government's legislative program, comes naturally for most of the ruling party's backbenchers. Perhaps they do so because the party leader's popularity boosted the margin of their own election victories, or they have received appointments to key committees in the Commons, or they aspire to becoming ministers. In time, however, this loyalty and support can become less steadfast. Prime ministers are aware of this, and that is a principal reason why they rely on their whips.

The Government chief whip is in charge of fifteen to eighteen whips. The whips' job is to maintain a cohesive party front in Parliament. To that end, at the close of every week that Parliament is in session, the chief whip issues *The Whip,* a document that briefly outlines what business awaits the House of Commons in the week ahead. Of particular interest to MPs are bills that will be debated in the Commons, when MPs are expected to vote on them, and most important, *how* they should vote on them. The measures listed are underscored with one, two, or three heavy lines; an item underlined three times—called a three-line whip—is one that members must support without fail. If the outcome of a vote is certain to be close, a backbencher who neglects to show up to vote, shows up but abstains from voting, or votes against the Government could fall from grace with the whips and the prime minister.

The fall from grace could be long and the impact hard. In all likelihood, it would mean that the backbencher would have to forget about becoming a minister—unquestionably so if the offence is egregious. The rebel's future as an MP might even be jeopardized if the party decides to withdraw the whip, that is, suspend the rebel from the parliamentary party for a period. This sanction is rarely used; however, John Major, in an unprecedented move, suspended eight MPs in 1994 when they abstained on a three-line whip measure that called for an increase in Britain's financial contribution to the European Union (EU). Major had put his reputation and his Government's on the line by declaring that he would regard defeat on the measure as tantamount to a vote of no confidence at a time when the Government had an overall majority of only a dozen. The Government won by a narrow margin; had it been defeated, it would have had to resign and Major would have had to call a general election. As for the "whipless eight," as they came to be called, their votes and behavior were closely monitored before they were reinstated in the parliamentary party five months later.

Not surprisingly, none of those suspended from the parliamentary party was part of the payroll vote, a term that applies to more than one hundred individuals who, because of their ministerial duties, are entitled to salaries above what they receive for their regular parliamentary responsibilities. This term also applies to the fifty to sixty MPs who serve as parliamentary private secretaries (PPSs), although they receive no additional salary. Because ministers and PPSs are members of the Government, they can be counted on to vote with the party. However, if a minister or PPS decides to vote against the Government or publicly take issue with a Government policy, convention requires that the individual tender his or her resignation to the prime minister before taking such action. That is indeed what two members of the Blair cabinet, Robin Cook and Clare Short, did to protest against the Government's decision to join the United States in invading Iraq in 2003.

Opposition Leader

It is as important for the leader of the Opposition to maintain party discipline as it is for the prime minister, so Opposition whips are as diligent as their counterparts in keeping a watchful eye on how their party colleagues vote. Every week, the Opposition chief whip issues an Opposition version of *The Whip*, which is "must" read for all in the parliamentary party, who know that failure to heed the whip's instructions on how they should vote will damage their prospects for promotion within the party. If they are members of the shadow cabinet, they will do nothing to risk demotion. If they are not part of the government-in-waiting, they will do nothing to spoil their chances of being promoted to the shadow cabinet, and later, to the cabinet after their party is returned to power.

Rebellious behavior is not countenanced, especially if the Government is hanging on to power by a slim majority, as John Major's did from 1992 to 1997. Tony Blair, then the Opposition leader, was acutely aware of the importance of Labour's maintaining discipline in this period. Not only had the Conservatives' overall majority gradually dwindled to single digits, divisions within their ranks, especially over controversial EU measures, made some Conservative backbenchers quarrelsome and the Government vulnerable. Under these circumstances, Conservative whips were determined to exact discipline to the strictest degree throughout the parliamentary party. But Labour's whips were equally determined. None could question that determination more than two front-bench foreign affairs spokespersons relieved of their responsibilities in 1995. This was the price they paid for failing to notify the Opposition chief whip of an inspection trip abroad that caused them to be absent for two key votes and to miss opportunities to question ministers on the day set aside for foreign affairs questions in the Commons.

Party Troubleshooter

Prime Minister

Hardly any troubleshooting would be required of prime ministers if all they had to do was announce their party's position, snap their fingers, and send party members trooping through the appropriate division lobby. (There are two division lobbies just off the Commons chamber through which MPs pass to register their vote—the Aye Lobby and the No Lobby.) As prime ministers Thatcher and Blair would attest, not even commanding majorities allowed them that luxury. Thatcher (overall majority: approximately 140) was reminded of how quickly a majority can dissolve when, in 1986, 68 members of her party contributed to the only defeat her Government suffered at the pivotal second reading stage of a bill that would have allowed shops to open for business on Sundays. Blair (overall majority: approximately 165) thought his Government might well suffer the same fate in 2004 when a bill raising university tuition fees by nearly 300 percent in two years' time was nearly defeated. So close was the vote at the second reading stage that had three Labour MPs switched their vote from "aye" to "no," the bill would have been defeated.

There are times when prime ministers troubleshoot by dispatching whips and ministers to opponents and fence sitters within the party to call attention to the error of their ways or, on the most important issues, by meeting personally with individuals and groups to win them over. Yet there also are times when the only way a prime minister can troubleshoot is by retreating from a previously announced position to limit the damage legislative defeat would certainly inflict on the Government (and on the prime minister's reputation). Even Tony Blair and Margaret Thatcher, neither of whom was inclined to shrink from controversy, proceeded with caution when the tide of opinion within their parliamentary parties was running against important Government legislation. In the 2004–2005 session, for example, the Blair Government did a U-turn on a measure when, after proposing a liberalization of the regulations on gambling, it later bowed to pressure to tighten them. In the Thatcher years, the Government in 1984 had to amend a bill that required increased parental contributions to their children's university education or face probable defeat by Thatcher's own Conservative backbenchers.

John Major, Thatcher's successor, also found it essential to stage legislative retreats. These were made all the more essential because of the slim majority over which he presided following the 1992 general election. In 1994, when he decided to press ahead with a controversial tax increase on home heating oil in the finance bill, several members of his party who had argued that it would impose an unreasonable burden on the elderly banded together to kill the measure. Defeat came as no surprise to the Government, however, which explains why the chancellor of the exchequer, who was determined to keep the budget in balance, had already prepared an amendment to the bill to introduce on the floor of the Commons to increase the tax on alcohol and tobacco. He promptly introduced the amendment and, just as promptly, the Commons agreed to it.

There are times, too, when a prime minister decides not to take a bill to the floor when support within the parliamentary party is so shallow that pressing ahead with it would risk defeat. An example is the Government's proposal in 1995 to privatize the Postal Service. A number of backbenchers cautioned Secretary of State Michael Heseltine, whose Department of Trade and Industry had drafted the proposal, not to proceed with the legislation. The whips took soundings in the Commons and confirmed what they had suspected—that backbenchers would oppose it. MPs feared a backlash from constituents convinced that vital postal services would be curtailed in villages all across the country. This bill, at one time a legislative priority for the parliamentary session, never went beyond the drafting stage.

A prime minister can ascertain rather quickly when opposition is building within party ranks. A Conservative prime minister learns of intraparty rumblings from the 1922 Committee, a body of back-bench MPs whose views are directed to the prime minister through the whips who attend the committee's various subject-matter meetings. A Labour prime minister learns of party opinion in meetings of the Parliamentary Labour Party (PLP), which is comprised of all the party's MPs, when it assembles to discuss issues and sometimes (unlike the 1922 Committee) votes on them.

Opposition Leader

The 1922 Committee and the PLP play just as important a role in alerting their respective party leaders to the sentiments of the party rank and file when they are in opposition. Like prime ministers, opposition leaders normally place a high premium on interacting with their parliamentary party colleagues. They also enjoy two advantages over prime ministers that assist them in their role as troubleshooters. One advantage is that they have no prime ministerial duties to divert them from interacting with their fellow party MPs. The second is that their offices at Westminster are more accessible to party colleagues than is the prime minister's at No. 10 Downing Street, and although the prime minister maintains an office at Westminster as well, he or she is rarely there.

Opposition leaders have a somewhat greater advantage over the prime minister in interacting with parliamentary colleagues; prime ministers, however, have a far greater advantage with respect to patronage and media attention. While opportunities exist for opposition leaders to bestow patronage or mete out sanctions, they are far fewer than those available to prime ministers. As for the media, the disproportionate amount of attention prime ministers receive in most cases helps them bolster their standing in the country, and in the afterglow of one or more highly successful media appearances, improve their chances of converting those within the party who are wavering on an issue.

Apart from these comparative advantages and disadvantages, opposition leaders, regardless of party, have gone to great lengths to cultivate acceptance of new ideas by their parties in Parliament. Margaret Thatcher embraced a robust troubleshooting role when, as Conservative Opposition leader from 1975 to 1979, she broke with mainstream party thinking by calling for reducing the role of the welfare state, pursuing hitherto untried economic policies to resuscitate Britain's economy, and privatizing nationalized industries and services. And when three successive Labour leaders—Neil Kinnock, John Smith, and Tony Blair—started to argue the case for distancing the party from the trade unions, abandoning socialism as a means to a just society, and scaling down the interventionist role of the state in resolving social ills, few were surprised when those on the left who felt marginalized by their leaders' calls for reform accused them of preaching political heresy.

Party Organizations in Parliament

The party whips, the 1922 Committee, and the Parliamentary Labour Party are pivotal to the work of the parties in Parliament. Indeed, they are the engines that drive the parties in Parliament and keep them on course.

Party Whips

Backbenchers call whips a variety of things. Some are complimentary, such as "democracy's unsung heroes," "confidants," and "problem solvers."

Others are not so generous, such as "the Gestapo," "bullies," and "black-mailers." It has been said they constitute a "brotherhood" lurking in the "shadowy world" of Westminster.[3]

It should come as no surprise that backbenchers use such characterizations in an institution in which political party comes before everything else. The whips' job is to deliver the votes. So determined are they to protect and promote their party's interests that they are bound to attract more criticism than praise from some quarters. Some say that the person who fills the position of whip is as intimidating as the term itself. "Whip" is a hunting expression, drawn from "whipper-in," the one whose job is to whip in the hounds that stray from the pack. Political whips perform a similar job. They are whippers-in in that they admonish, exhort, cajole, and even threaten colleagues who might be tempted to stray from the party's straight and narrow path. Backbenchers know that the whips speak for their party leader, because their leader appointed the chief whip, the deputy whip, and the fifteen or so assistant whips. The prime minister also confers with the chief whip daily when Parliament is in session. So crucial to the Government's legislative program is the work of the Government chief whip, deputy whip, and assistant whips that the Government chief whip sits as a member of the cabinet. All of this gives the whips considerable leverage when they attempt to convince fence-sitters and nay-sayers of the wisdom of their party's position before a whipped vote takes place.

The goals of the whips are to gather political intelligence, build party support, and advise the prime minister on ministerial appointments. It is one thing for a whip to require the attendance of MPs for a vote on a three-line whip, but quite another to demand that they vote with the party. Because some parliamentarians might be tempted to deviate from the party line, political intelligence is crucial. One way by which the whips tap the views of their "flock," as they call them, is by spending time in the Members' Tea Room in the House of Commons, where, as one former Labour MP put it, they "talk to members about everybody's opinion and everything." He continued: "They know what's going on. They know of any plots that are being hatched and they've got their ears to the ground all the time. All that intelligence comes to the chief whip and, if necessary … the prime minister."[4]

The Members' Tea Room is the ideal place for the whips to pick up scuttlebutt. They ply their skills there and elsewhere by dividing their responsibilities by subject matter and geographic region. As for subject matter, each whip is assigned a broad area of public policy, such as rural development, and monitors how party backbenchers react to issues that emanate from this policy area whenever they arise in standing and select committees. In addition, every whip is assigned to a geographic region—Yorkshire, for example. Party backbenchers who represent constituencies in that part of Britain constitute the whip's flock, and the whip regularly consults them about their reactions to bills covering not only rural issues, but also any number of additional issues soon to be debated in the Commons.

Political intelligence becomes the basis of the second goal, building party support. Some within the party are bound to be undecided about how they are going to vote, and others occasionally are tempted to vote contrary to their leader's wishes, so the whips use a number of sanctions, some positive and others negative. An example of a positive sanction is a whip's arranging for an MP to be absent from a vote when the MP has a pressing engagement elsewhere. Through a process called "pairing," the MP approaches the pairing whip, who consults the pairing whip in the other major party to ask if there are any backbenchers there who wish to be absent for the same vote. Usually there are, and if the vote is not on a bill with a three-line whip and the outcome would not be affected, the MPs can be paired, and thus accommodated. However, an MP who is absent without arranging for a pair—or worse, abstains from voting or votes against the party's position without first consulting the whip—contravenes a highly regarded norm. The offence will not escape notice. The MP can count on being subjected to a severe tongue lashing by the whips and scoffed at should he or she approach them for a favor in the near future.

Negative sanctions also can be applied. A dossier—a euphemistic term for what is referred to in the corridors of the Commons as a "black book" or "dirt book"—is kept on each MP. Some whips deny that such a book exists, but one scholar observed that "according to cynics, this produces a sophisticated form of blackmail whereby the keepers of the information (if it exists) deny they have it and yet profit from suspicions that they do."[5] A former whip confirmed that a form of black book does indeed exist and added that if a member refuses to vote with the party, "it is possible to suggest that perhaps it would be not in his interest if people knew [pause] ... something or other."[6]

Scheduling legislation is crucial to a Government's success. If the whips have succeeded in building party support for a measure, it can be scheduled for a vote. If their intelligence is inchoate or it demonstrates that support is shallow, the bill will probably be delayed until the whips can gather additional information, additional support, or (usually) both. When they muster sufficient backing to assure passage of the bill, scheduling proceeds through what is called "the usual channels." Involved are the Government chief whip's private secretary, who schedules meetings of the usual channels; the Leader of the House, a member of the cabinet with responsibility for seeing that the business of the House runs smoothly; the Opposition chief whip; and the shadow Leader of the House. Not much is known about how business is conducted in the usual channels meetings, except that it is thought that these four are scrupulous in adhering to the norm of fair play as they go about organizing Parliament's business for the coming week. Fair play or not, however, if there is interparty disagreement, it is the Government that has its way.

The third function performed by the whips is advising the prime minister on ministerial appointments. Because the whips are in regular contact with their flocks, they are in an ideal position to know the answers to certain key questions about those being considered. Are they party loyalists? Is there anything about their past that could embarrass the Government? Are they skillful in debate? The whips know the answers to these and other questions, and prime ministers attach great significance to their answers when the time comes for them to ponder which parliamentarian to promote to a ministerial post. The whips also offer their advice on which backbenchers are worthy of joining the Government as PPSs. These are the ministers' "eyes and ears" in the Commons and often speak on their behalf. Being selected as a PPS normally means that the MP is on his or her way to eventually becoming a minister. Whether higher office beckons, however, depends partially on how adept they are in assisting their ministers.

The Conservatives' 1922 Committee

The 1922 Committee takes its name from a group of Conservative backbenchers first elected to Parliament in 1922 who were frustrated by the failure of their party's front-bench members to consult them. To publicize their frustrations, these backbenchers formed a committee to appeal for "mutual co-operation and assistance in dealing with political and parliamentary questions, and enable new Members to take a more active interest and part in Parliamentary life."[7] Created in 1923, the committee expanded its membership in 1925 to include all Conservative back-bench MPs. Today, when the Conservatives are in power membership is restricted to the party's backbenchers; when they are in opposition, all frontbenchers except the party leader also become members. Whether the Conservatives are in power or not, the committee is run by an executive body of eighteen back-bench members elected by their fellow party backbenchers after a new parliament gets under way. One of the eighteen serves as chair.

The 1922, as it is commonly called, performs two functions, both of which are carried out behind closed doors. The first is to arrange for and supervise the nomination and election of the party leader and, if need be, the leader's removal. The second is to provide a safety valve for backbenchers determined to vent their concerns about a minister or a Government measure (when the party is in power) or a shadow minister or a party position (when the party is in opposition).

The 1922 meets once a week when Parliament is in session. When back-bench members gather they know they are free to air their concerns about ministers who exhibit poor judgment in carrying out official duties or who behave unbecomingly. They realize that such behavior could bring their party into disrepute and possibly even jeopardize their chances of winning reelection. For example, Foreign Secretary Lord Carrington exhibited poor judgment in 1982 when he refused to postpone a visit to Israel on government business at a time when an attack by Argentina on the Falkland Islands, a British protectorate, appeared imminent. He decided to keep his engagement despite his advisers' insistence that he remain in London to monitor events, and as it happened, the day after Carrington returned to London, Argentina did what British intelligence had predicted—it invaded the Falklands. When word reached Westminster that the foreign secretary had left the country at such an inopportune time, the 1922's executive decided to call a meeting. One backbencher after another rose to express dismay over Carrington's decision to absent himself. It did not take long for him to admit that, in hindsight, he had been remiss. Soon after the meeting, he submitted his resignation to Margaret Thatcher, lamenting that had he stayed, "there would have been continual poison and such advice as I gave you would have been questioned." Thatcher reluctantly agreed.[8]

Backbenchers also may lose confidence in ministers for exercising poor judgment in their private lives. One example is Michael Mates, a junior minister in the Northern Ireland Office who, when it came to light in 1993 that he had befriended a businessman who later absconded to Cyprus to avoid arrest, submitted his resignation to John Major. Major refused to accept it, but Mates stepped down anyway just hours before the 1922 was scheduled to meet to discuss his relationship with the businessman. Another example is David Mellor, the secretary of state for a department that at the time was called National Heritage. In 1992, the chair of the 1922 Committee advised Mellor that adverse publicity about his private life had so embarrassed the Major Government that support for him in the parliamentary party had all but disappeared. Mellor's response was immediate. Within the hour he contacted Major to say that he had decided to resign.

If it is rare that the 1922 registers unhappiness with a minister, it is decidedly less rare when it communicates its concerns about party policies. It normally communicates such concerns through one of its approximately thirty committees. The jurisdictions of roughly half of these committees are parallel to the departments of state; the rest deal with either crosscutting issues or issues that affect different geographic areas of Britain. When the party is out of power, shadow cabinet ministers chair most of these committees. When it is in power, chairs are elected. Many are members of the 1922's executive body, and some also chair the Commons' departmental select committees, that is, committees that oversee the work of departments.

Backbenchers are not assigned to committees and are free to attend any and to speak up at any. The number in attendance reflects the level of interest in an issue. Thus, when a committee attracts a large gathering, the leadership takes note, for it is likely a tip-off that problems are surfacing. To avoid dividing the party on issues, no resolutions may be proposed or votes taken either in committee or in plenary sessions of the 1922. The chair instead sums up the sense of the meeting. The whips observe the proceedings and report their findings to the party leadership if and when there is disquietude. The consequences can be significant. For example, the word disquietude or another word to that effect was certain to be found in the first line or two of a report the whips made in 1992, following a meeting of the 1922's Trade and Industry Committee. The committee had been discussing the Government's decision to close 31 coal mines, when a majority of party backbenchers—more than 150—descended on the meeting to demonstrate their disgruntlement with the decision. The whips lost no time in reporting their findings, whereupon the Government announced it had decided to think again about its closure policy.

Parliamentary Labour Party

The PLP is to the Labour Party roughly what the 1922 Committee is to the Conservative Party. Like the 1922, it began its life as a pressure group in Parliament. But instead of lobbying for more attention from the party's front benches, as the 1922 did, the PLP became a forum for Labour members to discuss upcoming legislation and decide who could best speak for the party when important bills were scheduled for debate in the chamber. It was a small parliamentary party at the beginning—only twenty-nine were elected in the general election of 1906, the year the PLP was founded—but its electoral fortunes improved markedly starting in the 1920s.

All Labour members are members of the PLP, whether the party is in Government or in opposition. It performs three functions, including participating in the election of the party leader and deputy leader. The PLP is one of three electoral college constituencies that elect these individuals, although Labour members of the European Parliament (MEPs) are included in the PLP's count. Thus, when Tony Blair was elected leader in 1994, 271 Labour MPs shared their one third of the vote with 62 Labour MEPs.

Labour MEPs, however, are not members of the PLP and therefore are not involved in performing the PLP's remaining two functions, which are electing the parliamentary party's executive and helping to shape party policy. When the party is in opposition, the PLP's executive, the Parliamentary Committee, is twenty-five members strong. Six seats are reserved for the party leader, the deputy leader, the chair of the PLP, the leader of the House of Lords, the chief whip in the Lords, and one other Labour peer. The PLP elects the remaining nineteen from within its ranks before the beginning of each parliamentary session, after which the party leader appoints them to various shadow cabinet positions. Thus, when Labour comes to power, its cabinet is already in place. Once in power, the Parliamentary Committee drops in number from twenty-five to fourteen. Four are its officers—the prime minister, the deputy prime minister, the Government chief whip in the Commons, and the chair of the PLP; the remaining ten include three ministers, six backbenchers elected by their fellow backbenchers, and one peer elected by back-bench Labour peers.

The third function of the PLP is to help shape party policy, which it does in its committees and its plenary sessions. Normally twenty committees form with jurisdictions that roughly parallel those of the departments of state; another eight deal with problems and issues specific to eight different regions of Britain. Each backbencher may join up to three of the first type of committee and one of the second. In addition to facilitating debate on leg-

113

islative issues, these committees help provide information and guidance to Labour MPs when they are in opposition so they can speak more knowledgeably on issues that arise in Parliament's standing and select committees on which they sit. The chairs of the PLP's committees invariably play an important role, whether Labour is in power or not. When it is in power, they are consulted by ministers assigned to the relevant departments; when Labour is in opposition and shadow cabinet members consult them, the chairs play an even greater role in party policymaking, for they are likely to have access to information and ideas that have not come to the attention of shadow cabinet members.

The PLP also shapes policy in its weekly plenary sessions. The Parliamentary Committee draws up the agenda for these sessions, during which the whips inform MPs about what business will be coming before the Commons, which bills will be assigned a three-line whip, and whether any are likely to be controversial. In contrast to the practice in the 1922 Committee, when contentious issues arise in PLP meetings, they are resolved by votes. Indeed, so contentious and so crucially important are some issues that the party leader might ask all front-bench members to be present at these meetings to demonstrate solidarity at the top of the party when a vote is taken. Some are not intimidated by such displays of unity, however, and when they fear the party is embarking on a foolish idea, they warn the leadership, knowing full well that, because PLP meetings are supposed to be closed, they probably can vent their concerns with the world beyond none the wiser.

The Parties beyond Parliament

The Labour and Conservative Parties also operate beyond Parliament as extraparliamentary parties. They perform a variety of functions. The most important are raising funds for party functions, recruiting new members, undertaking research on issues, contracting for party publicity, selecting candidates for Parliament, and running campaigns. There are some similarities between how the two parties organize themselves and what they do, but what stand out are the differences.

Labour Party

As Labour moved from mass movement to political party in the very early years of the twentieth century, its leaders were ever mindful of the party's origins and those whom they had pledged to serve—Britain's large population of working-class voters and the unions that spoke on their behalf. Like the leaders of other populist movements, the Labour Party's leaders organized mass meetings to which party activists regularly flocked to debate and vote on resolutions. Today, these meetings are staged every autumn and are called party conferences. These conferences were called "the parliament of the [labour] movement" early in the party's history, for union leaders and members dominated the conference sessions. Their views were prominently incorporated in resolutions delegates approved and sent to the Parliamentary Labour Party in Westminster to act on. In charge of the party between conferences was the National Executive Committee (NEC), a small body made up primarily of extraparliamentary party representatives, most of whom were elected by the conference. They were charged with two large and daunting responsibilities: interpreting conference policies and overseeing the work of the extraparliamentary party generally, including the party at the local level—the constituency Labour parties (CLPs).

Although the parliamentary party is represented on the NEC and many from the parliamentary party attend the autumn conference and speak there, the conference, the NEC, and the CLPs are the extraparliamentary parts of the Labour Party. This distinction between the parliamentary party and the extraparliamentary party has been upheld ever since the party's constitution was agreed to in 1918. Delegating as much power to the extraparliamentary party as the constitution does has occasionally given rise to clashes within the party. For example, party leaders (prime ministers in particular) and conference delegates see the political world through different lenses. Whereas conference delegates are eager to champion causes and win elections, party leaders are eager to win elections so that they can implement causes. To make matters more awkward, the causes they support often are not the same. From the late 1960s to the mid-1980s, there was considerable polarity within the party; the unions spearheaded policies at the conference that were radically out of step with electoral opinion. In the 1990s their voting power was reduced. Despite that, union officials have still made life difficult for party leaders from time to time, as have some CLP delegates at the conference and some members of the NEC.

The Autumn Party Conference

Labour holds two conferences every year—one in the spring and one in the autumn. The autumn conference is the one that attends to the party's most pressing business and receives the most publicity. Staged usually in a coastal resort, such as Brighton or Blackpool, it is an event to which more than two thousand of the party faithful flock. The delegates are trade union officials, activists involved in the party at the constituency level, and MPs. For several days they debate resolutions, cast votes, and rally around their leader.

Not only was the conference at one time called the "parliament" of the labor movement, it was also called the "fount" of the party. "Fount" aptly describes the purpose of the conference, for, according to Labour's 1918 constitution, it is from the conference that the party's work flows. From the 1960s through the early 1990s, however, different and sometimes conflicting strands of party thinking made it difficult for conference delegates to agree on what that work should be. Emotions ran high as debates degenerated into shouting matches, with those on the hard left of the party scrapping with those on the soft left and both groups scrapping with those at the party's center over what causes Labour should champion in the coming year. Every autumn, television viewers were treated to what one commentator called "astonishing acts of public, political self-mutilation."[9] One scholar put it less graphically but just as poignantly when he wrote that it was "one thing to believe in internal party democracy but quite another to parade party divisions remorselessly before potential voters."[10]

Beginning in the early 1990s, efforts were made to improve Labour's image. Until 1993 the unions, which were predominantly left of center, had been allocated 90 percent of the conference's vote on party policy and party governance. That generous percentage was reduced to 70 percent in 1993 and then to 50 percent in 1996. (Conversely, the percentages for local party delegates rose correspondingly on each occasion, first to 30 percent and then to 50 percent.) Nineteen ninety-six was also the last chance that Labour had to put on its best conference face before the next general election. The party had a popular new leader, Tony Blair; the left-leaning unions' voting power had been clipped; and the voting power of the more centrist-leaning local party delegates had been boosted. With Labour leading in the polls, a reform-minded party leadership was determined to keep that lead by stage managing its conference proceedings and even organizing training weekends for delegates that featured coaching sessions on how to behave before the cameras.[11] Since the 1990s, Labour conferences have been much more orderly, some would say even boring, by comparison with past conferences. To keep them orderly, however, party leaders are on the alert for signs that clashes will erupt on the conference floor; if necessary, they dispatch their lieutenants to the leaders of potentially warring factions to entreat them not to break ranks.

Winning adoption of a controversial party policy at the conference can be difficult. Obstacles to passage are left-of-center delegates (as most trade union delegates and some constituency party delegates are) and the conference rule that stipulates that adoption requires a two-thirds vote. Party leaders have been loath to press for the conference's approval of resolutions when they fear they will be defeated. They and their lieutenants have been known to go to great lengths to try to convince groups that they should refrain from going to the floor with resolutions that challenge their policy stands. But they have not always been successful, and when votes have gone against them, they have been known to disregard the outcome. Harold Wilson did so after the party conference rebuffed him in 1968 for pursuing his price and incomes policies and again after a special party conference in 1975 voted to oppose his stand that Britain remain in the European Economic Community.

Wilson's successor, James Callaghan, also chose to ignore certain conference decisions with which he disagreed, such as when the 1978 conference voted down his economic policies. Still another to ignore conference decisions was Tony Blair, Callaghan's Labour Party successor as prime minister some years later. One example was a decision taken in 2003 on a resolution that proposed a controversial package of reforms of National Health Service hospitals. The resolution was defeated by a combination of a majority of the 50 percent allotted to the trade unions (76 percent against) plus a minority of the 50 percent apportioned to constituency party delegates (36 percent against). Despite this defeat, a few weeks later Blair sent a draft bill to the Commons that incorporated the reforms and not long after, it was enacted into law.

How did Wilson, Callaghan, and Blair get away with it? It is probably on the strength of the argument Wilson marshaled when he responded to those who criticized him for ignoring conference decisions in the late 1960s. "A Prime Minister," he argued, "is responsible to the House of Commons ... and he *cannot* be from day to day *instructed by any authority other than Parliament.*" [12] [Emphasis this author's.] Despite Wilson's claim, party leaders are advised to tread carefully. They want to avoid triggering a repetition of the fractious conferences of the 1970s and 1980s and, just as important, they want to be seen as being in charge of events.

National Executive Committee

Just two days before the party conference defeated the resolution that favored the hospital reforms just referred to, Blair dashed off to an early morning meeting of the NEC, which was about to vote on the resolution commending the reforms to the conference. As party leader he was a member of the NEC, and his vote was thought crucial. Indeed it was, as demonstrated by the paper-thin sixteen to fifteen majority favoring the resolution.

Commending policies such as hospital reforms to the conference is just one function performed by the NEC, a thirty-three-member, mostly elective body on which representatives from the party's diverse corners sit. The major players are the unions (twelve representatives), local Labour parties (six representatives), and the parliamentary party (six representatives). The NEC's overall purpose is to supervise the work of the extraparliamentary party between conferences, a hugely difficult undertaking. Among other things, it involves organizing the two party conferences held every year plus any special ones, meeting with the cabinet (or shadow cabinet) to draft the election manifesto, overseeing the work of the general secretary (the official the NEC approves to manage Labour Party headquarters in London), looking over the general secretary's shoulder on party financing strategies, and screening candidates for elections to Parliament. Of these functions, two deserve closer inspection: recommending policies to the conference and screening candidates for election.

At one time the NEC played a key role in formulating party policy. Its committees submitted policy recommendations, and those the NEC favored it referred to the conference for debate and a vote. From the late 1960s through the early 1980s, the NEC acquired a reputation for promoting policy ideas that reflected the values of its left-wing membership, values often at variance with electoral opinion and the values of the party leader. Party reformers during the 1990s staged an end run around the NEC by convincing the conference of the need to shift policymaking from the NEC to three new bodies. One body was the National Policy Forum (NPF), which consists of 175 members drawn from all parts of the party. A second was a collection of bodies called policy commissions, each of which is made up of a small number of MPs and NEC members. Both of these function under the watchful eye of a third new body, the Joint Policy Committee (JPC), which consists of front-bench parliamentarians and NEC members and is chaired by the party leader. Since 1997 the NPF and the policy commissions have been involved in a continuous two-year "rolling programme" of policy development, with year one devoted to exploring a range of policy options and year two to selecting the best to send to the conference for debate and a vote. Over a two-year period policy documents are referred back and forth among the NPF, the Policy Commissions, and the JPC, giving party leaders ample opportunity to leave not only their imprint on the final draft, but their *imprimatur* as well.

The effect of these changes has been to give more control over party policymaking to the parliamentary party. In the meantime, even though the NEC has come close to disregarding Blair's position on some matters (such as the aforementioned hospital reforms), today it is rarely out of step with the party leader. Not only was its membership broadened in 1997 to reflect more centrist party views, it is no longer able to justify denying policy proposals access to the conference floor for debate if the party's new policy organs have done their job by commending proposals that are rooted in party-wide consensus.

The second function of the NEC that merits inspection is screening candidates for election to Parliament in constituencies in which no Labour incumbents are seeking reelection. It is the job of the local party, or constituency Labour Party (CLP), to select a candidate, but not before the NEC agrees that he or she is worthy of selection. The NEC has made a tentative judgment about some individuals even before the selection process begins. Any who wish to become candidates may declare their interest to the NEC; the names and biographical information of those considered worthy are kept on file at party headquarters in London for local parties to inspect. A CLP can rely exclusively on these files, or it can consider other individuals whose names are not on file but who have been nominated by a branch of the local party or an organization affiliated with it, such as a trade union. Before the CLP is allowed to draw up a short list, both the NEC and CLP's executive committees must approve every name on it. Having passed through these checkpoints, those on the short list are asked to address members of the local party at a selection meeting, after which members are balloted on their choice. At this point, the NEC is involved once again when it either accepts or rejects the local party's choice. Only rarely will it overturn the local party's decision. For example, in 1995 it turned down the choice of the Leeds North East CLP because it felt the candidate was too far to the left in her thinking. Another example occurred in 1996, when the NEC rejected the

Exeter CLP's choice of candidate for fear he would embarrass the party after the NEC learned that he had been involved in terrorist activities against South Africa's policy of apartheid in the 1960s.

As these examples demonstrate, the NEC, which today has a diverse but politically balanced membership, overrules a CLP's choice of candidate whose policy values are radically different from the party's core values or one with a past that could embarrass the party. Otherwise, its role in selecting candidates is indirect. By-elections, however, are an exception; in these the NEC plays a direct role. A by-election occurs after a parliamentary seat becomes vacant between general elections. The NEC takes more than a passing interest in these contests because of the exaggerated interpretations that spin doctors often place on the results. If the candidate of the party in power wins, the party's spin doctors are likely to claim that the result was a resounding public endorsement of the Government; if an opposition party candidate wins, the opposition's spin doctors are bound to assert that the party's return to power is only a general election away. What prompted the NEC to play a direct role in selecting by-election candidates was the party's embarrassing loss of a seat in Glasgow—until then, one of Labour's safest— to the Scottish National Party in a by-election in 1988. Ever since, the NEC has gone to great lengths to choose the best campaigner possible by interviewing would-be candidates, submitting a short list to the CLP, and then ensuring the CLP selects one as its candidate.

Constituency Labour Parties

Not to be overlooked is the party as it functions at the local level. The CLPs are found in 628 constituencies, that is, in all constituencies of the United Kingdom except the eighteen in Northern Ireland, where normally only parties indigenous to Ulster contest elections. It is important to add, however, that CLPs play an active role at the national level as well as the local level. They hold six of the thirty-three seats in the NEC, command 33 percent of the vote when there is a contest for party leader and deputy leader, and control 50 percent of the vote when resolutions on matters dealing with party policy and party governance are before the conference.

Every CLP is organized into branches; branches in turn are organized into wards. Each ward elects representatives to the General Committee, the ruling body of the CLP. The General Committee elects an executive committee to run the party's day-to-day affairs. It is the body that becomes heavily involved in selecting a candidate for the general election if there is no Labour incumbent or if the Labour incumbent decides not to seek reelection. In addition to selecting candidates, CLPs play a vital role in campaigning for their election. They know they must be poised to enter the electoral arena whenever a general election is called, and because one could be called any time within a five-year period, they have to begin planning for the next campaign once they have finished fighting the last one. However, it is one thing to plan a campaign and another to fund it, and thus fund-raising becomes a vital part of a CLP's work. Some CLPs benefit from the largesse of trade union contributions, but because they are never enough to cover all of a CLP's expenses, they engage in a variety of such fund-raising activities as bake sales, raffles, and socials to make up the difference.

Even before an election is called, CLPs rely on the work of party activists. Most are volunteers, and CLPs muster as many as they can. These nonpaid activists comb through the electoral register to identify the names and addresses of voters and then canvass electors to identify their party preferences. Later, in the ensuing campaign, they remind Labour sympathizers to complete and send in their postal ballots or exhort them to make their way to their polling stations.

That local party activists can make a difference in electoral outcomes has been well documented. In the 1987 general election, two scholars found a correlation between local Labour Party activism and support for Labour candidates in the election. Specifically, electoral support for Labour candidates fell below the national average in constituencies in which CLPs were relatively inactive but exceeded the national average in constituencies in which they were very active. On that same theme, in the 1992 election they found that had CLPs in twelve marginal seats boosted party membership by about 25 percent and raised the number of volunteers to match that of active CLPs, Labour would have prevented the Conservatives from winning an overall majority in the Commons.[13]

Conservative Party

The Conservatives' extraparliamentary party is not as organizationally complex as Labour's. Nor are there groups like trade unions or bodies like the NEC lying in wait to sandbag the party leader. The contrast between the two extraparliamentary parties is striking, although less striking today than it was before the 1990s, for both have moved toward centralizing their party operations while encouraging their rank and file to participate more fully in party decision making. The Conservatives' extraparliamentary party, which has been centralized for many years, is even more centralized today.

Conservative Central Office

Conservative Central Office—or Central Office, as it is called for short—is the party's national headquarters. It is headed by a chair (or co-chairs, on rare occasions) who is usually a sitting or former member of the cabinet and is appointed by the party leader. Central Office's reason for being is essentially what it was when Benjamin Disraeli founded it in 1870, which is to mobilize support for the party throughout the country so that it can win elections and sustain itself in power. With the passage of time, its work has changed to reflect the political requirements of the day.

Today's Central Office requires the chair to manage a complex organization that maintains contact with all parts of the party throughout the country, speak for the party, and transform Central Office into what the party leader hopes will be a campaign juggernaut during elections. In addition, the chair supervises the work of Central Office in undertaking research and analysis, raising funds to cover all of Central Office's expenses plus campaign expenses, and helping the Conservative constituency associations select candidates for election.

The Autumn Party Conference

For many years, annual party conferences were the responsibility of a body that functioned beyond Central Office called the National Union of Conservative and Unionist Associations. This was the umbrella organization of all Conservative constituency associations. It still performs that job, but in 1998 the National Union (as it is called for short) was merged with Central Office.

Labour's NEC plans and organizes party conferences, and so too does the National Union. Whereas the NEC organizes conferences for all sectors of the party, the National Union does so for the party's constituency associations, although the parliamentary party's senior members receive top billing. Moreover, despite the importance of Conservative Party conferences, they wield less power than Labour Party conferences. Labour conferences are empowered to direct the work of the party. Conservative conferences are seen by some, such as one former Conservative MP, as little more than occasions when the party faithful gather for four days at a seaside resort to revel in "a festival of some light and a little heat ... but whose proper purpose is to enthuse." [14] The "light" is the light that senior members of the party cast on major party policies in key addresses they deliver at the conference. When the Conservatives are in power, these policies are certain to be translated into legislative language and placed at the top of the Government's agenda for action. Whether the Conservatives are in power or not, the conference becomes a showcase of what the party stands for.

When Labour's party faithful gather at their conference, they speak for the organizations from which they are drawn—the various unions and local Labour parties—and they vote accordingly. When the Conservative party faithful gather, they do so not to vote, but to applaud their party leaders and the pronouncements they make from the conference podium. Proposing resolutions and balloting are dispensed with because, as one National Union officer explained, voting "highlights the size of minorities and implies a lack of trust in our leaders." He added that it is "far better to pass on our views in a polite and informal way and trust our leaders to sense the prevailing mood." [15]

How and when do the party faithful pass on their views if not at the autumn conference? Moreover, how can they be certain that their leaders are accurately assimilating "the prevailing mood"? One scholar found ample evidence that they passed on their views, particularly when they were restless about an issue, during the many regional party conferences held before the autumn conference. When party leaders responded to their concerns sympathetically at the autumn conference, they received "rapturous ovations." He reckoned these ovations occurred not out of deference for the leaders of the party, but from "a recognition that their speeches have acknowledged and articulated much of what they heard from the floor at earlier [regional] Tory conferences held that year."[16]

Researching the Issues

One of the most valuable forms of support for a political party is the analysis of issues that arise from public policy debates of the day. When a party is in power, it can marshal information and ideas from the civil service through ministers. When it is in opposition, it has no ministers to call upon. Research is vital to MPs when they assess what impact Government policies are likely to have nationally or on their constituencies. It is equally vital to MPs when they are assigned to a committee that is examining a bill or when they are sitting on a party committee's subject-matter committee to discuss a new policy to recommend to the party leadership.

In the case of the Conservative Party, research and analysis was the province of Central Office's Conservative Research Department (CRD) until it was abolished abruptly in 2006. Created in 1929, the CRD remained outside Central Office as an independent arm of research for the party until 1979, when Margaret Thatcher placed it under the control of party headquarters to create a renaissance in the party's thinking and policies. There it remained until Central Office's debts grew so great that maintaining a full complement of researchers and analysts became too much of a drain on the party's shrinking resources. Remaining behind were a few researchers from CRD who were put to work on issues taken up by the party's policy review commissions, which were created soon after David Cameron's election as party leader in 2005.

It is ironic that Cameron felt constrained to abolish CRD, for working there had helped many of the party's brightest activists, Cameron included, launch their political careers. As soon as he announced the creation of the party's policy commissions, CRD was expected to play a pivotal role in exploring fresh policy solutions to problems. Instead, most of CRD's staff was deployed to the House of Commons to help meet the research needs of the parliamentary party by working for shadow cabinet members.

Raising Money

Raising money to pay the Conservative Party's bills, plus meet its expenses for waging a general election campaign at the national level, is one of the most important tasks performed by Central Office, and one made all the more vital by the absence of state funding for political parties. Three sources of funds are available to Central Office—individuals, organizations, and Conservative constituency associations (CCAs). How much can Central Office count on raising? The answer depends to some degree on how the party is regarded and whether it is in power. Is the party riding high in the public opinion polls or is it approaching near-record lows? Is the party in power or is it in opposition and not likely to return to power any time soon? Probably the most consistent source of donations over the years has been the CCAs, which have long been required to contribute a fraction of their income to Central Office.

Far from consistent, however, are the amounts the CCAs have contributed. Local parties have enough difficulty raising money to fund their candidates' campaign expenses and keep their associations afloat; their difficulties are compounded by a shrinking income from a shrinking membership. Nationwide, membership has shrunk from an estimated 2.75 million in 1953, to 1.5 million in 1975, to 350,000 in 1997, to approximately 300,000 in 2006. Particularly worrying to Central Office in recent years is the decreasing percentage of the national party's overall income derived from local parties. In the 1960s and 1970s, CCAs contributed about 20 percent of Central Office's income; by 2005 it had dwindled to less than 5 percent. This dramatic downturn over the years is all the more reason why Central Office has been so eager to step up membership recruitment in recent years.

Selecting Candidates

Raising money is among the top functions performed by Central Office. So too is the initial screening of the many hundreds of hopefuls eager to be selected later by CCAs as the party's candidates in the next general election. Those who aspire to a seat appear before a Central Office selection board of high-ranking party officials for a rigorous round of interviews. The names of those who impress the board sufficiently are put on an approved list at Central Office.

Once on the approved list, would-be candidates begin their search for a constituency in which they think they have a reasonably good chance of being selected. If a candidate makes it onto a local party's long list and then progresses through successive stages leading to selection, Central Office reserves the right to ratify or veto the CCA's choice. In that regard, it functions like Labour's NEC by allowing itself a second, sober look at the qualifications of candidates. Also like the NEC, only rarely does Central Office turn down the local party's choice. It surely will do so if further information about a candidate comes to light that could embarrass the party. In the 1990s, for example, Central Office vetoed the selection of a candidate who had expressed anti-Catholic views in a rhetorical rant and another who had engaged in extreme right-wing activities.

Conservative Constituency Associations

Just about every large town in Britain has a building marked "Conservative Club," a tangible reminder to all that the party is important not just to those living in London, but also to those living even in the distant corners of England, Scotland, and Wales. Local party organizations, or Conservative con-

Speaking of . . .

Taking Sides on Funding Parties

The issue of funding parties gained momentum in 2006, in Tony Blair's third term, triggered by charges that peerages had been awarded to those who had given generously to the party and questions about whether the law allowed loans from party benefactors to be considered tantamount to contributions. Whatever reforms would eventually be agreed to, the unions were sure to oppose any proposed by the Conservatives that would disturb the unions' relationship with Labour. As *The Guardian*'s political editor writes,

> "We don't think people have realised just how radical and partisan the Tory proposals are.... Some people in Downing Street seem to have their own agenda."

"Union leaders have sent a warning to Tony Blair not to back Tory plans to impose a £50,000 [$90,000*] cap on donations to political parties, including from trade unions, saying such a move will cost the party £39m [$70.2 million] over four years.

"They say this would 'fatally undermine' the link between the unions and Labour and insist they will fight any such move, making Mr Blair's chances of creating a cross-party consensus on party funding unlikely.

"The unions sent their message in evidence to the [House of Commons'] constitutional affairs select committee, claiming proposals from [Conservative party leader] David Cameron to cap party donations at £50,000 a year would mean a cut in union funding to Labour from £42m [$75.6 million] in the last parliamentary cycle [2001–2005] to only £3m [$5.4 million], giving the Tories a huge advantage....

" 'We don't think people have realised just how radical and partisan the Tory proposals are. We are also not sure whether everyone in Downing Street yet wants to fight them. Some people in Downing Street seem to have their own agenda,' said Byron Taylor, the liaison officer of Tulo, the group that brings together the 17 unions affiliated to Labour....

"The proposals would mean the unions, Labour's chief source of funding, would only be able to provide £800,000 [$1.4 million] annually instead of the present £8m [$14.4 million] annually in affiliation fees alone....

"The unions ... warn that if the Cameron proposals are implemented 'the Labour party would be required to alter its structure, nature and membership, something never required of a party in a modern democracy without its prior consent'.

"They claim the changes would require the party to revise its conference, the election of its leader, its policy forum and the future of the national executive [committee].

"The [select] committee is examining state funding and caps on election spending and individual donations. The unions are concerned that the public and even Labour MPs have not yet seen the partisan nature of Mr Cameron's plans."

---

*Dollar equivalents are based on £1.00= $1.80, which was the approximate rate of exchange when this article was written.
Source: Patrick Wintour, "Unions Fight Tory Plan for Cap on Political Party Donations." Copyright Guardian News and Media Limited 2006.

stituency associations (CCAs), are found in every constituency in mainland Britain. They make every effort to achieve and maintain visibility by holding rummage sales, sponsoring dinner dances, and selling raffle tickets, and whatever profits they make from these activities they deposit into their association's coffers. Most of their profits do not remain there long, however, for the party treasurer has bills to pay. Monthly mortgage payments on the Conservative Club have to be met, as well as other expenses incurred to maintain the association. Moreover, the treasurer must put away funds to pay the annual contribution assessed by Central Office and to save for the next election campaign.

Except for CCAs that have no hope of seeing their candidates win, the general election campaign probably generates more enthusiasm among local party activists than any other activity. It is difficult to know exactly when the next election will occur, but once it is called, the constituency association knows it has to be ready, for a considerable amount of work has to be packed into the nearly four weeks allotted to campaigning. Therefore, even before the date of the election is announced, well-organized constituency associations already have recruited and trained volunteers to canvass supporters and distribute party literature during the campaign. As election day approaches, they are prepared to remind party supporters to send in their postal ballots or, on election day itself, to urge them to go to their polling stations.

Usually a year or more before a campaign begins, the local parties also select their candidates in those constituencies in which there are no Conservative incumbents seeking reelection. Approval of would-be candidates by a panel of party functionaries at Central Office is just the beginning. There are three further steps, all taken by the local party. First, the constituency association's selection committee trawls through background information kept on those whose names appear on Central Office's approved list to identify those it would like to interview. Next, once they have been interviewed, the committee invites the two or three who have impressed members the most to a CCA executive committee meeting to respond to questions, after which members of the executive committee are balloted on their choice. The third step entails mailing ballots to members of the association, for they make the final decision. Once the local party has taken these steps, the chair of the executive committee communicates the local party's choice to Central Office, which almost always accepts it.

On those rare occasions when Central Office has vetoed a local party's choice of candidate, CCAs predictably will communicate their irritation with Conservative Central Office. CCAs take seriously the job of selecting candidates. To many local party activists, it represents the culmination of all that they have toiled for. But just as there have been occasions when some constituency associations have been irritated by Central Office, so too have there been times when Central Office and parliamentary party leaders have been irritated by decisions the CCAs have made. For example, on the eve of the 1997 general election, the Tatton Constituency Association chose to ignore Prime Minister John Major's exhortations to de-select the incumbent because of allegations that he had gained financially from his position as a member of Parliament. And in 2004 several prominent Conservatives, including a former party leader, failed to persuade the Surrey Heath Constituency Association to change its mind about de-selecting the incumbent, a shadow minister, for falling out with his association officers.

Given the procedures governing the selection of candidates, the strains that surface every now and again between Central Office and local parties are probably inevitable. The solution to this problem, in Central Office's view, is to reduce the autonomy that CCAs claim in selection decisions. But the constituency associations have resisted such proposals because, they argue, they would infringe on what they consider to be their sovereign right. Even David Cameron, while in his honeymoon period with party activists following his 2005 election as party leader, was unable to persuade many CCAs to long-list, let alone short-list, potential candidates that Central Office thought were of star quality. Until Central Office and the CCAs negotiate a way of overcoming this impasse over the latter's proclaimed autonomy, Central Office's efforts to centralize its controls will be less than complete.

Conclusion

If there were no parties in Parliament, someone would surely invent them. The same could be said about those party organizations that function beyond Parliament, the extraparliamentary parties. Fortunately for today's political leaders the hard work of organizing parties, both in Parliament and beyond, was completed long ago. The first to organize was the Conservative Party, which traces its lineage to the Tories of the seventeenth century, a party that had its origins in Parliament. Labour, by contrast, first made its presence known in Parliament many years later, in 1900, although it did not adopt the name "Labour" until 1906. Also by way of contrast to the Conservative Party, the Labour Party had its origins outside Parliament. It was brought into being by the trade union movement, which formed a party of its own after concluding it could not achieve its objectives by working with the Liberal Party, and recruited candidates from its own ranks to run for Parliament.

Despite the differences in the age and origins of the two parties, they are remarkably similar in the way they are organized and carry out their work in Parliament. Both have organizations that could best be described as caucuses—Labour has its Parliamentary Labour Party (PLP) and the Conservatives, their 1922 Committee—and both have whips' offices. Labour was the first to create a caucus, in 1906. Conservatives followed suit in 1923 with their 1922 Committee. Two years later, the committee threw open its doors to all Conservative backbenchers. Today, the PLP and the 1922 Committee meet regularly and perform pivotal services for their respective parties. They alert their members to issues that are about to emerge, remind them of the importance of being present for votes on key bills, and ask ministers (or shadow ministers) to be present to respond to any questions and concerns they might have.

The whips' offices are the nerve centers of their party's organization. Whips are among the hardest working of all members of Parliament. It is hard to imagine how a party leader could function without them. They keep the leader abreast of backbenchers' opinions on major issues, give the leader their judgment on which backbenchers would be best suited to serve as future ministers (or shadow ministers), and work flat out to ensure that party colleagues are present and enter the correct division lobby when they vote.

As for the Labour and Conservative extraparliamentary parties, they are as different from each other as their parliamentary parties are similar. Whereas Conservative prime ministers Macmillan and Heath in the 1960s and 1970s inherited extraparliamentary party machinery that allowed them to lead in a relatively clear-cut, top-down fashion, Labour prime ministers Wilson and Callaghan in that same period were encumbered with a machinery that magnified divisions within the party and frustrated their ability to lead. Time and again, left-wing elements in the autumn party conference and on the NEC repudiated Wilson and Callaghan's policies. So divided was Labour that by the early 1980s it was seen as unelectable. Not until the 1990s did a series of major reforms spearheaded by Labour Party modernizers gradually enhance their leader's chances of exerting more influence within the extraparliamentary party. The voting power of the unions—that element in the conference that caused Labour prime ministers so much distress—was cut drastically, and the constituency Labour parties' voting power was increased. The NEC's policy development responsibilities were transferred to a newly created National Policy Forum, a larger body that represents a greater cross section of the party and over which the leader has more control. The autumn conference continues to be a hardy perennial, and the NEC's membership has even been expanded, but with rules changes for the conference and modifications in the NEC's responsibilities, the ability to frustrate party leaders is not nearly as great as it once was. In other words, the balance of power within Labour's extraparliamentary party has shifted.

The balance of power within the Conservatives' extraparliamentary party has changed as well, although not nearly as much. Although Conservative Central Office no longer boasts what was considered by many to be a premier research department, it continues to exercise the bulk of authority in the extraparliamentary party, especially after the National Union was brought under its roof. However, it has failed to achieve all the control it would like over its constituency associations in the role they play in candidate selection, which remains a prize they jealously guard.

The challenge that confronts the Labour and Conservative Parties today is not how to win elections, for they have won enough of them to know how to do it. Rather, it is how to create new ways to involve their members in their work at a time when their operations have become more centralized, and do so in a way that does not stymie the best efforts of their leaders.

6

Pressure Groups

A seemingly endless number and variety of pressure groups have taken root in Britain since the 1960s and 1970s. Why has this been the case? Are political parties no longer up to the job of representing the interests and needs of the body politic? Or do pressure groups perform these functions more effectively?

It is not surprising that these questions are raised today, for in their eagerness to address issues, political parties have been making manifesto pledges that are so broad and sweeping that they cannot possibly satisfy the specialized needs and single-issue concerns of individuals living in an increasingly pluralistic society. That probably explains why a multitude of diverse pressure groups have emerged. Indeed, so pluralistic have groups in Britain become that in a study of thirty-six democracies, Britain's was ranked as more pluralistic than those found in thirty-three other nations, with the United States trailing just behind, and Spain, Italy, and France further down the list.[1] Today there are so many pressure groups in Britain that one would be hard pressed to identify an issue that is not the concern of one or more pressure groups—with the lone exception that no group has yet been found lobbying to keep everything as it is! They have organized to promote everything from protecting birds to nuclear disarmament and to oppose everything from abortion to genetically modified food. And they represent all sorts—from asylum seekers to zookeepers.

Pressure groups have long been a major force in British politics. Their campaigns helped to abolish slavery, promote free trade, and win women the right to vote. Among the earliest major pressure groups was the Society for Effecting the Abolition of the Slave Trade. Soon after it came into being in 1787, the abolitionists launched a series of petition drives thought to have had a decided influence on Parliament's decision to outlaw slavery in Britain and its West Indian colonies. In 1839, the Anti-Corn Law League was organized to convince the government of the need to repeal laws that imposed heavy tariffs on grain imports. The free trade proponents accomplished their objectives eight years later, after leading a spirited campaign made noteworthy by the barrage of propaganda it directed to all parts of the country.

Probably the first women's suffrage group was the Women's Social and Political Union, founded in 1903 by Emmeline Pankhurst. Some of the most active suffragettes, as they soon came to be called, achieved widespread publicity when they chained themselves to railings, destroyed property, and staged hunger strikes after being hauled off to prison for their militancy. Ironically, however, their militancy set back the cause they so earnestly sought to advance. It was only after other women's suffrage groups emerged to pursue a more moderate course of action that Parliament enacted legislation in 1921 and 1928 that gave women the right to vote.

From these examples one might be tempted to conclude that pressure groups achieve all that they set out to do. But it is impossible to know how successful pressure groups have been over time, because the extent of their operations has been hidden from view. Indeed, in 1958, a British political scientist, Professor Samuel Finer, concluded that it was impossible to calculate what impact they had on public policy making.[2] He called upon other scholars to join him in investigating their activities. Responding to the call was an American political scientist who found that British pressure groups were "numerous, massive, well-organized and highly effective"—perhaps even more so than those in the United States. The principal reason for their previously having eluded the political scientist's microscope was that "British pressure groups work through channels far more inconspicuous and difficult to detect than those used by American pressure groups."[3] Most still do.

Through what channels, then, do pressure groups in Britain work? This is the dominant question that weaves itself through this chapter. To answer it, the focus is on the three Ts of pressure groups—their types, targets, and tactics. But first, it is necessary to pause to examine their functions and the phases through which they have passed since their "discovery" in the last century.

Functions

Pressure groups perform four functions in particular. They inform their members and the general public, represent the views of their members, prod the government of the day to keep its pledges to implement those programs they favor, and promote active citizenship by encouraging their members to participate in the political process.

To Inform

People join pressure groups for a number of reasons. One reason is that they wish to be kept informed of matters that interest or concern them. For example, the British Medical Association brings physicians up to date on medical research findings in its *British Medical Journal.* Information of such a specialized nature is not likely to arouse much interest in the general public. But when an issue could affect the lives of significant numbers, a pressure group is sure to lose no time in exploring ways to reach an audience many times larger than its members, especially if by doing so it thinks it can convert many to its way of thinking.

Ordinarily, groups communicate with their members through journals, newsletters, and fact sheets, but when they want to get the attention of the general public, they are likely to do something a bit more extreme. For example, the Fire Brigades Union stages sporadic strikes to demonstrate its unhappiness over levels of pay. Action on Smoking and Health (ASH) runs advertisements in newspapers that depict toddlers inhaling their parents' cigarette smoke to highlight the hazards of passive smoking, and a member of Fathers 4 Justice, a pressure group campaigning to convince authorities that fathers need more generous visitation rights with their children, dressed up as Batman and climbed up to perch on a ledge at Buckingham Palace. Whether groups use tactics that are orthodox or outlandish, their ultimate aim, of course, is to win public policy makers over to their side.

To Represent

Pressure groups also represent. Representation is the traditional preserve of political parties, but political parties cannot possibly be conversant with or reflect the range of thinking of all their members and supporters. Nor can candidates possibly know which of the many pledges bundled into their election manifestos were favored by their supporters when they voted, how strongly they felt about each, and what opinions their supporters have formed between elections. In all likelihood, their views have changed in the four to five years between these democratic exercises, and all the while new issues continue to emerge.

How might political parties overcome these deficiencies so that public sentiments can be systematically marshaled and channeled to public policy makers? The answer is they cannot. Pressure groups, however, can fill some of the gaps. They represent, and can speak knowledgeably for, certain "publics" in much the same way as the Trades Union Congress and the Confederation of British Industry do for the unions and for business and industry. Pressure groups also can speak for those who probably would not otherwise be heard, such as the homeless, or for causes that are not all that popular, such as penal reform, or they can represent the considered opinions of certain specialized organizations on highly complex issues, such as intellectual property law.

Whether a group is multi-issue or single-issue, its leaders are either already aware of the thinking of its members or, if they are not, can usually find out easily enough and communicate their findings to public policy makers. Public policy makers do not necessarily accede to the wishes of pressure groups. Whether they do so depends on several factors, including the extent to which the issue at hand is consistent with the governing party's policy objectives, the group's credibility, and the public mood as perceived at the time. Many pressure groups represent their members by having their say, but there is no assurance they will have their way.

To Prod the Government of the Day

Because pressure groups are eager to have their way as well as their say, they closely monitor the work of the government of the day. In this respect, they are like an opposition party or a House of Commons select committee formed to oversee the work of a government department. Although they are not political parties, do not sit in Parliament, nor constitute the official opposition or a select committee, they do prod the Government when it is slow to implement manifesto pledges consistent with their goals, and they do try to bring the Government back on course when it strays from or ignores other pledges it has made in which they have an overriding interest.

Their monitoring activities range across a broad front that includes everything from the initial stages of policymaking to various phases of policy execution. In the initial stages pressure groups attempt to convince the government of the day either to place an idea on its agenda or to refrain from doing so. During the execution stage, they keep a watchful eye on matters that could affect the outcome of a proposal they favor once it has made its way through Parliament. For example, which department or agency, and which officials within it, will be responsible for implementing the idea? Will enough money be allocated to administer it? What regulations will be drafted before it is put into effect? The answers to any one of these questions could make a material difference to a pressure group's campaign. That is why pressure groups are earnest about prodding the government of the day not only to implement pledges it has made that advance the goals of their members, but also to execute them in a manner that is consistent with these pledges.

To Promote Active Citizenship

Not all pressure groups call upon their members to help them in their lobbying campaigns. Some groups regard their members more as "subscribers" than "members" and expect them to do nothing more than pay their annual dues.[4] On the other hand, some groups promote an active form of citizenship by encouraging their members to help candidates who favor their causes by campaigning on their behalf, pressing members of Parliament or local councilors to act on them, organizing petition drives, or attending protest meetings. In this regard, pressure groups have filled something of a void, for as party membership has gone into steady decline since the 1970s, pressure group membership has risen dramatically. The apparent reason for this is that people derive greater satisfaction from joining a pressure group that focuses narrowly on one or a few issues with which they closely identify than they do from joining a political party that promotes a multitude of policies that their manifestos usually address superficially and even vaguely. In addition to promoting active citizenship, pressure groups allow activists to acquire a deeper understanding of the political system, and evidence indicates that the more that members of the public participate in these activities, the more knowledgeable about politics they feel they become.[5]

It is inconceivable that a representative democracy worthy of the name could operate without pressure groups, particularly in view of the functions they perform. First, they provide ideas and information that, when supported by credible research, contribute to the quality of debate on issues on which policymakers are expected to form judgments. Second, they facilitate the expression of opinion by representing the views of a wide assortment of interests that might otherwise fail to be heard during election campaigns or between elections. Third, when the government of the day distances itself from election manifesto pledges that certain pressure groups favor, they are likely to prod the Government to keep its promises. And fourth, when pressure groups encourage their members to participate in lobbying for a cause, such participation both enriches their members' understanding of democratic politics and enhances their self-worth as citizens in a representative democracy.

Phases

"The second half of the twentieth century might be regarded as the era of pressure groups in British politics," asserts one political scientist.[6] His was a judgment others might dispute, however, for a case could also be made that it was the era of enhanced prime ministerial power, of a rise in judicial activism, or of some other salient development in British politics. Certainly not in dispute were three facts about this period: (1) governments cultivated closer working relationships with pressure groups, (2) there was a marked expansion in the number of groups and their followers, and (3) their activities became much more visible. Phases in the development of pressure groups—that is, their relationship with government and their overall growth—can be linked to four relatively distinct periods.

Governments and Groups in Alliance (1940–1960)

During the Second World War, the Churchill Government forged an alliance with a number of pressure groups, in particular those that looked after the interests of employers, employees, farmers, and health care professionals. Putting the country on a war footing became a matter of great urgency that required the government to work in partnership with those who operated the nation's industries, grew its crops, and ran its hospitals. To that end, the Churchill Government created national bodies that consisted of representatives from business, industry, and the trade unions to advise it at the highest levels.

This alliance continued in the years immediately following the Second World War as Labour and Conservative Governments alike met the new challenges of managing a mixed economy, pursuing a policy of full employment, nationalizing industries, and introducing cradle-to-grave welfare policies. For a period starting with the end of the war, pressure groups that later became the Trades Union Congress (TUC), the Confederation of British Industry (CBI), the National Farmers Union (NFU), and the British Medical Association (BMA) were invited into government's decision making sanctums. Their interests were reciprocal: government counted on these groups for their advice and cooperation in delivering their programs, and the groups used their positions to try to win over governments to their points of view. The unions in particular shaped the thinking of the Labour Party, which gave credence to the view that Labour was "two-thirds trade union pressure group, one-third political party."[7] Indeed, there was so little difference between the two that when Labour was in power from 1945–1951, it was virtually impossible to determine whether many of its policies could be credited to the party or to the unions.

The Rise of Good-Cause Groups (1960–1979)

Just as noteworthy as the emergence of an alliance between groups and Governments between 1940 and 1960 was the rise in the 1960s and 1970s of groups promoting what they regarded as good causes. The Campaign for Nuclear Disarmament was the first of the major good-cause groups to form following the war; thousands joined it, and in 1961 one hundred thousand of its members marched on London to demonstrate the strength of support for its cause. The 1960s, but especially the 1970s, was a period when women's groups sought enactment of legislation to end such discriminatory practices as compensating women less than men for equal work and denying women maternity leave and the right to return to their jobs at the end of their leave.

At the same time, the membership rolls of such old-line environmental groups as the National Trust and the Ramblers' Association swelled, and new environmental groups, such as Friends of the Earth and Greenpeace, made their debut on the political stage. So, too, did an assortment of such good-cause groups as the Abortion Law Reform Association, the Child Poverty Action Group, the Disablement Income Group, and the Committee for Homosexual Reform, although they harbored little hope of enjoying as close a working relationship with governments as the unions and business.

These new good-cause groups first appeared on the political stage at a time when relations between governments, trade unions, and employers were especially close—so much so that in 1962 they became formalized in a tripartite body called the National Economic Development Council (NEDC). NEDC was Britain's experiment with corporatism. Corporatism can be described as both a body of representatives and working relationships: the representatives are drawn from the major economic interests and attempt to settle any differences they might have on economic matters that concern them and advance new ideas in the interest of achieving economic growth. Through the NEDC, cabinet ministers and senior civil servants consulted representatives of the TUC and the CBI in an effort to come up with solutions to revitalize Britain's ailing economy. Everything—inflation, un-employment, Britain's trade deficit—was high except economic growth. But probably nothing was higher than the expectations of those who hoped for more from this experiment in tripartite consultation, and they remained high until the late 1970s, when the experiment began to show signs of having run its course.

The End of the Alliance (1979–1997)

Even before the end of the 1970s, a growing number began to question how long Britain's experiment with corporatism could or should last. This arrangement had failed to dissuade the unions from making extravagant wage demands. Strikes contributed to the failure of Edward Heath's Con-servative Government to continue in power past the general election of 1974, and they paralyzed the delivery of many local public services during what became known as the "Winter of Discontent" of 1978–1979 that helped bring down the Callaghan Government the following spring. The unions were holding the government hostage—at least that was how the public saw it. Two parties in this triumvirate were "reluctant partners," as one scholar put it, for they were working at cross-purposes. As he explained, "The fundamental role of unions [the TUC] is to improve the pay and con-ditions of their members whilst that of businesses [the CBI] is to make profits for their shareholders."[8]

All of these concerns reinforced Margaret Thatcher's thinking that this tripartite arrangement was a political anomaly. She was convinced that the arrangement was undermining representative democracy and making the UK ungovernable, and when she became prime minister in 1979 the TUC and the CBI no longer found the welcome mat laid out for them at No. 10 Downing Street. The NEDC survived, but barely, for it was rarely convened. It was finally laid to rest in 1992. In the meantime, the TUC, now out of favor, was constrained by tough new Conservative trade union reforms, and the CBI was put on the sidelines. Favored instead were a host of other groups that Thatcher found more ideologically compatible. These were such groups as the Institute of Directors, whose members are directors of compa-nies; the British Roads Federation, reflecting her Government's preference for the automobile over rail transport; and even such right-of-center think tanks as the Adam Smith Institute and the Centre for Policy Studies.

Although relations between the Thatcher and Major Governments and many other groups continued at the individual departmental level, those groups whose agendas required more state intervention and increased public spending grudgingly listened to those who counseled them to bide their time until Labour was returned to power. The unions bided their time as well.

The Alliance Restored? (1997–Present)

As the 1997 general election drew closer, the trade unions began to wonder whether their long wait for Labour's return to power had been for naught.

Not long after the election, it became obvious that No. 10 Downing Street would not be issuing invitations to the unions for friendly discussions with the prime minister over beer and sandwiches as Labour's Harold Wilson did when he was prime minister in the 1960s and 1970s. Tony Blair was "New" Labour in more than just name, and this meant that his Government would no longer reserve places for the unions, or anyone else, for that matter, in its inner councils when industrial disputes erupted or other storm clouds appeared on the economic horizon.

Although the Labour-trade union axis of old was not to be resurrected, the unions soon learned they would at least fare better under Labour than under the Conservatives. So too would the CBI. No longer was it viewed with suspicion, as during the Thatcher years in the 1980s, for having played a role as a tripartite player. The Conservatives' loss of power in 1997 was a bonus to the CBI. There was another bonus as well: no Labour Government had exhibited more enthusiasm for cultivating a constructive working relationship with business than had Tony Blair's. Like the unions, the CBI was no longer ignored by No. 10 Downing Street. But also like the unions, it soon learned that the Blair Government would not be a pushover.

Steering a course somewhere between the unions and business was seen as an example of Blair's Third Way in action. Various good-cause groups felt the same, for even though they were no longer out of favor as during the Conservative years, they soon realized that their appeals, which required more government intervention and increased public spending, were receiving less sympathy than in the days of Clement Attlee, Harold Wilson, and James Callaghan. Sometimes history repeats itself. Not in this case.

Types

Of the many groups in society, the vast majority are interest groups and pressure groups, and of these most are interest groups. An example is the local Flora and Fauna Society (FAFSO), which meets once a month for slide-talks on plants and wildlife. That is FAFSO's only activity, and the interests its members share are what make it an interest group. To take this a step further, say that some members of FAFSO also are members of another group, a society organized to call attention to the need for more bird sanctuaries in a particular county. This group, which calls itself Save Our Disappearing Songbirds (SODS), gathers every month for slide-talks on birds. After each talk, its members devote the rest of their meeting to planning ways of convincing the Environment Agency to allocate more funds for sanctuaries. Lobbying the Environment Agency is the principal reason SODS was created, and lobbying is what makes it a pressure group.

Interest groups can easily transform themselves into pressure groups. To illustrate, say that those FAFSO members who also are members of SODS convince their FAFSO colleagues that their local club should combine forces with SODS in its lobbying mission to expand the number of bird sanctuaries in the county. Having been converted to the idea, FAFSO is now a pressure group, that is, until it concludes that the county has established enough bird sanctuaries and it has no need to wage further campaigns.

Distinguishing between interest groups and pressure groups is one way of classifying groups generally. How might pressure groups themselves be classified? There are large groups and small groups, well-known groups and groups most have never heard of, groups whose coffers are full and those that operate on a shoestring, and groups whose remit covers a range of issues and those that focus on just one concern. Some have members drawn from all parts of the UK and others only from the west side of town. There are ideological groups and groups with economic vested interests, groups that have an oligarchic structure and those boasting a democratic one, and those that work behind the scenes and those that prefer to make a scene. The list could go on and on.

To bring some order to this seemingly endless variety, some British political scientists devised a two-fold classification of pressure groups and called them primary groups and secondary groups. Primary groups are groups whose only purpose is to engage in political lobbying. An example is Liberty, a pressure group that lobbies to overcome human rights abuses. Secondary groups, on the other hand, are groups whose principal purpose is something other than political lobbying. The Union of Democratic Mineworkers is an example of such a group. Obviously a trade union, this group represents its members by negotiating with employers for higher pay and more generous pension benefits. It does have another, rather more secondary purpose, a political one that it sets in motion when it campaigns to strengthen government regulations dealing with mine safety or to oppose legislative proposals to raise the retirement age.

This two-fold classification encompasses such a vast variety of pressure groups that it is less useful than typologies that focus more narrowly on the differences among groups. Other typologies classify pressure groups by their overall aims, their relationship with the government of the day, and the strategies they pursue to accomplish their objectives—in short, by their purpose, their status, and their strategies.

Purpose

The vast majority of pressure groups can be classified as either self-promotion groups or good-cause groups. Self-promotion groups are pressure groups whose principal purpose is to protect and advance the economic, occupational, or professional interests of their members. They include employers' associations, for example, the Engineering Employers' Federation; trade unions, such as the British Airline Pilots Association; and professional bodies, including the British Dental Association. Some affiliate with umbrella organizations so that they can increase their influence. The most well-known of these are the CBI, which represents the interests of employers in the business sector, and the TUC, which speaks for the unions. Good-cause groups are pressure groups whose principal purpose is the promotion of the beliefs, values, and principles their members espouse. Examples are the Pro-Life Alliance, Amnesty International, and Friends of the Earth.

Self-promotion groups and good-cause groups appear to be mutually exclusive labels, but are they? Some argue that the British Medical Association (BMA) is as much a good-cause group as a self-promotion group, for although it negotiates for higher pay for its members, it also allocates some of its resources to wage campaigns to discourage teenagers from smoking. The Campaign for the Advancement of State Education (CASE) is an example in reverse. A good-cause group, CASE also could be considered a self-promotion group because many of its members are teachers in state-funded schools who might derive benefits from some of the group's lobbying campaigns. It cannot be denied that the BMA is a self-promotion group that also supports good causes and that CASE supports a cause that also potentially advances the interests of many of its members. The BMA and CASE are indeed dual-purpose groups. But the words "principal purpose" used in the definition of each term should nevertheless be borne in mind—that is to say that the *principal purpose* of the BMA is self-promotion and the *principal purpose* of CASE is the support of a good cause.

Status

Whether classified as self-promotion groups or good-cause groups, how well positioned are pressure groups to achieve their objectives? The answer depends in part on their status with the government of the day. Some work closely with government. These are called insider groups. Other groups have little or no working relationship with government. These are called outsider groups.

Insider groups are pressure groups that governments consult regularly because they have legitimacy. Their members play an important role in society, their leaders have a good sense of what is on their members' minds, and they do not identify so closely with one major political party when it is in power that they cannot work with the other when it comes to power. Their positions are supported by thorough and balanced research, they can be trusted to keep information to themselves that officials impart in confidence, and they demonstrate a willingness to compromise when negotiations on policy are approaching an impasse. A classic example of an insider group is the National Farmers Union (NFU). The government of the day consults it regularly on agricultural policy, and the Blair Government relied on it every step of the way in its efforts to eradicate the foot-and-mouth epidemic that swept through parts of England and Wales in 2001.

Outsider groups, or groups not consulted by governments, are outsiders for any number of reasons. One is that a government is not in sympathy with a group's objectives. Thus, the Home Office would consider it a waste of time to ask a group called Radical Alternatives to Prison for its recommendations on prison reforms. Another reason is that a group's "lobbying" methods are unlawful. Thus, if an animal rights group, such as the Animal Liberation Front, threatens to wage a campaign of terror at animal testing laboratories, it should not expect to receive an invitation from the Department of Health to respond to proposed new regulations pertaining to conducting experiments on rodents. Nor is it likely the group would accept an invitation if one were sent, for engaging in dialogue with government scientists about the welfare of laboratory animals would send a signal to its supporters that it had sold out to the political system with which it avowedly has no patience. Still another reason why some groups are not consulted by governments is that their leaders lack basic political skills to achieve insider status. They make too many demands, incorrectly assume they have automatic and immediate access to the top policymakers, neglect to back up their claims with adequate research, and fail to convince the officials who do see them that they are accurately voicing the opinions of their members.

Once pressure groups become insiders, there is no assurance they will remain so. Political events, such as a change of government, can alter their status, as the TUC discovered when Margaret Thatcher abandoned the practice of tripartite consultations soon after she became prime minister. Moreover, outsider groups need not remain outsiders. They can become insiders or move in the direction of becoming insiders. An example is Greenpeace. Since the 1990s it has begun to attach greater importance to backing up its claims with more in-depth research on environmental issues and has abandoned eye-catching publicity campaigns in favor of more conventional methods of lobbying that have made the government more receptive to its concerns.

Strategies

Strategies are master plans pressure groups devise to accomplish their objectives. A group's master plan can include the pursuit of a low-profile campaign, a high-profile campaign, or possibly both. A low-profile campaign involves a pressure group's working behind the scenes, primarily with the executive side of government. The group concentrates most of its campaign on civil servants in Whitehall (that is, the departments of government), because that is where ideas for future legislation are thrashed out, bills are drafted, and regulations are written. An insider group finds it an ideal arena on which to focus because it can almost always count on being consulted by a department or agency. And consultation, of course, allows the group to educate the department or agency to its way of thinking.

A high-profile campaign, as the term implies, is one that entails a group's churning out massive amounts of publicity for as many media outlets as will carry it in order to generate support for its position on a particular issue. Such a campaign could include organizing demonstrations and marches. A pressure group undertakes a high-profile campaign for two reasons: to increase public awareness of a problem it feels the government has ignored and to prompt members of the public to take up the issue with their elected representatives. Campaigners hope a high level of publicity will have a domino effect on all parts of the political system. They hope that it will be addressed at fringe meetings at the annual conferences of the political parties, that other pressure groups championing related causes will champion this one as well, and that all-party groups in Westminster will study it and then speak out on it. If it is an issue that touches on the work of local government, the group hopes that local government councilors will share their concerns with the relevant senior civil servants in Whitehall and that members of Parliament will press No. 10 Downing Street to come up with a solution.

A high-profile campaign is more likely to be adopted by outsider groups than by insider groups, for it is probably the only avenue available to them to attract the attention of public policy makers and impress them with the worthiness of their causes. As for insider groups, key to the decision to pursue a high-profile campaign is whether a group would jeopardize the good relations it has cultivated with government officials. That it would not is what persuaded the NFU, a long-time insider group, to encourage four hundred thousand of its members to join the Countryside Alliance, an outsider group, in a march on London in 2002. The NFU was confident the march would be peaceful and that alliance leaders would continue to be reasonable when pressing policymakers to address the problems of falling farm incomes and rural post office closures.

Targets and Tactics

What parts of the political system do pressure groups target, and once these parts are targeted, what tactics are used to win public policy makers over to their side? The answers to these questions reveal a great deal about where power and influence lie in the political system. That would be reason enough to search for the answers. But for now, there is a more pressing reason, and that is to examine how pressure groups work the system.

Of those parts of the political system targeted, singled out here are those institutions that are the most important in policymaking: political parties, Parliament, the executive side of government, the courts, and the EU. Some are more important than others. Moreover, when lobbyists focus their attention on one of these, they concentrate their efforts not on all parts of the institution, but on those that they consider the most useful; for example, with Parliament, it would be the House of Commons as opposed to the House of Lords because the Commons plays a more important role in lawmaking.

Political Parties

If a pressure group waits until after a general election to plan what tactics to use in its next lobbying campaign, it has very likely left it until it is too late. The groundwork for a successful campaign is laid before the leader of the winning political party forms a government and sets the date of the State

Opening of Parliament. Pressure groups are keenly aware that parties penetrate every aspect of political life in Britain. They select candidates for Parliament, decide what pledges to include in their election manifestos, form a Government if they win or become the government-in-waiting if they lose, determine what legislation will be debated in Parliament, and insist that their members toe the party line. Because political parties are so pervasive, the most experienced and resourceful pressure groups plan well ahead and attempt to influence the outcome of a general election and the policies that will follow by donating funds to the parties, backing candidates that support their causes, and helping shape party policies.

Donating Funds

Donations to political parties are made at the national level and the constituency level. Those who are particularly generous make their checks payable to the party at the national level. There is no limit to the amount they may give. That is why some observers express concern that when individuals and groups give large sums, they probably expect favors in return. However, after the piper has played his tune, will he be paid? It is often difficult to know the answer.

If a pressure group has the wherewithal to donate funds to selected constituency parties across the nation, it is participating in an effort that could lead to what it hopes will be an overall majority of seats in the House of Commons for the party that supports its causes. The trade unions have a long history of party giving, but only to the Labour Party—both to its headquarters and to its constituency Labour parties (CLPs). Since 1995, contributions to CLPs have taken the form of "constituency plan agreements." These are agreements that the unions make with CLPs where there are marginal seats, that is, seats for which the margin of victory between the winning candidate and the runner-up tends to be close. Roughly 15 percent of the total number of seats in the Commons are marginal; to give Labour candidates a boost, the unions contribute modest amounts from union funds that are pooled centrally. In exchange, these CLPs provide the unions representation on their general committees.

Backing Candidates

Serving on the general committees of CLPs provides an opportunity for trade union representatives to exercise influence over who is selected to stand as Labour candidates in the next election. Sitting alongside the unionists on general committees are other party members, some of whom may be active with other pressure groups, and although they are given no official status as union representatives are, they too have a say in selection decisions. Members of pressure groups also are likely to make their way onto local Conservative Party selection panels, although because the trade unions have never been political allies of the party, they have never drawn up constituency plan agreements with Conservative constituency associations.

Once the candidates are chosen and the election date is announced, members of pressure groups are encouraged to volunteer to serve alongside others as the party's foot soldiers for the duration of the campaign. On rare occasions a pressure group even fields candidates to fight an election under its own banner. One group, the Pro-Life Alliance, was so ambitious that it entered 57 out of 659 races in the 1997 election and 37 in the 2001 election. No one—not even the group itself—was surprised that it was defeated resoundingly in every seat it contested. But winning was not necessarily its aim. Achieving a higher profile was. And in that it succeeded.

Influencing Public Policy

Just as predictable as the approach of autumn is the approach of the autumn political party conferences. For the Labour Party, this conference allows the unions to exert some influence on party policy, for they are accorded 50 percent of the votes cast on policy. If the unions and the party leadership are at variance, the party leaders find themselves having to negotiate their differences behind the scenes to forestall a split that could embarrass the party and diminish its standing with the public.

Regular features of the party conferences are the exhibitions, receptions, and fringe meetings sponsored by Age Concern, the Scotch Whiskey Association, the Police Federation, and countless numbers of other pressure groups. Groups rent space at the conferences to make sure the messages they convey through their lobbyists' presence are not forgotten, even though it is questionable how much impact lobbyists have on these occasions on those who help shape party policy. If nothing else, they can get a sense of what opinions on issues are crystallizing among the party rank and file, as well as take advantage of the opportunity to establish at least superficial contact with ministers (or shadow ministers), nearly all of whom are present at this annual event.

A pressure group receives a major boost when a cause for which it has lobbied becomes a pledge incorporated in the election manifesto of the party that wins the election. Without this boost a pressure group's campaign can be stalled indefinitely. During the 1997 election campaign, the leaders of several good-cause groups had every reason to believe that their luck was about to turn. Not only had their causes been endorsed by Labour and incorporated into its manifesto, it looked like Labour was on the verge of defeating the Conservatives, who had shown little interest in their causes. It is understandable then, why those who had campaigned for the disabled, gay rights, electoral reform, human rights, and outlawing fox hunting with hounds were jubilant when Labour's victory was announced.

Parliament

Busy lobbyists may not always include the two houses of Parliament on their list of stops to make on their weekly rounds. They are certain to meet with ministers and civil servants, but stopping at Westminster normally does not have the same urgency as does doing business in Whitehall. Nevertheless, lobbyists know that it would be a mistake to overlook Parliament, for just as the executive side of government plays a leading role in public policy making, Westminster plays a supporting role, and sometimes more. Lobbyists set their sights on three targets: (1) back-bench members of Parliament (MPs), (2) committees in the House of Commons, and (3) the House of Lords.

Back-Bench MPs

Lobbyists seek out backbenchers in the Commons to enlist as their intermediaries with ministers. These intermediaries put in a good word with a minister, make introductions, arrange meetings with ministers, and ensure that a pressure group's position statements and research memoranda are in the minister's in-box. They perform an equally important role when they raise questions on behalf of lobbyists in the chamber during ministers' Question Time. Some questions demand a response from the minister at the dispatch box right then and there; others require written answers.

Intermediaries call attention to a pressing problem, attempt to find out what the Government intends to do about it, and try to determine when it will take remedial action. For example, an MP sympathetic to the problems of nurses might string these three reasons together and ask the following on behalf of the nurses' union: "In view of the critical shortage of nurses in our hospitals, will the Secretary of State for Health please tell this House what plans she has for overcoming these shortages and when she will put them into effect?" The minister's answer to this (and to all other questions, whether oral or written) is entered in *Hansard,* the official record of parliamentary proceedings. This means that if, after months have passed and there is no evidence that the department has addressed the problem, a delegation from the nurses' union could arrange to meet with the Health Secretary and read back her answer in *Hansard* to underscore the urgency of moving forward with a plan of action.

Backbenchers play an even more active role on behalf of pressure groups when they take the lead in circulating an early day motion (EDM) for interested colleagues to sign. Technically a motion that calls upon the government to do something, an EDM is very rarely debated. A lobbyist for the National Union of Teachers could ask a back-bench member of Parliament (ideally, a former union member) to initiate an EDM, which is in effect a petition, calling upon the Secretary of State for Education and Skills "to ensure that classes in all primary schools in England and Wales not exceed twenty-five pupils when the new school year begins." The more MPs who sign the EDM, the greater impact it is likely to have with the Government. One signed by fifty or more MPs is almost guaranteed to attract attention, and most certainly so if a majority of the signatories are members of the governing party.

The introduction of private members' bills (PMBs) is another way by which back-bench MPs attempt to promote the aims of a pressure group.

Once a year, at the beginning of every parliamentary session, backbenchers participate in a lottery to win a chance to introduce a bill. Only those whose names are among the top twenty drawn have an opportunity to do so, and once it is known who the twenty are, these MPs are inundated with requests from pressure groups to introduce bills on their behalf. Many groups have bills already drafted and have long waited for this day, hopeful that one of the winning MPs—preferably one of the first half-dozen, for there probably will not be enough time to consider them all—will sympathize with their cause.

Even if a pressure group can find a sponsor, however, there is no certainty the bill will become law, for if the Government opposes the bill it will kill it by denying enough time for it to be debated. Denying a bill enough time is what seals the fate of a majority of PMBs. An exception is the occasional bill that addresses an issue of "conscience," one that is so politically sensitive that it is presumed the Government would prefer not to sponsor it but in effect does so by allowing enough time for it to be considered. That was the case when PMBs inspired by good-cause groups led to the abolition of the death penalty and the legalization of abortion. If a PMB backed by a good-cause group fails, lobbyists hope that the campaign preceding the bill's demise has at least generated favorable media attention and that the government of the day will be converted to the need to incorporate it in future legislation.

Committees in the Commons

When pressure groups target back-bench MPs, in their peripheral vision is another target—the committees on which backbenchers sit. These include parliamentary committees, party committees, and all-party subject-matter groups. The parliamentary committees are of two types: standing and select. Standing committees are way stations to which bills are referred before they become law. MPs debate bills section by section and clause by clause, searching all the while for weaknesses and imperfections, and vote on amendments before sending them back to the whole house to await the next step in their consideration. This is the stage in the legislative process during which pressure groups have the best chance of influencing the outcome of legislation in the Commons. By consulting informally with committee members—with one or more backbenchers or the minister who will later pilot the bill through the house—lobbyists suggest ways by which the bill could be shaped to their liking. There is a good chance they will succeed if the bill is neither particularly controversial nor highly partisan and, most important, if the government of the day does not oppose the changes they propose.

The second type of parliamentary committee is the select committee. These committees scrutinize the policies of the government of the day to assess how well they are working and investigate why certain programs are not being administered effectively or efficiently. Committee members learn of implementation problems from many sources, among them lobbyists who represent those adversely affected by bureaucratic foul-ups. How likely is it that a pressure group will convince a committee to undertake an investigation? The answer depends on the committee chair's commitment to addressing the problem (it is often the chair who is the driving force on a committee), the committee's workload (there are only so many problems a committee can investigate), and its budget (normally committee budgets are modest). One or all of these factors could make it difficult for a pressure group to win a committee over.

On the other hand, it could be easier for the group to be successful if the issue troubling it is becoming the subject of growing public concern. If a pressure group is closely identified with the subject to be investigated, there is a strong likelihood its representatives will be invited to testify before the committee, an invitation the group would welcome in a day when select committees are receiving an unprecedented amount of media attention. But it is the grand prize that the group is holding out for, a prize that comes in two parts—first, a decision by the committee to incorporate the group's recommendations into its final report to the Government, and second, the Government's agreement to put them into effect.

Whether members of the governing party or of the Opposition, backbenchers sitting on parliamentary committees often are confronted with having to make important decisions without the benefit of any information other than what the government of the day chooses to share. In some cases government is the only source of information (for example, tax receipts, employment levels), but in others information can originate from a variety of sources, including pressure groups. If they are convinced that information in their possession will help their cause in a parliamentary committee, lobbyists will approach its members directly.

If lobbyists have not cultivated ties with these backbenchers, they could feed information to them through members they know who sit on two other types of committees—party committees and all-party subject-matter groups. Party committees are the creatures of the two major parties' back-bench organizations in the Commons, the Parliamentary Labour Party and the Conservatives' 1922 Committee. Each has approximately thirty committees, most of whose remits roughly parallel certain areas of jurisdiction in the departments of state. The second type of committee is the all-party subject-matter group. There are more than 150 such groups, and they are open to all MPs without reference to party. These form around an endless variety of subjects ranging from AIDS to wool. Both types of committees often are hungry for information, and lobbyists are eager to provide it. Some pressure groups help in other ways as well by deploying aides to assist some subject-matter committees with their research and even absorbing some of their operating costs.

House of Lords

The House of Lords is a third target for those who lobby Parliament, although for many years the Lords did not feature as one of the top three targets for most who lobbied Parliament. Starting in the early 1980s, however, lobbyists started to have second thoughts about the importance of the Lords to their work. Not only were peers becoming more active, as measured by the number of days they met and the number of hours they sat each session, they also were asserting themselves more and becoming more independent. No longer content to be regarded as a mere revising chamber that tinkered with legislation at the margins, they insisted on putting their imprint on selected pieces of government legislation. So assertive had the Lords become that from May 1979 to July 1998, it inflicted defeat on the Government's position on no fewer than 272 occasions.[9] Although some of its decisions were later reversed in the Commons, it was clear to the government of the day that the Lords had become a force to be reckoned with.

This revival of the Lords' independence and influence has become an enormous stimulus to pressure groups, good-cause groups in particular, to seek out peers to help them achieve their objectives. In some cases they do not have far to look; some peers are well known for the causes they support—such as human rights, the physically disabled, and animal welfare. Lobbyists gravitate to them if they are promoting the same causes. Lobbyists need peers, but the need is reciprocal. Peers are allocated no public funds to hire researchers, and therefore they have to carry out research on their own, rely on unsalaried interns, compensate researchers from personal funds, or, more likely, accept the research undertaken by professionals who work for pressure groups.

Filling a research need is one reason why lobbyists make themselves available to peers. A second reason why lobbyists target peers is that there are relatively few constraints imposed on how peers vote. Some are cross-benchers, that is, they are not affiliated with a political party. They vote as they please. Others, although members of a party, are not blindly loyal to it; many of these individuals also vote as they please. Not beholden to a party, a party position, or an electoral constituency, peers are under few constraints, and thus they introduce amendments during the committee stage of the legislative process with far greater freedom than their counterparts in the Commons. That is one reason why peers are a logical choice for lobbyists to turn to if they fail to get their way in the Commons.

The third reason lobbyists turn to peers is traceable to the standing orders, or rules of procedure, of the House of Lords. So few are the restrictions imposed by the standing orders governing debate that peers normally have the time to dot every i and cross every t. Peers' freedom to vote with relatively few constraints and to have ample time to debate work in favor of a pressure group's objectives. Beyond that, all that lobbyists need is a sympathetic group of peers to endorse their objectives and pilot them through the legislative process, step by step.

The Executive Side of Government

Not all public policies require Parliament's approval. Indeed, many receive no input from it at all. Whether Parliament approves them or not, almost all public policies have their origins somewhere in the executive. Where exactly is often difficult to pinpoint because the executive is more vast and organizationally complex than Parliament. It is a sprawling labyrinth of mazes that sometimes leads to dead ends and sometimes to endless numbers of offices, departments, interdepartmental committees, and agencies. Added to all of this is the culture of secrecy that permeates its work; the work of Parliament, by contrast, is transparent. Organizational complexity and secrecy are two leading reasons why pressure groups have to devote more time to lobbying the executive than to lobbying Parliament. But the overriding reason is that the executive, far more than Parliament, is the initiator of public policy, whether in its upper reaches—in the core executive—or in the individual departments of state.

The Core Executive

The core executive includes the prime minister, his or her office at No. 10 Downing Street, the cabinet, the Cabinet Office, cabinet committees, interdepartmental committees, and the Treasury, plus the Foreign and Commonwealth Office on overseas matters. All are involved in formulating and coordinating the major policies of government. Few pressure groups have access to the core executive, and those that do are insider groups that usually represent vast numbers, for example, WHICH? (formerly, the Consumers' Association), or key groups in society such as the BMA. They generally have a history of good relations with senior ministers and officials. Being close to the upper reaches of the executive puts them in a prime position, for they are sure to be consulted about any number of policies. Insider groups are keen to be consulted so that they can convey their views on policies as they are being considered and influence their outcomes.

Why do decision makers reciprocate by encouraging groups to consult them? There are three reasons. First, consulting pressure groups is a legitimate democratic practice in Britain; it fosters opportunities for those representing different interests to speak when a government is considering issues that concern them. Second, groups are often repositories of highly specialized information helpful to decision makers as they formulate policies. Third, productive consultations with the representatives of pressure groups can lead to the effective implementation of government programs. Ministers and senior civil servants know that if they can convince representatives of a large insider pressure group (such as the BMA) to agree to changes that its members are uncomfortable with (such as hospital reforms), the less likely it is that the group's members will balk when asked to put the changes into effect.

Nothing can be left to chance in the world of lobbying. For that reason, seasoned lobbyists know they must be attentive to three distinctive stages of consultation, every one of which could be crucial to their success. The first is the *fluid-and-flexible stage,* when decision makers are having their first thoughts about what should be included in a new policy and are at their most receptive to ideas from pressure groups as they cast about for options.

The next phase is the *green-paper stage*. A green paper is a document that outlines various options being considered by the government of the day. It is circulated to pressure groups for their comments, any one of which could be incorporated into legislation. Green papers are normally reserved for major policies. By this stage, decision makers are close to bringing some closure to what they would like to include in a government's policy.

Finally, a government reaches the *white-paper stage*. A white paper is a document setting out a major policy the Government has decided to embrace, and if legislation is required, interested groups are invited to comment. The Government is often reluctant to entertain changes to a policy once it has progressed through the green-paper stage, but even more reluctant after it has passed through the white-paper stage because it wants to avoid creating an impression of indecisiveness. This reluctance explains why lobbyists attach such importance to conveying their views to decision makers early in the consultation process, preferably during the fluid-and-flexible stage.

The Departments of State

Consultation at an early stage is just as important for lobbyists who focus their activities on a single Whitehall department as it is for those who work closely with the core executive and for the same reason. However, there are two important differences between the two levels. Policies that a department initiates are usually less urgent than those that originate in the No. 10 Downing Street/Cabinet Committee/Treasury complex of the core executive, and consultation is conducted less formally. Departments issue consultation papers, but they normally do not bear the trappings of a green paper or white paper.

Some departments and pressure groups have been interacting for so long that they constitute what has come to be known as a policy community. This is a policy in the macro sense, such as agriculture, health, or criminal justice, and one that has long been the province of a Whitehall department. "Community" includes a department's senior and junior civil servants and lobbyists from groups with long-standing relationships with the department, that is, groups that are by definition insider groups. These civil servants and lobbyists have essentially the same policy values, in that they often see problems in the same way and tend to come up with similar solutions or know when and where to compromise if they do not. Many are on a first-name basis and use their own code words when they interact.

Sometimes the relations between a department and one or more pressure groups are so close that the department is seen as vulnerable to "capture" by the groups. Capturing a department could lead to a conflict of interest. That is largely why, soon after Labour came to power in 1997, the Blair Government took the first steps to divest MAFF—the Ministry of Agriculture, Fisheries and Food, as it was then called—of responsibility for food safety and set up a free-standing, independent Food Standards Agency. Although MAFF

147

and the NFU were content to keep things as they had been, others were convinced that MAFF's mission of ensuring food safety was seriously compromised by its other mission of promoting agricultural interests.

Whereas a pressure group might not obtain all that it wants in the bill that Parliament approves, it might have greater success with the statutory instrument produced after the bill has been enacted. A statutory instrument is legislation made by a minister. A minister, who is delegated this authority in an act of Parliament, draws up the details of the statute and the regulations appropriate for putting it into effect. Increasingly, acts of Parliament require ministers to consult groups likely to be affected by the statutory instrument before it is drawn up. The rationale for consultation is that ministers and civil servants will benefit from the specialized advice experts from these groups can offer.

Ministers and civil servants make few policies without first undertaking consultations with outside interests. Pressure groups are not always pleased with the results or with the way the policies on which they were consulted are implemented. As with politics in general, some groups win and others lose. Groups that lose often are ready to begin their lobbying campaigns afresh. However, if they think they can gain from it, these groups take a government to court with the hope of achieving there what they could not achieve in the political thicket.

The Courts

A pressure group that gives serious consideration to taking the government to court knows what pitfalls lie in wait. The judicial process is long and drawn out, and the cost of litigation can rapidly drain a group's treasury. Moreover, there is no guarantee the judge will allow the group to have its day in court. The process starts when a pressure group initiates an application for judicial review. The application sets out the reasons why the court—the High Court of Justice in cases such as this—should review an action taken by a department or agency that the group claims is wrongful. If the High Court decides to review the case and finds that the action was illegal, irrational, or procedurally flawed, the court either stops it from happening or prevents it from continuing if it has already started. An example of a judicial review is one that Friends of the Earth (FoE) initiated when it claimed that the Environment Agency had wrongfully issued a license to a company to dismantle a fleet of old U.S. Navy ships in a breaker's yard. Because asbestos and other toxic materials had been used in the ships' construction, FoE argued that these materials would threaten the nearby breeding grounds of twenty thousand birds as well as mudflats that were the feeding grounds for several forms of marine life. The judge agreed with FoE's lawyers and invalidated the license because no assessment had been carried out to determine what impact breaking up the ships would have on protected wildlife in an area designated a "site of special scientific interest."

If pressure groups are prevented from having their way in one corner of the political system, such as Whitehall, they are likely to try another corner,

Speaking of . . .

When Two Friends Disagree. . .

Saving the environment takes many forms, but not all environmental pressure groups agree on what part of it to save. An example is how two environmental groups—Friends of the Earth and Friends of the Lake District—opposed each other on a plan to capture energy from wind through turbines in the county of Cumbria near the Lake District, one of England's most picturesque national parks. This is what David Ward of *The Guardian* wrote after he learned about the disagreement these two "Friends" had:

"Tackling global warming is critical but we must also nurture the immediate environment and wildlife."

"Climate change campaigners yesterday condemned the government for rejecting a ... plan to build 27 wind turbines each 115 metres (377 ft) high on a windy ridge just outside the eastern boundary of the Lake District national park.

"The energy minister, Malcolm Wicks, and rural affairs minister Jim Knight said they had accepted an inspector's conclusions that the need to protect the landscape outweighed the benefits of securing a source of renewable energy.

"The decision was denounced by bodies promoting wind power as part of the answer to the problems caused by climate change.... The Whinash scheme ... had divided campaigners, with Greenpeace and Friends of the Earth in support but the Campaign to Protect Rural England, the Council for National Parks and Friends of the Lake District against....

"The ministers' decision, which follows a seven-week public inquiry in Cumbria last year [2005], is likely to cause a rethink of the development of windpower in remote, windy parts of the country with a high landscape value....

"Commenting on the recommendation of the planning inspector, ... Mr Wicks said: 'Tackling global warming is critical but we must also nurture the immediate environment and wildlife. This is at the crux of the debate over wind energy. On this occasion, we agree with the independent inspector that the impact on landscape and recreation would outweigh the benefits in terms of reducing carbon emissions.'

"But Tony Juniper, Director of Friends of the Earth, said he was appalled by the decision. 'On the one hand, ministers say they support renewable energy and on the other turn down carefully worked-up proposals that would have minimal environmental impacts while helping to fight climate change—the greatest threat of all.'

" 'We are delighted,' said Andrew Forsyth, director of Friends of the Lake District. 'We feared that the requirement for renewable energy would outweigh questions of the damage caused to the site and Cumbria in general. But it is quite clear that the weight of evidence made it easy for ministers to decide it was the wrong development in the wrong place on the wrong scale.' "

Source: David Ward, "Climate Campaigners Outraged as Wind Farm Plan Is Axed." Copyright Guardian News and Media Limited 2006.

such as the courts. As it happens, pressure groups have turned increasingly to that corner—a trend that prompted one commentator to observe that groups

> as diverse as the Fire Brigades Union, the World Development Forum, the Child Poverty Action Group, parents' groups, Friends of the Earth, Spanish fishermen's lawyers, architectural conservationists and London residents angered by aircraft noise are seen celebrating political victories not outside Parliament but the High Court in the Strand.[10]

In addition to decisions resulting from judicial review, the Human Rights Act that took effect in 2000 has encouraged more good-cause groups, such as those representing the disabled, gays, and the aged, to try to win in court what they failed to win after lobbying the political parties, Westminster, and Whitehall. Pressure groups also examine European Community (EC) law to determine whether there is any basis for their taking the British government to court. The reason EC law is consulted is that when the UK joined the EU in 1973, it had to agree to abide by all EC laws, which meant that EC law had to take precedence over UK law whenever they were inconsistent. A threat to take the government to court for failing to comply with EC law is usually sufficient to convince government to think twice. For example, when the Major Government considered transferring responsibility for pollution control from the public to the private sector, it changed its mind when the Council for the Protection of Rural England, an environmental pressure group, threatened to take the Government to court for contravening EC law.

The European Union

By 1994, just twenty-one years after the UK joined the EU, up to one third of all laws in effect in Britain were thought to have come not from Westminster, but from the EU.[11] Because a substantial portion of British law is EC law, it comes as no surprise that British lobbyists have maintained a continuous presence in Brussels, the hub of EU operations. Some pressure groups have even established offices there as EC laws have expanded in scope and extended their reach. Chapter 13 is devoted to Britain and the EU; the focus here is on the major EU institutions that pressure groups are likely to lobby. Not to be overlooked, however, is the fact that lobbying the EU invariably involves lobbying in London as well as Brussels.

Making Laws

Much of the work of pressure groups focuses on making laws. That means their lobbyists are in regular contact with three EU institutions that play a role in lawmaking—the European Commission, the European Parliament, and the Council of Ministers. Ideas for laws spring from a multitude of sources, but the commission alone is responsible for initiating legislation. With Bulgaria and Romania joining the EU in January 2007, this is a body of twenty-seven, with one commissioner drawn from each member nation.

Among other things, the commission is in charge of approximately twenty-three directorates-general (DGs), organizations comparable to government departments that have different jurisdictional responsibilities, such as agriculture, industry, and the environment. The lobbyists target the DGs because DGs draft EC legislation. Their civil servants are often receptive to any help lobbyists offer, for they are hungry for information and ideas and the expertise that lobbyists can provide. Lobbyists are especially eager to help a DG draft a law because once work on the draft is completed, it becomes more difficult to change the draft as it makes its way up the commission hierarchy and then over to the European Parliament and the Council of Ministers.

After the commission approves the draft law, it refers it to the European Parliament. Here, lobbyists target the members of the parliamentary committee considering the legislation—its British members in particular—and buttonhole as many of the UK's seventy-eight elected members of the European Parliament (MEPs) as is feasible. Because the British delegation is less than 10 percent of the total membership of the parliament, representatives from pressure groups urge British MEPs to lobby their colleagues from other national delegations who sit alongside them as members of cross-national parliamentary political groups. Perhaps to their advantage is the fact that MEPs from Britain's two major parties are members of the two largest of the approximately seven party groups that sit in the European Parliament.

The European Parliament's approval of a proposed law, however, is only the penultimate step in the process; it may not become law unless it also wins the approval of the Council of Ministers. Exactly which minister attends a council meeting to debate and vote on a proposal depends on the nature of the legislation being considered. For example, if the legislation deals with a transportation issue, the Secretary of State for Transport attends. That means that lobbyists try to make their case with the appropriate minister and civil servants at the Department of Transport long before the proposed law reaches the council.

In addition to making contact with the major players in Whitehall, lobbyists attempt to impress British civil servants stationed in Brussels with the worthiness of their proposals. These civil servants have been posted to Brussels from Whitehall departments that deal with major EU issues. There are about fifty of them, and they are attached to a permanent representation, an organization comparable to an embassy. Every member government has one; Britain's is called United Kingdom Permanent Representation (UKREP). Sometimes pressure groups have more success winning over civil servants in UKREP to their point of view than they do convincing civil servants in Whitehall. However, of the two—UKREP and Whitehall—Whitehall is the key to successful lobbying at this stage, for it is Whitehall that has the final word on the position the British government takes. That is why lobbyists try to make their case to UKREP so compelling that UKREP not only accepts it but convinces Whitehall it should accept it as well.

Implementing and Enforcing Laws

Once an EC law has been agreed to, the next step is to implement it. This is the responsibility of member governments, but overseeing them is the job of the commission. Determining whether twenty-seven member governments are in compliance with every EC law and regulation is a massive undertaking. Pressure groups realize how daunting the job can be, and that explains why they are not at all shy about drawing the commission's attention to instances of implementation that are flawed or nonexistent in the areas of public policy that concern them. Of the different types of pressure groups, environmental pressure groups are especially vigilant in monitoring the implementation of EC laws; if they spot a government failing to comply, they waste no time in reporting this lapse to the commission.

Once the commission becomes aware of an instance of noncompliance, it serves notice on the errant government. A grace period is normally allowed, but if the government ignores the deadline, the commission may take it to the European Court of Justice in an infringement proceeding. If the court agrees that the government has failed to honor its obligation, it could insist that it come into compliance within a reasonable period or be forced to pay a heavy fine. The court is key to enforcing the law and its decision is final. Here again, a pressure group could play a role in this unfolding drama by taking information it has acquired to the commission, documenting the government's failure to act, and detailing the adverse effects flowing from its failure.

Conclusion

In September 1997, the Royal Society for the Protection of Birds (RSPB) enrolled its one-millionth member. This meant that there were more card-carrying members of a pressure group that promotes public policies protecting birds than there were of all three of Britain's top political parties put together. The criteria for becoming a party member were not difficult to meet. All one had to do was write a check for an amount which, as it happened, was not much different from the membership fee for the RSPB and one's enrollment in the party was automatic.

One should not infer from the foregoing that the British public has transferred its allegiances from political parties to pressure groups, for no evidence exists to confirm that. What can be confirmed, however, is that parties are not as salient to the public as they once were. The number of card-carrying members of Britain's top three parties (never high to begin with) plummeted from more than 9 percent of registered voters in 1964 to between 1 and 2 percent forty years later. Significant too is the fact that among those who identify with a political party, the number who identify very strongly dropped from 43 percent in 1964 to 13 percent in 2001. That does not mean that pressure groups will step in and take their place, for parties do something that pressure groups, by definition, cannot do. They pull together a broad range of public demands, translate them into manifesto pledges, and present them to the voters to choose from on election day. The party that wins a majority of seats becomes the party of government.

Pressure groups cannot take the place of political parties, but they nevertheless perform certain functions that complement the work of parties. They help inform the public, represent their members, nudge the party in power to act on its pledges, and promote active citizenship. These functions can all contribute in varying degrees to strengthening Britain's representative democratic form of government. Of these four, however, the function that probably makes the greatest contribution is the representation of group interests. But three questions need to be raised before one can make any definitive judgment about the degree to which this function enhances representative democracy.

First, there is the question of whether the opinions of the members of a pressure group are allowed to flow unimpeded to the top of the organization and are then communicated by the group's leaders to decision makers in an accurate and timely fashion. There are several factors that make tapping the opinions of members difficult, among them the complexity of an issue, the way a group is organized, and the size of its membership. There are ways of overcoming these difficulties, and unless decision makers are convinced they have been overcome, they are likely to be wary.

Second, there is the question of whether some deserving interests promoted by certain pressure groups will prevail over others that are more deserving. The vast majority of most good-cause groups are made up of middle-class and well educated members. The groups they join and the causes they champion reflect the values that they embrace. Among these groups are those that promote civil liberties, a clean environment, and the preservation of historic buildings. When their lobbyists communicate with MPs and civil servants, they communicate with decision makers who by and large have the same life experiences and share the same social values. However, campaigners who represent the less fortunate—the homeless and the learning or physically disabled—often are unable to recruit as many to their ranks and mobilize campaigns with the same success as groups that have more financial resources, more lobbying expertise, and more in common with decision makers.

Third, there is the question of whether the policy communities formed over the years are so hidden from public view that it becomes impossible to know who should take the credit or the blame for their handiwork. It is a long-standing practice for key decision makers to consult groups likely to be affected by the decisions that the government of the day is actively considering; however, there is no requirement that these consultations be undertaken in a public forum. Some maintain that nothing of major moment is decided in these consultations. That could be true. But unless they are made transparent, it is difficult for members of the public to know whom they should hold to account—those who speak for the government or those who speak for one or more pressure groups.

7

Campaigns and Elections

lections are political dramas. They have a setting, a cast of characters with established walk-on appearances, and three acts. The setting is the whole of the UK or parts of it. The cast of characters includes all those who make their stage entrances as candidates on the first day of a campaign. As for the three acts, Act I is the selection of candidates, Act II is the campaign for election, and Act III is the election itself. Hours after the final curtain has come down, the world learns how the audience—that is, the voters—evaluated the drama.

Before the curtain goes up, however, the stage has to be set. Thus, the first section of this chapter examines some basic points about elections in the UK. Having dealt with the selection of candidates in chapter 5, the second section focuses on campaigns for election: pledges the parties make to the voters, getting the message across to the electorate, and campaign finance. The third and final section deals with the election—the several different electoral systems that are used, the pros and cons of the system used to elect members of Parliament, the reasons why some people vote and others do not, and how voters vote.

Varieties of Elections

Until the end of the 1970s, British voters elected only members of Parliament and local government councilors. Today voters also choose politicians to fill an expanded array of newly created positions in a variety of elections, all of which are identified in Table 7.1. Not included in the table, however, are two other occasions when UK voters go to the polls. One is for a by-election. This is an election held to replace a politician who has died in office or has resigned. Also omitted is a referendum, which is not an election, although it brings people to the polls. Whereas an election asks voters to take a stand on which candidate to represent them, a referendum asks them to take a stand

Table 7.1	Elections in the United Kingdom		
Body	Election	Elected	Number
House of Commons	General Election	Members of Parliament	646*
Local Authorities	Council Election	Councilors	25,000 (approx.)
Mayor of London	London Mayoral	Mayor of London	1
Greater London Authority	Greater London Authority Election	Members of the Greater London Authority	25
European Parliament	Euro-election	Members of the European Parliament	78
Scottish Parliament	Scottish Parliament Election	Members of the Scottish Parliament	129
Welsh National Assembly	Welsh National Assembly Election	Members of the Welsh National Assembly	60
Northern Ireland Assembly	Northern Ireland Assembly Election	Members of the Northern Ireland Assembly	108

*This is the number elected in the 2005 general election and could change in the general election that follows.

on an issue. As of this writing, only one referendum has been held across the UK: in 1975, voters were asked if they wished the UK to remain in the European Union (then called the European Economic Community). Referendums also have been held in smaller jurisdictions. In 1997 Scottish and Welsh voters were asked if they favored having powers devolved to a Scottish parliament and a Welsh assembly, respectively, and in 1998 London voters were asked if they wished to have a mayor and an assembly.

Eight different types of elections are held in the UK. Seven of these occur with fixed regularity. The exception is the general election, which is an election in which candidates run for Parliament. Although there is no fixed date on which it is held, it must occur no later than five years from the date that members of the currently elected Parliament first sat. A council election elects individuals to local government law-making bodies called councils. Normally, these elections are held on the first Thursday of every May. Councilors serve four-year terms; however, because most of their terms are staggered, only a portion of the total number of seats is up for election every spring.

Two other local government elections are the London mayoral election and the Greater London Authority election. Both are held every four years and on the same day that local council elections are held. Next, there is the Euro-election, held every five years in June to elect the UK's seventy-eight members to the EU's European Parliament. Finally, there are Scottish parliament elections and Welsh National Assembly elections and, if the Government decides to restore devolved government to Ulster, the Northern Ireland Assembly elections. Elections to these three devolved institutions are held on the same day in May once every four years.

Electoral Arenas

When speaking of general election campaigns, one appropriately speaks in the plural, for while one campaign is waged by party leaders as they crisscross mainland Britain, others are waged by candidates in each of the UK's constituencies (646 of them in 2005). Although the number of constituencies changes slightly every decade or so, the number found in each nation of the UK is roughly proportionate to the number of registered electors in each. In 2005, England had 529 constituencies, Scotland had 59, Wales had 40, and Northern Ireland had 18. Scotland's constituencies were scaled back from seventy-two to fifty-nine before the 2005 election to bring the ratio of the number of constituencies to registered electors more closely in line with the other three nations. Although the House of Commons approves how many constituencies there should be and how and when they should be drawn up, it has always bowed to the recommendations of boundary commissions.

Boundary Commissions

Since 1944, four independent boundary commissions, one each for England, Scotland, Wales, and Northern Ireland, have kept the number of electors in each constituency roughly the same. It should be emphasized at this point that they do not try to equalize the overall population in each constituency, but rather the population of qualified electors in each. At one time, electoral rolls were updated once a year. But starting in 2001, under a process called "rolling registration," their numbers now are updated once a month. Thanks to rolling registration, boundary commissioners are able to draw on relatively current data when they draft their recommendations for redrawing constituency boundaries, which they do between eight and twelve years after submitting their previous recommendations to the House of Commons for its approval.

The commissioners' work begins once an electoral quota has been established. This quota, which is derived by dividing the UK's total number of electors by the number of constituencies in the four nations, is the number a commission strives to allocate to each constituency. To equalize the population of electors, it is sometimes necessary to adjust the total number of constituencies in the UK up or down slightly, which explains why, every ten years or so, the number of constituencies varies somewhat. Yet despite the best efforts of commissioners to maintain equality, there can be considerable variance in numbers from constituency to constituency. The reason is that there are factors in addition to the number of electors that have to be taken into account. For example, keeping whole communities intact by making constituency boundaries coterminous with local government boundaries usually is given greater emphasis than ensuring that there are equal numbers of electors in each constituency.

The political fortunes of more than a few ride on a boundary commission's recommendations. For example, in 2002, the Commons accepted Scotland's Boundary Commission's recommendation that Scotland's constituencies be reduced from seventy-two to fifty-nine for the next general election in order to bring the average number of electors per constituency closer to the average number elsewhere in the UK. This had two effects. First, three cabinet ministers were among those who lost their constituencies, and they were forced to seek reelection elsewhere. Second, because Scotland has long been a Labour stronghold, not only was the number of Labour MPs from Scotland reduced, the total number of Labour MPs in Westminster overall was reduced as well.

Because the relative strength of the political parties and the tenure of members of Parliament are at stake, it is not surprising that affected parties take a keen interest in the ways the boundaries around political jurisdictions are drawn. Changes proposed in the boundaries of a constituency represented by, say, a Conservative MP who won by the slimmest of margins in the last election are certain to attract more than just the casual interest of the incumbent, the local Conservative Party, and Conservative Central Office. Alarm bells will ring if the changes include replacing pockets of Conservative support with pockets of Labour support. Sometimes the effects of such changes cannot be avoided. But gerrymandering—the act of deliberately re-shaping constituency boundaries to bring advantage or disadvantage to a political party in an ensuing election—is scrupulously avoided. The law precludes such tinkering. That is why a guardian of the law, a senior judge, is one of five who are appointed to each commission. The judge presides over the commission meetings and oversees the work of a small clutch of civil servants, of whom the four most senior serve alongside the judge as commissioners.

Variations in Constituency Size

As impartial as boundary commissions are, they cannot help but create constituencies that sometimes vary dramatically in size. The two extremes in the 2005 general election were the Isle of Wight, off England's south coast, and the Western Isles in Scotland (renamed Na H-Eileanan An Lar after the 2001 election out of respect for the 70 percent of the islanders who speak Gaelic). Six candidates campaigned for the support of the more than 21,500 voters of Na H-Eileanan An Lar, the UK's least populated constituency, whereas five candidates took up the more daunting challenge of winning over the more than 109,000 voters of the Isle of Wight, the UK's most populated constituency. Despite the disparity reflected in this 5-to-1 ratio, it is a vast improvement over the 14-to-1 ratio that resulted from the work of England's first boundary commission in 1948.

There are several implications that flow from allowing constituencies to vary in size to such a degree. As far as elections go, however, the most important of these is that not everyone's vote carries the same weight. In the case of the Isle of Wight and the Western Isles, if the same percentage of electors in each constituency had voted in the 2005 election, the value of each vote cast by an Isle of Wight elector would have been about one fifth the value of a Western Isles elector's vote.

Calling Elections

There are no fixed dates for general elections; they may be held several months apart or five years apart. Elections have been held in successive years (as in 1950 and 1951) and even twice in the same year (as in 1974, when there was one in February and another in October). The 1997 election, by contrast, took place five years after the last one. Why is there such irregularity? There are three reasons. One is traceable to the Parliament Act of 1911, another to the Commons' lack of confidence in the Government, and the third to political and economic conditions of the day.

The Parliament Act of 1911

The Parliament Act of 1911 dictates that the life of a parliament ceases precisely five years after the date of its first meeting. That means that a general election must be held no later than the end of this five-year period. If the government of the day wishes to delay an election and thus extend the life of a parliament beyond five years, the House of Commons and the House of Lords both have to agree. This they did in two periods when the country was at war—for the Parliament that sat from 1910 to 1918 (a life of nearly eight years) and the one that sat from 1935 to 1945 (a life of more than nine years).

Before a general election is held, Parliament has to be dissolved for the duration of the campaign. Once it is dissolved, all its functions cease. Whether it should be dissolved and when are decisions the prime minister makes, normally after consulting his or her advisers. When an election date has been determined, the prime minister asks the monarch to issue a Proclamation of Dissolution. Monarchs may exercise little discretion in the matter, for refusing this request would surely invite criticism that the sovereign is engaging in conduct that convention does not countenance—meddling in politics. At one time, monarchs alone decided whether and when to dissolve Parliament. In the second half of the nineteenth century, however, Queen Victoria allowed this authority to pass from her hands to those of the cabinet, and since 1918 the convention has been that the prime minister alone decides whether and when Parliament should be dissolved.

The Commons' Lack of Confidence in the Government

The House of Commons can demonstrate its lack of confidence in the government of the day in several ways, but in two ways in particular. One is when it refuses to agree with a motion of confidence, in which case a general election might be held. The second way is when the Commons agrees with a motion of no confidence. If the Commons supports the latter motion, a general election must be held.

A motion of confidence is introduced by the Government. A government makes such a motion when its majority is either paper-thin or nonexistent, and it is eager to impress on party backbenchers the need to pull together or pay the penalty by having to return to the hustings and face an unhappy electorate if the motion is defeated. There have been three such motions introduced since 1945, and the Government has won on each occasion. For example, in December 1978, the Labour Government won a motion expressing confidence in its management of the economy by a margin of 300 to 290. There is no convention that clearly spells out what would have happened had the motion been defeated. Had it lost, James Callaghan, who was prime minister at the time, would have had three options. First, he could have stepped aside to make way for the Opposition leader to take power, but without an intervening election, just as Prime Minister Stanley Baldwin did in 1924 when the Conservatives lost a motion of confidence, and Labour's Ramsay MacDonald became prime minister. A second option was that Callaghan could have asked the Queen to dissolve Parliament, and a general election would have followed. The third option was that he could have done nothing and plodded on.

As it happened, Callaghan was lucky to scrape by with a ten-vote margin—lucky, for he was the head of a minority government. (He was head of the only British government in the twentieth century that lost its majority through by-elections while it was in power.) He also had been lucky in beating back three other motions introduced by the Opposition over the preceding two and a half years. Two of these were motions of censure, which are motions introduced by the Opposition that are highly critical of specific issues or sets of issues. If carried, however, such a motion does not necessarily lead to the resignation of a prime minister or force another election. The third motion on which Callaghan had been lucky was a motion of no confidence, which covers the Government's entire performance. A motion of no confidence was introduced in March 1977 but was defeated by a comfortable margin, thanks to support from the Liberal Party.

Two years later, however, in March 1979, the Callaghan Government's luck ran out. By then, the economy had gone from bad to worse, strikes were rampant, and the Scottish National Party was furious with the Government for its alleged lackluster leadership in championing devolving power to Scotland in a referendum that failed on March 1. Later that month, a motion of no confidence was introduced and put to a vote and, despite the Herculean efforts of the Government's whips, it passed 311 to 310. Had just one individual voted otherwise, Callaghan could have attempted new initiatives to satisfy his critics and held out until the early autumn, when the Parliament Act of 1911 would have required him to call an election anyway. But a defeat by one vote was still a defeat, and it was one that entered the record books. It was the first time in more than a century that a Government lost on a vote of no confidence. Within hours, Callaghan, in keeping with convention, met with the Queen to ask her to dissolve Parliament. An election was held in May, the Conservatives won, the Callaghan Government resigned, and Margaret Thatcher moved into No. 10 Downing Street.

Political and Economic Conditions of the Day

If the life of a parliament can be sustained for five years and if, within that period, it is so difficult for the Opposition to drive the Government from office with a motion of no confidence, why is it that as many as five of the sixteen general elections held from 1950 through 2005 were called well more than a year before the five-year limit? The answer lies in the nature of the political and economic conditions of the day. The conditions preceding the elections of 1955 and October 1974 are illustrative. The 1955 election was held approximately three and a half years after the previous election, and the October 1974 election a mere eight months after the previous one. Even though the election in 1955 could easily have been delayed another eighteen months, there was no way that the election in 1974 could have been delayed that long.

General Election of 1955

The period from 1951 to 1955 was one of relative social harmony. The ruling Conservative Party produced programs that generated little controversy. Public opinion polls and by-election results revealed that the public was generally satisfied with the Government's record. In 1955, a little more than a week after Winston Churchill resigned as prime minister, Churchill's successor, Anthony Eden, went to Buckingham Palace to ask the Queen to dissolve Parliament. There was no constitutional requirement that the voters endorse this change in prime ministers through a general election. Yet Eden thought his accession to the premiership coincided with political and economic news that was auspicious for a second successive Conservative victory that would keep the party in power up to five more years. His advisers agreed, Eden announced a general election, the Government steered an "electioneering" budget through Parliament for good measure, and the Conservatives netted thirty-six new seats, boosting their overall majority to fifty-four.

General Election of October 1974

By September 1974, Labour prime minister Harold Wilson had presided over a hung parliament for seven months, the first since 1929–1931. The general election that had taken place the previous February had failed to produce a majority for any party. Immediately after the election, Edward Heath, who had been prime minister from 1970 to February 1974, desperately sought the support of the Liberals so that he could form another government. Four days later, however, Heath had to admit defeat, and the Queen turned to Harold Wilson to form a minority government. Labour had won a few more seats than the Conservatives; however, it was thirty-five seats shy of an overall majority.

Severely handicapped, the Wilson Government suffered no fewer than twenty-nine defeats in Parliament in the two months preceding the summer recess. On the diplomatic front, when Britain approached officials of the European Economic Community (EEC) to renegotiate the terms of its membership in the EEC, so questionable was it that Labour could cling to power that one or two EEC governments were reluctant to begin discussions. Finally, after 199 days of governing without a majority, Wilson called an election, a decision that brought an end to the shortest parliament of the twentieth century. Wilson won his majority. But so insubstantial was it—a mere three—that he knew it was likely to slip away soon, and so it did eighteen months later.

Candidates and Parties

Anywhere from approximately 2,300 to 3,700 candidates have run for election in each general election since 1974. A total of 3,554 candidates representing 114 political parties ran in the 2005 election—335 more candidates than in the 2001 election but fewer than the record high of 3,724 who ran in 1997. Until the 1970s, a majority of seats in the UK were fought between just two candidates. Since then, no fewer than three have entered every contest. So steadily upward has the number of candidates climbed that in the 2005 election the names of five or more candidates appeared on ballots in 75 percent of the constituency races in the UK. In that same election, the Conservative and Labour Parties each fielded a candidate in every one of mainland Britain's 628 constituencies (except in the one represented by the Speaker of the House of Commons, which by tradition is not contested). So too did the Liberal Democrat Party, with the exception of the Speaker's constituency plus one other constituency. Conservative, Labour, and Liberal Democrat candidates, plus Conservative candidates who ran in three of Northern Ireland's eighteen constituencies, brought the grand total of candidates for the three parties to 1,883.

That accounts for a little more than half the candidates who ran in the 2005 election. What about the remaining number? Among them were 818 candidates representing three political parties who ran in two or more nations of the UK: 496 from the United Kingdom Independence Party, 203 from the Green Party, and 119 from the British National Party. In addition, nationalist parties in Scotland and Wales fielded ninety-nine candidates: a Scottish National Party (SNP) candidate ran in each of Scotland's fifty-nine constituencies, and a Welsh National Party (Plaid Cymru) candidate in each of Wales's forty constituencies. Another 105 candidates ran in Northern Ireland's 18 constituencies. Of the 105, 84 ran under the banners of Northern Ireland's five long-standing parties: the Alliance of Northern Ireland, the Democratic Unionist Party, Sinn Féin, the Social Democratic and Labour Party, and the United Ulster Unionist Party.

As for the rest of the roughly 650 candidates, 64 ran as candidates of single-candidate parties (such parties usually focus on a local issue), approximately 165 ran as independents, and the remaining were drawn from parties that stood for everything from the sublime to the less than sublime. Examples from the sublime side were the fourteen candidates of the Liberal Party who had refused to join the Liberal Democrats when the latter party was created in 1988, the twenty-one candidates of the Legalise Cannabis Alliance, and the four candidates of the Communist Party of Britain. Examples from the less-than-sublime side were candidates of the Vote for Yourself Dream Rainbow Ticket Party (twenty-seven candidates); the Official Monster Raving Loony Party (nineteen candidates); and the Death, Dungeons and Taxes Party (two candidates).

Although this rarely occurs in British elections, one independent and one candidate representing a single-candidate party were elected. After Peter Law, a Labour member of the Welsh National Assembly, quit the Labour Party, he ran as "Independent Law" and bucked the trend by scoring a stunning victory over five others, including a Labour candidate. The candidate of the single-candidate party was a physician, Richard Taylor, who was re-elected after campaigning for the first time in 2001 to oppose the closure of an accident and emergency facility in a hospital in his constituency.

Law and Taylor are obvious exceptions to the rule that candidates not backed by a well-recognized political party have no hope of winning, and all the candidates running in the 2005 election knew that before they signed up. Included were candidates who campaigned for single-issue parties, like the Free Scotland Party; for parties that sounded vaguely ideological, including the Independent Working Class Association; for parties whose names shed little light on what they stood for, as in the case of the Civilisation Party and the Peace and Progress Party; and for tongue-in-cheek parties, such as the Xtraordinary People Party, the Silent Majority Party, Your Party, and Their Party.

On the British mainland, unless candidates run as a Conservative, Labour, or Liberal Democrat, they have little hope of victory. When the Returning Officer, the constituency's top election official, announces the election results, candidates who are not members of these three main parties almost always are at or near the bottom of the list. Since 1918, candidates have had to pay an election deposit fee, which has remained at £500 since 1985 (in 2005, the equivalent of approximately $950) in the weeks prior to a general election. The fee is refunded to the candidate following the election on condition that the candidate wins 5 percent or more of the vote. Of the 1,880 Conservative, Labour, and Liberal Democrat candidates who ran in mainland constituencies in 2005, only three (two Conservatives and one Liberal Democrat) garnered less than 5 percent of the vote and lost their deposits. By contrast, 1,372—or 82 percent—of the remaining 1,674 who contested elections on the mainland lost their deposits.

Campaigns

Identifying the number of candidates and the political parties under whose banners they run helps convey a sense of the magnitude of a British general election. Once the political parties have selected their candidates, it is only a matter of time before the prime minister announces when the election will be held. Following the announcement, the candidates are only days away from a period of frenetic campaigning, frenetic because so many activities are packed into a campaign of short duration. Before the campaign can begin, Parliament is prorogued, that is, dissolved, for the duration of the election. (In other words, the parliamentary session ends, and a new session will begin when Parliament is reconvened soon after the election.) By law, the campaign must last no fewer than twenty-three days, weekends included. In 2005, Tony Blair announced on April 5 that the election would be held on May 5, and Parliament was dissolved on April 11. It is common practice for prime ministers to announce the date about thirty days before the election is held.

For more than three weeks, the drama of the campaign plays out. Once Parliament is dissolved, the political parties issue their manifestos. On most days, the media chase and report on the movements and utterances of the party leaders. The parties send eye-catching messages from billboards. Candidates dash from a speech to a photo opportunity to joining volunteers as they go from house to house canvassing for support. Public opinion pollsters track levels of party support among likely voters. Pundits look for trends and patterns and speculate on the outcome. Campaign advisers huddle to revise electioneering tactics when wrong turns are taken. Political advertising gurus are called in to bolster sagging party images and clarify obfuscated party messages.

The following sections explore four key aspects of campaigns. The first deals with the promises parties make to voters. The second addresses campaigning at the national level and the local level. The third looks at getting the message across to voters, and the fourth examines the raising and spending of campaign funds.

Campaign Pledges

Usually just a day or two after Parliament has been dissolved, the parties unveil their election manifestos. Formulated at the top of the party hierarchy, a manifesto is a document that identifies the policies a party pledges to implement if it wins power. At one time couched in rather general language, manifesto pledges became more specific and detailed starting in the second half of the twentieth century. Possibly because by 1997 Labour had been out of power for 18 years, its manifesto was bursting with 177 commitments in a 19,000-word document.[1] The party singled out the ten most important at the manifesto's launch, declaring them to be its "contract with the people."[2] All ten became grist for the party's election broadcasts and for the party's candidates in the campaign. Five of these ten were spelled out on a card the size of a driver's license and distributed by the thousands to likely voters.

The manifesto is a strategically important weapon to take into a campaign, and political parties pin their hopes on making their pledges credible, appealing, and memorable enough to galvanize electoral support. What a

163

manifesto pledges, and sometimes what it does not pledge, becomes a target for rival parties to attack. That is why party leaders and their ministers (or shadow ministers) give as much thought as they do to their manifestos as they are being written.

So serious are the parties about acting on their pledges that the manifesto of the winning party is regarded as a mandate. That means the governing party is expected to fulfill the terms of its "contract with the people" (to use Labour's expression again) or at least the most important ones. Some issues lose their currency and thus their relevance, such as Labour's manifesto pledge in 2001 to eradicate foot-and-mouth disease, the spread of which had been essentially halted just before the campaign began. Other pledges, even major ones, cannot be kept when they are overtaken by events. For example, massive flu outbreaks three winters in a row put such a strain on National Health Service hospitals that Labour could not honor its 1997 manifesto pledge to reduce patient waiting lists at hospitals by one hundred thousand.

Opposition parties are nevertheless eager to find fault with commitments the party of government fails to honor. They are likely to take aim in particular at policies that run totally contrary to what the winning party had pledged. For example, in 2004 the Blair Government spearheaded legislation that would raise tuition fees (called "top-up fees") at universities three years hence, even though its 2001 election manifesto had promised not to do so in that parliament. The Government's decision triggered howls of derision from opposition parties and embittered many Labour backbenchers; in the end, the bill barely scraped by in the Commons despite Labour's massive overall majority.

Governments require flexibility in carrying out their responsibilities, at times so much so that they have to delay implementing some manifesto pledges and ignore others. Despite that, British politicians have long prided themselves on making ideas the centerpiece of their election campaigns. For that reason, as one doyen of British elections put it, "there should be some moral and political pressure on politicians, first to exercise prudence in making promises and, secondly, to keep them when made."[3]

Campaign Fronts

The campaign proceeds on the national front and the local front in each of the UK's constituencies. Those who throw themselves into the campaign nationally are the party leaders and other key ministers from the cabinet and the shadow cabinet who fan out across the country to give speeches, greet people in town centers, and hold press conferences. This is the level of the campaign that attracts the most media coverage. The words and actions of the party leaders, as well as major campaign issues and events, become the subjects of lead stories just about every morning in the serious press and are nearly always the first news reported on national television and radio every morning, noon, and night. So much attention has been focused on the prime minister and the Opposition leader in recent years that it is as if their names are emblazoned on every ballot in the country.

The national campaign did not always attract so much attention. Before 1959, those who received their news principally from radio and television were treated to little more than reports of the speeches made by party leaders, followed later in the campaign by the weather forecast for election day. They might have even been given an update on Prime Minister Clement Attlee's progress during the 1950 election campaign as his wife drove him in his pre-war car on a one-thousand-mile journey through Britain, stopping along the way to give speeches. Campaigns, as most experienced them in the 1950s, were conducted at the local level and were limited to what candidates in their constituency said and did when they were on the stump. By 1959, however, the British Broadcasting Corporation (BBC) had developed the technology to transmit television coverage of campaigns all across Britain, and most of the nearly three-quarters of the electorate who had acquired television sets tuned in to receive it.

With the arrival of television, election campaigns underwent change, and as television coverage of campaigns became more sophisticated, so too did the campaigns themselves. With each passing election, national campaign organizers realized more and more the benefits that could be reaped from television, as well as the pitfalls that might await them.

The National Campaign

Labour's campaign coordinator takes charge of the campaign just before the opening salvos of the campaign are fired. The coordinator is assisted by the party's chair and its general secretary and draws upon the resources of Labour Party headquarters. As for the Conservatives, the chair of the party takes charge, with the staff at Conservative Central Office providing assistance at every turn.

The campaign is a flurry of activity from the start. Party headquarters concentrates on creating opportunities for the party leader to be seen in different parts of the country projecting his or her persona in a flattering light and emphasizing the party's commitment to its high-profile manifesto pledges. The campaign team—the party leader and a retinue of his or her advisers—along with security personnel, reporters, and camera crews hustle onto buses, helicopters, and jets to travel to parts near and far. Once the team reaches its destination, the party leader addresses local business leaders, interacts with youngsters in their classrooms, absorbs the concerns expressed by health professionals in a hospital, and greets workers as they pass through factory gates. Each activity is carefully choreographed down to the last smile and wave of the hand.

Media specialists put the final touches on party election broadcasts (PEBs), or campaign commercials. BBC television and the commercial television services provide five five-minute slots to the two major parties for their PEBs, four five-minute slots to the Liberal Democrats for theirs, and one five-minute slot to each minor party that sponsors candidates in fifty or more constituencies. Hardly a Sunday passes without a major television interview being conducted with a party leader. The following day, the press normally gives these interviews extensive coverage. Britain has not yet experimented with anything along the lines of the debates held between presidential nominees in the United States, although BBC television did broadcast a variant of the presidential debates during the 2005 campaign, one that could very well be used in national campaigns in the future. In a special edition of its weekly program *Question Time,* the three party leaders were brought out on the studio stage separately to be questioned by veteran BBC broadcaster David Dimbleby and the studio audience.

If 1959 was the first year for televised campaigns, 2001 was the first year of campaigns via the Internet. An estimated one third of the public had access to the Internet at home that year, and an untold number had access through work, school, and libraries. The two major parties developed Web sites designed to attract party activists, journalists, and the electorate in general. Party activists, including candidates, were given password access to "templates, logos, photographs and articles for use in newspapers, policy briefings for use during canvassing, and archives of news briefings."[4] The second audience, journalists, availed themselves of press releases and photos and were able to view Webcasts of press conferences. The electorate, the third audience, tapped into the parties' Web sites primarily to download copies of the parties' manifestos. Interest in Labour's manifesto was especially high; its site took so many hits when its manifesto was released that the site nearly ground to a halt.[5]

E-mail and cell phone communications were used on a limited scale in the 2001 campaign, although campaign workers preferred the latter over the former. Labour volunteers sent up to twenty-four thousand text messages to supporters who had left their cell phone numbers on the party's Web site. As cell phone technology advances and usage costs drop, one can imagine scores of party volunteers frantically sending text messages to tens of thousands of likely party supporters to remind them to mail their postal ballots or, on election eve, to urge them to show up at their polling stations the next day.

Local Campaigns

Constituency agents are to local campaigns what Labour's campaign coordinator and the Conservatives' party chair are to the national campaign. These agents are party activists who hold certificates from their national party headquarters that attest to their knowledge of election law and, on the strength of that knowledge, are put in charge of constituency campaigns. Their salaries are derived from two sources—a modest amount from national party headquarters, plus however much the local parties can pry from their budgets. Because the parties are usually strapped for funds, they cannot hire enough agents to work even part-time in all constituencies. Normally, an agent is assigned either to manage a campaign in a single constituency in which a close contest is predicted or to divide his or her time among several adjoining constituencies. Unfortunately for the agents, the lack of party funds means they have no hope of hiring a professional campaign staff. What staff they are able to muster are volunteers, and as the campaign draws near, agents direct their efforts to training these volunteers and keeping their spirits high.

Whether agents are on full-time or part-time salaries, are temporarily salaried, or are working without pay, they know that the nearly four weeks they devote to managing campaigns will be the busiest they will experience in the work they perform for their parties. A campaign headquarters has to be rented, a telephone system connected, stationery bought, and computers hooked up. Volunteers must be assigned duties, and the names and addresses of electors recently added to the electoral register need to be obtained. The candidate needs to identify his or her qualifications, single out manifesto pledges he or she considers the most salient, and put all of this into an election address. Plans for visits from key figures of the parliamentary leadership must be coordinated with the candidate's campaign commitments, and schedules must be organized for the candidate to visit shopping centers, greet commuters at the railroad station, make speeches to various community clubs, and canvass neighborhoods. On election day, appeals need to be made from sound trucks to urge voters to get to their polling stations. And after the election is over, the agent has to account for how campaign funds were spent.

Campaign Advertising

Campaign advertising received a huge boost when television came into its own in the 1950s, but there is more to advertising than television. Just what strategies the parties should adopt is based at least partly on the advice offered by a new breed of public relations firm that also came into its own in the 1950s—the *political* public relations firm. In PR parlance, the electorate is the "market." Those who do "market research" produce information about how best to persuade those in the market to "buy" the "products" being offered.

At one time, the thought of a political party hiring a public relations firm to help develop advertising for a campaign was unheard of; by the 1960s it had become commonplace. The Conservatives, in 1957, were the first of the two major parties to seek outside professional help. Labour followed suit a half dozen years later, but only after party modernizers had overcome resistance to the idea in the party hierarchy. Initially, Labour pursued a different course from the Conservatives by putting public relations professionals directly on the party's payroll before and during election campaigns. Later, before the 1983 election, it took yet another tack when it hired its own communications and campaigns director who recruited public relations experts, including speechwriters, researchers, art designers, and advertisers. Among other things, they

> provided a patriotic red rose as a logo. Labour party political broadcasts and leaflets were professionally designed; the party sought and

gained endorsements from pop and sports stars; leaders appeared on TV chat shows and [party leader] Mr. Kinnock even took part in a pop-song video.[6]

In 1993 Labour followed the Conservatives' lead and contracted for the services of out-of-house public relations consultants. By then, both parties had been convinced that the rising stars in the campaign consultancy firmament could make crucial contributions to their campaigns.

What has stood out is the work public relations firms have performed in scripting PEBs, creating billboard displays, and devising full-page newspaper advertisements. The only significant change in campaigns was a de-emphasis of newspaper advertising starting in 1997. At one time, this form of advertising was given a high priority. In the 1983 election campaign, the two major parties bought ninety-four pages. They doubled their spending again for the 1987 campaign, when they bought a record-breaking 319 pages. After that press advertisements started to pass out of favor. The two parties bought 113 pages for the 1992 election campaign and 39 for the 1997 campaign. For the 2001 campaign, press advertising became nearly nonexistent: Labour bought a mere seven pages, and the Conservatives bought none. The numbers rose slightly in the 2005 campaign, when Labour bought twenty-two pages and the Conservatives bought four. Overall, however, newspaper advertising no longer ranks high in the parties' budget priorities. It has become too expensive and is no longer considered cost-effective.

Are PEBs and billboard displays cost-effective? The Electoral Commission, an independent body created by law in 2000 to report on various election issues, contracted with MORI, a polling firm, to find out how much influence various factors had on how respondents voted. During the 2001 election campaign MORI found that 55 percent of respondents had watched PEBs, and 61 percent had seen billboards displaying party messages. As Table 7.2 shows, when the first two columns—"Great deal" and "Fair amount"—are added, PEBs tied for fourth place in importance to respondents, with 22 percent. Billboard advertisements ended up in eighth place, with 10 percent. In an especially close election, such results could make a difference between winning and losing.

Campaign Finance

Campaigns do not come cheap. Costs have risen dramatically over the years and not just because of inflation. To illustrate: the Conservatives spent nearly eight times more on their 1997 campaign than on their 1983 campaign. Labour spent more than nineteen times more.[7] Contracts with campaign consultants alone have added materially to campaign costs. So expensive have they become that, every now and then, financing them flares up as a pressing issue, one, in fact, that Labour promised in its 1997 election manifesto to address were it returned to power. With the state making no direct contributions to the parties, and party membership in steady decline with each passing elec-

Table 7.2	Sources of Possible Campaign Influence, 2001

Question: *Please tell me how much influence, if any, each of the following had on your decision about what you would do on the day of the General Election.*

	Great deal	Fair amount	Not very much	None at all	Don't know
Election coverage on TV	13	36	20	30	1
Election coverage in the papers	8	30	22	39	1
Parties' leaflets or letters	4	22	25	49	<1
PEBs on TV	6	16	20	57	1
Election coverage on radio	5	17	18	58	3
Views of friends or family	6	14	20	60	<1
Opinion polls	2	11	21	65	1
Billboard advertisements	2	8	17	72	1
Personal calls from the parties	2	6	9	80	3
Election coverage on the internet	1	3	5	87	4

Source: MORI poll for the Electoral Commission, June 9–18, 2001, as reported in David Butler and Dennis Kavanagh, *The British General Election of 2001* (Basingstoke: Palgrave, 2002), p. 215.

tion, membership fees were found to meet only a small fraction of a campaign's expenses. For example, for the 1992 election, membership fees paid for only 12 percent of the Conservative Party's campaign outlays and only 11 percent of Labour's. The day of mass parties, a day when members' dues paid for the entirety of their party's expenses, had long since gone.

Moreover, the two parties realized that they could no longer count on the largesse of their constituencies—the trade unions for Labour and the business community for the Conservatives. Trade union membership was in decline and, subsequently, union contributions to Labour were not as generous as they once had been. In addition, some unions scaled back their contributions to Labour after the new Labour Government refused to support all of the reforms they had lobbied for. The Conservatives realized they had to vie with Labour for corporate donations as business and Labour began to warm to each other. To make ends meet, the parties struggled under a stringent cost-cutting regimen. But try as they might, their accounts still slipped into the red, at least for short periods.

The search for funds triggered a series of charges that cast the Conservatives in a bad light when they were in power in the 1990s. Many of the party's benefactors and the amounts they gave were unknown because no law required that such information be disclosed. Left to its own devices, the party refused to divulge this information. Despite the party's policy of secrecy, every now and again names and amounts donated were leaked to the media, with the head of one company or another being identified as the recipient of a knighthood or peerage not long after reportedly making a particularly generous contribution. The media made much of these revelations, questioning whether wealthy contributors were attempting to buy titles or had something more in mind. The press made even more of the fact that some who had given generously to the Conservative Party were not even British, including at least two individuals who lived in Britain and later became fugitives from British justice. One got into trouble with the Serious Fraud Office, jumped bail, and left Britain by stealth; the other fled to Switzerland to avoid prosecution for tax fraud.

Labour too was singled out for conferring benefits on generous multimillionaires. It sustained the most serious attack six months after it came to power in 1997, soon after Tony Blair met with a wealthy racing car tycoon who happened to be a major party donor. It was seen as more than coincidental that a week after this meeting an announcement was made that a new rule outlawing tobacco advertising and sponsorship at racing tracks would be delayed for four years. This incident created an uproar, and not long after, the party returned every penny to the donor. As if to soften public criticism, the Government turned to the independent Committee on Standards in Public Life to ask for its recommendations on funding political parties.

A year later, this committee submitted its recommendations, most of which were incorporated in 2000 in the Political Parties, Elections and Referendums Act (PPERA). Broadly reflecting the views of the public as reported in opinion polls going back as far as the 1970s, this act of Parliament emphasized the importance of full disclosure by the parties of the sources and amounts of donations they receive. Under PPERA, all donations, whether in cash or in-kind (goods or services), must be declared publicly if they exceed £5,000 (roughly the equivalent of $9,000 in 2005) to a political party at the national level or £1,000 ($1,800) to a constituency party. Foreign donations are prohibited. The parties must adhere to stringent reporting requirements: reports are to be made once every three months during a nonelection period and once a week during an election campaign.

Even more radical than disclosure was the imposition of a ceiling on campaign spending at the national level. There has always been a limit on how much a constituency party could spend; for the 2005 election campaign, it was £7,150, plus either 5 pence per elector in an urban constituency or 7 pence per elector in a rural constituency. (Assuming a constituency of seventy thousand electors, which is only slightly larger than the average size, the total amounts are roughly $10,650 per urban constituency and $12,050 per rural constituency.) Until PPERA, there was no such thing as a ceiling on how much a party could spend on a campaign at the national level. With PPERA, general election year outlays for each political party were limited to £24,000 multiplied by the number of constituencies the party contests or, put another way, £15,048,000 ($27,086,400) if it contests every constituency (except the Speaker's) in mainland Britain. (An election year is defined as the 365 days preceding election day.)

Those who had hoped that PPERA would authorize the use of public funds to underwrite political parties and their election campaigns were disappointed. Nothing was mentioned to that end. Nor did the Blair Government drop any hints that it would consider state funding at a later date. Central government has nevertheless continued the practice begun in 1975 of providing funds every year to all opposition parties in the House of Commons. These funds defray only parliamentary, not campaign, expenses. The central government bears the cost of administering elections; beyond that, it subsidizes party meetings, party mailings, and the parties' use of the media during campaigns. Candidates are allowed to hold public meetings in school halls, and any costs are borne by local government. And even though the candidate or candidate's party pays for producing campaign leaflets, which usually include the all-important election address of the candidate, they may be mailed to every address in a constituency without charge to the party as long as each leaflet weighs no more than sixty grams (2.1 ounces).

Third, although parties are banned from buying air time on television and radio stations to broadcast political advertisements, any political party that sponsors candidates in fifty or more constituencies has an automatic right to broadcast one or more PEBs via television and radio free of charge. The cost of producing PEBs is borne by the parties, but the government's provision of subsidies to broadcast them is so vast that the consultant who directed Labour's advertising campaign in 1997 claimed that "the total value of free TV and radio broadcasts in and prior to elections in Britain 'dwarfs' the sums paid by the parties for all other types of campaign advertising put together." [8]

Finally, it is important to call attention to the Electoral Commission and its assessment of party funding. The commission, created by PPERA in 2000, is a body independent of government that oversees the implementation of party finance. In addition, it reports on the conduct of elections, makes proposals for electoral reform, and promotes public awareness of the electoral process. Addressing itself to public concerns about party funding, the commission found that it "did not become a significant issue in this [2001] election campaign." It went on to state that

Whether this was a direct result of the increased transparency of donations and the limits on expenditure is impossible to judge. Certainly, press reporting on the donations was generally favourable, with most of the broadsheet papers [serious newspapers] making regular use of the information provided on the Commission's website to highlight donations to the parties and welcoming the changes that required the publication of such data.[9]

Events relating to donations brought to light five years after these words were written suggested that the Electoral Commission would not be going out of business for lack of work. In 2006, charges were made that the Labour and Conservative Parties had approached some wealthy individuals to ask for loans to replenish their empty coffers. In the case of Labour, the *quid pro quo* was allegedly peerages for four of the lenders. Because nominating individuals for peerages in return for cash is illegal under a 1925 statute, Scotland Yard was called in to investigate. Whatever the outcome of this investigation (it was ongoing as this book went to press), these events point up the financial straits that the parties often find themselves in and underscore the need for the Electoral Commission or others to give thought to what further reforms might be pursued.

Elections

June 10, 2004, was called Super Thursday in the UK, a day when elections were held all across the four nations. At stake were the UK's 78 seats in the European Parliament, more than a quarter of England's nearly 20,000 council seats, all of Wales' more than 1,200 council seats, London's mayoral seat, and the 25 seats in the Greater London Assembly. It was "super" in that so many elections were contested simultaneously, so many candidates were in the running, and so many were to be elected to such a variety of posts. But it was "super" in another way as well: as many as six different voting systems were to be used to produce the winners.

Elections to Parliament continue to be the principal focus of this chapter. But because there is such a variety of voting systems in the UK, it is useful to know how each works and why each is used. The oldest system is that used for elections to Parliament, and although it has its critics, it also has its defenders. After looking again principally at parliamentary elections, this chapter goes on to investigate why most people vote, why others do not, and, just as important, how they vote.

Electoral Systems

A large number of voting systems are used throughout the world; in the 1990s, there were as many as seventy in twenty-seven democracies that were examined.[10] Some governments use more than one system for different jurisdictions, and the UK is one of them. Six were used in Britain on Super Thursday in 2004, which is the number presently used. (See Table 7.3.) The oldest is the single-member, simple-plurality system used to elect members of Parliament and most English and Welsh local government councilors. The newest system is the supplementary vote system used to elect the mayor of London.

Single-Member, Simple-Plurality System (SMSP)

The "single-member" in the SMSP designation means simply that an area, such as a parliamentary constituency or an English or Welsh council ward, is represented by just one member of Parliament or councilor. The "simple-plurality" part means that the winning candidate is the one who receives more votes than anyone else in that race, whether by a plurality or a majority. Perhaps it is helpful to conceive of it as a horse race—the first horse past the post wins. In fact, "first-past-the-post" is how SMSP is often referred to.

Table 7.3	Electoral Systems in the United Kingdom
Electoral System	Body Elected
Single-member, Simple-plurality	House of Commons Some English/Welsh local councils
Multimember, Simple-plurality	Some English/Welsh local councils
Additional Member System	Scottish Parliament Welsh National Assembly Greater London Assembly
Multimember List System	European Parliament (75 parliamentarians from England, Wales, and Scotland)
Single Transferable Vote	European Parliament (3 parliamentarians from Northern Ireland only) Northern Ireland Assembly Northern Ireland local councils Scottish local councils*
Supplementary Vote	London mayor The 11 mayors of English local councils

Sources: David Denver, *Elections and Voters in Britain* (Basingstoke: Palgrave Macmillan, 2003), p. 169; and Richard Kelly, Oonagh Gay, and Isobel White, "The Constitution: Into the Sidings," *Parliamentary Affairs,* vol. 58, no. 2 (April 2005): p. 222.
*Starting in 2007.

In a simple-plurality system, however, there is no post, or fixed finishing line. Thus, in a contest involving five candidates, one of the five could conceivably win by capturing a mere 20.01 percent of the vote. No one has yet been elected to Parliament with a percentage that low; the closest anyone has come to it in the four general elections held since 1992 was in 1992, when Sir Russell Johnston won the Scottish constituency of Inverness, Nairn, and Lochaber. Sir Russell defeated his closest rival by a little less than one percentage point—26.0 percent to 25.1 percent—and a second rival by a little more than one percentage point—26.0 percent to 24.7 percent. That Johnston was elected by the lowest percentage recorded by any winner in these four general elections made his victory unique. Far from unique, however, was that five candidates fought for that constituency—a number not atypical, for more than one quarter of all races in the 1992 general election were contested by five candidates, making it difficult for any one of them to win a majority.

Multimember, Simple-Plurality System (MMSP)

The "simple-plurality" in MMSP is the same as it is in the single-member system: the winners are those who receive more votes than anyone else. The difference is with the "multimember" part of the term. Wards in a minority of English and Welsh councils are represented by more than one councilor. These wards are almost always found in urban areas, such as Manchester, Birmingham, and Leeds, with high population densities. Electors in these areas are asked to vote for, say, three out of ten whose names are on the ballot, and the three who attract the most votes are declared the winners.

Additional Member System (AMS)

The additional member system of voting is used to elect members of the Scottish parliament, the Welsh National Assembly, and the Greater London Assembly. When voters appear at their polling stations in any one of these jurisdictions, they are reminded to cast two votes. The first one is for a constituency representative under first-past-the-post, just like it would be if they were voting for a member of Parliament. Their second vote is not for a candidate, but rather for a party list. Each party that contests the election prepares a list of its candidates, and voters cast a vote for the list they prefer. In London there is one party list for all of London; in Scotland, with its eight regions, and in Wales, with its five regions, each region has a different party list. Those elected from the party lists are the "additional members." Constituency members outnumber additional members in each of these jurisdictions; there are 73 constituency members out of 129 total members in Scotland, 40 out of 60 in Wales, and 14 out of 25 in the Greater London Assembly.

The election of the twenty-five-member Greater London Assembly in 2004 provides an illustration of what happens. Of the twenty-five, one was elected to represent each of London's fourteen assembly constituencies, and eleven were elected as additional members to serve London-wide. Conservatives were elected to nine of the fourteen constituencies and Labour to five. As for the eleven additional members, voters elected five Liberal Democrats, two others from the Labour Party, two from the Green Party, and two from the United Kingdom Independence Party. The results of this election would have been spectacularly different had voting been restricted to either the single-member or the multimember system.

And that brings us to the rationale for voting under AMS. AMS provides for proportionality, allows for the election of minor parties that would probably otherwise not be elected, and, through the fourteen assembly representatives, gives separate-but-equal status to constituencies that are not the overwhelming size of all of London. On the negative side, each list is "closed," that is, it is drawn up by the party. Voters are prohibited from adding other names to their ballots. Moreover, the party determines the order in which the names of candidates appear on the list, and those at the top are favored.

Multimember List System

The seventy-five members of the European Parliament (MEPs) from England, Scotland, and Wales are elected in the same way as additional members are, in that voters are asked to vote for a party list. The constituencies are huge and multimember. Scotland, with an electorate of more than 3.8 million, is one large constituency that elects seven MEPs. Wales is also one large constituency, with an electorate of more than 2.2 million, and four MEPs. As England is much more populated and spread out than Scotland and Wales, it is divided into nine constituencies. The Northeast, whose electorate of more than 1.9 million makes it the smallest constituency, is entitled to 3 MEPs; the Southeast is the largest with an electorate of more than 6 million represented by 10 MEPs. What commends this electoral system is that the number of seats each party receives is roughly equivalent to the share of the vote it wins. However, it also has a drawback: as with AMS, the parties—not the voters—decide whose names appear on the lists and in what order.

Single Transferable Vote (STV)

The multimember list system used to elect MEPs in mainland Britain and additional members under AMS are two versions of proportional representation (PR), a voting system designed to ensure that political parties win seats roughly equivalent to their share of the vote. However, in the view of the Electoral Reform Society, the most effective variant of PR is the Single Transferable Vote. Northern Ireland adopted it in the 1970s and continues to use it today to elect its three MEPs, council members, and (when and if London restores devolved status to Northern Ireland) the Northern Ireland Assembly.

As with all the electoral systems discussed so far (apart from SMSP), constituencies under STV are multimember. What makes STV distinctly different, however, is that although political parties decide which candidates appear on the ballot, voters rank their preferences of the candidates by signifying 1, 2, 3, etc., beside their names. The voters are able to make a choice not only among parties, but also among candidates. This feature gives voters a greater range of choice in another realm as well, for parties' candidate-selection committees tend to field more women and ethnic minority candidates under STV than they do under non-PR voting systems.

In addition, STV removes some of the confusion about constituency boundaries. Because these boundaries often are not at all obvious, it is not uncommon for constituents not to know which constituency they live in and therefore who their member of Parliament is. For example, one member of Parliament who had an office in Leeds just streets away from where his constituency bounded another was regularly visited by people who "turned up from the 'wrong' constituency," thinking he was their member of Parliament.[11] Had all of Leeds' constituencies been grouped into one, this problem would not have occurred. Moreover, voters would have been allowed a choice of MPs to consult. They could have turned to one MP from Leeds, to all MPs from there, or to one or two from that enlarged constituency whose party affiliation or ideological leanings within the party corresponded to their own.

Supplementary Vote

The supplementary vote is the newest electoral system to make its appearance in Britain. It was first used in 2000 to elect London's mayor. Voters in this type of election are asked to make a first choice and a second choice for mayor from a slate of candidates. Ideally, the victor wins a majority of first-preference votes, but if a majority fails to materialize, one is manufactured in a two-step process. First, all but the top two on the ballot are eliminated from the contest. Second, the ballots of those whose first-preference votes were for someone other than the top two candidates are re-examined, and any second-preference votes for either of the top two candidates are transferred to them. After the transfers are made, the winner is the one who accumulates the most votes. Before the winner could be declared in London's first two mayoral elections in 2000 and 2004, second-preference votes had to be examined and transferred in both instances. In the 2004 election the winner received 36.6 percent of first-preference votes cast; the runner-up got 29 percent. But the winner moved well beyond the 50 percent mark when second-preference votes were added to his 36.6 percent.

One could well wonder why there are as many as six electoral systems in the UK, but as one would expect, there is at least one reason behind each. For example, MEPs from England, Wales, and Scotland are elected by the multimember list system because the EU mandated that some form of PR be used. In Northern Ireland, STV was introduced in the 1970s to reduce clashes between the denominational parties and to encourage the rise of nondenominational centrist parties. London's mayor is elected by the supplementary vote because it was thought the mayor could lead more effectively with an electoral system that gave him or her a solid base on which to govern.

None of the voting systems used in the UK is perfect, but the benefits of each are seen as outweighing any flaws. Yet some regard one electoral system in particular as having more flaws than any of the others. That system is the single-member, simple-plurality (SMSP) system used to elect members of Parliament.

SMSP under Attack

True or False?

1. The party that forms a Government is the party that has won a majority of the popular vote.

2. In the House of Commons, the party that receives the greatest share of the two-party vote wins a majority of seats.

3. The percentage of seats a party wins in the House of Commons is a near-perfect reflection of the percentage of voters who supported the winning party in the election.

Question 1:   *The party that forms a Government is the party that has won a majority of the popular vote.* Answer: ***False.*** To win a seat in Parliament, the SMSP establishes no fixed finish line for a candidate to cross. To form a Government, however, there is a fixed finish line: the winning party must acquire one more than one half of the seats in the Commons or, at the very least, more seats than any other party. While most governments of the day from 1945 through 2005 won a majority of seats (the one exception being the February 1974 election), their share of the popular vote never reached, let alone surpassed, the 50 percent mark. (See Table 7.4.) Only twice since 1900—in 1929 and 1935—has a party won more than 50 percent of the vote, and in the seventeen elections from 1945 through 2005, the closest a party came was in 1955, when the Conservatives won 49.7 percent of the vote. Since 1945 the lowest percentage has been 35.2 percent of the vote, which Labour won in 2005 when it became the government of the day for the third time in a row. Until then the record low since 1945 had been 37.1 percent in the February 1974 election.

Question 1 is therefore false. Before moving on, however, one more point is in order. If one were to identify the number who voted for the party that formed a Government and then calculated that number as a percentage of all eligible voters—both those who voted and those who abstained—the result would be discouraging news indeed for those who prize democratic participation. The results for the elections of 1992, 1997, 2001, and 2005 dropped markedly with each passing election—from 33.3 percent to 31.7 to 24.8 to 21.6.

Question 2: *In the House of Commons, the party that receives the greatest share of the two-party vote wins a majority of seats.* Answer: *False.* Although it is generally true that the party that wins more of the two-party vote wins a majority of seats, the elections of 1951 and February 1974 make the answer to Question 2 false. In these elections the party that won the greatest share of the popular vote failed to become the government of

Table 7.4	The Conservative and Labour Parties at the Polls, 1945–2005			
General Election	Number of Seats		Percentage of Vote*	
Vote	Cons.	Lab.	Cons.	Lab.
1945	213	393	39.8	**43.8**
1950	299	315	43.5	**46.1**
1951	321	295	**48.0**	48.8
1955	345	277	**49.7**	46.4
1959	365	258	**49.4**	43.8
1964	304	317	**43.4**	44.1
1966	253	363	41.9	**47.9**
1970	330	288	**46.4**	43.0
1974 (Feb.)	297	301	37.8	**37.1**
1974 (Oct.)	277	319	35.8	**39.2**
1979	339	269	**43.9**	37.0
1983	397	209	**42.4**	27.6
1987	376	229	**42.3**	30.8
1992	336	271	**41.9**	34.4
1997	165	418	30.7	**43.2**
2001	166	412	31.7	**40.7**
2005	198	356	32.4	**35.2**

*Party that won the election is in bold.
Source: Dennis Kavanagh and David Butler, *The General Election of 2005* (Basingstoke: Palgrave MacMillan, 2005), p. 203–204.

the day. As Table 7.4 shows, although Labour won more votes than the Conservatives in 1951—48.8 percent to 48.0 percent—the Conservatives won twenty-six more seats than Labour. The same inconsistency occurred in February 1974, although this time the Conservatives won more of the popular vote than Labour—37.8 percent to 37.1 percent—and Labour won four more seats than the Conservatives.

The cumulative distorting effects of several variables explain this situation. First, elections are fought in approximately 650 constituencies (646 in 2005), not in one constituency embracing the whole of the UK. Second, the electorates are not equal in size. Third, the number of candidates in races varies. Given these variables, the party commanding the greatest share of the popular vote cannot always be assured of winning a majority of seats. An illustration of distortion in electoral choice can be seen in Table 7.5, which profiles the results of three constituency races in England in the 2005 general election.

In constituency A, the voters elected a Conservative candidate, and in constituencies B and C, Labour candidates. If these three constituencies were the only constituencies in the UK, Labour's two winners would form a government, and the lone Conservative MP would become the official Opposition. In these three contests the Conservative candidates captured the greatest share of the vote—5,307 votes more than the Labour candidates—but they failed to win a majority of seats. In short, this is what happened in the 1951 and February 1974 elections. A closer look at the data in Table 7.5 reveals why.

First, in constituencies B and C the races were very tight. The Labour candidate's margin of victory over the Conservative runner-up was only 163 votes in B and a mere 37 in C. Whereas those who voted Conservative and Labour in B and C were nearly equally divided, the contest was far from close in A, where the Conservative candidate won by a decidedly wider margin of 5,507 votes over his Labour rival.

Second, the three electorates are unequal in size. A is the smallest. It had more than 7,700 fewer voters than B and more than 10,100 fewer voters than C. One can only speculate about what might have happened had the English Boundary Commission in the mid-1990s re-drawn the boundaries of

Table 7.5	A Profile of Voting in Three English Constituencies in the 2005 General Election					
Constituency	Labour Vote	Conservative Vote	Other Party Vote	Number of Candidates	Eligible to Vote	Turnout
A Aldridge-Brownhills	13,237	**18,744**	7,575	5	61,761	64.05%
B Battersea	**16,569**	16,406	8,074	5	69,548	59.02%
C Crawley	**16,411**	16,374	9,188	7	71,911	58.37%
Total:	46,217	51,524	24,837			

Note: Party that won the seat is in **bold**.
Source: "Election 2005" supplement, The Times, May 7, 2005, pp. 67, 68, and 72.

these constituencies so that their electoral populations were roughly equal to the UK's average-sized constituency of approximately 68,400. If the commission had increased the population of A, a Conservative safe seat, and reduced the population of C, it could have re-drawn A's boundaries by incorporating a portion of Sutton Coldfield, a contiguous constituency whose population is considerably greater than A's. Re-drawn constituency A would undoubtedly continue to be a safe Conservative seat, however. As it happens, its new voters would have been drawn from a traditionally Conservative constituency. As for C, a Labour candidate won this seat by thirty-seven votes in a constituency surrounded by five safe Conservative seats. Because its electoral population of nearly seventy-two thousand exceeds the average population, the commission could have reduced its population by giving some of C's voters to Reigate, one of its five neighboring constituencies whose population falls short of the average-sized constituency. Would these boundary changes have affected the outcome of the election? It is difficult to know. If C lost many Labour voters to Reigate, a Conservative candidate could very well have won C, and the Conservatives would then have become the government of the day.

Third, the number of candidates in these races was not the same. There were five in A, five in B, and seven in C. What would have happened had two or three minor party candidates in B and C decided not to run? Put another way, did the minor party candidates siphon off many of the votes cast that could have otherwise gone disproportionately to the Conservative candidates in B and C? One can only speculate. Finally, to what extent did turnout affect the outcome? Again, one can only speculate.

Question 3:   *The percentage of seats a party wins in the House of Commons is a near-perfect reflection of the percentage of voters who supported the winning party in the election.* Answer: *False.* The full effects of distortion in electoral choice become evident when results similar to those in constituencies A, B, and C are repeated all across the UK, as they were in the elections identified in Table 7.6. Two findings about distortion emerge from the data shown in this table. First, the two major parties usually receive an electoral bonus in the form of a greater proportion of seats than popular vote, regardless of whether they win or lose the election. Second, the leading minor party wins far fewer seats than would be suggested by its share of the vote. This disproportionality is proof enough that Question 3 is false.

Of the five elections shown in Table 7.6, only the election of 1951 experienced minimal distortion. In that election the percentage of seats won by the three parties was close to the percentage of the popular vote they received. The same cannot be said for the other four elections. The most severe distortions occurred in the general elections of 1983 and 2001, when the winning parties captured less than 43 percent of the vote but amassed 61 percent and 64.2 percent of the seats, respectively. Ironically, the Conservatives won a slightly higher percentage of the vote in 1983 than Labour did in 2001 but

Table 7.6	Percentage of Votes and Seats in Five General Elections in Britain				
Party	1951	1974 (Feb.)	1983	1992	2001
Conservative					
Votes	**48.0%**	37.8%	**42.4%**	**41.9%**	31.7%
Seats	**51.3%**	46.7%	**61.0%**	**51.6%**	25.9%
Labour					
Votes	48.8%	**37.1%**	27.6%	34.4%	**40.7%**
Seats	47.2%	**47.4%**	32.2%	41.6%	**64.2%**
Liberal					
Votes	2.5%	19.3%	—	—	—
Seats	0.9%	2.2%	—	—	—
Alliance*					
Votes	—	—	25.4%	—	—
Seats	—	—	3.5%	—	—
Liberal Democrat					
Votes	—	—	—	17.8%	18.3%
Seats	—	—	—	3.0%	8.1%

*An electoral Alliance of the Liberal Party and the Social Democratic Party.
Notes: Party that won the election is in **bold**.
The parties above did not compete in Northern Ireland. These results are for Britain only.
Source: Dennis Kavanagh and David Butler, *The General Election of 2005* (Basingstoke: Palgrave MacMillan, 2005), p. 203–204.

had a smaller majority of seats—144 compared with Labour's 166—which suggests that SMSP worked to Labour's advantage.

If distortion rewards the winning party and runner-up party with a bonus of seats, it follows that other parties are penalized by winning less than their fair share of seats. When the Liberal Party and the then newly created Social Democratic Party joined forces electorally in 1983 to become the Alliance, the campaign the two parties waged together attracted a quarter of the popular vote—the highest vote for a minor party in sixty years—but a paltry twenty-three seats, 35 percent of the total seats in the Commons. Distortion was repeated for the Liberal Democrats in the 1992 and 2001 elections, but the margins of difference between votes and seats narrowed.

Some distortion in voter choice is a natural outgrowth of SMSP. High levels of distortion are inevitable when one or more minor parties becomes a serious contender in the electoral arena. Thus, the level of distortion in elections in the last quarter of the twentieth century is a concomitant of the emergence of more robust minor party challenges and electoral successes. The more support these parties attract, the greater the distorting effects the electoral system produces. An example drawn from the 1992 general election makes this point—but in reverse. The Liberal Democrats and the Scottish National Party in that election were the two parties against which the electoral system discriminated. But if the votes and seats both parties won were recalculated to exclude their wins from the final tally, the seats captured by both the Conservatives and Labour would have been in almost perfect proportion to the votes they received. The Conservatives would have won 52.2 percent of the vote and 53.5 percent of the seats, and Labour would have gotten 42.6 percent of the vote and 43.2 percent of the seats.[12]

To overcome distortion, a minor party needs to increase its distribution, but not necessarily its overall level, of support throughout the country. An example is the Alliance. In 1983 it achieved nearly the same level of support as Labour (25.4 percent for the Alliance and 27.6 percent for Labour); Labour, however, won nine times the number of seats (209 seats for Labour and 23 for the Alliance).

SMSP is frowned upon for several reasons. First, its distorting effects mean that the share of the popular vote that parties win is not reflected in their share of seats in Westminster. This system almost always gives a disproportionately higher percentage of seats to the winning party and the runner-up party; the minor party receives a disproportionately lower percentage of seats. What would happen, then, if one of the other voting systems presently used in the UK replaced SMSP? The objective, of course, would be to install a system that would give each party a number of seats roughly equivalent to the share of the vote it wins. One system that meets this standard of proportionality is the multimember list system used to elect members of the European Parliament in mainland Britain. A simulation model devised following the 2005 general election comparing the results of SMSP with the list system is found in Table 7.7.

The last two columns in Table 7.7 show that, for the 2005 election, there was little difference between the percentages of the popular vote the parties

Table 7.7 Results of 2005 General Election in Britain Had a PR List System Been Used

Party	Actual Results Seats No.	%	List PR Seats No.	%	Percentage of Popular Vote
Labour	355	56.5	239	38.0	35.2
Conservative	198	31.5	207	32.9	32.4
Liberal Democrat	62	9.8	140	22.2	22.0
United Kingdom Independence Party	0	0	11	1.7	2.2
Scottish National Party	6	0.9	11	1.7	1.5
Plaid Cymru	3	0.4	7	1.1	0.6
Green	0	0	5	0.7	1.0
Totals:	624	99.1	620	98.3	

Source: List PR results from Patrick Dunleavy and Helen Margetts, "The Impact of UK Electoral Systems," *Parliamentary Affairs*, vol. 58, no. 4 (October 2005): p. 865.

received and the percentage of seats they would have won had they been elected by the list system. However, significant differences emerge when the SMSP system is compared with the list system. In effect, SMSP gave Labour 18.5 percent more seats than it would have won under the list system; the Liberal Democrats received 12.4 percent fewer seats under SMSP than they would have under the list system. The Conservative Party would have fared about the same with either electoral system.

How would other political parties have made out had the list system been used? The Scottish National Party and Plaid Cymru would have gained five seats and four seats, respectively. The United Kingdom Independence Party and the Green Party, which won no seats in the election, would have won eleven seats and five seats, respectively. Finally, Labour still would have been the largest party in the Commons, but with 239 seats, it would have won 116 fewer seats than under SMSP and come up 85 seats short of capturing an overall majority.

A second reason SMSP is disliked is that it produces a greater degree of disproportionality in the various regions of Britain than across Britain as a whole. Because of this, representation by one party or the other has tended to be concentrated in selected parts of Britain. For example, in the 2005 election, Labour's victories were concentrated in the six most populated metropolitan areas outside London. Out of 124 seats in these areas, Labour won 110, or 88 percent. The Conservatives won five seats, or 4 percent. The remaining nine seats, 7 percent of the total, were won by Liberal Democrats.

Table 7.8 shows how concentrated one party or the other has been in six of eleven regions of Britain from 1992 to 2005. So concentrated are they that some contend that Britain is really two nations, not one. Labour has dominated the political map in Scotland, Wales, and Northern England. But it was a far different story for Labour in East Anglia, Southwest England, and Southeast England (apart from Greater London). In these areas it has come in first in only a minority of constituencies. The Conservatives, by contrast, have elected numerous candidates to Westminster from these regions. Nineteen-ninety-two was a banner year for Conservatives in the three regions: voters in these regions elected 170 Conservative MPs to Labour's 14. In 1997, the Conservatives lost a number of seats to Labour and the Liberal Democrats, but there has been no further erosion of Conservative strength since then.

Despite its shortcomings, SMSP has its defenders. First, voting under this system is easy to understand. Voters simply put an X on their ballots by the names of the candidates they prefer. Most voters have had little experience with the other electoral systems and their associated ballots. When voters went to their polling stations to vote in London's first mayoral and assembly election in 2000, many found their ballots difficult to understand, a problem that failed to go away for many of them when they returned to their polling stations at the next election four years later.[13]

Second, because SMSP is biased against minor parties, extremist parties find it next to impossible to win seats. Third, for the same reason, it is in-

Table 7.8	Distribution of Seats by Party in Selected Regions of Britain, 1992–2005											

	1992			1997			2001			2005		
	Number of seats			Number of Seats			Number of Seats			Number of Seats		
Region	C	L	LD	C	L	LD	C	L	LD	C	L	LD
Scotland	10	50	9	0	56	10	1	56	10	1	40	11
Wales	8	27	1	0	34	2	0	34	2	3	29	4
Northern England	6	29	1	3	32	1	3	32	1	2	32	2
SE England	112	5	0	73	36	8	73	35	9	83	27	7
SW England	39	6	6	22	15	14	20	16	15	22	13	16
East Anglia	19	3	0	14	8	0	14	7	1	15	5	2

Source: Ron Johnston, Charles Pattie, and David Rossiter, "The Election Results in the UK Regions," *Parliamentary Affairs,* vol. 58, no. 4 (October 2005): p. 793.

conceivable that a minor party would become a governing party; one of the two major parties is almost always certain to win a majority of seats in the election and act on the pledges it made in the campaign. Fourth, because one of the major parties is nearly always sure to win, SMSP is a huge deterrent to a hung Parliament, which as Table 7.7 reveals, would have resulted had the list system been used in 2005.

A coalition government, which is the likely consequence of a hung Parliament, should be avoided at all cost, SMSP's defenders assert. The parties could disagree on an important issue and pull out of the coalition at any time, and the need to compromise across party lines could lead to policies that are half-baked. In addition to the instability a coalition government would create, SMSP supporters add that the parties in the coalition could be required to jettison some of the major manifesto pledges they made to their supporters as a condition for joining the coalition, precipitating widespread disaffection among large segments of the electorate.

When Labour was in opposition in the 1990s, two successive party leaders, John Smith and Tony Blair, agreed that the time had come to reform the electoral system; in 1997 holding a referendum on electoral reform became a plank in the party's election manifesto. Soon after Labour came to power, Tony Blair appointed a commission chaired by Roy Jenkins, one of the country's elder statesmen, to recommend a suitable replacement for SMSP that could be presented to the voters for their approval in a referendum. The Jenkins Commission finished its work in late 1998 and recommended an electoral system based on a proportional system designed to achieve widespread support. After completing two terms, however, the Labour Government showed no signs of preparing for a referendum, probably because it had serious doubts about whether the party would do as well under such a reformed system. The Government's perceived U-turn on the referendum was reminiscent of what had happened a century before. In 1906, the Liberal

Party, a long-term proponent of PR, did nothing to dismantle SMSP in the four full years it was in power after having been swept into office by one of the largest landslides in British history, thanks in part to an electoral system it had committed itself to reform. History, it appears, really does repeat itself.

Voting

In June 2001 Labour won a second term after burying the Conservatives in a landslide of paper ballots. It was a spectacular victory and an historic one; until then, no party had won two elections in a row by such epic proportions. But as celebrants at Labour Party headquarters partied into the early morning hours, news of another historical fact spread that made the bubbles in their champagne go flat. Voter turnout had sunk to 59.4 percent, the lowest level since 1918. It had plummeted 12 percentage points and nearly five million voters from 1997. Turnout rose in the next election, in 2005, but by a less-than-impressive 2 percentage points.

Voter Turnout

As Figure 7.1 demonstrates, turnout has been irregular for some time. There are several reasons for this. For example, in 1970 the percentage dropped probably because the year before, eighteen-, nineteen-, and twenty-year-olds were given the right to vote for the first time, and in the election a year later they followed the familiar pattern of fewer young people voting than older people. (In the 1970 election, roughly twice as many eighteen to twenty-four-year-olds abstained than did forty-five to fifty-four-year-olds and fifty-five to sixty-four-year-olds.[14]) Up went turnout, overall, after the 1970 election, although not spectacularly, and then, in 1997, the percentage dropped again, this time to the lowest level since the Second World War. This was followed by the near-historic low levels of participation in 2001 and 2005. Why had so many stayed home?

Those who stayed home had their reasons, but a lack of interest in politics was not one of them. Polling data indicate that interest in politics did not slacken as turnout fell. Interest was just as high in the election years of 2001 and 2005 as it had been in previous election years when turnout was higher.[15] What, then, contributed to the decline in turnout? One factor was the perception that there was little difference between the two major parties, a perception that had been on the increase since 1987. Only 17 percent in 2001 and 21 percent in 2005 felt there was a "great deal of difference" between the Conservative and Labour Parties compared with 48 percent in 1979 and 56 percent in 1992. Not surprisingly, those who felt there was a great deal of difference were more likely to say they were "absolutely certain" to vote than those who perceived the parties as Tweedledum and Tweedledee.[16]

That the outcome of the election was a foregone conclusion was cited as a second reason for staying home. In a major poll published just a few days before election day in 2005, 78 percent predicted that Labour would secure

Figure 7.1 | Turnout in UK General Elections, 1945–2005

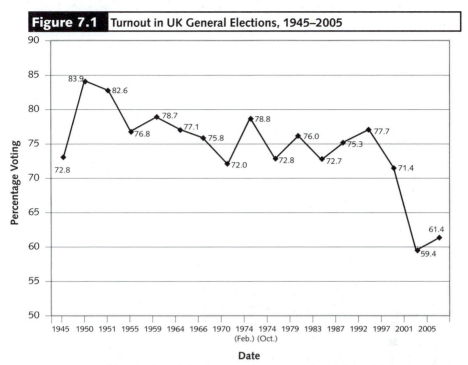

Source: David Sanders, Harold Clarke, Marianne Stewart, Paul Whiteley, "The 2005 General Election in Great Britain," a report for the Electoral Commission, August 2005, p. 4. (www.essex.ac.uk/bes/Papers/ec%20report%20final.pdf.)

enough seats to win a majority.[17] With support running that high for Labour, some who were hoping for a Labour victory stayed home because they felt their vote was not needed; others who were hoping for a Conservative win abstained because they felt their vote would be for naught. However, not all felt that way. Turnout was generally higher in marginal seats (seats in which the party of the winning MP beat the party of the runner-up candidate in 2001 by less than 5 percent) than in safe seats (seats in which the winning party had won by 20 percent or more in 2001).[18]

To these two reasons, research undertaken for the Electoral Commission following the 2005 election identified four additional ones. First, the electorate was disillusioned with politics and politicians; second, they were ignorant about politics and about what the political parties stood for; third, they thought the campaign uninspiring, stage managed, and negative; and fourth, they could not decide how to vote.[19] On this last point, part of the reason why it is so difficult for some to make up their mind is that the parties no longer serve as voting cues because voters' ties to a specific party have weakened.[20]

If these same reasons crossed the minds of those who did vote, they were not compelling enough to make them stay home. Their reasons for voting are documented in Table 7.9. When voters were approached, they were

Speaking of . . .

Where Have All the Voters Gone?

Voter turnout was often robust in the twentieth century. Only once did it dip below 71 percent. But no sooner had the first two general elections of the twenty-first century been held than psephologists began to puzzle over the startling drop in turnout, as it plummeted to 59 percent in 2001 and 61 percent in 2005. What did these worrying figures portend? The following is how the Electoral Commission saw things:

> If, as some academics have suggested, the first few elections they experience are crucial in shaping people's political outlook . . . then a degree of catching up could well be necessary. . . .

"The prognosis for future general election turnouts is not . . . entirely gloomy. However, there are some clear warning signs. Past research has shown weakening attachments to political parties, meaning that people are less predisposed to turning out for no other reason than to back 'their side'. In addition, younger age groups are much less likely than people in middle age and older groups to see voting as a civic duty and new analysis for us by the BES [British Election Study] team suggests the beginnings of a cohort effect with a generation apparently carrying forward their non-voting as they get older.

"Also of concern is the possibility that after two historically low turnout elections some people are now out of the habit of voting, or may not yet have acquired the habit, and must be won over. If, as some academics have suggested, the first few elections they experience are crucial in shaping people's political outlook, including the value of voting, then a degree of catching up could well be necessary at the next general election and throughout the crucial period between now and then.

"Finally, while we have found considerable variation in participation rates among different demographic groups and parts of the country, our research suggests that any attempts to re-engage people with politics, particularly voting, ought to be addressed to society generally, since non-voting and political skepticism is evident among all groups. There is also a clear need to reconnect people with politics, and vice-versa, beyond moments of (relatively) high political drama such as general elections."

Source: "Election 2005: Turnout: How Many, Who and Why?" London: Electoral Commission, October 2005, p. 54.

Table 7.9	**Why People Voted in the 2005 General Election**
	Question: *People have many different reasons for voting in general elections. Which of the statements on this card comes closest to your reason(s) for voting in the general election that was held on May 5?*

	Cited by (%)
It is my duty to vote	60
I wanted to have a say in who wins the election	51
It is my right to vote	49
I always vote	44
I wanted to support the party I preferred	40
I wanted to support the candidates I preferred	29
I wanted to send a message to the government	20
I wanted to vote against a party I didn't like	19

Source: David Sanders, Harold Clarke, Marianne Stewart, and Paul Whiteley, "The 2005 General Election in Great Britain," a report for the Electoral Commission, August 2005, p. 21. (www.essex.ac.uk/bes/Papers/ec%20report%20final.pdf.)

asked to identify any one or more reasons they thought relevant from the ones listed on the card they were handed.

A "duty to vote" was cited by respondents as the leading reason for heading to the polls. Not far behind was the "right to vote." So too was another reason that expressess essentially the same principle of "right" but with different words—"I wanted to have a say. . ." The right to vote also is suggested in two responses further down the table: "I wanted to support the party I preferred" and "I wanted to support the candidates I preferred." Although the table does not reveal this, 35 percent of the respondents cited both a "duty" and a "right" as reasons for voting. Twenty-five percent cited "duty" ("right" was not mentioned), and 15 percent cited "right" ("duty" was not mentioned). Twenty-five percent alluded to neither as their reasons for voting.[21]

The remaining reasons listed in the table are less positive: "[I voted because] I always vote," which drew an uncomfortably high percentage of responses, was neither positive nor negative. On the other hand, wanting to "send a message to the government" probably would be construed as negative, and wanting to "vote against a party I didn't like" is unquestionably negative. The only consolation to those who had hoped for higher ratings of a more positive nature is that these last two reasons came in last.

Voter Choice

Voter turnout has long fascinated political scientists, and so too has voter choice. Their research on the choices voters make and the reasons behind these choices has grown steadily over the years. Indeed, such a specialty has it become that in the 1950s a new term—psephology—was coined to identify the scientific study of elections. Psephology, derived from the Greek word *psephos,* meaning pebble, is an allusion to the way Athenians voted; they dropped pebbles into different jars to signify their choice of candidate.

Psephologists in Britain have explored many different aspects of voting, but this text touches on only a few of their major findings. How do Britons vote, and why do they vote as they do? The answers to these questions differ depending upon which of two eras one is referring to. The first is the era of alignment (1945 to 1970); the second is the era of dealignment (1974 to the present).

In the first era, there were two forms of alignment: partisan alignment and class alignment, and they were closely linked. With partisan alignment, Britons attached great importance to supporting one party or the other, and it should be emphasized that "one party or the other" meant the Conservatives or Labour. It was a period when the faith of the party faithful ran deep, and the partisanship of partisans ran high. Party membership was stable, party support reliable, and electoral outcomes predictable. Not only did the party rank and file show up at polling stations on election day, they also regularly voted for the party they had long rallied around.

The second way the electorate was aligned was along class lines. Class alignment had its beginnings with youngsters being socialized into adopting the views articulated by their parents and often reinforced by their peers. As a result of socialization, these youngsters who in time became young voters were inclined to accept that Labour stood for the working class and the Conservatives for the middle class. By and large they voted for the party they perceived as representing their interests, with the result that about two thirds of working class voters supported the Labour Party and upwards of four fifths of the middle class lined up behind the Conservative Party. Of course, not all voted in lockstep. Some, the "floating voters," floated between the parties; others decided to sit out one election or more; and still others, when their party adopted a string of policies they thought foolish, switched their allegiance to another party, or at least briefly so. A growing number of voters, called working-class Tories ("Tories" being the age-old term informally applied to Conservative Party members), started to deviate from the norm enough to prompt the authors of a seminal study on voting behavior to remark that "there were strong enough cross-currents in each class for partisanship not to have been determined entirely by class." They then hastened to add: "Yet its pre-eminent role can hardly be questioned." [22]

The second era was the era of dealignment, thought to have gotten under way in the late 1960s and early 1970s. It had arrived in no uncertain terms by the 1974 general election, and nothing has happened as of this writing to suggest it has run its course. It is a period when there has been a perceptible weakening of the two forms of alignment that prevailed from 1945 to 1970.

In the early 1970s, when the working class began to become somewhat more affluent, its attachment to Labour began to weaken, and some shifted their allegiance to the Conservative Party. This was the beginning of class dealignment and is reflected in the shifts found in Table 7.10. On the left of the table are two broad categories, "nonmanual" and "manual." These are

Table 7.10 Class and Party Choice, 1964–1966, 1997, and 2001	1964–1966 (mean)	1997	2001
Nonmanual			
Conservative	62%	36%	34%
Labour	25%	40%	38%
Liberal	12%	—	—
Liberal Democrat	—	19%	23%
Manual			
Conservative	29%	19%	20%
Labour	64%	60%	61%
Liberal	7%	—	—
Liberal Democrat	—	15%	14%

Note: Because votes for "others" are not displayed, the columns do not add up to 100 percent.
Source: Table adapted from David Denver, *Elections and Voters in Britain* (Basingstoke: Palgrave Macmillan, 2003), p. 68.

imperfect but conventional ways used for years to identify the middle class (nonmanual) and working class (manual). What becomes clear after examining the table is that from 1964–1966 through 2001 there was a sharp decrease in the percentage of middle-class Britons who favored the Conservative Party and a slight increase in those who favored Labour.

In a U-turn from the earlier period, more from the middle class supported the Labour Party than the Conservative Party in 1997 and 2001. Among manual workers there was a marked drop in the percentage of working-class Tories, which was accompanied by only a slight downward shift in the percentage who favored Labour. In the meantime, Labour appeared to profit from those in the middle class who defected from the Conservative Party. As for the Liberal Democrats, who did not exist before 1964 but trace much of their lineage to the Liberal Party, they received twice as much support from nonmanual and manual voters in 2001 as the Liberals did thirty-five years before. In other words, class no longer determined how people voted.

Partisan dealignment also was occurring as those faithful to one of the two major parties engaged in more than just a brief interlude of flirting with such minor parties as the Liberals, the Social Democrats, and later, the Liberal Democrats, as well as the Welsh and Scottish nationalist parties. None of these parties, it should be emphasized, fit the mold of class parties. No longer were the Conservatives and Labour attracting between 87 percent and 97 percent of the popular vote. Their support instead hovered around 75 percent. Indeed, only once between 1974 and 2005 did they win as much as 81 percent. Clearly, minor parties were on the rise.

One way to appreciate the extent of party dealignment is to examine trend lines in the degree to which the electorate identified with political parties. To what extent did they identify: very strongly, fairly strongly, or not very strongly? The answers are found in Figure 7.2. What is particularly

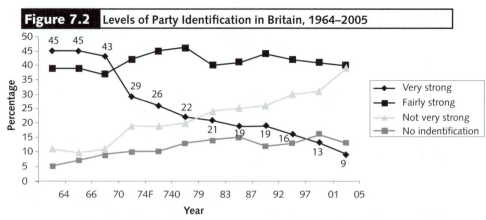

Figure 7.2 Levels of Party Identification in Britain, 1964–2005

Source: David Sanders, Harold Clarke, Marianne Stewart, Paul Whiteley, "The 2005 General Election in Great Britain," a report for the Electoral Commission, August 2005, p. 6. (www.essex.ac.uk/bes/Papers/ec%20report%20final.pdf.)

noteworthy about the trend lines as shown in the figure is the steady decline in the percentage of those who identified very strongly with a political party. In the mid-1960s, nearly five out of every ten respondents did so, but in the first half of the 1970s there was a precipitous drop—from 43 percent to 26 percent—followed by a steady, continuous decline from 1979 (22 percent) to 2005 (9 percent).

While Figure 7.2 focuses on the extent to which respondents identified (or did not identify) with a political party in general, it reveals nothing about their attachment to two parties in particular, the Conservative Party and the Labour Party. One could hypothesize that with the drop in support for the two major parties at the polls beginning in 1974, the electorate's attachment to them has been tepid. When put to the test (as shown in Table 7.11), not surprisingly, this hypothesis is proved correct. The percentage of those who identified with one or the other of these two parties declined slightly from the mid-1960s to 2001 (from 81 percent to 73 percent); however, those with strong attachments fell more dramatically, from 40 percent to 11 percent. As of 2001, although 73

Table 7.11 Party Identification, 1964–1966, 1997, and 2001

	1964–1966 (mean)	1997	2001
Identify with a political party	90%	93%	89%
Identify "very strongly" with a political party	42%	16%	13%
Identify with Conservative or Labour party	81%	76%	73%
Identify "very strongly" with Conservative or Labour party	40%	15%	11%

Source: Table adapted from David Denver, *Elections and Voters in Britain* (Basingstoke: Palgrave Macmillan, 2003), p. 74.

percent were Conservative and Labour Party partisans, all but 11 percent of these individuals were partisans without passion. However much avid partisans would wish otherwise, it is incontrovertible that political parties today do not have the salience with the body politic that they once did.

Much more consistent are trends in the percentage of those who described themselves as identifying fairly strongly with a political party. Thirty-nine percent did so in 1964, 40 percent did so in 2005, and there was no marked change between those years. In the meantime, however, there was a relentless rise in the percentage of those who did not identify very strongly with a party, with the percentage of those in this category climbing from roughly one out of ten in 1964 to four out of ten in 2005.

Conclusion

The changes that have taken place in British politics since 1945 have been nothing short of enormous. Triggering some of these changes has been a growing dissatisfaction with the two major parties. First, there has been a dramatic increase in the number of candidates vying for seats in Westminster. Until the 1970s most seats were fought between just two candidates, one Conservative and the other Labour. Years later, in the 2005 general election, by the Electoral Commission's count Conservative and Labour candidates were joined by candidates from 112 other parties. So steadily has the number of candidates climbed that the names of five or more appear regularly on ballots in more than three quarters of the constituencies from one election to the next. Among these candidates are those sponsored by the Liberal Democrats, who, because of the growing support they have received in recent years, could be considered more than a minor party today. They contest almost every seat in mainland Britain. Other candidates are drawn from the United Kingdom Independence Party and the Green Party, both of which sponsor candidates in a number of races across the country. In Scotland, the Scottish National Party and in Wales, the Welsh National Party (Plaid Cymru) have fielded candidates in every seat in their respective nations.

Second, unlike the Liberal Democrats and the Green Party, most minor parties are single issue in their orientation. Among single-issue parties is the United Kingdom Independence Party, whose objective has been to convince the public that the UK should withdraw from the EU. As time passes, it is likely that more single-issue oriented parties will emerge, for it appears that increasingly for some, voting is structured by one issue or other. Voting based on class and strong party preference has diminished, and the electorate is seen by one scholar as engaging in "judgmental voting," voting based less on broad swathes of policy than on specific issues and even the personalities of the party leaders.[23]

Third, there has been increased distortion in electoral outcomes, brought about by an increase in the number of candidates contesting parliamentary seats. One effect of a crowded field of candidates in a constituency race is that it is more difficult for one candidate, with SMSP, to win a popular majority. A second effect is that it rewards the two major parties by giving them a greater number of seats than they would receive were they apportioned seats in accordance with the popular vote.

Finally, a fourth knock-on effect of dissatisfaction with the two major parties is a decline in voter turnout. This decline prompted the Blair Government to undertake what amounted to an experiment with postal voting, one which made it possible for eligible voters starting in the 2001 general election to request and use a postal ballot without having to give a reason for doing so. As many as 12.1 percent of the UK's 44.2 million electors were issued postal ballots; those who completed and mailed them did so for a variety of reasons. It was convenient for them to vote this way, those in poor health were able to vote, and those who normally have difficulty finding the time to vote did so. Did postal voting have a measurable effect on increasing turnout in 2005? The Electoral Commission has concluded from its research that "turnout was edged upwards by increased postal voting but, for the most part, postal voters would have voted anyway."[24] From this one can only wonder whether this experiment will lead to a new way forward for elections in the UK and whether greater turnout will result.

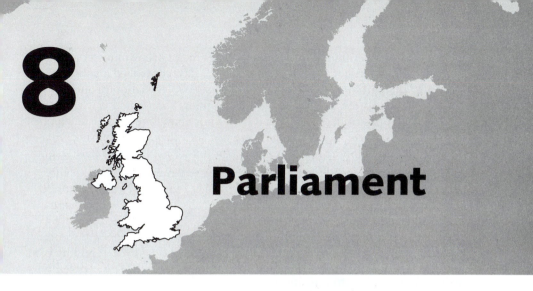

8

Parliament

Stretching for some distance along the banks of the River Thames in central London is the splendid Gothic Palace of Westminster, which until the sixteenth century was the chief residence of kings and ever since then has been the seat of Parliament. The House of Lords' chamber and offices are situated at one end of the palace, bounded by Victoria Tower, and the House of Commons' chamber and offices are located at the other end, bounded by the familiar clock tower housing Big Ben, whose massive bell tolls every quarter hour. Despite the fact that monarchs no longer live there, it is still called the Palace of Westminster, although one member of Parliament delighted in calling it the Palace of Varieties because of its 1,100 rooms, 100 staircases, 11 open courtyards, and 3 miles of passageways.[1]

It is one of history's ironies that Parliament today occupies the site that for five hundred years was occupied by England's kings and queens against whom it intermittently struggled. These struggles assumed epic proportions in the second half of the seventeenth century, when Parliament sentenced a king to death (Charles I, in 1649), governed England for the first four of the nearly twelve years when there was no monarch (1649–1660), declared the throne vacant after a king fled to France (James II, in 1688), and then insisted in law (in the Bill of Rights, in 1689) that monarchs not interfere with its rights. A parliamentary form of government began to take shape early in the eighteenth century, as cabinets, whose ministers were drawn from Parliament, gradually became a salient feature of government, and one minister who was selected by the king to chair its meetings in time came to be known as the prime minister.

Having finally prevailed in its struggles with the English monarchy, Parliament in the eighteenth century was "powerful but rarely assertive."[2] But rarely assertive became often assertive, and even spectacularly assertive, from 1832 to 1868. Parliament was then in its Golden Age, a period not seen before or since. The House of Commons at times became a fierce critic of the policies of the Government, that is, the policies of the prime minister and the cabinet. Parliament, not the government of the day, controlled a substantial portion of the parliamentary timetable of business; legislation proposed by the Government often was amended on the floor, abandoned if it encountered strong opposition, or defeated if it was not abandoned. Ministers were hounded from office. Governments were not sure they could muster a majority of votes to support their measures, for not all members of Parliament were members of a political party, some switched their party membership, and those who retained it could not always be counted on to toe the party line.

Like most golden ages, Parliament's was short lived. Ironically, it came to an end with passage of the Reform Act of 1867—ironically because the act nearly doubled the number of voters eligible to elect members to an institution that reformers thought would represent their best interests just as that institution was about to cede more influence to the executive side of government. Political parties quickly realized they had to organize themselves to appeal to the voters both nationally and at the constituency level and take a united party stand when voting in Parliament so that they could demonstrate that they delivered on their promises. Gradually, the cabinet reasserted control over Parliament, and voting cohesion increased markedly. Party votes, that is, votes on which 90 percent or more members of a party voted the same way, rose from 7 percent in 1860 to 76 percent in 1881.[3]

By the end of the nineteenth century and the beginning of the twentieth, this shift in the relationship between Parliament and the executive was all but complete, giving rise to what has come to be called the Westminster Model of Parliament. The cabinet had by then become the preeminent initiator of legislation. By then, too, political parties were becoming a *force majeur* in the Commons. The party in power controlled Parliament's timetable for scheduling its business; party whips exerted ever-greater influence over how their backbenchers voted; and Government ministers, supported by a parliamentary party majority, steered bills through Parliament from draft to enactment with backbenchers unable to shape the final form they took. In the meantime, individual parliamentarians were given few opportunities to introduce legislation of their own making, and parliamentary oversight of the executive was patchy and ineffective.

The received wisdom of the day about Parliament's functions was articulated by Leo Amery, a minister, when in his *Thoughts on the Constitution* he wrote, "The main task of Parliament is still what it was when first summoned, not to legislate or govern, but to secure full discussion and ventilation of all matters, legislative or administrative."[4] These words, penned in 1947, applied to the Parliament of Amery's day but can they be said to apply also to the Parliament of the early years of the twenty-first century? Apparently, they do. But today's Parliament does more than yesterday's. It could even be argued that the Westminster model is yesterday's model and needs to be replaced by a more fitting one.

What Is Parliament?

The Parliamentarians

Of the two houses of Parliament, only members of the Commons are elected, one from each constituency. Called members of Parliament (MPs), their numbers vary somewhat every two or three general elections as a result of boundary changes undertaken periodically to accommodate shifts in the population of electors. For example, there were 651 MPs in the 1992–1997 parliament, 659 in the two parliaments between 1997 and 2005, and 646 in the parliament that first sat in 2005. The Lords, by contrast, is a nonelected chamber. As of the end of 2006, it had 737 members, almost all of whom were peers. Approximately six hundred are life peers. These are individuals who have been appointed by the Queen on the advice of the prime minister and are "life" peers in the sense that after their death, their peerages cannot be passed on to their heirs. Another ninety-two are dukes, earls, viscounts, and other nobles who have inherited their peerages and are called hereditary peers. Among the life peers are twelve judicial peers, or Law Lords. These Lords of Appeal in Ordinary, as they are formally called, constitute the highest court of appeal in Britain (although they will no longer sit in the Lords once the judicial function of the Lords is transferred to a newly created Supreme Court in 2009). Life peers and hereditary peers are called Lords Temporal.

The remaining members of the House of Lords are not peers, but rather bishops and archbishops and are called Lords Spiritual. There are two archbishops and twenty-four bishops, all with the Church of England, and when they participate in debates in the Lords they normally confine their arguments to the social and moral dimensions of legislation. In the closing years of the twentieth century, there were more than 1,250 peers—approximately 750 hereditary peers and about 500 life peers. Now, however, the House of Lords is a slimmed-down version of its former self. In 1999, legislation reduced the number of hereditary peers from 758 to 92, and if the Labour Government acts on a pledge made in its 2005 election manifesto, the remaining 92 will be removed in time as well.

Tenure

The tenure of parliamentarians varies. Life peers serve for life, and bishops and archbishops only for the period they hold their bishoprics. The tenure of MPs, however, is the duration of a parliament. Parliament is an institution and a building. But a parliament—lowercase *p*—is a period of time, a period starting when parliamentarians convene for the first time following a general election and ending when Parliament is dissolved just before the next election. Because a general election may technically be held at any point, the tenure of an MP may be uncommonly short, as in 1974, when one general election was held in February and another the following October. Or it may

Speaking of . . .

Women in the House

All sorts of records have been broken by women in British politics in recent years. In 1979, Margaret Thatcher became the first woman prime minister; in the House of Commons, Betty Boothroyd was elected the first woman Speaker in 1992; and in the House of Lords, Baroness Hayman was elected the first woman Lord Speaker in 2006. In the meantime, the number of women elected to Parliament has risen sharply—from 41 in 1987 to three times that, 128, in 2005.

> "It was not until after the First World War that women, initially those aged 30 and over, won the complete franchise. And that only after winning the nation round by their efforts during the war."

Just one hundred years before the election of the 128, the suffragettes were engaged in intense struggles to win women the right to vote. A lot has happened since two suffragettes were jailed in 1905. *The Times* picks up the story from there:

"A century after the first suffragettes were sent to prison, women MPs complain that they are regularly patronised and insulted by their men colleagues. [Suffragettes] Christabel Pankhurst and Annie Kenney might look ruefully at the current position in Parliament as limited, yes, but also astonishing progress [has been made] in just 100 years. Arrested for a technical assault on the police after being thrown out of a Liberal Party meeting for demanding a statement about votes for women, the pair were jailed when they refused to pay a fine. Their actions, on October 13, 1905, were the first to attract national attention to the Women's Social and Political Union, founded two years earlier by Ms. Pankhurst and her mother, Emmeline, and home to the nascent militant suffrage movement. . . .

"The increasing militancy of the suffragist movement aimed itself at a Liberal Government under which no fewer than seven suffrage Bills were defeated. It was not until after the First World War that women, initially those aged 30 and over, won the complete franchise. And that only after winning the nation round by their efforts during the war. . . .

"Women may still be woefully under-represented at Westminster, but they are better represented than ever before. Of 659 MPs today [2004], 119 are women, 94 of these Labour. The Conservative Party's lamentable tally of 14 is set to slip still farther at the forthcoming general election [in 2005], in which women's votes will, as is now usual, be a key battleground.

"Yet concerns traditionally seen as female have never had a higher profile, with ministers from the Prime Minister and the Chancellor down championing flexible working and greater access to childcare. It is to the credit of the much disparaged women MPs that these issues enjoy the prominence they do, a status that must not be allowed to whither once the [general election] votes are counted this spring [of 2005]. And it is ultimately a tribute to those two women sent to prison just a short century ago."

Source: Reprinted with permission of *The Times* and NI Syndication Ltd.

last up to five years, the statutory limit, as in 1997, when Parliament was dissolved almost exactly five years after the previous general election. The vast majority of MPs represent safe seats, and if they run for reelection many times over, most are likely to enjoy long-term service in the Commons.

Legislative Powers

With certain exceptions, proposals for legislation are introduced, debated, and approved first in one body and then in the other. Because Commons-passed and Lords-passed versions of a bill must be identical before it can become law, when the two houses pass different versions there is considerable to-ing and fro-ing of the bill between the chambers as one house entreats the other to accept the compromise amendments proposed. These procedures are followed on many measures, but not all, for there are three limitations placed on the Lords' legislative powers. One is manifesto bills. The Salisbury convention—dating from 1945—dictates that the unelected House of Lords has no right to prevent the governing party in the elected House of Commons from enacting bills honoring commitments the party made in its election manifesto. Limitation number two is money bills, that is, taxing and spending bills. The Lords has only one month to agree to a money bill after the Commons has approved it. If it fails to agree, the bill automatically receives the Royal Assent.

Limitation three allows the Commons to ignore the Lords' refusal to approve other government-proposed measures the Commons has passed. All the Commons need do is pass the same bill again in the next session of parliament, after which the Speaker of the Commons may invoke the Parliament Acts of 1911 and 1949, and the bill then becomes law without the Lords' agreement. Looked at from a different perspective, this third limitation is a limitation on the Commons as well, for it allows the Lords to delay or threaten to delay the enactment of legislation for a period of at least thirteen months. This procedure helps to explain why the Speaker has invoked the Parliament Acts only four times since 1949; the Government may be more inclined to give in to the Lords and accept amendments that house insists upon than wait more than a year before the Parliament Acts are invoked. In this respect, the House of Lords has the upper hand. It has also long made a contribution as a revising chamber par excellence, offering not only substantive amendments but also procedural ones designed to clarify muddled legislative language and provide consistency with existing statutes. All things considered, however, the Commons almost always has the last word on legislation.

Accountability

Peers are not elected, and therefore they are not accountable to constituents, for they have none. If they align themselves with a political party (as most do) they will probably act in the interests of their party, although in the case of life peers, the party leader responsible for selecting them might regret it if they fail to vote or if they vote contrary to their leader's expectations. Other peers ignore party interests and act instead on what they regard as the interests of the nation as a whole or possibly the interests of an interest group or pressure group. There is no legal requirement that candidates for Parliament reside in the constituencies they hope to represent or to live there if they are elected. Nowadays, however, newly elected MPs are expected either to move to the constituency they represent or to establish a second home there to demonstrate their link to the constituency and their accountability to it.

Sessions, Space, and Staff

Not long ago MPs worked full-time, or nearly so, in banks, law firms, and other commercial establishments in London and only part-time in Westminster. Today, however, with the increase in their workloads, the vast majority of MPs work full-time in Parliament, a fact demonstrated in the number of days and hours that the Commons is in session. In the early years of the twenty-first century the Commons meets four to five days a week, and so too does the Lords. MPs are not expected to sit in the chamber all the time or even much of the time, however, for in addition to listening to and participating in debates, they have committee meetings to prepare for and attend; engagements to keep with ministers, constituents, and pressure group representatives; and a staff to consult and direct.

As the work of parliamentarians has increased, so too has their need for more office space. Although the Commons has responded to this need, it has taken no steps to enlarge the size of its chamber—even when necessity made it possible after a bomb destroyed it during the Second World War. The rebuilt chamber is no larger than it was before it was destroyed. So small is it that if all 646 MPs assembled for a debate, they would have to squeeze into a space designed for 346—or 427 if they spilled into the galleries that overlook the chamber. This is an arrangement that some regard as a logistical nightmare, but one which Winston Churchill thought lent intimacy to the proceedings.

As for office space, construction of Portcullis House was completed in 2000. Almost directly across from the clock tower housing Big Ben, this large building is the most dramatic example of the Commons' efforts to accommodate its needs. In the meantime, not only has the size of the Lords chamber remained the same, the need for further space for peers has led to a mix of limited leasing and conversion of office accommodation near Westminster. As it stands, the vast majority of peers have no offices whatsoever. They stake out a temporary claim to a chair in a quiet corner of one of several lounges in the House of Lords or in the Lords' library. Peers are not salaried (aside from party leaders), but they are provided a token daily attendance stipend and a modest secretarial allowance. No doubt some of the hardest-working among them cast an envious eye on the elected chamber, where MPs may employ two or three staff and can usually provide space for them to work.

Political Parties

When members of the two major parties gather in the Commons chamber, they take their places on two sets of several rows of benches, with the two sets facing each other. A central aisle divides the two sets of rows in the oblong chamber, with members of the party of Government to the right of the Speaker, members of the official Opposition party to the Speaker's left, and Liberal Democrats farther down on the left. That a debate is about to unfold becomes apparent to visitors in the public galleries above the chamber when ministers and members of the official Opposition shadow cabinet file into the chamber and take their places on the front benches opposite each other. The aisle stretching down the length of the chamber is bordered by a red line. Folk-lore has it that years ago, when MPs wore their swords in the chamber, during debate they were allowed to step up to the line and toe it but not cross it, and thus they had to settle their differences with those across the aisle not with their weapons but rather their minds and mouths. That MPs brought swords into the chamber is apocryphal, but there is a rule that when MPs speak from the front row of benches, they never cross the line. In the Lords, the party of Government and the Opposition party face each other as they do in the Commons, and although there are no lines down the chamber, a strictly enforced norm dictates that debate there proceed calmly, even dispassionately.

Party Discipline

Chapter 5 illustrated what length whips in the Commons go to gain the support of back-bench fence-sitters and naysayers on upcoming votes. Usually, MPs are so disciplined to vote the party line that only rarely is the party of government with an ample majority defeated on an important procedural motion. Party whips ply their skills of persuasion in the Lords as well. But enforcing party discipline poses a greater challenge there than in the Commons, for even though the whips appeal to peers' party loyalty, they can offer few incentives to ensure their support. Party loyalty is not slavish in the Lords, nor is it expected to be. Even if it were expected, the whips could not be assured of winning the day for their party, for no party possesses an overall majority, and 25 percent of the peers sit on the cross-benches to signify that they do not affiliate with a party.

Parliament and Government

Parliamentary government, as two scholars once put it, is "not government *by* Parliament, but government *through* Parliament."[5] [Emphasis this author's.] The Government—or the government of the day, as it is sometimes referred to—is the prime minister and the more than one hundred senior and junior ministers who are drawn exclusively from Parliament and who retain their seats in it. It would be impossible for them to govern without Parliament, however, for the legislation they propose must pass through Parliament and gain its approval before it can become law.

Not only is the Government drawn from both houses of Parliament, it is accountable to both houses. But because Government is primarily accountable to the elected chamber, it is the Commons from which prime ministers select the vast majority of ministers. The most senior ministers head the fifteen departments of government, such as Defence, the Home Office, and Health. All fifteen sit in the cabinet, a body of approximately twenty-two or twenty-three. Other ministers, of whom there are about eighty, are called junior ministers. They assist those senior ministers who head the departments. Ministers drawn from the Commons must appear before the Commons to answer for their work, and ministers from the Lords come before the Lords when they are called to account. (Ministers may not speak in a chamber of the house of which they are not a member.)

Their accountability assumes two forms. First, they respond to questions about the work of their departments that Opposition party spokespeople and backbenchers put to them at regular intervals in the chamber or in writing when members request a written reply. Second, they appear in their respective chambers whenever there are announcements to make about important developments taking place in their departments. In addition, they have responsibility for introducing Government bills and then piloting them through their respective chambers. MPs vote on legislation, but they do not confirm the prime minister's appointments to Government, ratify treaties, or make decisions about going to war. Those are crown prerogative decisions made by the cabinet, in which the driving force is almost always the prime minister. It is the prime minister, not Parliament, who makes the decision to hold a general election.

These are the key characteristics of Parliament. An examination of three key functions it performs conveys a fuller account of its workings—functions generic to most Western legislatures: representation, lawmaking, and oversight of the executive.

Representation

Context

Representation means different things to different people, including different legislators. That is why it is important to know what legislators mean when they use the term and how they act on any one of the various strands of the definition they identify. Studies of representation have accomplished this task by asking legislators a series of questions about how they carry out the job of representing and then allocating their responses to one of three role categories—trustee, delegate, and politico. The *trustee* role is reflected in Edmund Burke's classic formulation of the job of the representative in his address to the electors of Bristol after he won a seat there in 1774. The most-quoted line from this address leaves no question about Burke's conception of representation: "Your representative owes you, not his industry only, but his judgment;

and he betrays, instead of serving you, if he sacrifices it to your opinion." [6] This definition of the trustee role stands in contrast to the *delegate* role, which a legislator performs by giving expression to his or her perceptions of constituent opinion, whether or not he or she agrees with it. The delegate, then, *re*-presents the views presented by his or her constituents. The *politico* role is an it-all-depends role assigned to a legislator who acknowledges that he or she acts sometimes as a trustee and at other times as a delegate. Whether the politico acts as one or the other depends on the issue at hand.

Figure 8.1 shows the trustee, delegate, politico, and other representational roles of legislators, plus the type of constituency associated with each. It should be borne in mind that role types and the relationship between role type and constituency type are not as hard and fast as they might appear. Moreover, constituency types should not be regarded as mutually exclusive.

For many legislators, the electoral constituency is the most salient reference point when they give thought to how they will vote. But it is not the only reference point, and for some it is not the most important one. To the *partisan,* political party is the most important constituency; when he or she deliberates and votes in the legislative arena, the most important reference point is the party leadership. Other legislators regard the nation as a whole as their constituency and heed the opinions and interests of their electoral constituencies and political parties only when these are consistent with the interests of the nation as a whole. Interest groups are the primary reference point in representation for still other legislators. These legislators act for organized interests that operate in the electoral constituency or beyond by *re*-presenting their opinions and acting on their interests in the legislative arena.

Just as there are differences in the ways that legislators view their representational role and in the meanings they give to constituency, so also are there differences in the manner in which they perform the job of representing. One way is to debate and vote on legislation that furthers the interests of the constituency. That is what Edmund Burke had in mind when he spoke of representing the electors of Bristol. There was, however, little expectation in his day that MPs would take on what is now commonly known

---

Figure 8.1 Representational Roles and Constituency

REPRESENTATIONAL ROLE	CONSTITUENCY
Trustee	→ Nation
Delegate	→ Electoral constituency
Politico	→ Nation or electoral constituency
Partisan	→ Political party
Interest group agent	→ Interest group
Functional	→ Profession/occupation

Source: Roles taken from John C. Wahlke et al., *The Legislative System* (New York: John Wiley, 1962); and David Judge, *Representation: Theory and Practice in Britain* (London: Routledge, 1999).

as case work, the constituency service function of representation that legislators perform when they come to the aid of constituents who complain about inadequate street lighting, run-down public housing, and reduced postal services. Serving as ombudsman is a second way by which legislators represent constituents and has been ever since government began to assume a greater role in the lives of the body politic.

The House of Commons

Representation in the House of Commons has a national and an electoral constituency dimension. The national dimension is reflected in the voting behavior of MPs on bills formulated by the party the electorate has endorsed in the general election. The constituency dimension is seen in the assistance MPs provide their electoral constituencies overall or to individuals within them.

As for the national dimension, most MPs make political party and the nation their constituency. The two are almost always interchangeable. MPs are selected to stand for election by their local party, and they subscribe to the election manifesto drawn up by the national party. The election itself is fought along party lines in every constituency and focuses on national issues and policies. MPs sit in the Commons according to party, and they follow the party line when they vote, "more because they want to than because they feel they have to."[7] Moreover, their conception of what is in the national interest often coincides with the party's view, which explains why they joined the party in the first place and ran for election under its banner sometime later.

MPs adopt the role of partisan when they cast their votes. The opinions of their electoral constituencies on high-profile issues often reinforce the discipline imposed by the whips, and on rare occasions cause them to ignore the whips' instructions. However, not all bills are partisan: their contents may not create an obvious Labour-Conservative divide or drive parliamentarians from the major parties into opposing camps. For these bills the whips probably will not have assigned even a one-line whip. MPs nevertheless adopt a national view on these issues as well when they cast their votes, although the sentiments they perceive in their electoral constituencies could come into play.

Normally, the interests of the electoral constituency, the party, and the nation are seen as mutually inclusive, and thus only rarely do MPs regard a bill as pitting the interests of the electoral constituency against the interests of the other two. Almost all bills the Commons debates are introduced by Government ministers. These bills are always allocated time for debate, but on certain days in a parliamentary session a limited amount of time is given over to debating bills introduced by back-bench members of any party. These are called private members' bills (PMBs), of which only a limited number stand any chance of making it into law. Whatever their chances, even these bills, like bills introduced by the Government, deal with issues that are national in scope. They are not necessarily drafted with the electoral constituency in mind, but they are unlikely to arouse opposition there.

When MPs respond to the bells that ring out in Westminster summoning them to a vote, their whips expect them to follow the party line. How, then, do constituents expect to be represented? Those close to their constituents believe it is "not so much that they particularly want you to put their [policy] views over, but rather that when something goes wrong, there is somebody who will shout for them."[8] When MPs "shout" for their constituents by assisting them with problems they have with a government authority, most do it not to boost their fortunes at the next general election, but rather because they consider it an essential part of the job of representation. As one MP put it, "I do the constituent work, not for a political bonus, because there isn't a political bonus in it. I do it because it's part of the job."[9]

But not all MPs agree there is no bonus in constituency service work. Among them are incumbents from marginal seats who estimate that establishing a reputation as a diligent constituency ombudsman could attract anywhere from 500 to 1,500 additional votes. Such a cushion could make the difference between winning and losing on election day. Performing a constituency service function is not predicated upon how secure an incumbent's seat is, however, for research suggests that MPs who represent safe seats are as assiduous in helping their constituents as those who represent marginal seats.[10] What is more, whether or not an MP's seat is safe, a local party organization will look askance at an incumbent who fails to embrace the job of ombudsman by meeting regularly with constituents in what is called an "MP's surgery." Some have been so neglectful that they have incurred stern rebukes from their local party chieftains. A few have paid the ultimate price for their inattention by being de-selected, that is, denied an opportunity by the local party to serve again as its choice to fight the next election.

Thus, all MPs are expected to devote time to the constituency service function of representation. Some backbenchers even make it their first priority and emphasize one of two roles—that of Welfare Officer and Local Promoter. The role of Welfare Officer is performed by MPs who stress the importance of assisting individual constituents who have problems with government, such as housing, state pensions, and social security benefits. As one MP put it, his job was

> not so much representing the political views of constituents at Westminster, because you don't do that, but rather being able to bring the private trouble and complaint of a constituent to the notice of authority and get it put right.[11]

Local Promoters, on the other hand, are MPs who attach greater importance to addressing the collective concerns and needs of a constituency. These MPs press for a new wing on a local hospital, conduct a campaign to save a plant from closing, or try to persuade authorities to construct a road bypass.[12]

To summarize, MPs adopt one of several roles. When they debate and vote on legislation, they perform the role of partisan. Rarely do they regard the position of their party as contrary to the interests of the nation as a whole. On occasion, some take exception to their party's stance, and when that happens, they make a judgment independent of party and perform the role of trustee, even though their independent-mindedness is unlikely to ingratiate them with the party whips. Such action is prompted by their conception of what is in the national interest. However, it also could be derived from their perceptions of the preferences of their electoral constituents, although the role of delegate is not one that MPs enthusiastically or frequently embrace. MPs represent their electoral constituencies, but not by re-presenting their views in the arena of the Commons. Rather, they carry out this form of representation by interceding with government officials when individual constituents bring their problems to them or by mounting campaigns to promote the economic and social well-being of their constituencies as a whole.

The House of Lords

The representative function of the House of Lords has not been subjected to a great deal of empirical analysis by scholars, largely because the Lords is not seen as a representative body. Peers are not elected and are not required to account for their stewardship to anyone. Using such indices as education and occupation, they are far from representative of the British public, even less so than their counterparts in the Commons. Some might be tempted to conclude, facetiously, that they represent no one but themselves. To understand the representational role of peers, one might begin by formulating and testing hypotheses drawn from scattered anecdotal evidence. But quite apart from the methodological problems posed by anecdote-based research, there is a probability that reforms under consideration as this book went to press could give peers overt representational roles to perform for the first time since the House of Lords was created in the fourteenth century.

The first Lords' reform was undertaken in 1999, when the House of Lords Act reduced the number of hereditary peers from 759 to 92. Three further reforms were promised in Labour's 2005 election manifesto. The first of these three would remove the remaining ninety-two hereditary peers. The other two were not spelled out, but one would deal with the composition of a new House of Lords, and the other with how the membership would be formed—by election, by appointment, or by a combination of both. Presumably the powers and roles of a new House of Lords would remain the same as those in the old House of Lords. Whatever happens, the results probably will have an impact on how, or possibly even whether, a reformed House of Lords performs the function of representation.

Peers presently perform three representational roles: functional representation, interest group representation, and partisan representation. Functional representatives are those who have been appointed by the prime minister to represent the interests of two specific professions from which they are drawn, the ecclesiastical profession and the legal profession. These members take their seats on the cross-benches in the chamber to signify that they do not align themselves with any political party.

Those from the ecclesiastical profession are twenty-four bishops and two archbishops, all drawn from the Church of England. They concern themselves primarily with legislation affecting the Church of England, but they also debate moral and ethical issues, such as divorce and abortion and social issues that have moral and ethical overtones, such as political asylum and genetic engineering. They leave the Lords when they retire from their bishoprics and others are appointed in their place. The legal representatives are the Law Lords, or Lords of Appeal in Ordinary, who constitute the highest court in the United Kingdom. The Law Lords will no longer serve in the Lords once the judicial function of the Lords is divorced from the institution and transferred to a new Supreme Court in 2009. However, it is thought that those Law Lords who will have retired from the bench by then will choose to remain in the Lords and join other retired Law Lords to participate in debates dealing with the law (the judicial system, the administration of justice, and legal reform) and share their ideas on legal points arising from proposed legislation.

Interest group representatives are peers who act on behalf of one or more of a galaxy of interests reflected in the membership of the Lords. As one scholar has noted, "In part, it is a representative chamber, not according to any elective principle but simply through the accidental membership ... of doctors, practicing dentists, bee-keepers, opticians, accountants, lecturers, social workers, journalists, retailers, and so on." [13] It is not that peers are the agents of interest groups and act on their behalf because of the pressure *on* them. Rather, it is because of the pressure *in* them, pressure which has its origins in their membership in professional associations, their careers, their personal interests, and any causes they champion. Thus, on one occasion when there was a debate calling attention to issues pertaining to medical teaching and research in the National Health Service, among those who spoke up were

two former deans of university medical schools,

a practicing dentist,

a consultant obstetrician,

a consultant pediatrician,

a former general practitioner,

a former professor of nursing,

a former director of Age Concern (an interest group), and

the president of MENCAP (an interest group).[14]

Seeking alliances with peers friendly to their causes is not a new lobbying tactic of pressure groups. It was given greater emphasis starting in the 1970s and 1980s, when the Lords insisted on attaching numerous amendments to Government legislation and even defeated some major Government bills.

Most individuals whom the prime minister recommends to the Queen for appointment as peers are known supporters of the Conservative, Labour, or Liberal Democrat Parties nominated by their respective party leaders. When they are appointed, they are expected to be faithful to the party when they are called upon to cast their votes, for they are partisan representatives. But there is no certainty they will always toe the party line; even those appointed after spending many years in the Commons have no interest in supporting every party policy. Moreover, the whips hold few bargaining chips with which to persuade peers to support the party. Indeed, peers may choose to assert their independence by ignoring all manner of cajolery and coaxing. Although party discipline is weaker in the Lords than in the Commons and some peers may exhibit rebellious streaks, party cohesion in voting is nevertheless high for an institution that has prided itself on its independent-mindedness.

Lawmaking

Enacting bills into law is the oldest and most basic of the three functions of legislatures. Yet in the second half of the twentieth century, it was also the function most in decline. It still is. With few exceptions, legislatures are no longer the independent force they once were in initiating public policy. They instead look increasingly to the cohesive, resource-rich executive arms of government, which are eager to provide them ideas for legislation, establish their legislative priorities, set their agendas, and even help them guide bills through the legislative process. Table 8.1 depicts three types of legislatures: legislatures capable of making policy, legislatures capable of influencing policy but not making it, and those capable of neither.

Many legislatures, the British Parliament among them, are policy-influencing legislatures. One must approach these categories with caution, however, for there are times when one type of legislature tends to behave like another. For example, the U.S. Congress acts more like a policy-influencing legislature than a policy-making one in the political "honeymoon" period after a president is first elected and when his party controls both houses of

Table 8.1 Impact of Legislatures on Public Policy		
Policymaking	Policy Influencing	No Policy Influence
Legislature capable of formulating polices, amending and rejecting policies the executive proposes, and substituting its policies for the executive's.	Legislature capable of amending and rejecting policies the executive proposes, but will rarely formulate its own policies or substitute its own policies for the executive's.	Legislature not capable of formulating policies, amending and rejecting policies the executive proposes, or substituting its policies for the executive's.

Source: Adapted from Philip Norton, *Does Parliament Matter?* (London: Harvester Wheatsheaf, 1993), p. 50.

Congress. As for the British parliament, it has been inclined to act more like a policy-making body than a policy-influencing one when political parties are in coalition, as during the Second World War, than when the legislature is dominated by one party.

The House of Commons

The Government has the upper hand in driving its legislative program through the Commons—so much so that one former cabinet minister called governments of the day—any government—"elective dictatorships." [15] (He changed his tune, however, when he joined the cabinet again after his party was returned to power.) All of this is based on one overarching principle of British politics: the party that wins the general election is not only entitled to but is obliged to fulfill the pledges it made in its election manifesto. Moreover, those elected under the banner of the winning party are not ciphers, but rather are agents the voters have commissioned to help the Government enact its legislative program. However, not every bill the Government introduces is drawn from its manifesto and not every pledge it made in its manifesto, once transformed into a bill, contains provisions with which all party backbenchers agree. There are times, therefore, when there is underlying tension between backbenchers and their party leader, especially when the leader's popularity is beginning to sag in the opinion polls.

Back-bench rebellions have been on the rise since the 1970s and are possibly symptomatic of the disquietude that back-bench members have felt for some time over the increasing dominance of Government. In 1978, the House of Commons' Select Committee on Procedure warned that the balance of power between Government and Parliament "is now weighted in favour of the Government to a degree which arouses anxiety and is inimical to the proper working of our parliamentary democracy." [16] At the end of the 1992–1997 parliament, a majority of Conservative, Labour, and Liberal Democrat MPs polled agreed with the warning the committee had vented two decades before, and more than two thirds of that majority were certain that Government had become even more dominant in the intervening years. [17]

Government dominance comes into sharpest focus when ministers are steering bills through successive stages of the legislative process outlined in Table 8.2. A discussion of each stage is followed by an examination of whether back-bench MPs and opposition parties have any impact on legislative policymaking.

Government Bills

Several types of bills are introduced every parliamentary session, but nearly all—and certainly the most important ones—are public bills introduced by Government ministers. Government bills have priority in legislative scheduling and, like other bills, pass through at least five stages before they are prepared for the Royal Assent or are referred to the Lords for consideration. The cabinet, under the leadership of the prime minister, normally establishes the

Table 8.2	The Legislative Process in the Commons
Stage	Significance
FIRST READING	The minister introduces the bill. Its title is read, there is no debate, and a vote to proceed to the next stage is agreed to.
SECOND READING	Debate is held on the "principles" of the bill, i.e., its purpose and its major provisions. No amendments are allowed, but if a bill is controversial, a vote is usually taken to refer it to a standing committee.
COMMITTEE*	A standing committee is formed to examine the bill clause by clause.
	The committee then votes to report the bill to the Commons, along with any amendments it has approved.
REPORT	The committee reports the bill to the Commons, along with any amendments. The bill and any amendments are debated and voted on.
THIRD READING	The bill and any amendments agreed to in the Report Stage are put to a vote. No further amendments may be proposed at this stage.
LORDS' AMENDMENTS	If the House of Lords already has acted on the bill, any amendments it might have approved will be debated and put to a vote.

*Usually, this stage occurs in a committee room; all other stages occur in the chamber.
Source: Robert Rogers and Rhodri: Walters, *How Paliament Works*, 5th ed. (Harlow: Pearson, 2004), 189–205.

Government's legislative priorities. Three key players then become involved in legislative scheduling—the prime minister, the leader of the House of Commons, and the Government chief whip. The chief whip directs the whips to sound out backbenchers for their reactions to upcoming bills, and the leader of the house and the chief whip develop the weekly timetable after consulting their counterparts in the Opposition party through a process known as "the usual channels." If a bill is controversial, determining when to debate it can be crucial. The chief whip thus plays a major role in the decision and could recommend to the prime minister and leader of the House that the bill be delayed until the whips can win over those backbenchers who are undecided.

Once the Government has prepared a bill for introduction, it normally takes several weeks to reach the final stage of consideration in the Commons. The process starts with the First Reading. This stage is perfunctory and lasts no more than a few minutes as the minister introduces the bill and the clerk of the Commons reads out its title. Far from perfunctory is the Second Reading. This occurs two or three weeks later and is the first and possibly most important test for the Government, for this is when the principles and major provisions of the bill are debated. What took three minutes to accomplish in the First Reading could take as many as three days to complete in the Second Reading for a bill that is especially controversial. Amendments are not permitted at this juncture. The whips are particularly diligent in enforcing party discipline, for if there is a vote on whether to send the bill to the next stage and it is defeated, the bill dies. Rejection at this stage is rare, however, so rare that in the twentieth century it happened only three times. But the whips take nothing for granted. They will have issued a three-line whip the week before and they will be on the lookout for telltale signs of contrariness on the back benches.

Having survived the Second Reading, the bill almost always is referred to a standing committee for the Committee Stage. (One exception is the Terrorism Bill of 2005. It was referred to the Committee of the Whole, that is, to the floor of the House of Commons, for debate because of the high-profile nature of the issue.) Most standing committees in the British Parliament are ad hoc and temporary, just the opposite of committees in the U.S. Congress. In Westminster, a standing committee is created for one bill only and then is dissolved after it has completed its work on the measure. The permanent all-party Committee of Selection appoints twenty to twenty-five members to the standing committee, with the decision about how many to appoint from each party based on the relative strength of each in the Commons. A majority are backbenchers, most of whom are chosen because of their interest in and knowledge of the bill's subject matter. Rounding out the rest on the committee are one or more junior ministers from the department that will implement the bill after it has been enacted, their Opposition party counterparts, and a Government whip and an Opposition whip. A senior backbencher chairs the committee and may be from any party but must remain impartial throughout the proceedings. The Committee Stage can last anywhere from one short meeting to numerous protracted sittings spread out over many weeks.

The Government is almost always assured of success at the Committee Stage, for voting on amendments usually follows party lines. The minister might have to appease opponents of the bill in committee—or anticipate opposition later in the chamber—by accepting amendments in committee that accommodate backbenchers from the ruling party who voiced their discontent during the Second Reading or in committee. If discontent surfaces at either stage, the bill's future could be in doubt, especially if the Government's majority is slim, as it was from 1992 to 1997, during the Major Government. It is rare when a committee approves amendments contrary to the Government's liking, but if it does, the minister and the whips are certain to try to overturn them at the Report Stage.

Once the committee has finished its deliberations, the measure moves on to the Report Stage. The committee chair reports the bill to the Commons, and a minister then manages the bill on the floor. Amendments agreed to in committee are debated and put to a vote. Also debated are new amendments, among them ones offered by committee members who might not have been given the time to propose them in committee. This stage in the bill's consideration can last anywhere from a few minutes to a few days, depending on how complex and controversial the measure is.

The Third Reading follows. At this stage the amended bill is debated, usually immediately after the Report Stage. Debates often are brief and can be acrimonious, depending again on how controversial the bill is. Amendments are out of order during the Third Reading. But probably none is necessary at this stage, for to avert the bill's defeat, the whips would have instructed the minister to accept certain amendments from backbenchers to overcome some of their unhappiness with—and their opposition to—the bill's provisions at the Committee Stage or Report Stage. Only rarely has a measure proceeded through the previous four stages and then met its demise at the Third Reading. The last time it happened was in 1977.

Once the bill has been agreed to on the Third Reading, it is referred to the House of Lords. However, if the Lords already has approved the bill with amendments, the Commons next considers the Lords' amendments. The Commons then has four options: it can accept the Lords' amendments, amend the Lords' amendments, substitute one or more of the Lords' amendments with its own, or reject all of the Lords' amendments outright. If the Commons disagrees with any of the Lords' amendments, the Commons-passed bill is returned to the Lords, and the Lords normally accepts the bill as referred. On occasion, however, the Lords insists on its amendments being retained. When that happens and the Commons rejects them again, the bill shuttles back and forth until both houses can agree on one version. Once this is done, the bill is printed in its final form and prepared for the Royal Assent.

One variation on the theme of the Commons' consideration of legislation is the review by an ad hoc committee, a select committee, or a joint committee of a bill in draft form before the draft becomes a formal bill and is introduced in either chamber. An experiment initiated by the Blair Government soon after it took power in 1997, a draft of a bill is referred to a committee that examines it in some depth. If it spots weak sections in it, it points them out and suggests improvements. About 10 percent of Government bills from 1997 to 2003 were examined in draft form. As helpful as this pre-legislative review process is, several factors militate against a higher percentage of bills receiving the same treatment. One is the legislative clock, for the process can consume more time than the Government anticipated and slow efforts to clear the legislative pipeline before the end of the parliamentary session.

"Heckling the Steamroller"

Governments normally have little difficulty defeating those who oppose them in Parliament. Those who stand up to the government of the day, whether members of an opposition party or the occasionally disaffected from the ruling party, can do little more than "heckle the steamroller," as one Labour backbencher once put it.[18] For several reasons, the Government is almost certain to prevail. First, the arithmetic of power ensures that the government of the day almost always has the numbers to support its position, and its whips are diligent in consolidating that support. Second, the

Committee of Selection, which is made up of nine MPs, six or seven of whom are party whips, appoints as members of standing committees backbenchers certain to be loyal to their party when controversial legislation is being considered. Third, if a bill's progress is slowed, the minister can propose a *guillotine* motion in the Commons to cut short the time available to consider the bill in committee and at later stages. Fourth, ministers, with the assistance of the whips, can mount aggressive campaigns to overturn on the floor those amendments approved in committee that are not to the Government's liking.

Heckling the steamroller does not bring it to a stop, but it might slow its progress by diverting the driver's attention. Indeed, it is the driver's attention that backbenchers are trying to get when they sign an early day motion (EDM). Although it is highly unlikely to have much effect, as EDMs are very rarely debated, once one has been circulated and signed, it is printed in the Commons' *Daily Order Paper* with the names of the signatories for all to read—the party leadership included. Most EDMs arouse little interest, but if a majority of backbenchers of the party in power raise concerns about an issue in an upcoming bill, it does more than catch the eye of the Government chief whip. To ward off defeat of the bill, the whips can be persuaded to agree to amendments to accommodate the concerns of the disaffected before the bill proceeds to the next stage of deliberation. However, if the Government refuses to entertain amendments, with the names of the disgruntled and the probable reasons for their frustration in the open, the whips know whom to target and on which issues to focus when they try to bring them around to the Government's position.

Every now and again, backbenchers have a chance to effect changes in the provisions of a Government bill through an EDM. What chance, however, do they have to bring about change by introducing a bill of their own? If given the chance, are their bills likely to pass? The answer to the first question is "rarely"; the answer to the second is "not very." Bills introduced by backbenchers are private members' bills (PMBs). Like Government bills, PMBs are public bills. They are *Private* because backbenchers are private members, that is, they are not members of the Government. They are given the right to introduce a bill if they are among the top twenty whose number is drawn from a box in a kind of lottery competition at the beginning of every parliamentary session. Because the Government absorbs so much of the legislative timetable for its bills, little time is left for PMBs. Usually the first seven have the best chance of receiving consideration.

However, their fate and the fate of the PMBs that remain hinge on whether the Government chooses to support them. If the Government opposes a bill, it is sure to fail. The Government can kill the bill by arranging for a backbencher to rob it of what little time it has been allotted by filibustering it to death. Or the Government could instruct a minister to accept wrecking amendments (amendments offered by the bill's opponents that are designed to dilute its appeal), and then deny it the extra time it needs to progress beyond that point. On the other hand, if the Government supports a PMB, it is sure to release the additional time it needs. This the Government will do if a bill tidies up anomalies in existing legislation (often these are recommended by the Government to MPs in search of a bill to introduce), if it is minor and noncontroversial, or if it is so controversial that the Government may favor it but be reluctant to promote it. Examples of the latter are bills that abolished the death penalty and legalized abortion.

There are Government bills and PMBs, but there are no such things as Opposition party bills. The closest an opposition party can come to making a law is when one of its backbenchers, by the luck of the draw, introduces a PMB. The problem for an opposition party is that it operates under the continuous handicap of being in the minority. The only chance it has to have an impact on legislation is if it succeeds in amending a bill in committee or on the floor. Opposition parties are left to influence the course of legislation through four debate tactics. One, which was covered in chapter 5, is questioning ministers when they have their turn at the dispatch box in the Commons. The remaining three are extended debates following both the Queen's Speech and the Budget Statement and day-long debates on special "Opposition Days."

Debates of an extended nature become available to the opposition twice a year. The first is held on the Queen's Speech, a Government-prepared text read by the Queen in the House of Lords at the State Opening of Parliament that outlines the Government's legislative objectives for the parliamentary session. The debate lasts four or five days, after which the Opposition is entitled to offer one or two amendments. They are usually wrecking amendments, and votes cast in their support are treated as motions of no confidence. Should the Government lose a vote, it is obliged to resign or call a new election. The last time a motion of no confidence carried following a monarch's address was in 1924, when the Labour and Liberal Parties toppled the Conservative minority Government of Stanley Baldwin and Labour's Ramsay McDonald succeeded him as prime minister.

The next opportunity for an extended debate occurs usually in March, just after the chancellor of the exchequer has delivered his budget statement to the Commons. The statement gives the chancellor a chance to make pronouncements on the state of the economy and the government's finances and to urge the Commons to agree to various tax proposals. After the chancellor has finished speaking, it is customary for the leader of the Opposition to respond and, predictably, find fault with the chancellor's assumptions; question the wisdom of the proposed tax changes; and trumpet the virtues of the policies of the official Opposition. Three or four days of debate on the budget follow, and at their conclusion between fifty and sixty motions are put to a vote to give effect to the chancellor's proposals. The motions give opposition parties a chance to focus on a handful that they find the most disagreeable, although the outcome of the vote is never in doubt.

Spread fairly evenly through the session are twenty days set aside for two opposition parties to debate with Government ministers on issues on which the opposition parties wish to be heard. These are called Opposition Days, of which the lion's share—normally seventeen—are reserved for the official Opposition and the remaining three for the second largest opposition party, which since 1988 has been the Liberal Democrats. An opposition spokesperson opens each debate by denouncing the Government's failure to perform adequately on the issue at hand, and then his or her counterpart from the ministerial ranks rises to offer a spirited defense. The debate revolves around two motions, one offered by the shadow minister and the other by the minister. For example, the opposition spokesperson for health opens with a motion condemning the Government for its alleged failure to keep its pledge to the voters to reduce waiting lists for patients requiring treatment by the National Health Service. A minister from the Department of Health counters with a motion to amend the motion by affirming the Commons' confidence in the Government to deal with the problem. The minister's motion is certain to carry, but the opposition on this and future Opposition Days hammers away at the Government's alleged incompetence in various policy realms in an attempt to embarrass the Government. If the exchanges draw the attention of the media, as the opposition hopes, they could shake the public's confidence. Moreover, if the Government also is shaken, it could decide to review and possibly think again about its policies and procedures to deflect charges from opposition parties on the same issue on later occasions.

The House of Lords

As discussed earlier in this chapter, money bills and bills formulated to honor the winning party's manifesto commitments are given relatively free passage through the House of Lords. The same cannot be said for some other measures. The Lords gives many Commons-passed measures a second sober look and, in keeping with its reputation as a revising chamber of considerable stature, seeks to leave its imprint on the bill by successfully entreating the Commons to accept amendments it has approved. A majority of these amendments tidy up unclear and confusing language. On other measures, however, the Lords may take exception to more than language and refuse to accept what the Commons proposes. It is then that the government of the day may have to negotiate the differences or even accept defeat.

The Lord Speaker, as the Speaker of the House of Lords has been called since 2006, presides over the Lords from the woolsack (a large cushion filled with strands of wool from Britain and the Commonwealth nations), has no cause to shout "Order! Order!" as his counterpart, the Speaker of the House of Commons, often must. Debates in the Lords are far more restrained and often are delivered in the measured tones of a lecturer holding forth in a university lecture hall. This far more relaxed, less frenzied style of debate in the Lords is in part a function of the absence of time constraints and in part the less interventionist role of party leaders. Parliamentary rules impose few time strictures on debate and thus foster an environment conducive to unhurried, thoughtful argumentation. The lack of rigid time constraints also allows peers more opportunities to propose and debate amendments than their counterparts in the Commons. Whips in the House of Lords, although keen to speed bills on their way to passage and achieve party cohesiveness in the process, tolerate the slow pace and threats from colleagues to depart from the party line. After all, whips in the Lords are peers too, and they can only hope that the arguments made in debate will bring the naysayers around to the party's position.

Because the Commons is the elected chamber, convention dictates that manifesto bills, money bills, and most major bills that are controversial are introduced and considered there first. In the meantime, the Lords considers relatively minor measures at the beginning of a session. As the session wears on, and the Commons passes one controversial measure after another, a bottleneck of Commons-passed bills is created in the Lords; as a result, some bills are left behind because peers have no time to consider them before the end of the session. Bills may not become law unless both houses agree to them by the end of the session, so scheduling decisions are important. For that reason the leader of the Commons and leader of the Lords coordinate the work of their respective houses. In a session with a particularly heavy workload, the leaders are very likely to decide that this convention has to be relaxed and thus some major bills are introduced and considered first in the Lords.

The legislative process in the Lords is nearly identical to that in the Commons. A bill is introduced and given a First Reading. A Second Reading follows, providing peers time to debate the bill's principles. Amendments are considered next, in the Committee Stage, after which the bill is reported. At the Third Reading, a vote is taken on the final version, but not before further amendments are put to a vote. Offering amendments at the Third Reading is prohibited in the Commons. It is one of three major differences in the legislative process between the houses, each of which warrants a brief examination.

Motions to cut, or guillotine, debate are permitted in the Commons but not in the Lords. Resorting to such a tactic, even if permitted by the rules, would be repugnant to peers, who cherish time for debate that is relatively unrestricted. Yet this freedom from constraint rarely tempts peers to engage in filibusters, principally because repeated abuse of the privilege to speak for a reasonable period could lead to a tightening of the rules.

In addition to guillotine motions, there are two other differences in the legislative process between the Lords and the Commons that affect the freedom of debate. They appear at two junctures in the process—at Committee Stage and at the Third Reading Stage. Committee Stage in the Lords contrasts sharply with Committee Stage in the Commons, for whereas bills in the Commons are almost always considered in standing committee, in the Lords, they are considered by the Committee of the Whole. This means that debate on a bill's provisions takes place on the floor of the chamber, peers in attendance automatically become members of the committee, and any who wish to introduce amendments may do so and expect them to be debated. Thus, while whips in the tightly controlled standing committees of the Commons can ward off unwelcome amendments from backbenchers, whips in the Lords are confronted with a more difficult challenge: they have no idea which peers will show up, whether they will offer amendments, or how they will vote.

As already noted, amendments may be offered at the Third Reading Stage in the Lords. Thus, peers are provided an opportunity denied their counterparts in the Commons to offer substantive and procedural amendments to a bill before the minister managing the bill proposes a motion that "the bill do now pass." Peers also use this stage to offer amendments that have the intent of fine tuning a bill by dispelling any lingering doubts about its purpose or by making its language more intelligible.

Revising legislation is regarded as the Lords' most important contribution to Parliament's lawmaking function. In an especially busy session, peers may introduce as many as three thousand amendments.[19] As one scholar put it, "If the productivity of the House were to be measured in terms of the number of amendments passed, then its record is impressive."[20] Amendments emanate from three sources—individual peers, opposition parties, and the party of government. Identifying what proportion of the mix can be credited to each is difficult, but according to one study, the majority originated with the Government, and of these, most were agreed to.[21]

Amendments designed to correct technical imperfections, such as clarifying legislative language, are dealt with cooperatively between the two houses. The same cannot be said of most substantive amendments. Thus, ministers hope that peers will defeat those the Government deems unwelcome. But if they do attract widespread support in the chamber, ministers generally accept them, for mounting an assault on the amendments delays a bill's enactment or even can lead to its demise. Giving in to these amendments, however, does not necessarily mean that ministers are abandoning the Government's position. Once the bill bearing the Lords-passed amendments is returned to the Commons, Government whips press backbenchers to reject them.

In the end, it is not unusual for the Lords to bow to the Commons. Since the 1970s, however, it has inflicted an increasing number of defeats on the government of the day by insisting on amendments that the Government opposes but has chosen not to overturn in the Commons for the sake of expediting a bill's passage. As Table 8.3 demonstrates, the number of Government climb-downs has risen steadily from 26 in the Heath Government in the 1970s to about five times that many—128—in Blair's first Government and more than nine times that in Blair's second Government.

Ironically perhaps, defeats were inflicted on Conservative Governments from 1970 to 1974 and from 1979 to 1997, years when there were more Conservative peers than peers of any other single party. Equally ironic is the great number of defeats that the Blair Government suffered from 1997

Table 8.3	Government Defeats in the Lords
Parliament	Number of Defeats
1970–1974 (Heath)	26
1979–1983 (Thatcher)	45
1983–1987 (Thatcher)	62
1987–1992 (Thatcher/Major)	72
1992–1997 (Major)	56
1997–2001 (Blair)	128
2001–2005 (Blair)	245

Sources: For 1970–1974 and 1979–2001: Robert Rogers and Rhodri Walters, *How Parliament Works*, 5th ed. (London: Pearson, 2004), pp. 215–216. For 2001–2005, written communication from Rhodri Walters to this author.

through 2005, despite Blair's appointment of a host of new Labour peers and the expulsion of more than 650 hereditary, primarily Conservative peers in a move to reform the Lords. One can attribute this lack of party loyalty during Conservative Governments to the independent-mindedness of peers. As two high-ranking aides in Parliament have suggested, "Some of the defeats are on matters of principle that command some support from the ranks of back-benchers in the Commons and from the country at large." For that reason, they continued, the Government "accepts amendments of this kind graciously rather than risk unnecessary unpopularity for itself among its own supporters both inside and outside Parliament."[22]

The tangle of rules governing Parliament's lawmaking function can be said to be politically neutral. Not so the results of their use, for the arithmetic of power means that Governments can almost always count on having their way, especially in the Commons. Parliament can be likened to "a bridge between bills and laws."[23] Governments might encounter checkpoints on the bridge, but there are few obstacles even when their numbers in the Commons dwindle to a less-than-comfortable overall majority. Whatever the margin, only rarely do members stage a direct confrontation with their party leaders to urge them to abandon positions they judge to be politically untenable. When they do, it is behind closed doors where they can speak with candor. But these confrontations are invariably leaked to the press and can amount to a series of politically self-inflicted wounds. British voters have little patience with a party that is divided and even less patience if the divided party is the party of government.

Oversight

Context

Work on a bill does not grind to a halt once it is enacted into law. The next step is implementation, and having devoted time and energy to debating and then passing the bill, legislators try to keep an eye on the progress of the program or policy that the new law has created. Will its objectives be met? Is it being administered effectively and efficiently? What should be done to overcome any problems that might arise? Are there major unexamined aspects of public policy that require attention? These are questions that loom large in the minds of at least some legislators once a bill has been passed, especially if it has sparked controversy.

Apart from new programs and policies, how well administered are programs and policies generally, whether new or old and whether based on law or executive discretion? There are many demands competing for legislators' time; keeping an eye on how well the executive administers programs and policies is not normally a high priority unless legislators can gain politically from doing so. Thus, if ever-increasing numbers of constituents complain to their legislators about repeated problems they are having with the same program of government, or if legislators learn that a department has wasted massive amounts of taxpayers' money on a project whose worth was questioned from the start, they would probably seize the opportunity to investigate.

When legislators investigate, they involve themselves in one or more of these activities—oversight, supervision, or control. Although "oversight" is used here to refer to all three activities, oversight in its narrowest sense is the most modest form of action legislators take. It means merely to see over or monitor the way in which a program or policy is carried out. When oversight reveals a problem that greatly concerns legislators, they ratchet up their involvement by engaging in supervision. This process includes calling upon the executive to institute changes in the administration of the program or policy and then evaluating the effects of the changes. Supervision also can take the form of legislators reviewing all or parts of a bill to call attention to its deficiencies before they approve it or even before it is introduced.

Control is a third level of activity. There might be so many deficiencies in how a program or policy has been implemented that legislators demand that the executive devise strategies to overcome them or risk having their budget cut in the next fiscal year. Legislators might even threaten to revamp the law itself. Demands and threats such as these are made from time to time by key members of the U.S. Congress in their relations with the executive branch. If members of most other Western democratic legislatures acted similarly, their demands and threats would fall on deaf ears, for they have little or no authority to control the executive body by withholding funds or initiating other sanctions to make it comply with their wishes.

Yet many legislatures are capable of engaging in varying degrees of oversight and supervision, the British Parliament among them. However, because political party in Britain is the dominant factor in decision making, to what extent do political party considerations dictate what the Commons oversees and in what depth? For example, might legislators from the party in power be dissuaded from overseeing a department, executive agency, or regulatory body if they have reason to think that their findings could embarrass the governing party? If they do think that, why would Parliament be inclined to engage in oversight in the first place?

The House of Commons

Until the last quarter of the twentieth century the Commons' oversight of the executive was superficial and fitful. Attempts were made to monitor by putting oral and written questions to ministers, initiating and signing EDMs, and challenging the Government on Opposition Days. But these efforts had little impact. Somewhat more effective was the work of several select committees commissioned by the Commons to scrutinize the executive. These developed haphazardly, their work was sporadic and patchy, and their remit was so limited that large swathes of executive activity escaped Parliament's scrutiny. To overcome weaknesses in its oversight capability, the Commons introduced two key reforms in the 1970s and 1980s. It created select committees to scrutinize the ways every department of government administered policies, and it established the National Audit Office to assist another select committee, the Public Accounts Committee, in its review of public spending. A third key reform was instituted by the Commons and the Lords together when they created the Joint Committee on Statutory Instruments to enhance Parliament's oversight of delegated legislation.

Administering Programs and Policies

The Commons made a significant overhaul in its infrastructure for overseeing the executive in 1979 when it replaced an assortment of moribund select committees with a string of departmental select committees. From that day to the present, a select committee has been in place to "examine the expenditure, administration and policy" of every department of government, as well as each department's executive agencies and any regulatory units that fall under the jurisdiction of each. Today, there are fifteen departmental select committees—one to oversee each of the fifteen departments.

Whereas most Commons' standing committees are temporary creations, select committees have permanent status. The same members—all backbenchers—remain on them for the duration of a parliament. The committees are small; most have eleven members, and the party divisions on each reflect the party divisions in the Commons. The Committee of Selection, some members of which are whips, decides who sits on the select committees but not who chairs them. That decision is left to each committee. A chair is drawn from within the ranks of each committee; usually it is a colleague from the party in power, although it is not uncommon for it to be an opposition party MP. Once appointed, committee members are supported by a full-time staff of five or six; the committee can augment this number by contracting for the assistance of outside specialist advisers.

Because select committee members work together closely over the life of a parliament, they usually defer to the norm of holding partisan instincts in check when choosing issues to investigate, determining which strategies to adopt, and deciding what line of questioning to pursue with ministers, civil servants, and others who appear before them. So prized is committee consensus that a chair will avoid dividing committee members by calling for votes or encouraging minority reports as members ponder what findings to include and recommendations to make in reports to the Commons. These findings and recommendations are referred to the relevant department. A report that is less than unanimously supported, they realize, carries little weight with the executive.

In addition to departmental select committees, there are several select committees whose jurisdictions cut across the boundaries of various departments. One is the Public Accounts Committee, discussed in the next section. There is also the Environmental Audit Committee, which assesses the progress made by the government in achieving standards established to protect the environment. Another is the Public Administration Committee, which has investigated such crosscutting issues as the powers and conduct of Government ministers and the proper roles of the prime minister's press officers and special advisers and their relationships with their opposite numbers in the departments. Still another is the European Scrutiny Committee, which examines EU policies and proposed European Community laws (about which more is taken up in chapter 13). Of all the select committees that deal with crosscutting issues, the one that stands out is the Liaison Committee. This committee, whose members are the chairs of approximately thirty other select committees, is a housekeeping committee that sees to the administrative needs of the other select committees. What makes it stand out is that since 2002, the prime minister has subjected himself to in-depth questioning twice a year by its members on a variety of domestic and foreign affairs issues in sessions lasting two-and-a-half hours.

So coveted have assignments to departmental committees become in recent years that the number lobbying for seats has far exceeded the number of slots available. This popularity derives in part from the reputations the committees have achieved from probing such issues as the Home Office's response to the rise in the number of asylum-seekers, the use and effects of setting performance targets in all sectors of government, and the adequacy of the Ministry of Defence's provision of military gear and ammunition for British troops fighting in Iraq.

Job satisfaction is another reason why committee assignments are sought. First, committee members are at liberty to probe whatever policy issues they wish and to determine what methods of investigation to employ. Second, these committees offer backbenchers an effective way to acquire insights into the departmental policies they investigate. Third, because their findings and recommendations have attracted media coverage, these committees have raised the public's awareness and understanding of certain major issues. Fourth, their work allows members brief moments of national exposure. And fifth, perhaps the greatest source of satisfaction of all is getting an executive body's attention, for after a committee has submitted its report, the executive, that is, a department or agency, or even No. 10 Downing Street, is expected to respond to its recommendations within two months. Committee members know that at the very least their reports are read by those ministers whose departments are under scrutiny.

Having read their reports, do ministers act on their recommendations? There is no requirement that they do so. On the other hand, they dare not risk alienating their party colleagues on the back benches. This is how two senior officers of Parliament summarized the impact of committee reports:

> If the committee has put forward challenging recommendations, the government is likely to be cautious rather than to accept them right away. But the "delayed drop" effect of select committee reports should never be underestimated. Ambitious recommendations may change the whole public debate on a subject; they may be taken up by public bodies and pressure groups; and months (or sometimes two or three years) later they may contribute substantially to a major shift in government policy. Similarly, the effect of justified criticism may not be immediately apparent; but a department may be quietly changing its procedures to avoid making the same mistake again.[24]

Departmental select committees and crosscutting committees have made it possible for the Commons to engage in systematic and comprehensive oversight. Yet there are several obstacles that prevent these committees from reaching their full potential. Not surprisingly, one is the executive. For example, the Blair Government vetoed two proposals put to it by the Liaison Committee. One would have given more time to the chairs of select committees to report their findings on the floor of the Commons; the other would have made it possible to offer debatable motions permitting the Commons to endorse select committee reports. These proposals would have contributed to parliamentarians' awareness and understanding of specific cases and the causes of maladministration and probably would have increased the pressure on Government to act on the committees' recommendations—all reasons, no doubt, why the Government turned the proposals down.

The other obstacle preventing departmental select committees from reaching their full potential is the Commons itself. In 2002 a vote was taken on a motion that provided for an alternative to the Committee of Selection for choosing the members of departmental select committees. Those who spoke for the motion argued that Government whips who sit on the Committee of Selection are bound to choose backbenchers who they believe will refrain from embarrassing the Government by finding fault with its programs and policies. Most of those who spoke in the debate argued for a more open system of selection. When a vote was held, however, the motion was defeated by a narrow margin, with a large minority of Labour MPs voting against it. Robin Cook, then leader of the House, had argued for this change and explained what he thought was the reason for its defeat:

> Most MPs are deeply ambivalent about their primary role. I include myself in that case of confused identity. MPs usually recognize that somewhere in their job description is a responsibility to protect the privileges and independence of Parliament. At the same time all MPs

bar one [an Independent] are elected on a party ticket and came to Westminster not as independents but as partisans. This dual identity of MPs ensures a constant struggle between the perception of the role of Parliament and their sense of belonging to the party faction. On this vote a large minority of Labour MPs resolved that they would rather back control of committee membership by party than Parliament.[25]

Most backbenchers agree that departmental and crosscutting select committees have introduced greater rigor in the Commons' oversight of the executive. Yet they also are aware that the demands placed on backbenchers are so great that they have little time for the job of oversight. Add to this the frustration of extracting information from ministers and civil servants who are "economical with the truth," as one official once put it. Moreover, the skeletal force of professionals on these committees is no match for the army of civil servants who work for a department. The choice of issues to investigate is seen as another shortcoming. So controversial are some that committees studiously avoid them lest they be criticized for being partisan. Finally, committees focus on issues of policy implementation often to the neglect of acting on another aspect of their jurisdictional responsibilities—examining departmental expenditures. Perhaps they look upon this part of their remit as politically unrewarding and are not embarrassed to admit that the Public Accounts Committee is far more suited than they to accomplishing this task.

Spending Public Funds

The Public Accounts Committee is Parliament's financial watchdog. Its job is to determine whether funds allocated to departments have been used in a manner consistent with what Parliament has authorized and whether they have been spent efficiently and effectively. The committee has functioned since 1861, but it was not until 1983 that the Commons shored up the committee's function of monitoring executive spending by setting up an auditing arm external to the executive side of government called the National Audit Office (NAO). Today, the sixteen members of the committee, which has always been chaired by a backbencher from the official Opposition, are supported by teams of NAO auditors and investigators.

The law gives NAO auditors access to departmental accounts, and they work under the direction of the comptroller and auditor general (C&AG), an officer of the Commons who reports to the committee. If auditors identify instances of irregularity or waste in a department's spending, they report their findings to the C&AG, who in turn alerts the committee. If their findings expose serious deficiencies, the committee is sure to launch an investigation, which could include summoning the permanent secretary, a department's most senior civil servant, to the committee for questioning. With the NAO's support, the committee has acquired a reputation as the hardest working of all the Commons' select committees. It issues approximately fifty reports a year, and so seriously are they taken by the executive's financial watchdog, the Treasury, that no time is lost in demanding that a department faulted in a report undertake whatever is necessary to correct the cited deficiencies.

Delegating Legislation

When Parliament passes a bill and it becomes an act of Parliament, it is known as primary legislation. However, there is more to this new law than first meets the eye. While an act of Parliament sets out in general terms *what* objectives are to be met, determining the details of *how* they are to be met is delegated by the act to a minister under whose responsibility the act will be administered. Examples of these details are rules for driving motor vehicles, safety regulations in the workplace, and manufacturing standards. Omitting these details in bills saves parliamentarians from having to debate the minutiae of legislation and gives the government of the day more time to make progress with its legislative program.

The details devised after passage of primary legislation are incorporated into what is aptly called secondary, or delegated, legislation. Both terms are interchangeable in general with a third, somewhat more formal term, statutory instrument (SI). About 1,500 SIs are drawn up every year for presentation to Parliament; another 1,500 or so, which pertain to local areas and are usually in effect for short periods only, are not required to be submitted to Parliament.

The number of SIs presented to Parliament has grown from fewer than 1,000 a year before 1970 to between 1,300 and 1,600 a year since the 1990s. Translated into numbers of pages, the 1,373 SIs presented to Parliament in the year 2000 filled 10,755 pages and a noticeable amount of shelf space.[26] The law stipulates that Parliament is to deal with SIs by a negative procedure or an affirmative procedure. As Table 8.4 shows, the negative procedure is used in the vast majority of cases, but as a rule, the most important SIs require the affirmative procedure. SIs that require the negative procedure take effect automatically at some point in the near future unless either the Commons or the Lords votes to annul them within forty days after they are submitted to Parliament. Under the affirmative procedure, by contrast, SIs do not go into effect until or unless both houses agree—usually within twenty-eight to forty days after Parliament has received them.

With all these SIs and the importance attached to many of them, how do backbenchers monitor them? For some years, only the Select Committee on Statutory Instruments scrutinized SIs in the Commons. But in 1973 the Joint Committee on Statutory Instruments was created with members drawn from both houses. Today this joint committee is made up of fourteen members, seven from each house, and is chaired by an opposition party member from the Commons. The vast majority of SIs are referred to both houses, but the joint committee's seven Commons members meet alone as members of the Select Committee on Statutory Instruments when certain SIs that pertain only to the Commons (such as financial matters) are referred to it.

Table 8.4	Statutory Instruments (SIs) Considered by Parliament, 1998–2002	
Parliament	Affirmative Procedure	Negative Procedure
1998–1999	178	1,266
1999–2000	180	1,241
2000–2001 (short session)	123	717
2001–2002 (long session)	262	1,468

Source: Robert Rogers and Rhodri Walters, *How Parliament Works*, 5th ed. (London: Pearson, 2004), p. 231.

The fourteen members of the joint committee usually meet once a week and focus only on the technical aspects of SIs. Assisted by a staff that includes three specialist lawyers, they seek answers to key questions as they analyze the more than one thousand SIs referred to them every year. Are the regulations found in an SI consistent with the dictates of its parent act? Is the language of the SI clear? Does the SI prescribe rules of procedure faithful to the basic principles of due process? These are just three questions that members and staff raise; if the answers to any concern them, the joint committee reports its concerns to both houses. If an SI is defective, neither the joint committee nor the Commons has the authority to amend it. For this, the minister responsible for the SI must withdraw it and present a corrected version to the Commons, which is something that happens fairly regularly. If the minister disagrees that the SI needs to be revamped, both parties persist in their disagreement, and the minister refuses to withdraw it, the Commons makes the final decision.

Negative procedure SIs go into effect unless a majority of the Commons votes to annul them. Only rarely is one referred to a standing committee, where members may debate the merits of the SI. This happens only if the relevant minister makes a motion that it be referred. Rarer still are debates on negative procedure SIs on the floor of the Commons. And most rare of all are those instances when one is defeated. The last time it happened was in 1979.[27] An SI that requires the affirmative procedure is referred automatically to a standing committee. The merits of the SI are debated, but they cannot be amended. The SI is then referred to the Commons, where MPs are asked to decide whether it should be approved, but, again, without amendment and without the benefit of further debate. Only occasionally is an affirmative procedure SI allowed to circumvent a standing committee to be debated on the floor.

The Select Committee on Statutory Instruments and the Joint Committee on Statutory Instruments were created to strengthen Parliament's hand in overseeing delegated legislation; however, five factors impede this work. First, Parliament is prohibited from amending SIs; if parliamentarians have cause to override one, they can only hope that a revised SI that the executive body in question could submit later will take their objections into account. Second, although SIs are supposed to be limited to rules and regulations, they have been used increasingly to introduce policies in ways that go beyond what Parliament approved in the parent act. Third, because nine or ten SIs on average are referred to Parliament every day it is in session, the joint committee has little time to review them closely and report its findings in time to meet the twenty-eight-to-forty-day deadline. Fourth, the committee's findings are rarely opened up to debate on the floor of the Commons. And fifth, because no guidelines governing the classification of SIs exist, some which in the past required Parliament's affirmative vote have been downgraded to negative procedure SIs, which Parliament pays less attention to, and some negative procedure SIs have been downgraded to SIs that Parliament is not required to see at all.

The House of Lords

The Lords also oversees the work of the executive, although it does so somewhat differently from the Commons. The Commons has had a Select Committee on Statutory Instruments for some time. The Lords has had the comparable Committee on the Merits of Statutory Instruments since 2003. However, the Lords does not have anything comparable to the Commons' Public Accounts Committee or its departmental select committees. Peers carry out most of their oversight activities through three permanent select committees—the European Union Committee, the Science and Technology Committee, and the Delegated Powers and Regulatory Reform Committee. From time to time, the Lords creates ad hoc select committees of seven to twelve peers to investigate issues that fall outside the jurisdiction of the three permanent select committees, such as unemployment, sentencing provisions for murder, and legalizing cannabis for medical reasons.

The Lords' oversight of the executive through the mechanism of permanent select committees did not begin until the 1970s. Its first was the European Union Select Committee, created just after Britain joined the EU. Its purpose today is the same as it was then—to examine legislation drafted by the European Commission before representatives of the British government and the governments of the other member nations meet to consider such legislation in the Council of Ministers. The committee's oversight of the British government's position on European legislation is more pre hoc than post hoc, since it submits its reactions to EC proposals to the Lords and the appropriate departments before votes are taken in the Council of Ministers.

A second select committee, Science and Technology, was formed in 1979 and given a broad jurisdiction. Its reports focus on both short-term and long-term aspects of Government policy and sometimes fill as many as two or three volumes on such diverse topics as hazardous waste disposal, priorities in medical research, agricultural and food research, and decommissioning oil and gas installations. In 1992 a third permanent select committee was created, one that reflected the mounting concern of many peers, especially the Law Lords, over the increasing authority primary legislation gave to ministers to draft delegated legislation. Called the Select Committee on

Delegated Powers and Regulatory Reform, its reports to the parent chamber focus on provisions in draft legislation that propose giving ministers the authority to devise statutory instruments. Should the bill propose that negative procedures be used when, in the committee's view, the provisions of the measure are so significant that affirmative procedures should be used instead? What is more, should it be proposed in a bill that a minister be given the authority to draw up statutory instruments when, in the committee's judgment, all of the bill's provisions should be included in the primary legislation? The committee also recommends whether the house should accept, amend, or reject Henry VIII clauses in draft legislation. (The term for these clauses comes from the Statute of Proclamations of 1539, which gave Henry VIII the power to legislate by proclamation.) These are clauses in primary legislation that empower ministers to alter or repeal specific acts of Parliament.

The three permanent select committees in the Lords operate much like their counterparts in the Commons, especially in the emphasis they give to issuing reports they can endorse unanimously. However, there are some minor differences in size, organization, and the criteria used in assigning members. Because the scope of their jurisdictions is so far-reaching, the European Union and the Science and Technology committees are larger than the Commons' departmental select committees, and they operate primarily at the subcommittee level. The European Union Committee's nineteen members are divided into seven subcommittees, and Science and Technology's fifteen members into two. Membership on both committees increases when additional peers whose knowledge of the subject matter under investigation are asked to enhance the quality of the committees' work. As a result, at any one time as many as seventy peers may sit on the European Union Committee and thirty on the Science and Technology Committee. The Delegated Powers and Regulatory Reform Committee, by contrast, is smaller with only a dozen members. It functions at committee level only and does not co-opt peers on a temporary basis.

Finally, as important as party is in assigning peers to committees and subcommittees, experience and knowledge usually are regarded as more important. For that reason, political party and cross-bench strength on committees and their subcommittees does not always reflect the distribution of political party and cross-bench strength in the parent chamber. Undoubtedly, background and knowledge were deemed more important than political party when in 2003 peers were assigned to the European Union Committee's Subcommittee on Common Foreign and Security Policy. Among its members were a former chief of the Defence Staff, a former cabinet member, a former senior foreign policy adviser to the government, a former attorney general, a former secretary general of the European Commission, and a former member of the intelligence community.[28]

The oversight activities performed by the Lords complement those of the Commons. Whereas each of the Commons' departmental select committees is restricted to focusing on the work of a single department, the Lords Select

Committee on Science and Technology and its ad hoc committees can examine policies that cut across departmental boundaries. It is significant that these committees investigate policies that are often broader in scope than those that the Commons' departmental select committees examine. It is just as significant that the Committee on Delegated Powers and Regulatory Reform, like the European Union Committee, is empowered to examine legislative proposals *before* the Government sends them on their way for approval. Through the permanent and ad hoc select committees, well more than one hundred peers are involved at any one time in overseeing the executive. They report on fewer policy issues than their counterparts in the Commons; however, they select issues that the Commons has less time and perhaps less inclination to investigate. Moreover, they examine them in greater depth and take a longer-term view of their implications.

Conclusion

"Parliamentary sovereignty" is the term used to refer to Parliament's exclusive authority to make laws. The term's origin is not known, but it probably could be traced to the seventeenth century, when Parliament was struggling with the monarchy. By the end of that century Parliament had won the struggle, and more than halfway through the next century, an MP proudly proclaimed Westminster "the mother of parliaments"—a fount of legitimate authority at home and a model copied in many parts of the world.

Parliament was then in its Golden Age, a period that lasted from 1832 until 1868. Parliamentarians introduced significant legislation on their own and voted on measures as they saw fit. But this resurgence was short-lived; in the 1870s and 1880s Parliament passed into a new relationship, this time not one with monarchs, as in the past, but with the executive. Britain's parliamentary form of government was becoming increasingly executive-centered, if not executive-dominated, buttressed by increasingly disciplined political parties. This arrangement, it should be added, was grudgingly accepted by some parliamentarians and gladly welcomed by others. The realists among them undoubtedly thought that the responsibilities of governing had become so much more demanding and complex that relinquishing to the cabinet the role of the dominant force in legislative policymaking was not only sensible but ineluctable.

At the beginning of this chapter it was suggested that the Westminster Model might not be as fitting a model as it once was to describe Parliament's relationship with the executive side of government. The 1970s, 1980s, and 1990s were decades of salient change in Parliament. It became a stronger institution. The momentum for change had begun even before then. By the 1970s, Parliament had just about seen the last of the amateur MP. It was the professional backbenchers of both major parties in the Commons who became restive and found reasons to defy their whips when they were summoned to vote. The Lords, in the meantime, was asserting its independence by leaving its imprint on Government legislation or by delaying it and at times even defeating it. In the elected chamber, MPs demanded opportunities to decide for themselves how to vote on major "conscience" issues of the day. Parliament, the Commons in particular, was reasserting its right to engage in systematic oversight of the programs, policies, and expenditures of the executive by organizing departmental select committees and expanding the investigative resources of the Public Accounts Committee.

How far has the momentum for change taken Parliament? It is a stronger institution today than it was before the 1970s. Is it significantly different from what it was before the 1970s and if so, is it also sufficiently different to justify replacing the Westminster Model with a more appropriate one? The record suggests that, for a litany of reasons, it is not sufficiently different. Parliamentarians have successfully lobbied governments to introduce changes in some major bills and have even come close to defeating them on important measures. However, these instances have been rare. Governments continue to control a substantial portion of Parliament's timetable of business. Government whips continue to dominate backbenchers. They make sure their flock is herded through the correct voting lobby; they sit on the committee that assigns backbenchers to ad hoc, standing, and select committees; and they recommend to the prime minister those backbenchers they feel are most deserving of junior ministerships. As for oversight, because it is normally not a politically rewarding pursuit, many issues are ignored. Moreover, when an issue of importance looms, members of the governing party think twice before agreeing to investigate it if it could embarrass the Government. As for statutory instruments, so numerous are they that backbenchers have no time to examine them all; most are not even debated in the Commons chamber. If they are debated and fault is found with them, the fault cannot be removed because amendments are out of order.

There has always been a degree of tension between the governing party in Parliament and the government of the day, and it appears to have been exacerbated in recent years as the balance of power between Parliament and Government continues to shift to favor the latter. Parliamentarians were feisty in the last three decades of the twentieth century and have remained so in the early years of the twenty-first, and although they have supported changes that have strengthened Parliament, the changes are too few and unremarkable to convince observers that the Westminster Model no longer has relevance. Indeed, the British parliament can probably do no more than carry on as it has, because in a parliamentary form of government invigorated by a strong two-party system, parliaments are the instruments of power, not its holders, and government is "not government *by* Parliament, but government *through* Parliament." [29]

9

Prime Minister and Cabinet

When television correspondents report on a fast-breaking political event in the UK, they invariably use one of Britain's most famous doors as a backdrop. Apart from the police officer who always stands outside it, there is nothing extraordinary about this door. It is black and has a door knocker above an inscribed brass plate, and a house number—No. 10—with the "0" distinctly askew. The cul-de-sac on which it is found, Downing Street, is equally unremarkable. Indeed, everything that comes into view is unremarkable—except the inscription on the brass plate, which reads: "First Lord of the Treasury." This was the title conferred for the first time in 1715 on Robert Walpole, whose successors some years later came to be known as "Prime Minister." No. 10 Downing Street, or No. 10, as it is called for short, is used today for the same purpose it was used for when Walpole took up residence there in 1735: it serves as the office and residence of the head of government of the United Kingdom.

It is from this door at No. 10 that a prime minister emerges to travel in a Daimler to nearby Westminster every Wednesday that Parliament is in session to answer Prime Minister's Questions, make major announcements to waiting reporters, or greet heads of government when their limousines draw up. No. 10 is the center of power in British politics. The portraits of former prime ministers that adorn the walls within, however, are sober reminders that prime ministers do not remain at the center of power indefinitely. (For a list of prime ministers since 1945, see Table 9.1.) Their tenancy is only as long as the voters and the party in government wish it to be. When they leave office not by their own choice, the cameras focus on this door to record their departures—as they did when Margaret Thatcher emerged from it and was tearfully chauffeured from Downing Street after stepping down as prime minister in 1990, and when John Major passed through it to make way for his successor, Tony Blair, in 1997.

No. 10 has not always been the most important political address in Britain, but seismic changes in British politics since Robert Walpole's days there have made it such. Walpole became the first to exercise a power that those who later became prime minister would exercise with great regularity: chairing the cabinet. The cabinet at that time was a small group of advisers to the King drawn from Parliament; in 1717, when George I gave up attending its meetings, Walpole, First Lord of the Treasury, assumed the position of chair. By the end of the eighteenth century, the cabinet had become the most preeminent executive decision-making body in British politics. Its members were equals (*pares*), decisions were made collegially, and he who chaired its meetings was first among equals, or *primus inter pares*.

British government was cabinet government in that the decisions of government were the decisions of the cabinet and not just the prime minister. Little changed from that point, even after the position of prime minister became firmly established by convention in the early part of the nineteenth century. The monarch had long since relinquished responsibility for appointing members of the cabinet. This task, plus those of convening the cabinet, chairing it, and serving as its spokesperson constituted the prime minister's principal duties until the first half of the twentieth century, when two world wars (1914–1918 and 1939–1945) demanded more.

When Britain was at war, two prime ministers, David Lloyd George in 1916 and Winston Churchill in 1940, emerged to provide the highly

Table 9.1	Prime Ministers since 1945	
Prime Minister	Party	Period
Clement Attlee	Labour	July 1945–February 1950
		February 1950–October 1951
Winston Churchill	Conservative	October 1951–April 1955
Anthony Eden	Conservative	April 1955–January 1957
Harold Macmillan	Conservative	January 1957–October 1959
		October 1959–October 1963
Alec Douglas-Home	Conservative	October 1963–October 1964
Harold Wilson	Labour	October 1964–March 1966
		March 1966–June 1970
Edward Heath	Conservative	June 1970–February 1974
Harold Wilson	Labour	February 1974–October 1974
		October 1974–March 1976
James Callaghan	Labour	March 1976–May 1979
Margaret Thatcher	Conservative	May 1979–June 1983
		June 1983–June 1987
		June 1987–November 1990
John Major	Conservative	November 1990–April 1992
		April 1992–May 1997
Tony Blair	Labour	May 1997–June 2001
		June 2001–May 2005
		May 2005– ?

Source: Chambers Book of Facts (Edinburgh: Chambers Harrap Publishers, Ltd., 2005), 407.

focused, personalized leadership required to galvanize the support of the nation and inspire its troops. The locus of power did not shift from the cabinet to the prime minister in this period; however, the *persona* of the prime minister loomed large and dominated the British polity, just as William Gladstone and Benjamin Disraeli's had in the closing decades of the century before. This president-like image was thought out of place in the aftermath of each conflict, however, and quickly receded.

This background is vital to bear in mind to appreciate fully the significance of the changes that have occurred in political leadership in Britain, especially since the general election of 1979. The 1980s was the decade of Margaret Thatcher and of the revival of the president-like persona of the prime minister. Under her leadership, three consecutive general elections gave her Conservative Party thumping majorities in the Commons and gave her the longest uninterrupted lease to No. 10 of any prime minister in the twentieth century. Even more remarkable was the fact that Thatcher achieved a preeminence of leadership in peacetime that rivaled that of Churchill's in wartime. As one scholar put it, in her determination "to change the face of Britain," Thatcher "in effect *became* the face of Britain" and government became "the institutional embodiment of her personal ideas and drives."[1] [Emphasis this author's.] Cabinet government remained the dominant feature of British politics, but even members of her own party whispered their concern that she had reduced its standing. The cabinet appeared to be dwarfed by her.

As the end of the 1980s approached, however, Thatcher's political fortunes began to sag. Some of the policies with which she was personally identified ended in failure, public opinion polls revealed that the electorate had become disenchanted with her leadership, and the grandees of the party feared she would draw it into a vortex of defeat at the next election. The issue of whether she should continue as leader started to emerge in 1989. It came to a head in 1990 after she failed to win an outright victory on the first round of voting when Conservative MPs were balloted to choose between her and a former member of her cabinet who challenged her for the leadership of the party. Before the second round of voting was to take place, she met one evening with her cabinet colleagues one by one. Nearly two thirds of them delivered a verdict that she had hoped she would not hear: she would be defeated. She realized she had to step down, and step down she did the next morning. "I had lost the Cabinet's support," she later wrote in her memoirs. "I could not even muster a credible campaign team. It was the end."[2]

Before Thatcher's decline as prime minister, her premiership prompted academics and political commentators to ask whether leadership in British politics lay primarily with the cabinet or the prime minister. Did her prime ministership give rise to a British "presidency," as some have called it? If so, did that not make cabinet government obsolete, or at the very least, obsolescent? Or, because she had "lost the cabinet's support" (as she put it), did her departure signify that cabinet government was still a viable force?

The question "What have we—cabinet government or prime ministerial government?" had been raised before Thatcher entered No. 10 and was raised during John Major's prime ministership from 1990 to 1997 as well, although less frequently. It was not until soon after Tony Blair took office in 1997 that it was raised with the same ringing intensity as in the 1980s. The question is still there to be answered. But other questions need to be answered first—questions about the powers of the prime minister, the staff on whom the prime minister relies to exercise those powers, and factors that help or hinder a prime minister's efforts to lead.

The Powers of the Prime Minister

"Headmasters have powers at their disposal with which Prime Ministers have never yet been invested."[3] When prime ministers are forced to cope with an especially vexatious problem, they would probably agree with this sentiment, expressed some years ago by one prime minister who knew something about power—Winston Churchill. Exaggerated though Churchill's lament was, the powers of British prime ministers nevertheless pale by comparison with those exercised by many other heads of government. The prime minister's powers are not spelled out in statutes or judicial decisions. Rather, they flow from an accumulation of conventions that have evolved from repeated practice over the years.

The Cabinet

A prime minister's most important powers are those dealing with the cabinet. It is the prime minister who forms a government by appointing cabinet ministers. In addition he or she approves the cabinet's agenda, convenes it, chairs it, summarizes whatever conclusions it reaches before it adjourns, and creates its committees and subcommittees. In addition to chairing several of these committees and subcommittees, the prime minister decides which cabinet ministers should sit on the rest of them.

Appointing, promoting, demoting, and dismissing ministers are among the most far-reaching of a prime minister's powers. Because prime ministers are not required to rely on Parliament or any other body to confirm cabinet appointments, they have a relatively free hand in giving form to the top of political Britain's executive hierarchy. How free that hand is depends on party rules and a variety of practical political factors.

When Labour comes to power, a party rule dictates that the prime minister appoint all those whom the Parliamentary Labour Party (PLP) elected to the shadow cabinet the year before and were returned to Parliament after the general election. This limits the scope of choice, although the prime minister is free to appoint those elected by the PLP to whichever posts he or she deems appropriate. Only at some unspecified interval after the general election is a Labour prime minister at liberty to make substitutions in a cabinet reshuffle. A new Conservative prime minister, on the other hand, is not lumbered with this restriction, although he or she is likely to appoint to the cabinet many whose leadership was tried and tested on the Opposition front benches.

Except for these differences, prime ministers, whether Labour or Conservative, follow the same steps in appointing cabinet ministers. Prime ministers cast a wide net in Parliament, the Commons in particular, in search of worthy candidates. They look for such attributes as knowledge of public policies, political acumen, administrative skills, previous experience in Parliament, adroitness in parliamentary debate, loyalty to party, and a willingness to be a team player. Requiring ministers to possess every one of these attributes in ample measure narrows the pool.

Narrowing this pool further is the practical political necessity of including in the cabinet leading figures in the Commons who are thought to be the prime minister's rivals and who command the support of party factions. They may not be among the prime minister's first choices; however, the prime minister's advisers will make the case that bringing them into the cabinet, where uniting behind a single position is a cardinal norm, is preferable to allowing them to remain on the back benches to snipe at the prime minister and incite revolts. Above all, it is in the prime minister's interests to unite the various factions of the party by appointing their leaders, for the British public has shown little tolerance for a government whose party is fraught with division.

Once appointed to the cabinet, ministers are beholden to the prime minister for selecting them. Winning a seat on the cabinet is an ambition to which they have long aspired. Not only have they won the prime minister's confidence to serve as senior members of the Government, they can be fitted out with the trappings of office, be called "Right Honorable," and receive a substantial boost in their salary. Moreover, they can nourish the hope that if they bide their time, they themselves could be in pole position to become prime minister one day. In the meantime, they are acutely aware that their political futures are in the prime minister's hands. As one scholar observed, the prime minister can

> advance the careers of those he favours and check those he dislikes according to the positions he gives them, for some offer the chance to make a good reputation, while others can bring the holder little esteem. Thus a minister who wants to climb is dependent on the prime minister, and the easiest way to earn his gratitude is to serve him loyally.[4]

Serving the prime minister loyally is one test that ministers must pass to remain in the cabinet. It is not the only one, however. At some point, a prime minister assesses the performance of the government and takes stock of the effectiveness with which ministers have helped to achieve results. If a few are seen as "not up to the job," as Prime Minister Clement Atlee (1945–1951) once put it to a minister he dismissed, a cabinet reshuffle is likely to be in the offing. One or two are likely to be dispensed with, a few will probably be reassigned to different posts in the cabinet hierarchy, and a talented junior minister or two or possibly a backbencher will be brought in to fill any vacancies. All prime ministers realize, however, that a reshuffle incurs some risk. Prime Minister James Callaghan (1976–1979) put it best when he noted, "You make an enemy of the man sacked and disappoint a dozen MPs who hoped for promotion."[5]

Cabinet reshuffles produce other risks as well. Apart from arousing animosities within the cabinet and the party, a prime minister wishes to avoid admitting publicly that the Government has performed poorly. A prime minister is hardly likely to admit to such, yet that is indeed how the public might construe a reshuffle. At the very least, therefore, prime ministers avoid sacking popular ministers for the same reason that they appointed them in the first place—to prevent them from mounting rearguard actions on the back benches. Just as important, if there is a reshuffle, prime ministers do not dismiss too many ministers at one time. Although Prime Minister Harold Macmillan (1957–1963) was astute in holding potential rivals in check by keeping them in his cabinet, he failed to demonstrate the same level of foresightedness on "the night of the long knives," a summer evening in 1962 when he abruptly purged a third of his cabinet. The political fallout was enormous. "Mac the Knife," as he was later called, was seen as sacrificing seven talented, loyal ministers to achieve one transparent objective: to invigorate his image as a decisive prime minister when there was a slump in his popularity and that of his Government. His dismissals had the opposite effect. They cast doubt on his judgment, angered members of his party, and diminished the Government's popularity even more.

Reshuffling the cabinet is one way by which prime ministers exert power. Convening and chairing the cabinet are two other ways. If crises erupt, prime ministers can demonstrate their decisiveness as head of government by summoning the cabinet into emergency session. Otherwise, ministers can expect to meet with the prime minister at the usual time most Thursday mornings. Before these meetings, the cabinet secretary, a civil servant, calls upon the prime minister to approve the agenda and add to it any items of importance. The prime minister then directs that certain documents be distributed to ministers so that they are properly briefed on matters relevant to the next meeting. Not all prime ministers chair the cabinet in the same way. At the very least, however, they are expected to raise issues, ask ministers for their views, and decide whether to refer certain problems that need thrashing out to any of the cabinet's nearly fifty committees and subcommittees. Only rarely does a prime minister ask for a vote on an issue, and at the end of the session he or she sums up whatever conclusions the cabinet has reached. A day or two later, the prime minister approves the minutes of the meeting submitted by the cabinet secretary.

These are the *pro forma* powers that conventions confer on prime ministers once they have formed a cabinet. But these powers mask certain limitations. The power to approve the cabinet's agenda does not give the prime minister license to reject it. Any changes the prime minister makes are usually only at the margins. To do more than that could risk arousing animosity, especially if the prime minister deletes agenda items on which some ministers expect to be heard and about which others need to be informed.

Just as risky is it for a prime minister to undertake changes in the pattern of business that ministers have come to expect. Before they can speak in unison beyond the cabinet room, which they must, ministers need information that is normally exchanged in the cabinet. Often this information is derived from reports by the foreign secretary on international developments, updates from the chancellor of the exchequer on economic news, briefings from other ministers on one or more thorny domestic issues, or from a run-down from the Government chief whip on the legislative business before Parliament.

It does not take long for prime ministers to realize that they do not hold their cabinets in an iron grip. That is why prime ministers may choose not to announce their position until their ministers have divulged theirs, or they may remain silent when it is clear the tide of opinion has turned against them. Margaret Thatcher was an exception. She "would invite the responsible minister to introduce the subject, then state her own view and argue with anyone who disagreed with her." [6] At the beginning of her premiership, she rarely tried to hold her cabinet in thrall. As her time at No. 10 wore on, however, the number of times the cabinet overruled her mounted and some policies with which she was personally identified failed.

The result was that she gradually became remote from her colleagues, intolerant of their disagreements, and heavy-handed in chairing meetings. All of these contributed to her downfall. In 1989 her actions prompted the resignation of the chancellor of the exchequer. A year later, the deputy prime minister also resigned. When a third disaffected minister, who had resigned from the cabinet some time earlier, challenged Thatcher in a leadership contest, she withdrew from the race after failing to win reelection on the first ballot.

Not all prime ministers go to the lengths to which Thatcher went. However, they may stretch their powers to get their way or to preserve harmony in the cabinet. They may persuade departmental ministers to keep controversial items off the cabinet agenda. On occasion, they might delay raising a sensitive issue until the closing moments of a meeting and then insist it be decided immediately. They may circumvent the cabinet by referring contentious issues to cabinet committees that either they or one of their trusted cabinet allies chair. Short of that, they might attempt to orchestrate agreement in cabinet by meeting beforehand with ministers, one-on-one, to convince each of the correctness of their position.

When prime ministers have no need to resort to such tactics, they almost always look to cabinet colleagues for counsel. It is often in their interest to do so, for when ministers are encouraged to participate freely in discussions, they are likely to commit themselves to decisions they have helped shape, and the prime minister can be assured of receiving more than just their token support. Even ministers who persist in taking issue with a decision after colleagues fail to bring them around by the force of their arguments satisfy themselves that they at least had their say.

Whether or not all ministers are of one mind on a cabinet decision, the convention of collective cabinet responsibility requires that all ministers, dissenters and supporters alike, close ranks and accept it as Government policy. The cabinet shrouds its deliberations in secrecy; any dissent expressed in the cabinet room remains there. Those who disagree must take every precaution not even to hint at their dissent in public. So iron-clad is this convention that Prime Minister Lord Melbourne (1834–1841) once admonished his cabinet: "It doesn't matter a damn which line we take but we had better all be in one story."[7] A minister who finds a position taken in the cabinet indefensible might be tempted to tender his or her resignation. Resignations are rare, however, and a minister who considers taking this step usually thinks long and hard before taking this action, for the opposition will surely exploit any resignation as of a fissure in the otherwise smooth bedrock of cabinet solidarity and trumpet assertions that the Government is in a shambles.

Rounding out the prime minister's powers over the cabinet is the ability to create committees, chair them, and appoint committee members and chairs. An elaborate standing committee system has been in place for some years and has served prime ministers well. However, prime ministers are at liberty to dissolve committees and create new ones, either other standing committees or ad hoc ones, if they find it expedient. To achieve the results they want, prime ministers have been known to refer potentially divisive issues to committees of trusted allies or to chair these committees themselves. They also have been known to create ad hoc committees and stack their members with their supporters. These cabinet subsystems are likely to have the last word on an issue, for, although the most important decisions are almost always reported back to the cabinet, only rarely are they referred back to it for its approval.

Appointments

Once a newly elected prime minister has appointed a select group of parliamentarians to the cabinet, the job of filling other major posts is next. From the ranks of Parliament, prime ministers appoint junior ministers and approve ministers' appointments of parliamentary private secretaries. They also approve or reject candidates recommended to fill the top posts in the civil service and senior positions on the judiciary when these positions become vacant.

Junior Ministers

Junior ministers are mostly MPs (the others are peers), the vast majority of whom the prime minister appoints to some fifteen departments of state. There are about eighty such ministers, and they are "junior" only in the sense that they do not sit in the cabinet but instead work under the direction of those cabinet ministers who serve as heads of departments (who are, formally, secretaries of state). Roughly half of the junior ministers work in the more senior ranks as "ministers of state"; the remaining half work just below as "parliamentary undersecretaries of state." Secretaries of state give junior ministers the job of troubleshooting problems across a full range of a department's responsibilities or, as is more often the case, one or two major areas of operation within a department. Whatever job they perform, junior ministers report to their secretaries of state.

When a prime minister casts about for worthy candidates to fill vacant junior ministerial posts, there is a limited pool from which to choose. As the demands on secretaries of state have mounted over the years, they have come to rely on junior ministers all the more, and their spheres of responsibility have expanded as a result. A knock-on effect is that the number of such posts has proliferated; prime ministers have had to intensify the search for greater numbers of talented MPs who can be counted on to advance the interests of the government. Ideal candidates are those who can "grasp the basic issues, inject the Government's political priorities into their department's thinking and subject officials' proposals to the litmus test of political acceptability."[8] Above all, they must be bound to the decisions of the cabinet.

With experience, junior ministers themselves become a valuable pool to which the prime minister turns when cabinet positions become vacant. Because most ministers nourish higher ambitions, they are driven to serve with diligence and loyalty. The prime minister's power of appointment is a powerful tool and the prospects of advancement to cabinet level, limited though they are, are tantalizing enough to junior ministers to help prime ministers keep their Governments in line.

Parliamentary Private Secretaries

Parliamentary private secretaries (PPSs) might be called ministers' "spear carriers." Every member of the cabinet, including the prime minister, has one, and junior ministers usually share one per department. There are between forty and fifty total, all of whom are appointed by ministers from the back benches of the majority party, subject to the approval of the prime minister once they have survived rigorous screening by the Government chief whip. Unlike cabinet ministers and junior ministers, PPSs are not members of the Government, although if they intend to defy the whip's instructions in an upcoming vote, they are first expected to resign as a PPS.

Duties vary, depending upon the minister, but normally they include arranging to pair their minister's vote with that of a member of the opposition party so that the minister can keep an urgent engagement, attending meetings for which the minister has no time, and keeping the minister informed of back-bench opinion. No pay and little prestige are attached to these positions. But it is the first step on the ladder. There is no guarantee PPSs will ascend to the next rung; however, they are mindful that a high percentage of junior ministers once served in the same position and that some among them now are being groomed as ministers-in-waiting. For that reason, they have a strong incentive to excel in their work. All of this enhances the prime minister's ability to build cohesion in the parliamentary party.

Other Appointments

Other appointments prime ministers make are to positions filled by individuals drawn from outside Parliament. The most important of these are the top two civil service posts in each of the departments of state and judicial positions on Britain's two highest courts. There is no "spoils system," and therefore newly elected prime ministers are prohibited from making a clean sweep of those at the top and installing those to whom they might owe favors. Apart from cabinet ministers and junior ministers, prime ministers in fact make few, if any, appointments immediately after they take office. Usually, as in the case of the top two positions in the departments of state and the judicial positions, they must wait until posts become vacant.

Even when they become vacant, however, the choice of candidates is limited. For permanent secretaries and deputy secretaries in the civil service, prime ministers are expected to choose only from those whose names have been submitted by the Senior Appointments Selection Committee, which is chaired by the cabinet secretary, who is also head of the Home Civil Service. Prime ministers are determined to select individuals who will offer wise counsel to ministers and oversee the effective administration of programs, so they expect candidates to have a proven record of problem solving, managing scarce resources, and implementing policies. But never may party preference be a consideration, for filling the top posts of the civil service with major party patrons would seriously violate the long-standing and carefully guarded convention of preserving the political neutrality of the civil service.

This convention applies with equal rigor to the appointment of judges to the Court of Appeal and the Appellate Committee of the House of Lords (or the Supreme Court, starting in 2009) whenever vacancies occur. Here too the choice of prime ministers is circumscribed—in this case by the lord chancellor and the Judicial Appointments Commission (JAC). The JAC recommends the name of one candidate to the lord chancellor, and if the lord chancellor finds the candidate suitable, he or she recommends the candidate to the prime minister. (If the lord chancellor is not happy with the choice, the JAC is asked to make another recommendation.) The prime minister then recommends the appointment of the judicial candidate to the monarch, who automatically confers the appointment of the crown.

Calling a General Election

Another power of the prime minister is that of choosing the date of the next general election. Prior to 1918, a convention gave this power to the cabinet, but since then to the prime minister alone, although prime ministers normally do not set the date until after they have consulted their closest cabinet colleagues. Once a date has been determined, convention dictates that the prime minister ask the monarch to dissolve Parliament, after which, according to protocol, a formal press release is issued by No. 10 announcing that the monarch is "graciously pleased" to honor the prime minister's request.

Setting the date of the general election is a substantial power. But there are checks on this power, as there are on other powers prime ministers wield. One check is that an election must be held no later than five years from the date that Parliament convened for the first time following the last election. If political and economic conditions are favorable, this requirement becomes less a check than an opportunity, for it gives a prime minister leeway to call an election any time before the five years have run their course. Margaret Thatcher seized this opportunity in 1983 after one term in office, and Tony Blair did the same in 2001. In each case an election was called approximately a year before the prime minister had to. The standing of their respective Governments in the public opinion polls allowed them to forfeit what remained of the time allotted and hold an election to capitalize on the popularity of their Governments so they could lock into a further four or five years in office. In the case of Thatcher, Britain was still basking in the patriotic afterglow of its defeat of Argentina the year before, after Argentine forces seized the Falklands, a British crown colony. With Blair, the economy was robust and the Conservative Opposition was not a threat. In each case, the election produced handsome majorities for their party.

Political and economic conditions might not always be favorable, as John Major found in the 1992–1997 parliament. Not long after the 1992 election, his Government's popularity ebbed and then took a downward slide. Major nevertheless soldiered on, all the while hoping he could reverse his party's fortunes. As the end of the fifth year approached, his party still had not succeeded in overcoming Labour's commanding lead in the opinion polls. But time was running out. Soon it would become the longest peacetime Parliament in nearly ninety years. He had to call an election, and the voters inflicted a massive defeat on the Conservative Party.

Even when conditions appear favorable, determining when to call the next election can be fraught with uncertainty, so much so that Churchill called it a decision "in which Luck and Hazard enter on a remarkable scale."[9] It was hazard, not luck, that befell prime ministers Edward Heath in 1974 and James Callaghan in 1979. Many believe that, had Heath called an election earlier, the voters would have given him another lease to No. 10. In Callaghan's case, he rejected the advice of his advisers to call an early election, but was later forced to do so after his Government was brought down by a vote of no confidence.

The examples of Heath, Callaghan, and Major demonstrate that the power to set the date of the next election carries no guarantee of success. This fact is poignantly borne out by the results of the general elections held between 1945 and 2005: seven of the seventeen elections held in this period were lost by the party whose prime minister had called (or had to call) an election.

Support Staff

Were visitors allowed through the gates barring entry to Downing Street to get a view of No. 10, they would probably think its size far too modest to accommodate the family and principal staff of one of the world's leading heads of government. But No. 10's façade is misleading. Not only is the building larger than it looks, it also is linked to another building behind it by a corridor, at the end of which those with clearance may gain access with the swipe of a card. The outside entrance to the building behind No. 10 is around the corner at No. 70 Whitehall, the address of the Cabinet Office. Sequestered within this complex are the principal staff of the prime minister and of the secretary of the cabinet. These two large buildings provide space for a sizeable number, but not enough to accommodate all of the estimated 175 individuals who work for No. 10 and the more than 1,600 who work for the Cabinet Office. Many of these are forced to work nearby.

Prime ministers are free to organize No. 10 in any way that suits them. Aside from Harold Wilson (and Tony Blair some thirty years later), however, most have done little more than tinker at the margins of the organization chart. For some years, No. 10 was organized into four units. First, there was the Private Office. This office, headed by the prime minister's principal private secretary (who was also the prime minister's adviser), provided information and advice on domestic, economic, and foreign policy and parliamentary affairs. In addition, the office's staff stood athwart the paper flow and flagged the most important items for the prime minister, coordinated the prime minister's engagements, drafted speeches, and helped the prime minister prepare every week for Prime Minister's Questions.

A second was the Political Office, which consisted of the political secretary and the prime minister's parliamentary private secretary. The PPS kept the prime minister abreast of backbenchers' reactions to the latest issues. The political secretary maintained contact with party headquarters and local party organizations in order to inform the prime minister about what the rank and file were thinking.

The Press Office was the third office. The press secretary briefed The Lobby (a group of more than two hundred accredited political correspondents), coached the prime minister on how to impress viewers when appearing on television, and made sure press officers in the departments were given the Government's position on issues so that their briefings were consistent with the Press Office's. No. 10's fourth office was the Policy Unit, created by Harold Wilson soon after Labour was returned to power in 1974. Different prime ministers used it differently. Wilson and Callaghan used it to analyze the medium- and long-term effects of policies, especially economic ones. Thatcher utilized it to monitor government economic strategies and to develop new policy ideas, and John Major turned to it for recommendations on new policy initiatives, but especially for its evaluation of policy ideas proposed by the departments.

No. 10 continues to perform the functions associated with these four offices, but their names have changed. The Press Office, Private Office, Policy Unit, and Political Office no longer appear on No. 10's directory. They have given way to the Strategic Communications Unit, the Policy Directorate, and the Government Relations Unit. The first to give way was the Press Office, which became the Strategic Communications Unit during the first Blair Government. In addition to giving twice-a-day briefings to The Lobby, this unit coordinates Government news announcements across Whitehall to produce consistency.

To eliminate overlap between the Private Office and the Policy Unit, Blair merged both into a new unit called the Policy Directorate early in his second term. The new unit is headed by his principal private secretary and overseen by his chief of staff. Lastly, the Political Office was renamed the Government Relations Unit, the head of which oversees relations with ministers, the parliamentary and extra-parliamentary party, the devolved governments, and business interests, and coordinates the prime minister's schedule. These and other lesser reforms of No. 10 introduced later were far from radical, but they were significant enough to send out the message that the prime minister was taking a no-nonsense approach to commanding a government from the center whose legacy would be the timely provision of improved public services.

Tony Blair did more than tinker at the margins of the cabinet office as well. Although this office had been created in 1916 to serve the cabinet as a whole, prime ministers have relied on it more than other ministers, primarily because prime ministers chair the cabinet. Indeed, so reliant had prime ministers become by the closing decades of the twentieth century that some started to question whether its original purpose had given way to serving the prime minister to the near exclusion of all other cabinet ministers. Increasingly, it seemed, prime ministers were using the swipe card at the end of the corridor of No. 10 to gain access to the Cabinet Office so that they could expand their theater of operations. In 1971, Edward Heath (1970–1974) created a think tank, the Central Policy Review Staff (CPRS), placed it in the Cabinet Office, and used it more than anyone else in the cabinet. The CPRS was dissolved in 1983, but not before Margaret Thatcher created the Efficiency Unit, first to identify ways to cut government expenditures and later to devise a plan to speed the delivery of public services. Thatcher's successor, John Major, used the Cabinet Office as well, giving it responsibility for overseeing the Citizens Charter initiative, a program designed to improve the quality of public services, about which more is said in the next chapter.

Blair was as eager as his predecessors to improve the quality of public services: upgrading public services became a refrain heard throughout his premiership. To that end, in 2002 he created three units and placed them in the Cabinet Office at the same time that he reorganized No. 10. The first of these, the Strategy Unit, was the prime minister's think tank, an office that differed from No. 10's Policy Directorate in that it looked at issues ten to twenty years in the future, whereas the Policy Directorate focused on short-term policy issues. The second of the new Cabinet Office units was the Delivery Unit, which was commissioned to oversee the timely provision of such public services as health, education, and transportation. The third office, the Office of Public Service Reform, was given responsibility for evaluating the full range of public services to determine whether staff could deliver the services the public expected. Yet a fourth unit was added at the end of 2006: the Office of the Third Sector was launched to help improve public services by drawing on the strengths of the not-for-profit sector.

No longer were all those in charge of these prime ministerial creations in the Cabinet Office expected to report to the prime minister through the cabinet secretary. Instead, some reported directly to the prime minister. In the meantime, the cabinet secretary increasingly was seen as the prime minister's permanent secretary. As one seasoned political correspondent put it, the Downing Street operation alone had been

> reorganized and expanded to resemble the Executive Office of the President [of the United States], albeit on a much smaller scale. There is a chief of staff, a policy directorate, a strategy unit, directors of communications, government relations and political operations and what amounts to a national security adviser.[10]

Performance

The powers conferred on prime ministers cannot guarantee a premier success as a leader any more than his or her staff can. That both are crucial to a prime minister's ability to lead is self-evident. But a stream of factors, some of which a prime minister has little or no control over, can help or hinder the head of Government's performance. Three of the most important are resources, events, and leadership style.

Resources

Of all the resources available to a prime minister, none is more critical than a parliamentary majority. By definition, a party leader becomes prime minister when the voters elect an overall majority of the leader's party to the Commons. What happens if voters fail to elect a majority of any party? Two Labour Party leaders—Harold Wilson and James Callaghan—were denied a parliamentary majority in the 1970s as one and then the other moved into No. 10. In the election of February 1974, the voters gave Labour more seats than the Conservatives, but thirty-five short of an overall majority. Wilson agreed to head a minority government, and in the parliamentary session that followed, his Government suffered a string of defeats. In an effort to shore up his ability to lead, he called another election in the autumn that boosted the number of Labour seats to an overall majority of three. Eighteen months later, by-election defeats robbed the Government of this threadbare majority. Callaghan, who had just replaced an ailing Wilson, soldiered on for yet another three years, with some support from Liberal MPs, before being forced to call an election after his Government narrowly lost a vote on a motion of no confidence.

Much more fortunate were Thatcher and Blair, who formed governments with thumping parliamentary majorities. Thatcher started her second term in 1983 with a majority of 144, and Blair began his premiership in 1997 with an extraordinary majority of 179. Both exploited the opportunities these numbers gave them by embarking on ambitious programs of reform. Before long, however, backbenchers began to sense that Thatcher had isolated herself from them. As she began her second term (1983–1987), Thatcher no longer socialized in the Commons tearoom as she had in her first term, and, apart from mandatory appearances at Prime Minister's Questions, parliamentarians rarely sighted her in the Commons.

Rarely sighted too was Tony Blair not long after he began his first term in 1997. He made even fewer appearances than Thatcher in Westminster, and when he did appear, usually only for Prime Minister's Questions, he rarely lingered to mingle with his party backbenchers. He seemed to evince little interest in the Commons. So, too, it appeared, did several of his cabinet colleagues, who were upbraided by the Speaker on more than one occasion starting in 1999, for announcing major policy initiatives to the media before doing so in the Commons. This serious breach of a long-standing convention so irritated MPs that the leader of the Commons reminded her cabinet colleagues that flouting this convention gave "unnecessary credence to . . . complaints that the Government is treating Parliament with contempt."[11]

However small or large, a parliamentary majority is a resource prime ministers cannot do without. Moreover, they cannot take their party in the Commons for granted, even a parliamentary party of sizeable proportions. A failure to nourish good relations with backbenchers, if prolonged, can dampen enthusiasm for the leader and ultimately breed discontent. Discontent, when it is coupled with a growing anxiety about the popularity of the Government and the re-electability of the party, as in 1989 and 1990 under Margaret Thatcher, usually means it is only a matter of time before the prime minister falls prey to challengers.

Events

"Events, dear boy, events." That is how Harold Macmillan once responded when he was asked what challenged him most as prime minister. Events, both planned and unplanned, can indeed challenge, especially if they foreshadow turbulence. They can even hinder a prime minister's ability to solve problems. But not all events signal the approach of storm clouds. Some can bolster a prime minister's leadership. A robust economy, for example, can contribute to a "feel good" factor in the body politic that boosts a prime minister's position. With additional tax revenues available, the prime minister's standing can be enhanced all the more when he or she announces that individual income taxes can be reduced or more funds can be released for spending on public services. War too, under the right conditions, can galvanize public support and bolster a prime minister's standing, as it did when Britain went to war with Argentina in 1982 after Argentine forces seized the Falkland Islands. The public strongly backed Thatcher's decision to recapture the Falklands, and she basked in the afterglow of Britain's victory for several months.

Not all events, however, contribute to a prime minister's ability to lead. In the early 1970s, much of Edward Heath's premiership was plagued with one emergency after another, including strikes by miners, an upturn in violence in Northern Ireland, grueling inflation, and a quadruple increase in the price of oil following the Arab-Israeli war that led to power cuts and a three-day work week. Soon after negotiations broke down between the Government and the National Union of Miners over miners' salaries in the winter of 1973–1974, Heath, in a showdown with the miners, called an election, lost his parliamentary majority, and was unable to form another Government.

Widespread public protests over controversial government policies and how prime ministers respond to such events also can affect a prime minister's ability to lead. For example, soon after the Thatcher Government introduced a new form of local tax in 1990 called the community charge (or poll tax, as it was commonly referred to), about one hundred thousand people streamed into the streets of London to denounce the tax as punitive, and left widespread property damage in their wake. Despite the public outcry and the intensity of the protests, Thatcher refused to relent, and her inflexibility was one of several factors that contributed to her resignation several months later.

Protestors also threw down a challenge to Blair's Government in 2000 over another tax, the duty on fuel for motor vehicles. As oil-rich nations cut their exports in the summer and autumn, the price of oil shot up, which attracted increased attention to the Government's duty on fuel at the pump, the highest in Europe. Hardest hit were truckers and farmers, who dramatized their plight by blockading oil depots to prevent tankers from making their deliveries. Inconvenienced though the public was, it nevertheless sided with the protestors, who carried on with the blockade for six days. Before calling it off on the seventh, they threatened to resume their action sixty days later unless the Government acceded to their demand to reduce the tax.

This event triggered charges that the prime minister was out of touch with the public and contributed to the sharpest one-month slump in support of a Government ever recorded by a polling firm. Blair appeared to be gripped by a problem he could not solve: capitulating to the protestors would make him look weak, but doing nothing would incline people to think he was showing arrogant disregard for their difficulties. Just before the sixty-day deadline, the head of Britain's Treasury, Chancellor of the Exchequer Gordon Brown, defused the issue when he announced a modest cut in the duty on a cleaner form of fuel that would become available in the following fiscal year, and he made other concessions to truckers. These changes took the steam out of the protest movement, and in the meantime, the Government adopted a get-tough approach with the oil companies, especially after they reported large end-of-year profits. Two months later the price of oil began to drop. Soon after the price drop, opinion polls recorded a sharp rise in the Government's public approval ratings.

Leadership Style

A contemporary historian in 1994 spoke of how difficult it would be for a prime minister to possess all of the many traits and talents thought desirable in a prime minister "exhausting week after punishing year." If it were possible, the result would be a composite of

> someone with the dedication to duty of a Peel, the physical energy of a Gladstone, the detachment of a Salisbury, the brains of an Asquith, the balls of a Lloyd George, the word-power of a Churchill, the administrative gifts of an Attlee, the style of a Macmillan, the managerialism of a Heath and the sleep requirements of a Thatcher.

And then, not surprisingly, he added: "Human beings do not come like that."[12] Neither do prime ministers. As the historian suggested, prime ministers possess distinctive personal attributes that affect the way they lead. A closer look at Thatcher, Major, and Blair illustrates this point.

Margaret Thatcher was a conviction prime minister. Her convictions suffused her style of leadership. She held tenaciously to her beliefs and became combative when challenged. Making decisions by consensus was anathema, for, as she put it, it required "abandoning all beliefs, principles, values and policies in search of something in which no one believes, but to which no one objects."[13] She used her premiership in a messianic promotion of individual initiative and entrepreneurship and as a crusade to reverse what she believed was Britain's steady economic decline. She thrived on detail, possessed boundless energy, and required only four hours of sleep a night. The major policies of the 1980s were largely those for which she delighted in taking credit and responsibility, and which, when strung together, acquired the status of an -ism: "Thatcherism." Many of these policies were highly contentious, and she hectored with righteous indignation those who opposed them, scrapped with ministers, circumvented the cabinet, and even attempted to micromanage the work of ministers in their departments. Not since the Second World War had a prime minister so dominated the political stage. In the end, however, it was her dominance that brought her down in 1990 after the public became increasingly irritated with her abrasive manner and inflexibility.

John Major, who succeeded Thatcher, adopted a style of leadership that was the polar opposite of his predecessor's. Major was a consensus prime minister. His party colleagues saw him as unifying the party by attracting the backing of both Thatcher's supporters and detractors. This enhanced the party's standing with the public in the run-up to the next election. Unlike

Thatcher, he attached great importance to collegial decision making in the cabinet. He convened the cabinet regularly, sought out the views of ministers, and achieved agreement by compromise when opinions diverged. When he occasionally kept his own counsel and made decisions without consulting the cabinet, his colleagues did not resent him for it, "because genuine collective discussion was his normal and preferred practice." [14] Both his standing and that of his party rose after he replaced the highly controversial poll tax instituted by his predecessor with one that was more acceptable, negotiated terms favorable to Britain when he met with other heads of government to approve a new EU treaty, and dispatched troops to the Persian Gulf to join in putting a stop to Iraq's incursions into Kuwait. Before long, Major's ratings soared to near-record levels, higher than any other prime minister since Churchill.

They did not remain there. Shortly after the Conservatives won the election of 1992 with an overall majority of twenty-one seats, some intractable issues about Britain's membership in the EU surfaced and then intensified. They dogged Major for much of what remained of his premiership. The cabinet was no longer united and neither was the parliamentary party; Euroskeptics pitted themselves against Europhiles, and the Government's approval ratings plummeted. Leadership by consensus, once thought to be Major's strong point, came to be seen as vacillation. From 1992 until the end of his premiership, the Major Government appeared at times to have no determinative agenda. The prime minister was accused of dithering, especially on issues dealing with the EU. His former chancellor of the exchequer called him "in office but not in power," and some longed for the return of a no-nonsense style of leadership reminiscent of the Thatcher model.

When the Labour Party emerged victorious after the 1997 election, few doubted that Tony Blair would lead his party in government any differently from how he had led it in opposition in the previous three years. In opposition, he was as determined to reform his party as Thatcher had been to transform Britain in the previous decade. Soon after he moved into No. 10, it became apparent there was something very Thatcher-like about his style of leadership. Not short on convictions, zeal, or energy, he lost no time in acting on his pledge to lead vigorously from the center. As one scholar put it, he became a command and control prime minister. [15]

Within days of the 1997 election, the Government announced a shift in monetary policymaking: no longer would interest rates be set by the prime minister and the chancellor of the exchequer, but instead by the Monetary Policy Committee of the Bank of England. Taking politics out of the setting of interest rates was a significant reform in monetary policy making. Just as significant was the fact that the prime minister chose not to discuss this initiative with his cabinet first. This announcement foreshadowed Blair's decision-making style. Decisions would not be made collegially by the cabinet, as they had been under Major, but rather bilaterally by Blair and the cabinet minister in charge of the department responsible for carrying out the policy.

One senior minister likened Blair to the chief executive of various subsidiary companies who held his ministers accountable for the work of their departments.[16] Performance objectives were devised for every department, increased funding for departments was made contingent upon achievement of their objectives, and ministers were required to clear all their media interviews, speeches, and press releases with No. 10. No. 10 issued a steady stream of news about the Government's accomplishments on all fronts. So clear was it from the beginning of Blair's premiership that he would be the driving force behind decision making that one seasoned commentator was prompted to proclaim, "Goodbye cabinet government, welcome the Blair presidency."[17]

Blair kept his pledge to lead vigorously from the center. When opinion polls in the fourth year of his premiership began to register the public's discontent with certain public services, however, a cabinet minister close to the prime minister admitted in a major speech that the Government had been responsible for inflating public expectations. Leading vigorously from the center had failed to take into account the time the departments required to implement policies. "The enthusiasm of our rhetoric did not help," he acknowledged, and "we were all a bit guilty of letting some of our sense of the possible get out of sync with the pace of change on the ground." The lesson the Government had learned, he continued, was not to exaggerate what it could do. Labour's manifesto for the next general election, he intimated, would be much more cautious.[18] As indeed it was. Some Blair loyalists began to concede that there were limits to Blair's command and control premiership.

The Cabinet

At the close of the nineteenth century, the cabinet was the nation's high command for decision making. It was at the cabinet table that ministers thrashed out their differences, established priorities, and agreed to the policies of the government of the day. Their tasks were onerous, but not nearly as onerous as they are today. Governing then carried fewer responsibilities, and ministers were able to carry out their work at a relatively leisurely pace. But the pace soon picked up. With the outbreak of the First World War in 1914 and the introduction of the first stages of the welfare state in the decade both before and after the war, cabinet workloads mounted. By the 1930s, the pressures on ministers had grown so much that prime ministers began to refer issues their cabinets could not handle alone to one or more ad hoc committees. These cabinet subgroups, each made up of a handful of ministers, were charged with examining issues in some depth and then reporting their recommendations to the full cabinet for further discussion and final approval.

The pressures on cabinet ministers mounted again with the onset of the Second World War in 1939 and the dizzying pace of reconstruction that followed. As Clement Attlee's Governments (1945–1950, 1950–1951) assumed further roles in managing the economy and nationalizing industry and stepping up efforts to expand the welfare state, departments grew in number and size. With the work of government becoming more specialized and complex, ministers relied all the more on an ever-expanding network of ad hoc cabinet committees—as many as 250 between 1945 and 1951. When cabinets convened, much of their time was taken up considering their recommendations.

Prime ministers in this period after the war used cabinets in different ways, depending on how they viewed both their role and that of the cabinet and how they sized up events of the day. For example, Attlee (1945–1951) used the cabinet as a clearinghouse for reports from cabinet committees and position papers from ministers' departments and demanded snappy decisions from his colleagues. Only rarely did he encourage the cabinet to engage in wide-ranging discussions of major issues and policies that cut across departmental boundaries. Winston Churchill (1951–1955), on the other hand, was much less eager to press ministers for final decisions on day-to-day issues and instead used the cabinet as a "sounding board for broad sweeps of policy."[19] He chaired meetings in a much more relaxed manner than Attlee and took greater care in drawing out ministers' views. So different from Attlee was he in presiding over the cabinet that one observer of the day was prompted to remark that Churchill ran the cabinet in a manner "reminiscent of bygone times."[20]

In the years following Churchill's post-war premiership, cabinet agendas became more crowded. By the 1960s, increasing numbers of issues were referred to cabinet committees for consideration—and final settlement. The authority of the full cabinet was devolved to these ministerial subgroups, which by then had achieved a status that bordered on the permanent. In effect, they became mini-cabinets. Although they continued to report their decisions to the full cabinet, so final were their recommendations that Harold Wilson in his first two Governments (1964–1966 and 1966–1970) ruled that they could not be appealed to the full cabinet for reconsideration unless the minister who chaired the committee agreed. Those who followed Wilson continued this practice.

Another variant of devolved decision making reduced the role of the full cabinet even further. It took the form of bilateral agreements struck by the prime minister and one or more cabinet colleagues whose judgments the prime minister valued. This practice was nothing new. Attlee had consulted selected cabinet colleagues individually, in particular his foreign secretary. Later, Harold Macmillan did the same with his foreign secretaries and chancellors of the exchequer. Bilateral consultations became much more common with Wilson. However, every now and again they made ministers restive. Although Wilson reported the results of his consultations to the cabinet, his ministerial colleagues felt that on some issues they should have been drawn into discussions, and drawn in at an early stage.

Trends in the way cabinets functioned in the thirty years following the Second World War have become hallmarks of the cabinet today. Cabinets meet less often—not twice a week, as in the past, but usually just once a week. Meetings are shorter and fewer decisions are made in cabinet, as suggested by the sharp decline in the number of background papers circulated to ministers before meetings. So anodyne have most cabinet meetings become that noncabinet ministers regard cabinet minutes as "among the least important parts of their weekly reading."[21] Cabinet committees are now the centers of government policymaking. Their decisions usually are final and are not always reported to the cabinet. In the meantime, decisions struck bilaterally by the prime minister and selected cabinet ministers, either in person or by correspondence, have become standard practice. They too are not always reported to the cabinet, let alone thrashed out there.

Because of these developments, cabinets today have become deeply fragmented. Meetings held once a week last sometimes little more than an hour and afford little time for ministers to take in all of the complex policies reported and to grasp fully all of the issues on which the prime minister might ask them to comment. So grueling have the demands on cabinet members become that ministers lack the time to take as much interest as they once did in what is happening in other departments. In the meantime, a cabinet norm has evolved that discourages ministers from speaking up in cabinet about matters that deal directly with the responsibilities of their colleagues lest they be seen as interfering. Ministers feel their reputations depend "far more on their ability to represent their own departmental interests in cabinet and its committees . . . than on any contribution they may make to collective decision-making."[22]

Cabinet committees and bilateral dealings have fostered fragmentation. Ministers with responsibilities within one broad sphere of government activity rarely interact with ministers whose work falls within another broad sphere of activity. For example, the secretaries of state for Health and for Work and Pensions, both of whom sit on the Domestic Affairs Committee, seldom come into contact with the secretaries of state for the Foreign and Commonwealth Office and for Defence, who sit on the Committee on Defence and Overseas Policy. "Such fragmentation," concludes one scholar, "corrodes the collegiate nature of government. Cohesiveness is lost. The Cabinet loses strategic vision; it cannot stand back and consider its policies in the round."[23]

The same also could be said for bilateral decision making. "Creeping bilateralism" (coined by a former member of Thatcher's cabinet in the 1980s)[24] became a rampant form of decision making starting in the early days of Blair's premiership. As one veteran observer of the political scene put it,

> No Prime Minister since the nineteenth century has spent more time avoiding formal meetings with Cabinet colleagues than Tony Blair. When they happen, they are brief. The real deals are done elsewhere,

usually in the Prime Minister's study with only three or four people sitting around: and, as often as not, with only two. "We are not a very collegiate government," said one Cabinet minister, just before he was sacked. "I'm afraid we don't really see very much of each other. It's a strange outfit."[25]

With rampant bilateralism the modus operandi, ministers were left in the dark more than ever about what had been agreed to by the prime minister and a minister. Said one former minister of the Blair cabinet, bilateralism "runs quite counter to the whole concept of joined-up government," for "ministers who have a legitimate role or responsibility . . . don't know what's happened or what has been decided."[26]

In 2002, there was the appearance of a return to cabinet government, probably because the prospect of Britain's joining the United States in invading Iraq was so controversial that Blair realized he needed to assemble his colleagues regularly to convince them of the worthiness of this cause. The cabinet met often in the twelve months prior to the start of the war in March 2003, and Iraq appeared on its agenda twenty-four times and arose tangentially as a topic in cabinet meetings on several other occasions.[27] That was one of many findings released in 2004 in the Butler Report, the product of an investigation commissioned by the prime minister and headed by Sir Robin Butler into the intelligence that led Britain into war. Another finding was that while ministers received oral briefings in cabinet meetings on Iraq's putative weapons of mass destruction, they were not issued the "excellent quality papers" on the subject written by civil servants in the intelligence community as background documents either before or during these meetings.[28] Moreover, the cabinet Committee on Defence and Overseas Policy was not convened once in this period.

Thus, what appeared to be a return to cabinet government was a return to its form, not its substance. Decisions were made about Iraq not in the cabinet room, as the Butler panel discovered, but rather in a Downing Street sitting room, with the prime minister presiding from a sofa over a meeting attended by "a small number of key Ministers and officials and military officers." No minutes were taken. In the twelve months before the war, there were twenty-five such "sofa-style" meetings, as some called them later. Butler and his four colleagues on the panel found this revelation disturbing. For ten years a cabinet secretary when Thatcher, Major, and then Blair were at No. 10, Butler was a stickler for procedure. So much of a stickler was he that he urged Blair to ask that a civil servant accompany him during the many times the prime minister met to discuss business with Gordon Brown, the chancellor of the exchequer, so that records could be kept for future reference. It came as no surprise, then, that the Butler Report registered concern "that the informality and circumscribed character of the Government's procedures which we saw in the context of policy-making towards Iraq risks reducing the scope for informed collective political judgement."[29]

Speaking of . . .

The Prime Minister, the Cabinet, and Iraq

Tony Blair made several changes in the Cabinet Office in his second term, most of them in the months preceding the run-up to the invasion of Iraq in March 2003. As it happened, the changes had a potential impact on the capability of the cabinet to respond to the emerging crisis.

Although the full cabinet was convened on several occasions for briefings on Iraq in the pre-invasion period, in the end, the cabinet that appeared to carry any weight was not a cabinet, but rather a select few from the cabinet who were invited by Blair to join a handful of unelected others. Their venue was not the Cabinet Room, but a sitting room in No. 10, where the prime minister presided over the small gathering from a sofa.

> "[O]pportunities were negated by the prime ministerial preference for informal, small group decision-making. . . . Yet . . . [cabinet] ministers must bear their own share of responsibility for allowing themselves to be carried along in the flow so uncritically."

In what follows, Professor Christopher Hill touches on the most important changes that Blair made in the Cabinet Office; suggests that, quite apart from these changes, the prime minister preferred the informality of "small group decision-making" in the No. 10 sitting room; and argues that Blair alone cannot be blamed for the comparatively minor role that the real cabinet played on Iraq.

"The Cabinet was the key site where debate and forensic analysis might have restrained the Prime Minister [from the decision to invade Iraq]. But its position, even in these favourable circumstances for participation (that is, a long-drawn out period of gestation, with ample opportunities to seek information and to debate options) had been structurally weakened by five years of confident prime ministerial leadership. . . . Blair had replaced Robin Cook as foreign secretary with a more pliable figure in 2001. He had also weakened the key post of Cabinet Secre-

Lord Butler, interviewed for the first time a few months after he submitted his report, lamented the fact that "the Cabinet now—and I don't think there is any secret about this—doesn't make decisions." When asked, "Wasn't that also the case under Margaret Thatcher?" he replied: "She certainly wanted to get her own way, and she was very dominant, but she certainly took the view, as Harold Wilson did, that important decisions should be taken by Cabinet." Butler then added:

> I think what tends to happen now is that the government reaches conclusions in rather small groups of people who are not necessarily representative of all the groups of interests in government, and there is insufficient opportunity for other people to debate, dissent and modify.[30]

Shifting the decision-making arena from the cabinet to what Butler described as "small groups of people who are not necessarily representative of all the groups of interests in government" runs counter to the Ministerial Code, which reads in part:

tary by hiving off intelligence matters to a special 'security and intelligence coordinator', who does not, however, attend Cabinet. Furthermore, two key posts in the Cabinet Secretariat, those of the head of the Defence and Overseas Secretariat and head of the European Affairs Secretariat were combined with those of the Prime Minister's personal advisers on foreign affairs and European affairs respectively. The net effect was that the Cabinet Secretary, who traditionally has served the Cabinet as a whole and not just the prime minister, was unable to carry out effectively the functions of ensuring that proper papers were written for Cabinet and its committees (the Defence and Overseas Policy sub-committee did not meet during this long crisis), that full minutes were kept, and that informal inner groups did not have an unfair advantage. As W.G. Runciman has argued, '. . . the decision to go to war was taken without the extent of informed discussion in Cabinet that would have been normal in the past'.

"Unfortunately the Cabinet in the past has not always had the 'informed discussion' on foreign policy that would have been desirable. But in this case the opportunities which had been created by virtue of prolonged public debate, were negated by the prime ministerial preference for informal, small group decision-making, dignified with the label of a 'War Cabinet'. . . .

"Yet . . . [cabinet] ministers must bear their own share of responsibility for allowing themselves to be carried along in the flow so uncritically. They were, after all, for the most part experienced and hard-nosed. It is difficult to know why a momentum of concern did not build up."

Source: Christopher Hill, "Putting the World to Rights: Tony Blair's Foreign Policy Mission," in *The Blair Effect: 2001–5,* ed. Anthony Seldon and Dennis Kavanagh (Cambridge: Cambridge University Press, 2005), pp. 400–402.

The business of the Cabinet and Ministerial Committees consists in the main of . . . questions which significantly engage the collective responsibility of the government because they raise major issues of policy or because they are of critical importance to the public.

Who had the authority to shift the decision-making arena from the cabinet room to the sitting room? Only the prime minister. The code is the prime minister's dominion, and only the prime minister may interpret it, revise it, enforce it—or ignore it.

"He [Tony Blair] simply cannot imagine how a government can function with a Cabinet having to be consulted regularly." [31] That was how one political analyst summed up Blair's view of cabinet government. Cabinet committees, bilateral meetings with a minister in the Downing Street garden, or multilateral meetings with a select group of ministers and several nonelected individuals in a Downing Street sitting room—each of these is a venue Blair found more congenial than the Cabinet Room. His preference for these locations contributed to a loss of cabinet collegiality and solidarity. Contributing also to this loss was an unprecedented entente concluded by Blair and Brown three years before Labour was returned to power to divide government policies into two spheres, with Blair presiding over one sphere and Brown over the other:

> [T]here were "Gordon's areas" (notably the economy, welfare, industrial policy and international development) and "Tony's areas" (notably education, health and defence), and areas where they overlapped and often clashed, notably Europe, and increasingly, the direction of public service reform. The boundaries shifted as Blair became more involved in the second term with Africa and with pensions.[32]

Dividing policies into "Gordon's areas" and "Tony's Areas" represented Blair's fulfillment of one of three sets of understanding reportedly concluded between Blair and Brown in 1994 in the event Labour won power in the next general election—which it did. The other two sets of understanding are thought to be that Brown would become chancellor of the exchequer and that, were Labour re-elected, Blair would step down from his premiership before the end of his second term, but not before making Brown his heir apparent.[33] As it happened, Brown became chancellor of the exchequer when Labour won power in 1997.

But as Blair's second term drew to a close and there were no signs of his imminent departure from No. 10, Brown's patience wore thin. Feeling betrayed by Blair, he became rancorous, and his relationship with the prime minister took an antagonistic turn. When the cabinet met, it was as if two prime ministers were present, one an actual prime minister and the other an increasingly impatient prime-minister-in-waiting, each wishing they were somewhere other than in a cabinet meeting, and both with agendas that were not always in harmony.

Finally, in the autumn of 2006, the tensions between the two started to ease. It was at that time, sixteen months after Labour's third election victory, that Blair agreed to announce his departure. Although he had said at a 2004 party conference that, if reelected, he would serve a full third term but not seek a fourth, pressure began to build within the Parliamentary Labour Party: Blair would have to leave before the next election. Furthermore, he would have to announce his departure date. As it happened, he agreed to cut short his premiership and to leave office at some unspecified date before the autumn 2007 party conference.

From that point on, cabinet ministers reportedly looked to two for leadership in the cabinet room. They not only turned to the prime minister, they also looked to Brown, who now was decidedly more than just a prime-minister-in-waiting. Brown's election as party leader was seen as a foregone conclusion, and ministers could not afford to ignore his views if they wished to remain in the cabinet after Blair's departure.

As the cabinet has grown weaker as a decision-making body, the Cabinet Office has become stronger. This is contrary to what one might expect, but it can be explained by the fact that the Cabinet Office has gone to great lengths in recent years to ensure that the policies made from on high are carried out in a faithful, efficient, and timely manner. There can be a wide chasm between policymaking and policy execution. This is where bridges must be built, and those who engineer them and keep them in good repair are found in the Cabinet Office.

The Cabinet Office

Historically, the most effective bridge builder has been the Cabinet Office. This office, which had its origins in the First World War and has grown in size and stature ever since, assists the cabinet as a whole but increasingly aids the prime minister. Its staff consists of some 1,600 civil servants, many of whom are drafted for two- or three-year stints from various departments, and most of the rest of whom are recruited from the private sector for similar periods. All work under the direction of the cabinet secretary. As noted earlier, the Cabinet Office is located around the corner from No. 10, and the cabinet secretary's office is on the other side of the back door of No. 10, just a few steps from the prime minister's. Such propinquity is not accidental. One of the prime minister's most trusted advisers, the cabinet secretary sits to the prime minister's immediate right in the cabinet meetings, distributes documents to ministers before such meetings are held, writes the minutes of cabinet meetings, briefs the prime minister on the work of cabinet committees, and counsels the premier on ministerial dismissals. Although the head of Government and government's chief public administrator have pursued different professions and are driven by different incentives, they share the same objective—to ensure that whenever cabinet decisions are made, they are accurately communicated to the departments and are effectively enforced there.

"The Cabinet Office is a Ferrari, built for speed and action," said one former minister. He might have gotten carried away a bit with his metaphor and even exaggerated the office's abilities, but he essentially was correct when he wrote:

> It services the Prime Minister and knows his wishes. It is in constant contact with all government departments and is aware of everything that is going on there. Almost at the drop of a hat, it can produce documents, aircraft, communications networks, plans.[34]

To produce these and other services, it is organized into the following six secretariats:

- Economic and Domestic Affairs

- European

- Defence and Overseas
- Civil Contingencies
- Ceremonial
- Joint Intelligence and Security

The first four assist the cabinet overall, including its nearly fifty standing committees, ad hoc committees, and subcommittees, which are listed in Table 9.2. The Economic and Domestic Affairs and the Defence and Overseas Secretariats have long been part of the Cabinet Office. The European Secretariat, on the other hand, is a relatively new addition. Formed after Britain joined the EU in 1973, it deals with countless numbers of issues that bear on Britain's membership. Newest of the secretariats are the Civil Contingencies Secretariat and the Ceremonial Secretariat. For some years, the Civil Contingencies Unit, which developed plans for dealing with civil emergencies, was not central to the Cabinet Office's concerns, but it was elevated to a secretariat in the wake of the terrorist threat in Blair's second term. The Ceremonial Secretariat prepares the prime minister's twice-a-year honors list, and the Joint Intelligence and Security Secretariat assesses intelligence and advises the cabinet secretary on the coordination of those units of government that acquire and use foreign and domestic intelligence.

As prime ministers focused more on the timely and effective implementation of their Governments' policies, it did not take long for them to realize that the No. 10 machine was not up to the job of pressing departments for rapid results. Increasingly, they have relied on the Cabinet Office to play a troubleshooting role. This it does as it attempts to accomplish three objectives: to overcome bureaucratic inertia, if not intransigence; improve management systems so that new programs can be implemented quickly and effectively; and coordinate the work of several departments when all are expected to participate in achieving one overarching policy. The objective that poses the greatest challenge is the last one, for departments often focus narrowly on their work and pay scant attention to related responsibilities performed by other departments. To deal with this problem, which is colloquially referred to as "departmentalitis," the Blair Government created the prime ministerially directed but Cabinet Office-based Delivery Unit. Departmentalitis precipitates turf battles between departments when one claims it is more competent than another in dealing with a program or issue. Here, the Cabinet Office involves itself in the work of departments by arbitrating disputes.

The Cabinet Office today performs many tasks the cabinet itself performed long ago, at a time when the pressures on ministers were fewer. It assists the cabinet and its committees and subcommittees, enforces Government policies both within and across departments, and arbitrates disputes that arise between them. It is a bridge builder par excellence. There is another bridge builder as well—the Treasury—whose engineers complement the work of the Cabinet Office.

Table 9.2	Cabinet Committees, Cabinet Subcommittees, and Ad Hoc Committees

Standing Committees:

■ Anti-Social Behavior

■ Asylum and Migration

■ Civil Contingencies

■ Constitutional Affairs

  • Subcommittees on Electoral Policy

    –Freedom of Information

    –Parliamentary Modernization

■ Intelligence Services

■ Defence and Overseas Policy

  • Subcommittees on International Terrorism

  • Protective Security and Resilience

  • Iraq

  • Conflict Prevention and Reconstruction

■ Domestic Affairs

  • Subcommittees on Aging Policy

    –Children's Policy

    –Communities

    –Legal Affairs

    –Public Health

■ Economic Affairs, Productivity and Competitiveness

■ Energy and the Environment

  • Subcommittee on Sustainable Development in Government

■ European Policy

■ European Union Strategy

■ Housing and Planning

■ Identity Management

■ Legislative Program

■ Local and Regional Government

  • Subcommittee on Government Strategy and Performance

■ National Health Service Reform

■ Public Services and Public Expenditure

■ Electronic Service Delivery

■ Public Services Reform

■ Regulation, Bureaucracy and Risk

  • Subcommittees on Regulatory Accountability

    –Inspection

■ Schools Policy

(continues)

Table 9.2	(continued)

- Science and Innovation
- Serious and Organized Crime and Drugs
- Social Exclusion
- Welfare Reform

Ad Hoc Committees:
- Restructuring of the European Aerospace and Defence Industry
- Animal Rights Extremism
- Olympics
- London
- Efficiency and Relocation
- Data Sharing
- Influenza Pandemic Planning
- Post Office Network

Source: www.cabinet-office.gov.uk. List as of 2006.

The Treasury

If "knowledge itself is power," as the English philosopher Francis Bacon once put it, money runs a close second. The Treasury possesses both powers. It has a knowledge of what policies the departments are implementing and the money to implement them. So powerful is the office that not one, but two, ministers sit as members of the cabinet—the chancellor of the exchequer, who heads the Treasury, and the chief secretary of the Treasury, who oversees annual budget negotiations with departmental ministers. Of all ministers, historically it has been the chancellor with whom a prime minister has the most frequent dealings, although their relations are not always cordial.

The Treasury is the place where policy and money meet. The departments of state have long been required to obtain annual clearance for policies from the Treasury before receiving authorization to spend public funds. This has given the Treasury an opportunity to exercise immense control over departmental policies by vetoing proposed policies if they are too expensive or if they are inconsistent with other overarching policies of the government of the day or, alternatively, by allocating generous levels of funding to support them. The centrality of the Treasury allows its officials to take in the "big picture" of government departments and their policies and expenditures, and scores of Treasury expenditure controllers are trained to "perceive and make connections between policy issues and expenditure items which have arisen separately in different programmes."[35]

From the start of the first Blair Government, the chancellor of the exchequer, Gordon Brown, tightened the Treasury's control over the release of funds like no other chancellor since the end of the Second World War. The

Treasury's power of the purse takes two forms: a triennial comprehensive review of departmental spending and public service agreements struck between the Treasury and the departments. To qualify for further funding, departments must demonstrate that they have achieved the policy outcomes set out in their public service agreements. Their progress is monitored by the cabinet's Committee on Public Services and Public Expenditure, chaired by the chancellor. Blair's command and control premiership is underpinned by the Blair-Brown axis, with its emphasis on the rapid delivery of public services. Brown is not just the chancellor, but the "iron chancellor," for the departments of state realize what penalties they must pay for failing to achieve policy results on their own or in conjunction with other departments. In that respect, the Treasury is equipped to do what the Cabinet Office cannot do—rein in the departments by threatening to impose financial strictures on them if their performance falls short.

Conclusion

So does Britain have a cabinet government or prime ministerial government? Few questions have generated more debate among British political scientists. That prime ministers exercise more power today than before is accepted by most political scientists as a given. Where they divide is on the question of whether prime ministers have stretched their powers to such an extent that cabinets no longer play a significant role in national policymaking.

One scholar likened the powers of the prime minister to the elastic properties of a rubber band.[36] Activist prime ministers stretch the elastic until there is little, if any, give to it. The cabinet is the countervailing agent in the elastic that prevents it from being stretched too far or to the breaking point. When a less activist prime minister assumes office, it snaps back. Once stretched, however, the properties of the rubber band are such that it never fully reverts to its original state. The next time an activist prime minister stretches it, there is less resistance in the elastic. It is significant that there has been a pattern of more activist prime ministers following less activist prime ministers into office. Margaret Thatcher, a very activist prime minister, took office after the more quiescent premiership of James Callaghan, and Tony Blair, a prime minister in the Thatcher mold, has been far more activist than his predecessor, John Major. Just as significant, activist prime ministers have stretched their powers to a greater degree than the activist prime ministers who have preceded them.

The incremental and at times subtle ways in which prime ministers have stretched their powers is largely an outgrowth of the changing political environment of governing. Increasingly, these changes have thrust the prime minister front and center on the political stage. Television camera crews and sound technicians position themselves to capture a prime minister's every word and gesture, whether the occasion is the once-a-week Prime Minister's Questions or the once-a-month prime minister's press conference. Pollsters regularly tap the opinions of the public for an assessment of the prime minister's perform-ance. A No. 10 Downing Street Web site provides information on the prime minister's most recent pronouncements, and when there is an election, the prime minister shapes the contents of the party's manifesto and attracts the most attention as he or she campaigns up and down the country. All these changes have contributed to making the British political system a system dom-inated by the prime minister. There is no turning back the clock. A history of the intermittent stretching of the powers of the prime minister cannot be re-versed. As one scholar has observed, "If evolution means never escaping from the inheritance of the past, it also means that it is impossible to return to the conditions of the past," and as a result, the powers of the prime minister have grown "in accordance with the compulsive inheritance of the past and with the present imperatives of a changing political environment."[37]

Where does this leave the cabinet in the prime minister-cabinet relation-ship? Have prime ministers stretched their powers to such an extent that, as one official put it just before the close of the last century, "the old model of Cabinet government is dead as a doornail"?[38] He chose his words carefully, for his reference was to the *old* model of cabinet government. Like the office of prime minister, the cabinet has evolved and continues to evolve from what it once did and therefore from what it once was.

No longer do ministers gather around the cabinet table week after week to thrash out every issue, agree on every course of action that government should take, coordinate every major activity of government, and resolve every dispute that arises between departments. Rather than regularly shape the most important decisions and policies of the day, the cabinet today de-volves many decisions to cabinet committees, which are "the continuation of cabinet government by other means";[39] resolves interdepartmental dis-putes if the relevant ministers or officials in the Cabinet Office cannot settle them on their own; expects the Cabinet Office to coordinate the implemen-tation of policies across government departments; and deliberates on what to do whenever a crisis occurs.

Cabinets today are too small and too inexpert to deal effectively with the Goliath of big government. What is more, ministers are stretched to the limit. They struggle with the demands placed on them by their work in the departments, by their responsibilities in the Commons, by their efforts to troubleshoot for their constituents, and by the decisions they must make when they travel to Brussels to represent their Government in the EU's Council of Ministers. Little time remains for them to focus thoughtfully on the increasingly specialized and contentious issues of government that, if brought to the cabinet table, concern only a few of their colleagues at any one time. Meanwhile, the Cabinet Office, through its secretariats and other units, has played an increasingly vital role as the long arm of the cabinet.

In 1926, ten years after he left office, Prime Minister Herbert Asquith wrote in his memoirs that "The office of Prime Minister is what its holder chooses and is able to make of it."[40] Few would challenge Asquith's assertion in his day or in this. The key word in this passage, it must be emphasized, is *able*. Activist prime ministers often find the powers of the office too constraining and are unable to do all that they wish. They may lack a large and robustly supportive majority in the Commons, but if they are lucky enough to call upon this resource, they are always constrained by the mood and the thinking of the party and the cabinet. The cabinet, above all, represents a cross section of the party, and prime ministers who repeatedly attempt to stretch the elastic too far by circumventing the cabinet to achieve objectives contrary to what it finds acceptable to the party overall soon find that they have overstepped their bounds. As one scholar wrote, "A prime minister who can carry his colleagues with him can be in a very powerful position, but he is only as strong as they let him be."[41]

10 Administering Government at the Center

arliament enacts a law, the law receives the Royal Assent, and it is then returned whence it came—the department that discussed it, drafted its language, and watched it progress from public bill to public law. Having come full circle, the law proceeds to the next stage in the policy-making process—the implementation stage, which is dominated by bureaucrats and bureaucracy.

"Bureaucracy" is one of the deadliest words in the English language. It conveys images of workstations occupied by individuals wearing green eye shades who religiously follow rules that make no sense, store documents that are no longer useful, and are neither inspired by their work nor an inspiration to their coworkers. Those who have had any experience with the British civil service know that this cynical typecasting of civil servants and the world they inhabit bears no resemblance to reality. More than half a million civil servants are entrusted with administering government programs that affect the lives of sixty million people. They help find jobs for the unemployed, manage the economy, subsidize farmers, run prisons, collect taxes, administer state pensions, staff embassies, and much more. Their work is indispensable; without them, government would soon grind to a halt. In addition, they are poised to implement new policies initiated by whichever party comes to power. Here again, their work is invaluable, for without civil servants the party of the government of the day would be unable to carry out the pledges it made in the last election. Every Government is results-oriented, and unless the departments and agencies deliver on the promises its party made to win the last election, the voters could well deny it the right to govern after the next one.

With No. 10 Downing Street and the Cabinet Office at the top of the hierarchy, the executive side of government consists of fifteen (sometimes sixteen) departments, approximately 140 executive agencies, various regulatory bodies, and a seemingly endless number of entities called quangos and quagos. Whitehall, an area of London stretching from Trafalgar Square to Westminster, is where some of these units—the departments—are headquartered. Indeed, "Whitehall" is the shorthand term used to refer to the departments collectively. Found in various locations throughout the country are the executive agencies, bodies that have been set up in relatively recent years to implement Whitehall's programs. Regulatory bodies, quangos, and quagos perform yet a different set of functions, and all operate at arms-length from the departments.

Whitehall Departments

Whitehall departments devise and oversee the implementation of the policies of the government of the day. Where do these policies originate? The most important ones originate from the manifesto of the party of government; others come from the departments themselves. Minor proposals normally require only the approval of ministers, but the more important ones need the approval of Government and Parliament. The number of departments rises and falls as some are consolidated and others are created. Each is headed by a cabinet minister, or secretary of state, and each secretary of state is assisted by two or more junior ministers. All ministers, whether senior or junior, are appointed by the prime minister and are accountable to Parliament. Immediately below the secretary of state is the permanent secretary, the highest civil servant in a department. He or she is at the apex of a hierarchy of civil servants, all of whom are answerable to ministers. Unlike ministers, all civil servants, including the permanent secretary, are required to maintain a politically neutral stance and are expected to serve the ministers of whichever party is in power without favor and with equal fervor.

Because differences exist among cabinet departments, it is difficult to generalize about them, although they do share certain characteristics. Among the most salient are the following:

• they vary in size and function,

• most are reorganized from time to time to achieve certain objectives,

• they are headed by ministers and staffed by civil servants,

• they make policies and then oversee their implementation, and

• they are called upon to coordinate cross-cutting policies.

Variety in Size and Function

Table 10.1 shows that not all fifteen departments of state are called departments. Three are called offices, one is a ministry, and another an HM (for Her Majesty's) Treasury. Nomenclature aside, what makes these units of the executive distinctive is that each is headed by a cabinet minister, and in what follows all are referred to as departments.

Table 10.1	Cabinet Departments and Civil Servants
Department	Number of Civil Servants
Department for Communities and Local Government	5,740
Department for Constitutional Affairs	34,090
Department for Culture, Media and Sport	620
Ministry of Defence	87,260*
Department for Education and Skills	4,170
Department for Environment, Food and Rural Affairs	13,100
Foreign and Commonwealth Office	6,160
Department of Health	6,100
Home Office	73,010
Department for International Development	1,780
Northern Ireland Office	140
Department of Trade and Industry	10,000
Department for Transport	19,150
HM Treasury	1,160
Department for Work and Pensions	117,180

*Nonuniformed personnel
Note: Numbers, which are full-time equivalent, are effective as of September 2006.
Source: www.civilservice.gov.uk/management/statistics/index.asp (link: "Public Sector Employment Statistics").

Differences in the size of departments, as measured by the number of civil servants who work in each, are quite striking. These numbers, however, suggest little more than how extensive or limited a department's operations are. For example, the Ministry of Defence, which employs more than eighty-seven thousand nonuniformed personnel, is engaged in far-flung activities at home and abroad that range from maintaining strategic petroleum reserves to planning new missions for NATO and organizing logistical support for British troops stationed abroad. By contrast, the diminutive Northern Ireland Office, created in 1972 when Britain imposed direct rule following the resumption of militant activities by the Provisional Irish Republican Army (IRA), employs no more than 140 civil servants. This is the smallest department of government, but it struggles with one of government's largest challenges—overseeing implementation of the peace initiatives agreed to in 1998, which includes encouraging Ulster's principal political parties to work together to restore the now-suspended devolved government first put in place in Belfast in 1999.

Size alone provides little insight into how influential departments are. For example, the two most senior departments—the Treasury and the Foreign and Commonwealth Office—together employ barely more than 7,300 civil servants. The Treasury employs fewer than 1,200—third from the bottom in terms of size—but wields influence way out of proportion to its size. Charged with keeping the nation's economic growth on course, it also serves as the government's financial manager. It conducts annual spending rounds with the other departments to set their budget ceilings and approve their program objectives; draws up the Government's annual budget, which the head of Treasury, the chancellor of the exchequer, delivers and defends in the Commons; and through the year monitors departmental expenditures and the policies and programs they are intended to support. All other departments are dependent on the Treasury, the Government's check writer.

Foreign policy responsibilities reside with a department not much larger than the Treasury. The Foreign and Commonwealth Office has barely more than six thousand employees, a number of whom are in postings around the globe. Although the basic functions of these two departments have remained essentially unchanged over the years, the same cannot be said about most of the other departments. Their functions have been altered, sometimes frequently.

Reorganizing Whitehall

The number of departments has remained relatively constant over the decades; invariably new ones are created, some are renamed, others are consolidated, and a few are dissolved. At times, reorganization occurs at a dizzying pace. For example, so extensive were the changes Prime Minister Harold Wilson made from 1964 to 1970 that it could be said he was in the vanguard of an administrative revolution, for not for fifty years had a prime minister done so much to reconstruct the face of Whitehall. At the end of this "revolution," and the one that followed from 1970 to 1974 under Prime Minister Edward Heath, eleven departments had been merged into five, seven new departments had been created, one department had been split, and another had been dissolved—all within a period of eleven years. More recently, in 2001, Prime Minister Tony Blair spearheaded a revolution that rivaled Wilson's. Within days of Labour's reelection, Blair jolted Whitehall by announcing sweeping changes that involved reshuffling the functions of ten departments and restructuring and renaming four of them.

Reorganizing a department requires only that a prime minister issue an executive order called an Order in Council. Unlike the U.S. Congress, Parliament has no vote on reorganization initiatives. The arguments advanced for reorganizing departments can be compelling, but implementing change is often complex and time-consuming. It disrupts the normal flow of work and produces confusion, at least initially. Why, then, do prime ministers do it?

One reason is that their party's election manifesto requires them to. When Harold Wilson created a cabinet-level Welsh Office following the election of 1964, he did so to fulfill a pledge made in the Labour Party's manifesto. At the same time, he created the Ministry of Technology, not because it was called for in the manifesto, but because he was convinced that only a new, singularly focused department could give effect to his party's manifesto pledge to generate what it called the "white heat of a technological revolution" to spur economic growth. As he saw it, with cash to back technological advances, a Ministry of Technology would be the means to that end.

Not all reorganization plans are the progeny of manifesto pledges. Prime ministers may wish to accommodate an ambitious colleague by creating a high-powered position in the cabinet. Creating a niche was what Wilson did in 1968 when he merged two departments—Health and Social Security—into the Department of Health and Social Security. Prime ministers also are mindful of the need to achieve ideological balance in a cabinet. Thus, Wilson in 1974 split the Department of Trade and Industry into two departments and created a third, the Department of Prices and Consumer Protection, thereby producing portfolios for three cabinet ministers—one from the Labour Party's ideological left, one from its right, and one from its center.

Another reason prime ministers reorganize departments is to portray their Governments as problem solvers. In 1974, in the aftermath of severe economic dislocations caused by OPEC's drastic curtailment of oil, Heath transferred the energy functions of the Department of Trade and Industry to a new Department of Energy just weeks before an election. It was an eye-catching display of a government of action. Another example is his creation of a Department of the Environment four years earlier, done in part to alleviate growing public concern about conserving water resources, reducing pollution, and cleaning up Britain's beaches. These and related issues were entrusted to a freestanding department to serve as an institutional reminder that the Heath Government was the keeper of the nation's environmental conscience.

Less overtly political is departmental reorganization set in motion to achieve greater administrative efficiency and enhance the quality of public services and speed their delivery. These objectives were what Blair had in mind when he revamped Whitehall departments immediately after the 2001 election. Smarting from the sting of public criticism that key reforms of public services instituted in his first term (1997–2001) had had little impact, he concluded that the existing administrative structure was ill equipped to accelerate the delivery of services. He therefore set about reshuffling key functions among several departments and restructured four others. He transferred all education functions from the Department for Education and Employment (DfEE) to a new Department for Education and Skills. All employment functions of DfEE, plus all the cradle-to-grave benefits programs of the Department of Social Security, went to a new Department for Work and Pensions.

Blair was well aware that the electorate had supported him for a second term to continue the work he had begun in his first. His victory was "an instruction to deliver," as he put it, and within days after acknowledging that point, he announced the first of many steps to reorganize Whitehall so that his Government could act on the electorate's instruction. Once the changes were in place, however, he, like all prime ministers before him, had to rely on his ministers and civil servants.

Ministers and Mandarins

Without civil servants, a department's work would never be done; without ministers, a department would never receive the direction necessary to act on the pledges the party in power made to the public that elected it. Ministers rely extensively on their civil servants, especially the most senior, about 3,500 individuals who are sometimes called mandarins, a term that harks back to the wise counselors who staffed the civil service of imperial China. As wise as they are, however, how is it that after a change of government, a newly appointed minister can rely with confidence on mandarins who worked faithfully for a minister of the previous Government that had a different, if not contrary, political party agenda? Within days of the 1997 general election, when Harriet Harman, Labour's first secretary of state for Social Security (now called Work and Pensions) in eighteen years, arrived at her desk on her first day on the job, she quickly absorbed the brief that her civil servants had placed in her red folder. At the top of an otherwise blank sheet of paper, it read: "New Deal for Lone Parents" and "Help to the Poorest Pensioners." Later, in an interview, she confessed to having found it "amazing" that her civil servants had so accurately anticipated two key goals she hoped to accomplish during her tenure. As she put it, her civil servants

> think just like I do! They'd read all my speeches, all my parliamentary questions—it wasn't just the manifesto they'd gone through line by line, and there they were in our first meeting with their pens literally poised to write down and implement what I wanted to do.[1]

From this interview, three things can be concluded about civil servants. First, they are *permanent*; those who welcomed her had worked for her predecessor, a Conservative minister. Second, they are *politically impartial*; these civil servants were as prepared to work for a Labour minister as for a Conservative minister. And third, they are *anonymous*; Harman referred to no civil servant by name.

In these three respects, ministers are the polar opposites of their civil servants. Ministers are *transient*, in that they remain in their posts for an average of about two years. They are *partisan*, for they are, after all, politicians and have a partisan agenda. And they are *publicity conscious*, because politicians who shy away from publicity do little to advance their party's causes.

Ministers rely on their civil servants for several reasons. Because civil servants remain in their posts after changes of government, there is no break in their service. Those mandarins attached to what is called the minister's private office not only have a thorough knowledge of the policies their departments administer, they also know how to turn the wheels of bureaucracy to put new policies into effect. They either possess information that is important to act on or know where to acquire it, they have a thorough knowledge of subjects of which most ministers have only a passing acquaintance, and they can advise ministers on how practicable or impracticable it would be to implement policies that are being actively considered.

So too do mandarins rely on their ministers. Only ministers can defend their departments' interests both at the cabinet table and in cabinet committees. Only ministers can argue for their departments' fair share of funding in annual spending rounds with the Treasury and guard their departmental fiefdoms when interdepartmental disputes arise. And only ministers can explain their departments' work when they speak from the dispatch box in the Commons and attempt to foster good relations with the media so that their departments are seen in the best light.

At the top of every department is a secretary of state, and below the secretary are two or more junior ministers. For example, the secretary of state for the Foreign and Commonwealth Office is assisted by four junior ministers. Three are ministers of state: one for Europe, one for trade, and one for the Middle East, Afghanistan, and South Asia. The fourth is a parliamentary undersecretary of state, who is drawn from the House of Lords to allow peers to question him or her on aspects of the department's business that concern them.

In all departments, authority flows from the minister down to the rank and file. Accountability rises from the bottom back up to the minister. When a minister is appointed to head a department, he or she is given a copy of the Ministerial Code, a brief but key part of which reads: "Ministers have a duty to Parliament to account, and be held to account, for the policies, decisions and actions of their Departments." Imbedded in this terse passage lies a cardinal principle of the British constitution, which is the Government's accountability to Parliament. It is also a major part of the constitutional convention of ministerial responsibility.

A minister's responsibility to account to Parliament is not the same as the minister's being held to account by Parliament. Ministers *account to* Parliament when they appear at the dispatch box at question time in the Commons to keep parliamentarians abreast of what their departments are doing and, when called upon by a select committee, to explain their actions and those of their civil servants. But also they are *held to account* by Parliament. This phrasing conveys a different meaning but it is one that has become mired in ambiguity as government has become more complex. It means that ministers must accept responsibility for the actions of their civil servants. This is required of ministers because civil servants themselves are not accountable to Parliament, for, as a recent head of the Home Civil Service put it, they have "no constitutional responsibility or role, distinct from that of the minister."[2] Everything civil servants do is done for and in the name of the minister, including "every stamp stuck on an envelope."[3]

Until the 1990s, this form of responsibility was interpreted to mean that if a civil servant made a mistake, a minister had to accept responsibility for that mistake as if he or she had made it. If a mistake was made, the minister could then expect to hear calls from the opposition to resign. However, the practice was that unless the prime minister or the parliamentary party had lost confidence in the minister's ability to carry out departmental policy, the minister was under no obligation to resign, especially if he or she neither knew nor could be expected to know of a civil servant's blunder. Nevertheless, it was expected that a minister would inform Parliament of any blunder, report what steps had been taken to discipline the civil servant, and announce what would be done to prevent the mistake from happening again.

Starting in the closing decades of the twentieth century, ministers became increasingly restive about accepting blame for such mistakes, whether the ministers became aware of them or not. This interpretation of the convention, they maintained, had made sense when it originated back in the mid-nineteenth century. Departments then were small enough for ministers to manage with little difficulty. But with the growth of government in the second half of the twentieth century, they argued, it was fatuous to perpetuate the fiction that they were capable of monitoring every decision made by their civil servants.

The issue of whether ministers should be blamed for errors made by their civil servants is poignantly illustrated by events following the 1991 escape of two IRA prisoners from London's Brixton Prison with the aid of a gun that had been smuggled into the prison. Soon after news of the escape broke, those on the Labour Opposition benches quickly called for the home secretary's resignation, arguing that he should have known that the prison lacked an acceptable level of security. The home secretary, Kenneth Baker, countered by drawing a distinction between policy and administration, arguing that a policy failure was a resigning matter but an administrative failure was not—and that the prison break had been an administrative failure. As he put it,

> the Home Secretary is responsible for *policy* in prison matters. The *administration, development* and *running* of the prisons are the responsibility of the director-general [of the prison service] and of individual prison governors.[4]

Baker disclaimed responsibility not only for the lax security arrangements but also for what was later revealed as a failure to transfer high-risk IRA prisoners to more secure prisons. Determining the most appropriate facility to which prisoners should be sent, he contended, was not his responsibility, but rather that of the director-general. In the end, after he received the support of the prime minister and his party in Parliament, calls for Baker's resignation grew fainter, and he remained in his post. The heads of two mandarins rolled instead: Brixton's prison governor took early retirement, and the head of the Directorate of Custody was reassigned elsewhere in the Home Office.

This issue and similar ones generated a heated debate in the 1990s as politicians and others sought ways to make the convention of ministerial responsibility compatible with the realities of governing in the modern age. The issue was resolved in 1995—although not to everyone's satisfaction—by the so-called Butler doctrine. Proposed by Robin Butler, then-cabinet secretary and head of the Home Civil Service, it held that Parliament may call upon a minister to account "for everything which goes on within his department," including any "major failures," but that the minister cannot be "personally blameworthy when delegated tasks are carried out incompetently, or when mistakes or errors of judgement are made at operational level."[5]

The Butler doctrine troubled many, among them the members of the Commons' Public Service Select Committee (now called the Public Administration Committee). They contended that a clear distinction could not possibly be made between policy and administration, because "Ministerial responsibility is not composed of two elements, with a clear break between the two."[6] Troubled also were two political scientists who performed a "democratic audit" of British political institutions and processes. They argued that this interpretation blurred responsibilities between ministers and civil servants, for "the making of 'policy' and its implementation ('administration') are two interdependent parts of the same process."[7] So artificial was this distinction that ministers could absolve themselves from blame by construing as implementation that which others insisted was policy.

According to one authority on ministerial responsibility, in the Brixton Prison case Baker should have been aware of the need to transfer high-risk prisoners to high-security facilities but chose instead to distance himself from any knowledge of such matters.[8] If that were indeed the case, the question is whether Baker distanced himself from a policy issue or an administrative issue. There is a substantial grey area between these two interdependent poles, and because there is, the Butler doctrine remains mired in ambiguity. Until or unless it is clarified, mandarins run the risk of having to accept blame for some actions for which only ministers were once considered accountable.

Making Policies and Making Them Work

Not only do departments oversee the implementation of policies, they also help formulate them. The most important are those derived from pledges the party of government made in its election manifesto. These pledges proceed in two stages: translation and transformation. Their language is often highly generalized, so ministers invariably call upon their mandarins to advise them on how best to translate them by fleshing out particular details. A political philosophy on which the policy is grounded is not the concern of civil servants; they are expected only to offer advice that will produce the desired result. Once the details of the policy are negotiated, the minister turns to his or her civil servants for advice on how best to transform them into action. Civil servants outline various options that can be pursued, identify what administrative and financial resources will be required to carry out the policy, and consult parties who will have a hand in implementing it. If legislation is required, the minister calls upon civil service lawyers to draft a bill, and later, if required, a statutory instrument spelling out what procedures must be followed to implement the law.

Because ministers cannot realistically cope with involving themselves in every aspect of formulating policy, senior civil servants also determine policies, but only with the implicit approval of their ministers. However, officials know their boundaries; they may not stray beyond the general policy framework dictated by the government of the day. Because ministers must divide their time among Whitehall, Westminster, the cabinet and its committees, their constituencies, and Brussels, they have little time to focus on more than a few policy issues at a time. As a result, mandarins often are left to make assumptions about what their minister wants. When the minister's position is apparent, civil servants have the discretion to act. When it is not, they are free to proceed only after they have nailed it down. When confronted with a choice, they realize they are in a potential "lose-lose" situation. If they make assumptions that are wide of the mark, they are likely to be criticized for having usurped the minister's authority. But if they wait until the minister's position becomes known, they will be seen as lacking initiative or even preventing the government of the day from achieving its objectives.

Despite the criticism of civil servants heard from time to time, it would be misleading to suggest that ministers and mandarins operate in a climate of conflict. Some of the harsh words emanate not from ministers but from No. 10 Downing Street, especially when a Government's term is wearing on and the prime minister is impatient to produce results before announcing the date of the next election. In 1999, more than halfway through his first term, Tony Blair complained about the "scars on my back" inflicted over two years from prodding departments to speed the delivery of reforms in such core public services as education and the National Health Service.[9] He aimed his criticism not only at his ministers but also at their civil servants, despite the fact that ministers and their mandarins had been increasingly frustrated by the time it took Blair's overworked advisers in No. 10 to approve major initiatives proposed to them to improve the delivery of public services.

Because ministers work closely with their mandarins and depend heavily on their advice, they often spring to their defense when they are criticized. That is not to suggest, however, that strains in their relationship do not surface from time to time, for ministers and public administrators come from two different worlds, each nourishing a different culture. Politicians see themselves as change agents and ask, "Why not?" Civil servants, the gatekeepers, invariably ask, "Why?" Mandarins have a duty to offer the best advice they can to ministers and then ensure that what is agreed to is implemented in the most effective manner possible; however, they are keenly aware of what is feasible and what is not. If they regard a plan as impracticable, they are likely to balk. One minister, Gerald Kaufman, warned his successors that civil servants "will smother you with protestations as to why the thing is simply not possible technically."[10]

Kaufman's warning and variations on it have been familiar refrains heard when ministers gather and swap stories. Norman Tebbit, secretary for Trade and Industry in Margaret Thatcher's second term, could empathize with Kaufman's lament when he encountered massive resistance from his civil servants after Thatcher announced that her Government would privatize Britain's state-owned telephone company. The civil servants argued that it would be too complex to put into effect. But Tebbit had the last word. His civil servants grudgingly accepted the decision, struggled to figure out how best to make it work, and then set about implementing it. John Major's secretary of Transport also was faced with overcoming similar resistance. The transport secretary had to expend enormous efforts to transform the department's bureaucratic culture from one that favored road building to one more sympathetic to environmental concerns in transportation policy.

Both of these examples reveal that secretaries of state operate in a world vastly different from that of their civil servants, with each world nourishing a culture distinct from the other. Ministers are appointed to serve as change agents. But they work in a slow-as-you-go culture that prizes conservative values and time-honored ways of doing things.

Coordinating Policies within Whitehall

Ministers are not in office long before they become acutely aware of one value in particular that pervades many quarters of the civil service. This value, ironically, is one that ministers themselves defend if they remain in the same post for long. It is called departmentalism, although one former minister likened it to an affliction that he called "departmentalitis." A major symptom of departmentalitis is, as the minister put it, "a preoccupation with the [work of the] department . . . to the exclusion of all other considerations, including the fortunes of the government as a whole."[11] He could well have added that ministers and civil servants with this affliction also resist efforts that prod them to think strategically about how to mesh policies for which their departments are responsible with related policies that cut across the jurisdictions of other departments.

Departmentalism severely handicaps a Government's attempts to come to grips with broad problems that transcend any one department's remit, such as homelessness, poverty, and discrimination. There is no Department for Homelessness, nor is there one for poverty or discrimination, and when representatives from several departments meet in interdepartmental committees in search of solutions to such wide-ranging problems, they are rarely inclined to offer recommendations that transcend the narrow remits of each of their departments. As a result, there is a tendency for the committee to agree to solutions that are more higgledy-piggledy than systematic and comprehensive.

Short of radically amending departmental remits, rejiggering departments, or creating a host of new ones designed to give comprehensive attention to broad policies, a cabinet committee, such as the Committee on Domestic Affairs, will ask departments that fall within its jurisdiction to consult with each other and coordinate their efforts. All too often, however, attempts to achieve interdepartmental coordination fail even before they start. There is little interest in arranging interdepartmental meetings, and, as one minister put it, "Officials do not like the idea of ministers talking to each other or sorting things out in case you sell out the departmental interest." [12] Such institutional logjams are the bane of new prime ministers, who soon realize that some of the pledges they made in their campaign are going to be difficult, if not impossible, to transform into action. Prime ministers have thus had to resort to enlisting No. 10, the Cabinet Office, and the Treasury to join forces to produce what in Blair's first term came to be popularly known as "joined-up government."

To achieve "joined-up government," Blair pressed the Cabinet Office and the Treasury into taking a much more assertive role in coordinating policy than they had in the past. The cabinet, through its committees, was the government's lead player in coordinating policy long before Blair moved into No. 10, but its success was patchy. Ministers who sat on cabinet committees could not find additional hours in their day to plan and monitor the coordination of policy across departmental lines. Moreover, such tasks often are not high on their list of priorities. Blair was thus persuaded that cabinet committees were not part of the solution.

Cabinet committees might have proved not to be the best vehicles for coordinating the work of the departments, but Blair was convinced that the lead had to be taken at the top. Joined-up government, he and his aides reasoned, would produce joined-up policies. But joined-up policies were needed first. To produce the caliber of policy positions required to address wide-ranging problems, Blair created the Social Exclusion Unit a few months after the 1997 election. The unit, which he placed in the Cabinet Office, was organized into policy action teams and interdepartmental groups, with staff drawn from both the public and the private sectors, and was linked to a network of ministers and civil servants. Pleased with the unit's work, Blair decided to continue its lease after he was reelected in 2001. Further change was required, he was convinced, and thus he gave the deputy prime minister responsibility for overseeing this unit along with the Policy Delivery Unit, a new creation whose purpose was to prod departments to deliver crosscutting departmental policies.

The Treasury also took a more aggressive role. Shortly after the 1997 election, it initiated a policy of releasing additional funds to departments contingent upon their achieving certain policy-delivery objectives negotiated with the Treasury in the form of Public Service Agreements. As part of this new way of doing business, the Treasury reviewed departments' progress in coordinating policies that cut across departmental lines. Those that met their performance objectives were rewarded with further funds. Today, the Treasury exercises tight-fisted control over funds for crosscutting policies. As its role as enforcer has expanded, it has become apparent that such control was the best antidote to ward off departmentalism.

Reforming Whitehall

In an earlier era, when managing the operations of government was much less demanding, creating cabinet departments represented the orthodox way of organizing to get the jobs of government done. As time passed and governing became more complex, less conventional forms of organization were created to implement government policies. The most important of these were executive agencies. These agencies are relatively new, having been created in the 1980s and 1990s and a few since then, but there is nothing new about the functions they are commissioned to perform. What is new is that these agencies are headed not by ministers, but by individuals contracted from the public and private sectors to manage selected functions of government at arm's length from ministers. These semi-independent agencies were initially referred to as Next Steps executive agencies—"next" because they were a logical follow-on to Margaret Thatcher's efforts to reform Whitehall in the first half of the 1980s.

Steps to Reform

It was no secret that Margaret Thatcher was convinced that government spent too much money and that the civil service was too large and labored under outmoded methods of management. Soon after she became prime minister in 1979, she established the Efficiency Unit in the Cabinet Office to identify ways of cutting costs and achieving greater value for money. Her Efficiency Unit responded by organizing a team to scrutinize departmental expenditures. After uncovering examples of glaring inefficiency, the unit embarked in 1982 on a second phase in the campaign against waste by launching the Financial Management Initiative (FMI). Under FMI, departments were to define their objectives, devise methods of measuring their progress in meeting them, and then, based on the results of these exercises, allocate their resources more efficiently. Just how successful FMI was in eliminating waste is debatable, although one study estimated that measures it introduced produced savings of £1 billion (roughly $1.5 billion) between 1982 and 1987.[13]

Realizing savings, however, was only one of Thatcher's objectives for reform. The other was to improve the delivery of public services. To accomplish that, she was convinced that nothing short of root-and-branch reform would be required to strengthen the ways departments managed their programs. In 1986, she turned again to the Efficiency Unit for its recommendations; a few months later, it submitted a report entitled "Improving Management in Government: The Next Steps." However, the steps in "Next Steps" reforms could not be taken until other steps were taken first, steps to manage the reforms.

Managing Reform

So controversial were the Efficiency Unit's recommendations that Thatcher decided to keep them under wraps until after the 1987 general election. When she unveiled them several months later, the reason for the delay became clear. Not since 1870 had a panel recommended such radical reforms of the organization of government and the terms of service of government employees. Civil servants feared for their jobs upon learning that the report called for a massive downsizing of departments and the creation of a host of new, semi-independent executive agencies. These new agencies, the next steps in reform, would manage a myriad of government services, such as collecting taxes, issuing driver's licenses, and processing passport applications.

It was expected that by 1998, 75 percent of all civil servants would be working in these new agencies. The 25 percent that remained, the mandarins and their support staffs, would continue to work in the core departments, but no longer have responsibility for managing many public services. Instead, they would be free to advise ministers in making departmental policies. Thus the Department of Transport would continue to make policies governing road safety, highway design, and vehicle inspection, but no longer would it issue driving licenses and collect road taxes. Those jobs would fall to an executive agency, the Driver and Vehicle Licensing Agency.

Thatcher endorsed most of the proposed Next Steps reforms, and the first executive agency was created in 1988. When Thatcher left office in 1990, only a dozen agencies employing more than ten thousand civil servants had been established, but the pace accelerated under her successor, John Major. By 1998, the putative last year of the agency-creation phase of the Next Steps initiative and the tenth anniversary of the birth of the first agencies, 76 percent of the civil service workforce—338,000 individuals—were at work in 138 agencies.[14] The original target of 75 percent had been met and surpassed.

Executive agencies range widely in size and scope of operations. The largest of the seven agencies attached to the Department for Work and Pensions is Jobcentre Plus, which in 2005 had a staff of approximately seventy-seven thousand deployed in nearly nine hundred offices across the country to help the unemployed find work and to provide income support to those unable to work. This agency, plus the department's six others, employ more than one hundred thousand individuals. Approximately eleven thousand individuals work for the Child Support Agency, which in 2005 dealt with 280,000 cases assessing absent parents' support payments and simplifying the collection of these payments, thus saving active parents from having to go to court to petition for enforcement orders. Even larger than the Child Support Agency is the Pension Service. Its eighteen thousand civil servants are responsible for administering a state pension system that provides payments to eleven million retirees and helps those nearing pensionable age prepare for retirement. And the Rent Service's eight hundred civil servants determine the fair rental value of housing for landlords and tenants as the basis for setting the appropriate level of payments for those eligible for housing benefits.

All of the agencies discharge important functions, but, as Table 10.2 shows, while some support a central, or mainstream, mission of a department, others play only a marginal, or peripheral, role. Still others perform a regulatory function for a department or provide specialized services for several. The larger the agency, the more likely it is to perform a function of overriding importance to a department.

Table 10.2	Next Steps Agencies: Types and Functions		
Type	Function	Agency	Parent Department
Mainstream	Agency supports a central function of a department	Pension Service	Work and Pensions
Regulatory	Agency performs a regulatory function for a department	Driver and Vehicle Licensing Agency	Transport
Specialized Services	Agency provides specialized support services to many departments	Meteorological Office	Defense
Peripheral	Agency performs only a marginal role for a department	Royal Parks Agency	Culture, Media and Sport

Source: Efficiency Unit, *Making the Most of Next Steps: The Management of Ministers' Departments and Their Executive Agencies* (London: Her Majesty's Stationery Office, 1991), Annex A. (Names have been updated.)

Reforming Management

Separating the public service delivery functions from the policy functions of government, reformers thought, would allow executive agencies to pursue innovative methods of management in implementing policies. Moreover, creating smaller, discrete units of government would allow politicians to single out more easily which agency should be held responsible when blunders were made. Government would be made more accountable, but only if these agencies operated with clear-cut objectives. For that reason, ministers and mandarins from parent departments met with agency chief executives (ACEs) to negotiate agency goals, delivery targets, and performance indicators. Once these were agreed to, their understandings were incorporated into what are called "framework documents." ACEs were warned that agency performance would be subjected to rigorous scrutiny; to help them meet their goals, boards of management with members drawn from the world of business—one board for each agency—were assigned to help agencies adopt the most effective management methods.

ACEs accepted the challenge of managing important functions of government with a relatively free hand. They had vied for their jobs in open competition, been hired on three- or five-year contracts by their parent departments on the strength of their records as managers, and were compensated handsomely. Moreover, if their agencies met their objectives, they could expect to receive generous bonuses and a renewal of their contracts. In the meantime, the sting had been taken out of the revolutionary changes that agency civil servants initially feared. They came to realize that reform promised not only more responsibilities and greater career flexibility, but higher salaries as well.

274

No longer would they be pegged at uniform civil service pay scales; salary increases would be linked to performance.

The public, too, would be involved in assessing how well agencies managed their responsibilities, first through the mechanism of Citizen's Charters in John Major's Government and then through the Service First initiative in Tony Blair's. The Citizen's Charter program, launched in 1991, took the form of agencies making clear, forthright statements about the standards of service members of the public should expect from the agencies and how the public could complain if services fell below these standards. Agencies that excelled in meeting standards of service were awarded the Charter Mark; those that fell short had to devise a plan of action to deal with their shortcomings. When the first director of the Citizen's Charter program appeared before a Commons select committee, he emphasized that the pledges were "the next stage after Next Steps." He continued: "Next Steps gets management sorted out and now we are saying with greater clarity what we want management to deliver." [15]

When John Major left office in 1997, forty-one charters were in force in central government. His successor, Tony Blair, took a different approach to prodding the agencies to improve their efficiency and effectiveness with a program called Service First. Claiming he would consult the users of public services more aggressively than Major, he scrapped the Citizen's Charter program and arranged to create a so-called People's Panel of five thousand randomly selected individuals to provide feedback on the quality of agency performance and the speed with which it was delivered. In addition, public service users (who were invariably called "customers") were invited to register any complaints they had with an agency by following instructions provided on that agency's Web site.

Verdicts

Well into the agency-creation phase of Next Steps, one seasoned Whitehall observer remarked that "Government departments before the Next Steps programme were essentially 1830s technology." The reforms, he continued, were "a long-delayed recognition that the nature of state provision had changed." [16] A bold reshaping of the executive landscape was being put in place to produce conditions conducive to managing the public sector more effectively. The verdicts of practitioners soon trickled in, and they were generally positive. The (now defunct) Benefits Agency was meeting its deadlines for issuing Social Security checks, the Passport Agency was processing passport applications more quickly, and the Driver and Vehicle Licensing Agency was issuing licenses faster than ever.

Despite these advances, many parliamentarians remained skeptical. What concerned them was the absence of a requirement that ACEs be accountable directly to Parliament. Indeed, the Next Steps report had recommended that they be accountable to parliamentary select committees as well as to ministers. Margaret Thatcher had rejected that proposal, and those who came after her had in effect agreed. Ministers alone would be accountable. To emphasize that point, the first sentence of the Blair Government's Ministerial Code cautioned ministers that they had "a duty to account, and be held to account, for the policies, decisions and actions of their Departments *and Next Steps Agencies.*" [Emphasis this author's.] However, parliamentarians felt it fatuous to believe ministers could be accountable for actions delegated to agencies operating with a considerable degree of autonomy far removed from their supervision. Lord Nolan, the chair of the Committee on Standards in Public Life, voiced the view of the skeptics when he delivered a university lecture. "This is a much more complex public service than ever before," he remarked, "and it demands greater attention to accountability." He continued:

> If accountability is only through ministers, in respect of an agency with hundreds of offices and thousands of clients, the chain is too long, the person who should be answerable—perhaps at a local level—remains shielded from public view, and true accountability is weakened.[17]

Despite the concerns of skeptics, ministers alone continue to be accountable to Parliament for the policies the agencies implement. For the time being at least, the executive has resolved the issue of accountability on its terms. But its position continues to trouble many MPs who see this arrangement as weakening the convention of ministerial responsibility all the more.

Regulatory Bodies, Quangos, and Quagos

Not all units of government operate under the aegis of departments, although some units, the executive agencies, operate with relatively free rein within them. Other units function beyond departments and at an even greater distance from ministers. These are the regulatory bodies and the quangos and quagos.

Regulatory Bodies

What Margaret Thatcher had in mind in the 1980s when she spoke of reforming government was making government more efficient and reducing its size. She was convinced that her second objective, reducing its size, could be accomplished by eliminating the state's responsibility for the vast state-owned industries nationalized by the Attlee Government from 1945 to 1948. Arguing that "the state should not be in business,"[18] she devised a strategy to return these industries to the private sector by floating them on the stock exchange. The plan to privatize was as bold as it was ambitious, with pitfalls lurking at every turn. Despite them, however, Thatcher and her successor John Major succeeded; by the year 2000 more than fifty major state industries had been sold. They included oil companies, automobile manufacturers, an airline, a railroad, and utility companies. Privatization was hailed as a triumph and represented one of the most radical reforms undertaken in Britain in half a century.

Privatization led to a fundamental reordering of the responsibilities of government. Releasing publicly owned industries to the private sector freed government from having to fund and manage them. Once privatized, however, they were exposed to the same market forces as any other business in the private sector. In the meantime proceeds from the sales flowed into the Treasury's coffers. Government borrowing was then reduced, inflation checked, the civil service work force downsized, and the public awarded tax cuts.

The public needed more than tax cuts, however. It also had to be protected, since privatizing state industries—the utility companies in particular—could not be undertaken unless government took steps to prevent the abuse of market power that might otherwise ensue. The concern was that the giant utility companies, pressed to attract private investors, would maximize their profits to the detriment of consumers. To restrain these companies, regulatory bodies were created to ensure that standards of service and reasonable pricing policies would not be compromised and to encourage new companies to form and compete with these erstwhile state monopolies.

Each episode of privatization was accompanied in most instances by the creation of a regulatory body; as a result, since the mid-1980s regulating privatized industries has been one of the fastest growing sectors of the public service. Today, more than thirty regulatory bodies oversee organizations once owned and run by the state. Among them are OFWAT for water, OFCOM for broadcasting and telecommunications, and OFGEM for gas and electricity markets. Each of these was created to police the giant utility industries, which constitute 20 percent of the economy.

The authority to regulate each utility industry is usually vested in a ministerially appointed regulator, called a director general, for a fixed term. Once appointed, directors general wield substantial discretionary powers—more even than agency chief executives—and with little ministerial interference. Anything short of that, it was thought, would cause nervousness in the financial markets. These individuals also operate at arm's length from Parliament. It is rare, then, when ministers or regulators are asked to appear before a parliamentary select committee to address a regulatory issue. When they do appear, they usually do so in response to concerns that are peripheral to a regulatory function, such as the public outcry that followed the announcement of a regulatory body's awarding an excessive bonus to its director general in the 1990s.

Regulating business is nothing new in Britain. Government has been engaged in regulatory activities for several centuries. What is new is that these powerful regulatory bodies were created to operate free from government controls. That they were made to be free represents what one political commentator called "a very British response to the problem of how to privatise monopoly utilities on terms which would attract private investors while also safeguarding consumer interests."[19] Regulatory bodies are also a constitutional anomaly, but so too are quangos and quagos.

Speaking of . . .

Freedom of Information?

In his book, *Secrecy in Britain*, Clive Ponting wrote that "Britain has one of the most extensive systems to control the flow of official information of any Western democracy" (p. 1). In 2005, fifteen years after Ponting wrote these words, Britain brought a Freedom of Information Act into effect, its first-ever law of this kind. The law allows the public access to information held by departments, agencies, local governments, the armed forces, academic institutions, regulators, and quangos, among others. Did this new law signal an historic shift in the British government's control of information? Reporters and commentators are probably among the first to know, for they were among the first to test its limits. One who tested it on several occasions over the course of the law's first six months was Michael Evans, the defense editor of *The Times*. In his view, the Ministry of Defence (MOD) "probably wishes the Freedom of Information Act (FoI) had never passed." In what follows he sets out the reasons for this view:

> "The FoI Act was supposed to have brought in a new era of openness, but . . . there remains a fear of giving away any secrets, and the Act has too many, ready-made exemptions available for officials to seize on. . . ."

"My attempts to breach the MOD freeze on such interesting subjects as the sinking of the Argentine battle cruiser *Belgrano* in the Falklands conflict in 1982 . . . produced zero results.

"In each case, the final decision to reject my requests under FoI exemptions took several months. Just when you are wondering if the MOD is ever going to reply, you receive an e-mail from an official apologising for the delay and seeking

Quangos and Quagos

Like those who work in governments elsewhere, politicians and civil servants in Britain have a penchant for compressing awkward terms into acronyms. One is *quangos*, which stands for quasi-autonomous nongovernmental organizations. Translated, quangos are nondepartmental bodies composed of non–civil servants appointed by ministers to carry out public functions relatively free from ministerial control. However, "nongovernmental" is a misnomer, for it suggests that quangos are not part of the formal organization of government. Some are; some are not. For those that are not, the term is accurate. They are advisory bodies organized beyond the boundaries of government to which ministers turn when they need advice, usually on technical subjects.

The term is wholly inaccurate, however, when it is applied to organizations that operate within the formal structure of government. Some years ago, it was felt that a more accurate taxonomy was needed, and thus another acronym was introduced and is sometimes used: *quagos*, or quasi-autonomous government organizations. As the name implies, quagos are indeed part of government. They are executive bodies that make important decisions, but like quangos, at some distance from ministers.

more time in order to consult with other government departments and other countries before making a 'substantive' response. Yet when the substantive response comes along, the e-mail is full of empty words.

"Replying to my request for the documents relating to the decision made by the Government of Margaret Thatcher in 1982 to change the rules of engagement, allowing a Royal Navy nuclear-powered submarine to attack the *Belgrano* outside the British-imposed exclusion zone around the Falkland Islands, the MOD official wrote:

" 'Section 27(1) of the Act states that information is exempt from disclosure under the Act if its disclosure would, or would be likely to, prejudice, (a) relations between the United Kingdom and any other State, (c) (sic) the interests of the UK abroad, or (d) the promotion or protection by the UK of its interests abroad.'

"The FoI Act was supposed to have brought in a new era of openness, but the MOD has totally failed to get to grips with this notion. There remains a fear of giving away any secrets, and the Act has too many, ready-made exemptions available for officials to seize on if they have any doubts about handing over information.

"There is an appeal system, all the way to the Information Commissioner under the provisions of section 50 of the Act. But it's a long process and by the time the MOD has carried out an internal review of the handling of an individual request, the motivation for pursuing a potential story might begin to wane. Perhaps that's the MOD's game."

Source: Reprinted with permission of *The Times* and NI Syndication Ltd.

Operating at a distance from ministers is vital, especially for quagos. Two examples of quagos are the Equal Opportunities Commission (EOC) and the Commission for Racial Equality (CRE). (The EOC and CRE operated separately until 2007, when they and the Disability Rights Commission were consolidated into one quago, the Commission for Equality and Human Rights.) The CRE promotes interracial harmony; investigates discrimination based on race, religion, or national origin; and, if necessary, initiates legal proceedings against those who discriminate. The EOC investigates instances of sex discrimination and may even take those who discriminate to court. So controversial are certain issues that are dealt with by the CRE, the EOC, and a few other quagos that the government of the day is quietly grateful that the law requires it to maintain an arms-length relationship.

However, maintaining an arms-length relationship occasionally causes some discomfiture for a Government, for there have been instances when the CRE and EOC have taken a Government to court and won. For example, on one occasion the EOC went to court after the Royal Air Force discharged a pregnant servicewoman, and on another occasion after the Department of Health persisted in allowing women to qualify for free prescription drugs at an earlier age than men. Had the EOC functioned under the tightfisted control of a department, it possibly would not have been free to act without fear or favor to fulfill the terms of its remit.

Quangos also play an important role in government decision making, but do so as specialized advisory boards to ministers. Some, such as the Board of Governors of the British Broadcasting Corporation (BBC), function with a high profile; others, such as the Advisory Committee on Historic Wreck Sites, are so obscure that they are seldom heard of. Creating a quango is the prerogative of a minister whose work will benefit from its advice. The Cabinet Office advises ministers to inform Parliament when they create one; however, they are not obliged to do so or to divulge the names of those they appoint.

Quagos and quangos, often called boards or committees, are nothing new. They surfaced in the eighteenth century, when they were pried from departments to undertake public functions with a minimum of control from ministers. How many there are is not known, and estimates vary widely and wildly. As of 2003, the Cabinet Office estimated that there were one thousand quangos; the House of Commons' Select Committee on Public Administration thought the number nearer to nine thousand.[20] Just before the close of the twentieth century, two academics came up with what are probably quite accurate numbers: approximately 5,600 quagos, mostly at the local level, and about 675 quangos at the national level.[21]

Where quasi-public bodies exist in other democratic regimes, they are provided for in law. In Britain, only quagos that spend public funds are creatures of statute. Most quagos are statutory bodies, but only about half of all quangos are. Even when these quasi-public bodies are established by statute, the law lays down no criteria that ministers must honor when they make appointments other than that their members possess a knowledge of the subject matters of these bodies. Since the mid-1990s, however, some discipline has been introduced into the appointments process: in 1995, a commissioner for public appointments took office, and in 1996 a code of appointments practice was devised. With a commissioner and a code, the appointments process today is more transparent and greater emphasis is placed on candidates' qualifications. Nevertheless, there is no requirement that ministers appoint a set number from the three leading political parties in the interest of creating a party balance on these bodies. As a result, quago appointments are seen as political plums available to the party in power to distribute to those it thinks are predisposed to advancing its wishes.

Appointing individuals to quango and quago boards and committees creates opportunities to find "jobs for the boys," as the expression goes. Jobs such as these, however, also can lead to conflicts of interest, either potential or actual. Because the members of these specialized bodies are drawn from interests that have a direct or indirect stake in the outcome of the decisions they report to ministers, they are seen as protective of these interests. For example, several who sat on the Committee on the Safety of Medicines also served as consultants to pharmaceutical companies or held stocks in them.[22]

This finding has led to charges that some committee members are captives of the industries in which they have an interest. Whether they are is difficult to ascertain, for their decisions are made behind closed doors, and the Medicines Act of 1968 makes it a criminal offense to divulge their recommendations. This requirement for secrecy prompts the question all the more of whether the advice that these committee members offer is driven by a concern for the public interest—or their own interest. The same could be said of another form of conflict of interest created when a quango is partially funded by a private organization that could benefit from the advice it gives a Government. For example, it was found that the advice the Pesticides Safety Directorate gave to ministers on spraying crops with pesticides was scientifically flawed, and as it happened, the directorate's work was funded in part by the pesticides industry.[23]

Quangos and quagos are constitutional anomalies, for it is often all but impossible for Parliament to hold ministers to account for the work of these quasi-autonomous bodies. Quagos are created to make decisions independent of ministerial control, and quangos must offer advice to ministers free from outside pressure. In recent years, recommendations have been proposed to make the work of quangos more transparent and ministers more accountable to Parliament for their decisions. But reformers are not optimistic that their recommendations will be taken seriously, let alone agreed to, at any point in the near future.

Conclusion

Two themes thread their way through this chapter. One is implicit—the accountability of the Government to the electorate. The other is explicit—the accountability of the Government to Parliament. These forms of accountability are two parts of the same cornerstone laid in the eighteenth and nineteenth centuries.

The first of these, the accountability of the Government to the electorate, is a reciprocal relationship that involves the governors and the governed. Having made pledges to the voters in its campaign for election, the party that wins enough support to form a Government is committed to implementing them. Yet implementing electoral pledges is often difficult, especially if it entails breaking new ground and devising new methods of delivery. Implementing bold initiatives and improving old ones requires more time than would-be prime ministers normally appreciate when they are on the campaign trail. Change agents by temperament and profession, they do not always anticipate the obstacles that lie in wait.

Legislative ideas have to be carefully thought through, drafted, and introduced in Parliament, where they are then debated and eventually enacted. All of this takes time. So too does implementation. Funds must be allocated; new departments possibly created, and the responsibilities of others reshuffled; plans to implement the ideas must be devised; statutory instruments need to be written and approved; and units of government and civil servants geared up to carry them out. As initiatives are launched, officials are involved at every stage. Disagreements over ends and means emerge along the way, but once they are negotiated and the implementation phase finally begins, still more time is needed before the initiatives filter down and their impact is fully felt by a public in waiting.

As government has become more complex, Government's accountability to the electorate has become more difficult to achieve. Even more difficult is accountability to Parliament through the convention of ministerial responsibility. Without this convention, the public's elected representatives would be denied opportunities to hold ministers to account for their stewardship of programs, many of which form the basis of their Government's electoral pledges.

This convention has been steadily weakened since the 1980s. Ministers continue to keep Parliament regularly informed of their departments' work; however, they have increasingly abdicated responsibility for overseeing the administration of programs, partly because of the greater complexity of these programs, but also because of the emergence of at-arm's-length executive agencies, regulatory bodies, quangos, and quagos. Ministers are hard put to monitor the work of these expanding quasi-autonomous bodies; that, in turn, detracts from their responsibility to account to Parliament for their activities. So weakened has the convention of ministerial accountability become that some question whether it can any longer be regarded as a bedrock of the constitution. That is an issue that awaits the judgment of constitutional experts at some point in the future.

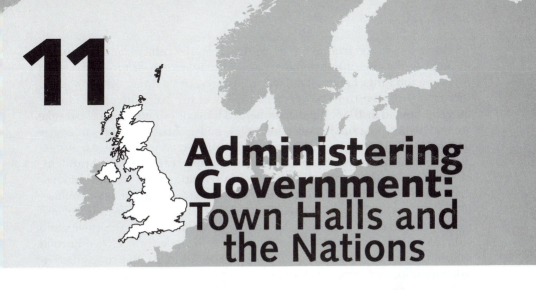

11

Administering Government: Town Halls and the Nations

Not all programs of government are administered at the center. Many, such as those that help the unemployed find jobs, answer taxpayers' questions about their taxable assets, and advise farmers on changes in agricultural subsidies, are run by the central government in regional and local offices all across the UK, close to those they serve. This form of geographic decentralization is called deconcentration, which means merely that government services are not concentrated at the center in London. A second form of geographic decentralization is what this chapter is about. It is called devolution, and it is manifested in two realms. The first is in local governments, euphemistically called "town halls" here, but technically called local authorities. The second is in governments headquartered in the capitals of Scotland and Wales, and intermittently, in Northern Ireland.

Because Britain has a unitary form of government, the authority to govern is vested in one all-encompassing center. But there is nothing that prohibits central government from devolving authority to layers of government below it, provided it is agreed to in law by Parliament. The difference between Britain's unitary form of government and a federal form such as that in the United States is that Britain's devolved governments have no *constitutional* right to exist. On the other hand, they have a *legal* right to do so, unless Parliament revokes that right. Parliament also may alter their organization and powers and has done so with regularity over the years.

Local Government

Local government in the UK has a long history, longer even than central government and Parliament. Its early beginnings and development closely paralleled major turning points in English and British history, starting with the

Anglo-Saxon period from the sixth to the eleventh centuries and continuing through to the rise of the welfare state in the twentieth. It took root when Anglo-Saxon kings divided England into shires, or counties, and appointed sheriffs to oversee them. After William I and his Norman invaders conquered England in 1066, the sheriffs helped him consolidate control over the country by keeping order, collecting taxes, and resolving disputes in courts of law. In the thirteenth and fourteenth centuries, when the feudal system disintegrated and towns burgeoned, royal charters were issued to boroughs, or townships, authorizing them to establish various units of local government, and they set about providing such services as road maintenance, bridge repairs, and tax collection. With the onset of the Industrial Revolution in the eighteenth century, as rural folk streamed into the towns and cities to seek work and settle, borough governments were stretched beyond their limits as they struggled with the problems of inadequate housing, unsafe factories, and rampant disease.

It was not until the right to vote came within the grasp of increasing numbers of local householders following passage of the Reform Act of 1832 that central government began to pay more than token attention to alleviating any of these concerns. Two years later, in 1834, Parliament passed the first law authorizing the election of local representatives. They sat as members of local Boards of Guardians, who carried out their work under the watchful eyes of commissioners appointed by the central government. Not until the twentieth century did government at the center assume a vast number of new responsibilities. As it did so, it pressed local governments into service to administer many of them, primarily those that dealt with education, housing, and social services.

Today, more than twenty-two thousand locally elected politicians called councilors take responsibility for the work of local authorities, or councils, all across the UK. Nearly two million individuals work for the councils, and they spend about a quarter of the UK's total government budget on such functions as:

- Social services

- Education

- Libraries, museums, and galleries

- Housing

- Land use planning

- Highways, traffic management, and transportation

- Playing fields and swimming pools

- Parks and open spaces

- Refuse collection and disposal and street cleaning

- Industrial promotion and development

- Consumer protection

- Environmental protection

- Police and fire

Local government has a long history, employs a high percentage of the UK's workforce, and spends vast sums on numerous public services. But why has central government devolved responsibilities and so many of them? Is it not a huge waste of time, money, and manpower to ask local government to do what central government itself is perfectly capable of doing on its own? Why have local government to begin with?

Why Local Government?

Central government could dispense with elected councilors, press local officials into service as its administrative agents, and carry out all the services currently performed by local authorities without any disruptions of service. Schoolteachers would continue to teach, planning regulations would continue to be enforced, public housing still would be built, streets still cleaned, and fires still put out. Efficiency would reign. Or would it? One cannot be certain, for Britain has never been governed along those lines, and thus it is an argument based on assumption, not experience. However, if central government were to abolish local authorities avowedly to achieve greater efficiency, any efficiency it would gain would probably not compensate for the loss of benefits derived from local government.

The first benefit is that local government serves as a counterweight to the uniformity of state provision. Central government polices standards of safety in the workplace, makes sure that roads are repaired, and ensures that meals-on-wheels are made available throughout the UK; however, central government realizes that the need for these and a multitude of other services varies from locality to locality. That is why Parliament provides local authorities with a measure of discretion in decision making. Local authorities are permitted to allocate their resources within reasonable parameters as long as when they do so, they adhere to the spirit and letter of the law.

Second, locally elected politicians are better placed to decide how policies should be applied to the communities they represent than policymakers who work in the bowels of a department in the far-off capital. It makes little sense for a minister or civil servant in London to dictate how to organize the disposal of household refuse, determine whether to pedestrianize a town center, or decide between adding a wing to the local library or purchasing land to hold Sunday afternoon cricket matches. These are responsibilities best left to councilors. Not only do they have a knowledge of the needs of their communities, as elected representatives, they also are accountable to their communities. That means they have acquired a legitimacy to speak for them and act on their behalf.

Third, local government promotes a culture of democracy. It is more than just axiomatic that when decisions are made closest to the communities where they take effect, citizens will approach their councilors to vent their views and lodge complaints about the quality of existing local public services. Access is vital, and councilors and local officials are far more accessible than MPs, civil servants, or ministers. The public is also more likely to consult them, as borne out in the findings of a major survey of political participation in Britain. (See Table 11.1.) The results show that the public is more than twice as likely to contact councilors and local officials than MPs and civil servants. Further survey evidence suggests that the public trusts local authorities more than central government "to do what is right." [1] When citizens appeal to politicians and officials at the local level, they have a greater sense of involvement in the affairs of their community, and few would disagree that such involvement is an essential ingredient in the recipe for democracy.

If these arguments have any legitimacy, how is it that, as one scholar claimed, local government today is "close to being no longer local, and to being no longer government"? [2] The short answer is that central government has imposed so many controls and restrictions on local authorities that they have much less discretionary authority to act on matters. But this answer begs another question: Why has central government diluted the powers of local government? The answer to this question is more complex, and parts of it are found in the relationships that have evolved between central government and local authorities over the years.

Whitehall and Town Halls

The relationship between Whitehall and local authorities is best identified by tracing four periods in the life and times of local government. These are:

- the Golden Age of local government (1830s–1920s),

- reining in local autonomy (1930s–1979),

Table 11.1 Frequency of Citizen Contact with Decision Makers		
Point of Contact	At Least Once (%)	Often/Now and Then (%)
Central Government		
MP	9.7	3.4
Civil Servant	7.3	3.1
Local Government		
Councilor	20.7	10.3
Official	17.4	8.9

Sources: Geraint Parry, George Moyser, and Neil Day, *Political Participation and Democracy in Britain* (Cambridge: Cambridge University Press, 1992), p. 423; and Geraint Parry and George Moyser, "More Participation, More Democracy?" in *Defining and Measuring Democracy*, ed. David Beetham (London: Sage, 1994), p. 47.

- local government under siege by the Conservatives (1979–1997), and

- local government under siege by Labour (1997–present).

Local Government's Golden Age

Local government's Golden Age was the first and longest of the four periods. It started in the 1830s and continued through the first two decades of the twentieth century. Local government was the only tier of government that experienced any profound growth in this nearly one-hundred-year period, but for two reasons its growth did not in any way threaten the good relations that had evolved between central and local governments. First, central government had little time for local government matters as it was preoccupied with the affairs of the empire and the defense of the realm. Second, local governments placed few demands on central government. They had ample tax-raising powers, and the revenue they collected usually covered all of their expenses. When they came up short and had to look to central government for grants to top up their income, central government usually provided them with few strings attached. Overall, local governments administered their programs with a considerable degree of autonomy, for London had little interest in micromanaging their operations and rarely interfered with their agendas, priorities, and methods of work.

Reining in Local Autonomy

The Golden Age came to an end in the 1930s, and a new phase emerged in its wake. This was a period when central government took back some of the functions it had delegated to local government and imposed limitations on others. For example, Parliament transferred responsibility for major road construction from local government to a central government department. Parliament also required local governments to use means tests on the unemployed, that is, tests to determine eligibility for public assistance by assessing whether individuals had the means to support themselves without gainful employment. Actions such as these represented the beginning of a pattern of a loss of local autonomy that continued for about the next fifty years.

There were two reasons in particular for central government's reining in local autonomy. One was the proliferation of welfare programs; central government needed to supervise their implementation closely to ensure that benefits were distributed uniformly across the UK. A second reason was that councils became increasingly reliant on grants from central government to cover the gap between revenue they were able to generate from their own local tax base and further funds needed to deliver public services. The more the gap grew, the more central government either took back programs that had been the province of local governments or reduced local governments' discretionary authority by imposing new restrictions on the way they administered funds. The latter was the more common course of action. By the mid-1970s grants exceeded locally generated revenue by a margin of two to one, and the prospect of an even higher proportion of grants, together with whatever strings would be attached, prompted fears that local government was likely to become little more than a submissive agent of central government.

Local Government under Siege by the Conservatives

These fears were partially realized soon after the Conservatives returned to power in 1979. Before that, laws that affected local government had contributed to what one scholar described as "a general and flexible framework" within which local authorities and central government consulted each other and negotiated any differences they had.[3] Almost always, they entered into negotiations in a spirit of partnership shaped more by accepted administrative practices and good will than law. However, all that started to change in the early 1980s.

From 1979 to 1997 local authorities were the subject of more than two hundred acts of Parliament that gave ministers "literally thousands of direct powers over local authorities."[4] Nearly every one of these laws reduced the discretionary powers of local government. They included provisions that instituted radical new controls over local financing, required local authorities to invite bids from the private sector to carry out selected functions of local government, and transferred certain other functions to newly created non-elected quagos. These changes bore the imprint of Margaret Thatcher, whose premiership dominated the early years of this period. Her antipathy toward local government was well known. In her view, government in the UK was too big, too inefficient, and too wasteful. It was local governments' alleged shortcomings in particular that aroused her passion for reform.

Financing local government drew Thatcher's greatest attention, and her Government imposed three extensive reforms on local governments' authority to spend and tax. The first brought about a radical break from the past. Councils were prohibited from setting their own annual spending levels; these now were set by central government. Nearly as radical was a second reform that limited the amount of revenue that selected councils were allowed to levy through local taxes, called domestic rates. "Rate capping" was followed by a third change: although local governments continued to collect business rates (taxes on business property), all receipts went to central government to dispense to local authorities based on need. The effect of these reforms was that local authorities were left with a shrinking tax base, greater dependence on grants from central government, and less flexibility to fund projects that they deemed urgent.

The sting of the Thatcher Government's reforms was felt in two other realms as well. First, in keeping with Thatcher's efforts to privatize state industries and involve the private sector in administering selected functions of government, the Government inaugurated a system of compulsory competitive tendering (CCT) for local government. It had been a long-standing practice for local governments to invite bids ("tenders") from the private sector for certain services they occasionally needed from such professionals as architects and building contractors. With CCT, local governments for the first time were required to invite bids from the private sector for certain services that were the traditional full-time, in-house responsibilities of local authorities, among them refuse collection, vehicle maintenance, and food catering. The objective was to save money, and if a private firm could provide a service of an acceptable standard but at a lower cost than a local authority, the firm was given the contract. Contracting for blue-collar personnel was followed by a similar requirement instituted in John Major's premiership for certain white-collar and technical personnel, in particular, lawyers, accountants, and computer specialists. CCT produced savings, but savings apart, there was a downside to CCT: it removed yet one more chunk of authority from local governors.

The last sting from the Thatcher Government's reforms was felt when central government transferred several major policymaking and implementation responsibilities that had been the preserve of local authorities to a vast number of new local government quagos called qualgos, or quasi-autonomous local government organizations. Quagos, it will be recalled from chapter 10, are government bodies that make executive decisions but at arm's length from government leaders. Most quagos are qualgos, and they make decisions affecting housing, schools, and employment training, among other things. The greatest number of qualgos—more than 2,600—are housing associations, which provide accommodation for low-income families, the disabled, and the elderly. There are as many as sixty-five thousand "quangocrats," as they are sometimes called—nearly three times the number of elected councilors—and they spend nearly as much as local authorities.[5]

Qualgos have profoundly changed the face of local government. Like quagos, they operate in realms removed from democratic controls. Their members are not elected but instead are appointed by local councilors and ministers. Moreover, qualgo members' names and addresses are not on the public record, and they usually are not required to live in the areas served by the bodies on which they sit. Most are not expected to consult members of the public, and they are accountable not to local government, but rather to central government. With the transfer of many local government responsibilities to qualgos, the lines of accountability have blurred, and citizens have been left confused about whom to praise or blame for decisions that affect their communities. For these reasons, qualgos represented one more assault on local government.

Local Government under Siege by Labour

Despite Labour's assertion in its 1997 election manifesto that "local decision-making should be less constrained by central government," the reforms Labour instituted after winning power suggested that it was not about to restore to local government the autonomy it had lost during the Thatcher and Major years. Instead of central government's loosening its grip on local government and its operations, Labour pressed ahead with reforms of a different nature that were intended to "modernize" (Labour's word) local government. By "modernizing," Labour meant (1) improving the quality of services administered by local government, and (2) revitalizing leadership at the local level by introducing new political structures to drive home their improved services.

Among the most important reforms adopted to improve public services at the local level were the Best Value program in Tony Blair's first term, and in his second term, local public service agreements and comprehensive performance assessments. Best Value prodded local authorities to manage services in the most economical, effective, and efficient ways possible and without regard to the provider. Thus, if a private firm could manage a service less expensively, more effectively, and more efficiently than a local authority, the private firm could be invited to do the job. In any event, the work of local government had to conform to standards of performance stipulated by central government and be subject to its scrutiny.

Scrutiny took the form of inspecting *how* government programs were working and *how well* they were working. Before long, inspectorates became a cottage industry under Labour at the local level. There are inspectorates for social services, police, fire, public assistance fraud, and educational standards, and since 2000, for Best Value. "Inspectorate" has become a familiar word in the lexicon of local officials as inspectors fan out across the country to investigate what progress programs have made. If a local authority's efforts fall short of what central government has prescribed, central government can ask it to adopt a new plan of action. Or if a program is managed so poorly that it slips woefully below an acceptable level of performance, central government may even transfer management of the program to the private sector, as it did on four occasions with schools in 1999 and 2000. "Death by inspection and hit squads" is how one official referred to decisions as extreme as this.[6]

Local public service agreements (LPSAs) are a logical extension of Best Value. Whereas Best Value focuses broadly on programs across the whole spectrum of local government, LPSAs focus narrowly on projects with lives of relatively short duration. Councils map out their plans for projects and argue their case for approval and financial backing from the relevant department of central government. For example, one county council negotiated a plan with the Department of Transport to cut substantially the number of people killed and seriously injured while traveling on certain county roads on which the number of deaths and injuries exceeded the county average. Councils that win departmental backing for their projects and then successfully execute them (as this one did) are awarded modest additional amounts to spend on projects of their choice.

Best Value and LPSAs were the first two of three flagship initiatives for local authorities that Labour inaugurated in its first eight years of power. Contributing to their development was the Audit Commission, which was created in 1983 to examine local governments' efforts to achieve value for money. The commission also conceived and developed a third initiative called comprehensive performance assessments (CPAs). CPAs grade each council's performance across a range of functions and, because the results are presented in league table form, central government has comparative data to consult when it wishes to reward high-performance councils for their accomplishments and isolate those that need to upgrade their work. Having hard evidence on which to draw to make its case is a boon to central government, but it could be anything but a boon to some local authorities. The methods by which league table data are collected and presented are thought by some to be seriously flawed, and league table results, which usually are published in the national press, are seen as "naming and shaming" exercises that have a demoralizing effect on councilors and officials of local authorities whose ratings are especially low.

"Modernize!" was the challenge that Tony Blair laid down to local governments as he entreated them to embrace Best Value, LPSAs, and CPAs as ways to raise the standards of public service. But that was not all that "Modernize!" meant. It also meant rejuvenating leadership at the local level by creating new political structures to entrench the reforms that were underway and to pave the way for others that would follow. In 2000, local authorities were asked to consult their communities for their choice of one of three options: (1) a directly elected mayor form, (2) a mayor and council manager form, or (3) a cabinet with leader form. The Blair Government had signaled its preference for the first option—the most radical of the three forms—but the overwhelming majority of local authorities plumped for the least radical of the three, the leader and cabinet form. By the end of 2005, aside from the mayor of London, there were only a dozen elected mayors in England and Wales. Among them was one who had campaigned in a monkey suit, and one "candidate" was a local football club's mascot. Why this frivolity? *The Economist* probably explained it as well as anyone could when it observed:

> The lack of enthusiasm or seriousness with which the idea of mayors has been greeted probably has more to do with the electorate's understanding of the powerlessness of local government than with the apathy that politicians bemoan.[7]

In the absence of any public enthusiasm for embracing the directly elected mayor form of government, Blair turned his attention again to the delivery of public services. Councilors had no quarrel with central government's expectations that they take the lead in upgrading the quality of public services. Yet they came to regard Whitehall's involvement with their affairs as excessive and meddlesome. The relevant departments micromanaged. They dominated the drafting of performance targets, undertook inspections that councilors considered unfair, and threatened to relieve councils of certain responsibilities when the councils failed to meet standards the departments had laid down. What many councils had hoped for when Labour came to power in 1997 was to win back some of the financial

Speaking of . . .

"TIME TO LET GO. . . ."

Filling out forms has been a way of life for local government officials as they respond to edicts from central government to report on what their councils are doing and how well they are doing it. The forms are crucial for the Blair Government's reforms to move forward, officials are told. But so intense have central government's demands become that some officials are convinced it thinks that local government's purpose is to fill out forms, not help govern the country. Is there a tipping point? Secretary of State for Communities and Local Government Ruth Kelly thinks so. In what follows, the political editor of *The Guardian* reports on why she thinks it is "time to let go. . . ."

> "Now is the time to start trusting local government and to start trusting local people to make decisions for themselves so they are able to set local priorities that deliver according to local need."

"Whitehall interference in local councils is to be hacked back by the new local government and communities secretary, Ruth Kelly, after she released figures showing that the government and its agencies collectively demand that councils report on 566 separate performance criteria.

"Speaking to the *Guardian,* she disclosed research showing that councils were spending 80% of their performance effort reporting upwards to Whitehall departments, rather than being held to account by local people.

" 'We need to turn that round dramatically so local government can be responsive to the demands of local people, rather than always looking up to try to meet the targets set by central government.

" 'Now is the time to start trusting local government and to start trusting local people to make decisions for themselves so they are able to set local priorities that deliver according to local need. We need fewer targets and fewer driven by the centre.'...

"The performance regime costs a typical council £1.8m a year [roughly equal to $3.3 million], according to research by PricewaterhouseCoopers. The research found that councils regarded this often duplicatory effort of reporting upwards as a 'disproportionate use of scarce resources'.

"Speaking ahead of a speech to the Local Government Association annual conference, Ms Kelly said: 'I think we have reached a devolution tipping point.'

"She defended the tough interventionism of the first two terms as necessary to raise standards in councils and drive workforce reform.

" 'But now is the time to let go, with public services improved and an overwhelming number of councils competent or excellent,' she said."

Source: Patrick Wintour, "Kelly to Reduce Number of Whitehall Targets for Councils." Copyright Guardian News and Media Limited 2006.

autonomy they had lost over the years. In the mid-1970s government grants exceeded locally generated revenue by a margin of two-to-one. Thirty years later the margin had grown to four-to-one. With the increase in central government grants came an increase in the number of strings attached to local government spending, and an increase, too, in the doubts harbored by many councilors that they could serve effectively the communities that elected them.

Organization and Functions

Table 11.2 suggests that mainland Britain has a confusing array of local authorities and a variety of names for them. Scotland and Wales have unitary councils; England has unitary, county, district, and borough councils. Added to these are the joint authorities found in all three nations, plus the Greater London Authority and London's borough councils. Aside from joint authorities, there are 441 units of local government in England and Wales (to which the reader is spared exposure to all 441!). Six forms of government—unitary, county, district, borough, joint authorities, and the Greater London Authority—are each touched on briefly, as well as two forms not yet alluded to: parish councils and community councils.

Unitary councils are the easiest form to take in. They were introduced throughout all of Scotland and Wales and in parts of England in the mid-1990s to simplify government organization and make government more efficient than the cumbersome two-tier county/district form of government they replaced. There are currently forty-six unitary councils in England, thirty-two in Scotland, and twenty-two in Wales. As the far right column in Table 11.2 shows, they provide "one-stop" government in that each is responsible for almost all local government functions. The exceptions in Scotland and Wales are police and fire services, which are organized under separate joint authorities, with each having jurisdictions that overlap a number of unitary council boundaries.

In England, the picture becomes a little more complicated. Leaving aside England's forty-six unitary councils, joint authorities, and local government in London, Table 11.2 shows that there are county councils, district councils, and borough councils. Next, England's local governments are divided into metropolitan areas and nonmetropolitan areas, with the greater number found in nonmetropolitan areas.

In nonmetropolitan areas, local government is organized either as unitary councils or as two-tier councils. In two-tier councils, the county council is the top tier and the district council the bottom tier. The 34 county councils are divided into 238 district councils, with an average of 7 district councils per county council. The two-tier arrangement was introduced to distinguish the level of service that each provides: counties provide services that apply to an entire county; districts cover those of a more local nature. Thus, while county councils are responsible for collecting refuse, district councils are given the task of disposing of it. Some other services are performed dually by

Table 11.2 The Division of Local Government Responsibilities in Great Britain

RESPONSIBILITY	ENGLAND				LONDON		SCOTLAND, WALES, and ENGLAND	
	Metropolitan		Nonmetropolitan					
	Joint Authorities	Borough Councils (36)	County Councils (34)	District Councils (238)	Borough Councils (32)	Greater London Authority	Joint Authorities	Unitary Councils (100)
Social Services		•	•		•			•
Education		•	•		•			•
Libraries		•	•		•			•
Museums/Art Galleries		•	•	•	•			•
Housing		•		•	•			•
Planning—Strategic		•	•			•		•
Planning—Local		•		•	•			•
Highways		•	•	•	•	•		•
Traffic Management		•	•	•	•	•		•
Passenger Transport	•		•		•	•		•
Playing Fields/Swimming Pools		•	•	•	•			•
Parks/Open Spaces		•	•	•	•			•
Refuse Collection		•		•	•		•	•
Refuse Disposal	•	•	•		•	•	•	•
Consumer Protection		•	•		•		•	•
Environmental Health		•		•	•	•	•	•
Police/Fire	•		•		•	•	•	•

Source: Adapted from Tony Byrne, Local Government in Britain, 7th ed. (London: Penguin Books, 2000), pp. 84–85 and 53 ff.

294

a county council and a district council. For example, each will take responsibility for its own parks and swimming pools.

Next are England's seven metropolitan areas. In addition to Greater London, the major conurbations (and cities) are the West Midlands (Birmingham), West Yorkshire (Leeds), South Yorkshire (Sheffield), Merseyside (Liverpool), Greater Manchester (Manchester), and Tyne and Wear (Newcastle-on-Tyne). Each of these six areas is divided into boroughs. There are thirty-six total, with the most populated (Greater Manchester) having more (eleven) than the least populated (South Yorkshire, with four). As Table 11.2 reveals, each of these thirty-six boroughs provides nearly all the services of local government. The exceptions are passenger transport, refuse disposal, and police and fire services, all of which fall under the jurisdiction of joint authorities.

Joint authorities, which function not only in England's metropolitan areas but in Scotland and Wales as well, were organized to provide a common service throughout areas that extend beyond the boundaries of a single borough or unitary council. For example, a joint authority is responsible for planning an integrated system of public transport to facilitate travel to and from suburbs and cities. Joint authorities for police and fire services are two further examples. The police often need to cross neighboring jurisdictions in hot pursuit of criminals, and the fire-fighting resources of several jurisdictions may well be called upon to put out a major fire. Joint authorities, it should be added, are often organized as qualgos.

London's local government deserves separate treatment from the form of local government found in the six other metropolitan areas of England. Greater London is the only metropolitan area with an elected mayor. Its first-ever elected mayor took office in 2000 along with the Greater London Assembly, a twenty-five-member council to whom the mayor is accountable. In addition, there are thirty-two borough councils having responsibility for the various parts of London's center (inner London) and the suburbs beyond (outer London). As Table 11.2 reveals, most local government responsibilities are borne by Greater London's boroughs, although some are the responsibility of both the Greater London Authority (the mayor and the Greater London Assembly) and the individual boroughs. However, the Greater London Authority alone has responsibility for strategic planning, passenger transport, and police and fire for all of the London area.

Finally, there are the parish councils of England and community councils of Scotland and Wales. They are found at the grassroots level, primarily in rural areas. There are as many as 8,000 parish councils in England, 1,100 community councils in Scotland, and 750 community councils in Wales. Their functions are limited, however. In all three countries they convey the views expressed by those living within the boundaries of the small areas they serve to unitary councils or district councils. (In those few instances in which they have formed in urban areas, they report to borough councils.) As the lowest tier of local government in England and Wales, parish councils have limited administrative responsibilities. They maintain community halls and construct bus shelters, spend modest amounts from public funds on local projects, and offer their reactions to local planning applications.

Noticeably absent from this survey is local government in Northern Ireland. This is largely because, with the Good Friday Agreement of 1998, either new local authorities will be created or the powers exercised by existing local authorities will be expanded. As of this writing, Ulster's local government is organized into twenty-six elected district councils and nine appointed area boards. The councils are responsible for environmental services, recreation, and consumer protection. The boards divide their work between health and social services and education and libraries.

This brief sketch of the structures of local government has offered a look into what they are and some of the functions they perform. But it has offered nothing about the role of political parties and the politicians and officials who make the wheels of local government turn. The following section investigates how political parties pave the way for the election of Britain's twenty-two thousand councilors, what councilors do, and the role that parties play in councilors' work. It then examines the work of the nearly two million officials who assist the councils by implementing their many programs.

Political Parties, Politicians, and Officials

Proportional representation is used to elect councilors in Northern Ireland, in Scotland, and in London to the Greater London Authority; in other jurisdictions councilors are elected by the single-member, simple-plurality (SMSP) system, otherwise known as the first-past-the-post (FPTP) method. All councilors serve for fixed four-year terms, but not all are elected at the same time. Their terms are staggered, and thus on any given local government election day (usually the first Thursday of every May), only a fraction of seats are contested. The election timetable is set by law, so candidates are not left to wonder when the next election will be held as candidates for Parliament are. Fixed-date elections allow candidates for local office to prepare themselves to enter the electoral arena on the first official day of the campaign with their volunteers, posters, and literature all at the ready.

Political parties pave the way for the election of would-be candidates by screening and then selecting slates of candidates from which the voters later choose. All too often, however, the pool of would-be candidates to which the parties turn is restricted. The reason is that except for those whose game plan is to use a council seat as a steppingstone to Parliament, the incentives are few. The job of councilor is part-time. More often than not, it intrudes on councilors' full-time jobs. It provides no salary, but rather a modest allowance for attending to official duties. In addition, it is difficult to inspire the public-spirited to contest elections when many voters pay scant attention to what they stand for and treat local elections as mini-plebiscites to vent their displeasure with the government of the day, predictably, to the disadvantage of council candidates of the same party. If they do choose to run and they succeed, they realize they will be bombarded with endless streams of regulations and guidelines from Whitehall that are bound to frustrate their efforts to improve the well-being of the areas they serve. All of this helps to explain why there are a number of seats unfilled from one election to the next.

As grim as this picture is, it does not apply to most councils. The average number of candidates per council seat has risen from two to three in recent years, largely because of the emergence of the Liberal Democrats, and the queues for selection by local parties can be anything but short for some seats. Competition is keen for safe seats on councils on which one party has a clear-cut majority, as the Conservative, Labour, or Liberal Democrat Parties did in more than one third of the English and Welsh councils in 2006. The scent of victory lures more would-be candidates of the dominant party because they realize that selection is usually tantamount to election. Queues for selection by the underdog party, on the other hand, are normally nonexistent; the party considers itself fortunate if it succeeds in persuading a few to go through the motions of campaigning, even though the outcome is known before the campaign begins. However, the underdog party is not always successful in coaxing some to run, and that is largely why the overall number of uncontested seats can run sometimes as high as 20 percent.[8]

Councilors are part-time. According to one survey of English councilors undertaken in 2004, they devote an average of 21.6 hours a week to their public duties. Table 11.3 identifies what duties they perform and how they allocate their time to each. Half of their time each week (10.8 hours) is spent attending council meetings, seeing to other council business, and traveling on council business. Constituents are important, too: councilors spend 5.1 hours a week meeting with constituents in constituency surgeries and carrying out other constituency business.

Councils are the decision-making bodies of local government. But for reasons that will become clear, not all decisions are made by the full council.

Table 11.3 Average Hours Spent Each Week by English Councilors on Their Duties

Activity	Hours per week
Attendance at council meetings	6.6
Attendance at party/group meetings	1.7
Attendance at civic functions	1.0
Other internal council business	2.3
External meetings and seminars	1.8
Surgeries and dealing with constituents	3.4
Other constituency business	1.7
All traveling related to council business	1.9
Training	0.6
Other	0.6
Total	21.6

Source: "National Census of Local Authority Councillors 2004" (London: Employees' Organisation for Local Government, 2004), p. 20. (www.lga.gov.uk/documents/briefing/censusofcllrengland2004pdf.)

First, some councils are so large, with sixty-five councilors and more, that they are too unwieldy for effective decision making. Second, because they rarely meet in plenary session for more than a few hours about five times a year, councilors are deprived of sufficient time to debate issues and resolve them by vote. And third, so technically complex can some problems be that most councilors lack the expertise necessary to nail down effective solutions. For these reasons, councils delegate much of their work to committees and subcommittees, where councilors can call on experts for their counsel as they thrash out various options. After a committee has reported its recommendations to the council, councilors debate them, agree to them, amend them, or return them to the committee for further consideration. This is the norm, but not all local authorities work the same way; some insist on voting on every recommendation committees make and others are content to vote only on the most important and allow the rest to stand as decisions of the full council.

Because British politics is party politics, parties dominate just about every facet of the work of most local authorities. Only in a small minority of cases is their presence less keenly felt. These are councils on which independents control a majority of the seats. Following local elections in 2006, 10 of the 410 councils in England and Wales were controlled by independents. One was evenly split between independent councilors and regular party councilors. Five of these ten were councils on which independents held 60 percent or more of the seats, and although the number of independent councilors has increased gradually over the years, the number of councils they control is dwarfed by the 185 councils on which two parties dominate. (See Table 11.4.)

Political parties function somewhat differently in different councils, and for that reason it is difficult to generalize about their operations. There is a pattern, however, in urban councils. Each party has a leader, and the one whose party commands the most seats usually serves as leader of the council; this leader in many instances has a cabinet. The runner-up party serves as the party of opposition, and the parties deploy whips to enforce party discipline. In these respects, political parties work in councils much as they do in Parliament: each party elects its leader, and the leader of the party commanding an overall majority of seats becomes the leader of the council. The parties elect their chief whips and the chairs of committees as well. They also might elect members of a policy committee, although it is common today for the party in the majority to allow the council leader and committee chairs to assume the functions of a policy committee and thrash out party issues and plan strategies and tactics much like a cabinet does. In opposition is the party that came in second in the election, and when it disagrees with a position taken by the party in power it invariably counters it by proposing its own. Councils conduct most of their business along nonpartisan lines; when an issue takes on a partisan flavor, the party leaders are likely to dispatch their whips to enforce party discipline. Indeed, this is certain to be the case when the council leader's party has only a slim majority and the outcome of a vote is in doubt.

Table 11.4	Party Systems in 375 of England and Wales' 410 Councils Following Local Elections in 2006		
Party System	Councils No.	%	Definitions
Nonparty	5	1.3	60 percent or more seats are held by Independents.
One-party Monopolistic	29	7.9	80 percent or more seats are held by one party.
One-party Dominant	121	32.2	60-79 percent of the seats are held by one party.
Two-party	185	49.3	Two parties predominate. The leading party has fewer than 60 percent of the seats.
Three-party	35	9.3	Three parties, the smallest of which holds 20 percent or more of the seats.
Total	375	99.8	

Note: Percentages in this table are based on 375 councils. Excluded from the 410 total count are 35 councils with independent councilors and councilors who represent such a variety of minor parties that several new and rather meaningless categories would have to be created to accommodate them.
Source: Taxonomy from Tony Byrne, *Local Government in Britain*, 7th ed. (London: Penguin, 2000), p. 160. Data for 2006 provided to this author by Neil Bishai, Local Government Association.

Once a council has made a decision, it relies on others to carry it out. Those who do so are called officials or officers, not civil servants. Within each council there is a division of labor and a hierarchy of positions. At the top is the chief executive officer (CEO). Close behind is the chief finance officer, and below are chief officers, senior administrators, specialists (for example, accountants, architects, and engineers), and clerical officers, all of whom are supported by an army of personal assistants, secretaries, and receptionists. Among the officers, the CEO is responsible for the overall management of the council's executive operations, and the chief finance officer oversees its finances. Most chief officers head a department of the council. In that capacity, they oversee the execution of policy, advise the council's committees, and work with other chief officers to coordinate the implementation of policies that cut across a council's departmental boundaries. In two-tier councils they liaise with the council below or above theirs, interact with chief officers in neighboring councils on matters of mutual interest, and consult with civil servants in London or in one of Whitehall's regional offices.

Like civil servants, local officials are barred from holding political office in the council in which they work. They are recruited to their positions on merit, are not expected to resign their posts when control of the council passes to another party, and must avoid being partial to any political party. They also must avoid the appearance of being partial, although this is not always possible for some officers, chief officers in particular. Because they have a duty to advise councilors who sit on committees, chief officers are drawn inexorably into a world in which the administration of policy shades imperceptibly into the making of policy. This is hardly surprising. Chief officers are experts by dint of their training and experience, and councilors, most of whom are generalists, rely heavily on their advice. So reliant are they that one study found that in two thirds of the public authorities, chief officers were reported as making a "significant" contribution to initiating policy and, in nearly a quarter, a "major" contribution. That they had to fill a void is revealed by a further finding: only a minority of councilors who sat on committees made any "real contribution"; 30 percent to 40 percent were described as "useless." [9]

Most councilors admit to being amateurs when it comes to making policy; nonetheless, they expect the experts to tread cautiously. All too often, chief officers find themselves walking a tightrope. If they offer advice that councilors regard as breaking new ground in policy realms, they could be either applauded for making an important contribution or reproached for usurping the prerogatives of the politician. When their advice is seen as impeccably neutral, they run the risk of being criticized for failing to provide recommendations that satisfy those councilors who are thinking only of the next election. Because of the pitfalls that await them, chief officers realize the need to cultivate and sustain good relations with the councilors who sit on their committees, their chairs in particular. In the end, these good relations are crucial, for nothing of any consequence receives the imprimatur of the council unless it first earns the blessings of its committees.

This concludes the examination of local government, a form of devolution that has survived in one guise or another since the days of the Anglo-Saxons before the Normans invaded in 1066. Now the discussion turns to another form of devolution, one set in motion at the close of the last century. Its implementation marked an historic break from the past, so much so that one scholar, Vernon Bogdanor, hailed it as "the most radical constitutional change this country [Britain] has seen since the Great Reform Act of 1832."[10]

The Four Nations

The radical constitutional change that Professor Bogdanor referred to was the devolution of legislative and executive powers to Scotland and Wales. In 1997, four months after Labour came to power, a question was put to the voters in referendums in both nations. Scottish voters were asked whether they favored the creation of a Scottish parliament, and Welsh voters, a Welsh National Assembly. A significant majority (74.3 percent) of Scottish voters agreed, and a paper-thin majority of Welsh voters (50.1 percent) did so as well. In 1998, Parliament spelled out what form devolution would take in the Scotland Act and the Government of Wales Act. Elections were held a year later, and soon afterward, 129 members of the Scottish parliament and 60 members of the Welsh Assembly took their seats in Edinburgh and Cardiff.

Devolution for Scotland and Wales was an experiment, but it was not the UK's first experiment with devolution. Westminster had devolved powers to Northern Ireland as long ago as 1921, although the Government of Edward Heath suspended them in 1972 when savage sectarian strife brought turmoil to Ulster. The nature and extent of the power devolved is different in each of the three nations; paradoxically, aside from local government, devolution in England itself is nonexistent. Why this is so is dealt with later. So, too, is the UK's second experiment with devolution for Northern Ireland in 1998.

Scotland and Wales

It will be remembered that when Parliament enacted legislation devolving powers to Scotland and Wales, it did so to slow the momentum that had been building in both nations to break away from England and become na-tion-states on their own. In Scotland in particular the currents for independence had been running swift and deep, and for that reason, Parliament conferred more power on Edinburgh than on Cardiff.

Beginning in the 1960s, the Scottish National Party (SNP) took a vigorous lead in the campaign for an independent Scotland. It invoked images of such Scottish folk heroes as William Wallace, aka Braveheart, who had in times past beaten back English invaders before the Scots in 1707 grudgingly agreed to the treaty that joined them to England. The SNP reminded the Scots that they had their own legal and judicial systems, their own education system, their own established church, and a relatively robust economy made even more robust by North Sea Oil. They had their own military regiments and football teams, and when they were "at war and on the football field they were invariably Scottish first and British second."[11]

Most Scots were not in the habit of electing Conservatives to Westminster, and in the 1980s and 1990s they chafed under successive Conservative administrations that refused to entertain their demands for a Scottish parliament. So disaffected were they that in 1990, 60 percent of those polled in Scotland agreed that if the Conservatives were to win the next election, Scottish Labour MPs should withdraw from Westminster to force the Government to devolve powers to a Scottish parliament. That never materialized, nor did it have to; little more than nine years later Scottish voters flocked to the polls to elect members of their own parliament for the first time in nearly three hundred years.

Demands for independence were heard in Wales, too, although less so than in Scotland. Most of the demands, indeed the most strident, came from the north of the country, where Welsh nationalism was most in evidence. Many there felt that it was only a matter of time before all things Welsh would be overshadowed by all things English. They feared for their way of life and in particular for their Welsh language, which many saw as embodying the richness of their culture. These individuals recoiled from the thought that one day the compilers of a new edition of the *Encyclopedia Britannica* might be tempted to use as the entry for Wales the one that had been used in a nineteenth-century edition: "For Wales see England." [12] As support for independence gathered momentum, Wales' nationalist party Plaid Cymru (meaning "Welsh Party") made a compelling case with Labour for a halfway measure, that is, devolved powers for Wales. After all, Plaid Cymru leaders argued, if Labour were to win the election in 1997, could it not do for Wales what it was planning to do for Scotland?

Labour's leaders were convinced that the stirrings for independence in Scotland and Wales could not be ignored, which explains why the party was prepared to pave the way for devolution so soon after it took office in 1997. Because the movement for independence had generated so much support in Scotland, Edinburgh received the greater measure of power. When Parliament agreed to the Scotland Act of 1998, it stipulated that all powers not specifically reserved for Westminster, such as foreign affairs, defense, currency, and immigration, would be devolved to the Scottish parliament. Members of the Scottish parliament (MSPs) would have full authority to enact primary and secondary legislation covering a broad band of Scottish domestic affairs, including agriculture, housing, education, health, the environment, legal affairs, and local government. Moreover, MSPs were authorized to adjust the basic rate of individual income tax in Scotland by up to or down to 3 percent of the rates levied elsewhere in the UK.

By contrast, there is no reserve clause for the Welsh Assembly. Moreover, assembly members have no authority to enact primary legislation or to adjust the level of individual income tax. Their powers are instead strictly confined to secondary legislation, that is, legislation that sets out the rules and regulations that accompany primary legislation passed by Westminster that pertains to Wales. The far greater powers conferred on the Scottish parliament perhaps explains why Scotland's legislature is called a parliament and Wales' legislature is called an assembly. However, in what follows, both are referred to as legislatures.

Both the Scottish parliament at Holyrood in Edinburgh and the Welsh Assembly at Cardiff Bay are unicameral, and their members are elected for fixed four-year terms. The SMSP system, used for elections to Westminster, was rejected; two variants of proportional representation (PR) were chosen instead. The reason for adopting PR was that while PR was likely to produce a hung legislature, it would nevertheless reflect more accurately a cross-section of electoral choice. In addition, it was thought that the legislatures would be more inclusive of all parties, large and small, and equally important, take their first steps as newly devolved bodies without the likelihood that one party would win an overall majority and be tempted to run roughshod over the others.

The first elections to the Scottish parliament and Welsh Assembly, in 1999, produced hung legislatures in both bodies. As Table 11.5 shows, Labour became the largest party in both Scotland and Wales and the nationalist parties—the SNP and Plaid Cymru—the second largest. Trailing behind were the Conservatives and the Liberal Democrats. The first major question facing

Party	Scotland 1999	Scotland 2003	Wales 1999	Wales 2003
Table 11.5 The First Two Elections to the Devolved Legislatures of Scotland and Wales				
Labour	56	50	28	30
Scottish National Party	35	27	—	—
Plaid Cymru	—	—	17	12
Conservative	18	18	9	11
Liberal Democrat	17	17	6	6
Green	1	7	—	—
Scottish Socialist	1	6	—	—
Independent Labour	1	—	—	—
Independent	—	4	—	1
Total	129	129	60	60

Source: Taxonomy from Tony Byrne, *Local Government in Britain*, 7th ed. (London: Penguin, 2000), p. 160. Data provided to this author by Neil Bishai, Local Government Association.

the new legislatures was how could one party govern effectively if none clinched an overall majority of seats? The answer was that it could not, not unless the largest party, Labour, went into coalition with another party, which is what it did. In Scotland, Labour formed a coalition with the Liberal Democrats soon after the election and did the same with the Liberal Democrats in Wales, although not until nearly a year and a half after the election.

Once the elections were over, the executive side of the devolved governments took shape. Each of the legislatures elected a First Minister, and soon afterward the Queen confirmed their appointment. Next, the First Ministers formed their cabinets; in each case the minister reached beyond the Labour Party to fill ministerial posts. Scotland's Donald Dewar chose three Liberal Democrats and nine Labour members to sit on his twelve-member cabinet. Wales' Alun Michael asked two Plaid Cymru, one Liberal Democrat, and one Conservative to join him and two other Labour members on his seven-member cabinet. Apart from the First Minister, almost all ministers are given responsibility for heading departments. Among the departments found in both governments are those having responsibility for education, finance, health, social services, agriculture and rural affairs, local government, and economic development. All of these departments are staffed by civil servants, who remain part of the UK's civil service.

The second elections to the two devolved bodies, held in 2003, produced few changes. Labour and the Liberal Democrats continued in coalition in Scotland. Dewar, the "father" of the Scottish parliament, had died, and Frank McConnell was now First Minister. In Wales, however, Labour had no need to continue in coalition with the Liberal Democrats or with any other party. Although it won only thirty of the assembly's sixty seats, the party nevertheless constituted a majority because the assembly's presiding officer and deputy presiding officer, Plaid Cymru and independent members, respectively, could not vote. This meant that the most votes the opposition parties could muster was twenty-eight. Aside from that, the names of the major players changed. Rhodri Morgan took the place of Alun Michael as First Minister.

When the Blair Government set out in 1998 to draft radical constitutional reforms to transfer responsibilities from central government to Scotland and Wales, civil servants became engaged in an activity that had preoccupied their predecessors years before when Britain set its colonies free, developing a sophisticated form of state building. It was an experiment, or to be precise, two different experiments, for devolution took on a different guise in each of the two nations. Those at No. 10 Downing Street who drew up blueprints for reform in Northern Ireland had the benefit of consulting the model for Northern Ireland devised by David Lloyd George's Government nearly eighty years before. That model was helpful, but an important ingredient was missing.

Northern Ireland

Devolution in Northern Ireland first emerged in the aftermath of a tempestuous period in Irish history that led to Ireland's partition in 1921 and the creation of Northern Ireland. Ulster, the six counties in the north of Ireland, remained in the UK; the rest of Ireland, known today as the Republic of Ireland, became an independent nation-state. With partition, a parliamentary system largely modeled on Westminster was established in Ulster, with a parliament located in the Belfast suburb of Stormont. The Stormont parliament was a bicameral body with a fifty-two member House of Commons elected by a form of PR and a twenty-six member Senate, twenty-four of whom were elected by the Commons. The parliament was empowered to enact primary legislation on most Northern Ireland affairs. Left to Westminster, however, was authority to raise or lower taxes and to legislate on foreign affairs, defense, external trade, and coinage and currency. A prime minister was drawn from Stormont, as were members of a cabinet, who headed a half dozen departments.

Stormont was a model of devolved government. Its legislative output was prodigious, and Westminster refrained from meddling in its work. But as parliamentarians went about their work in the peaceful surroundings of the suburb, sectarian riots erupted a few miles away in the streets of central Belfast. Curfews became a way of life there until 1924. As innovative as devolved government for Northern Ireland was, the Stormont parliament could not have been expected to resolve quickly the conflicts that had for so long divided Ulster's Catholic minority (the Nationalists) and its Protestant majority (the Unionists). Sharpening the division was Stormont's Unionist Party, the party of government. In 1929 it abandoned PR for fear that a proportional electoral system would diminish its political fortunes and introduced the SMSP system in its place. The Unionists thus scrapped the very electoral system that had been designed to reflect more accurately the representation of Ulster's Catholic minority; as a result the Unionists entrenched themselves as the majority in Stormont for the next forty years.

By the late 1960s, Northern Ireland had become a garrison state about which the world was reminded one Sunday in January 1972 when British paratroopers fired on participants in a banned civil rights march in Londonderry. Fourteen marchers were killed, allegedly in response to the paratroopers being fired on by some of the marchers. The day became known as "Bloody Sunday" and produced a further casualty of a different kind when Edward Heath's Government shut down Stormont and imposed direct rule on Northern Ireland.

In 1996, after years of violence committed by the Irish Republican Army (IRA) and Unionist paramilitary groups, representatives from the Nationalist side (most notably Sinn Féin, the political arm of the IRA) and the Unionist side agreed to gather at the same table to discuss ways of ending the violence and building peace. What followed were months of protracted peace talks, chaired by former U.S. Senate majority leader George Mitchell. As the months wore on and discussions deadlocked, hopes for a settlement faded. Finally, in the spring of 1998, near Easter, Mitchell was able to announce a breakthrough: both sides had resolved their differences, and the negotiators had signed an historic accord, the Good Friday Agreement. A significant part of this agreement pledged a return of devolution to Northern Ireland.

The form of devolution agreed to represented a departure from what had been provided for in the years before direct rule was imposed, although there were some similarities. A Northern Ireland Assembly, a unicameral body, would be installed at Stormont. Aside from the usual powers reserved to Westminster, such as taxation and defense matters, law and order, policing, and criminal justice, the assembly would have the authority to enact primary and secondary legislation bearing on Northern Ireland affairs. A first minister, a deputy first minister, and ten other ministers would be elected by the assembly to serve as the Northern Ireland Executive, which would make decisions collectively and by consensus and oversee the work of ten departments covering a swathe of economic and social matters. On the surface, this arrangement sounded like what Parliament had provided for Edinburgh and Cardiff—Edinburgh in particular—and for that matter, for Stormont from 1921 to 1972. But there was an overriding difference, one designed to overcome the age-old conflicts that had divided Ulster's two communities. It centered on one word—"power-sharing."

Negotiators were determined not to repeat the mistakes made by the David Lloyd George Government nearly eighty years before when it allowed Stormont to replace PR with the SMSP system, locking the Unionists into a permanent majority and frustrating the Catholic minority's ambitions to win seats for many years to come. Power-sharing, the negotiators were convinced, would prevent that from happening again. The concept was applied to two institutions, the assembly and an executive body. The size of the assembly was large—108 members; in proportion to population, it was three times larger than the Scottish parliament. The purpose behind such a large assembly was to maximize the opportunity for more than just a few parties to win seats. This objective was realized on election day in 1998, when candidates from eight parties and the Women's Coalition won seats. Once elected, the winners were required to declare their allegiances: fifty-eight registered as members of the Unionist group, forty-two as members of the Nationalist group, and eight as "other." One of the ingredients essential for power-sharing had therefore been put into the mix. All that was left was another ingredient: power-sharing among members of the Northern Ireland Executive. But as it happened, they produced results that threatened the future of devolution in Northern Ireland.

To comply with the provisions of the Good Friday Agreement, the Executive's first minister and deputy first minister had to be elected by a triple majority, that is, by a majority of the full assembly plus a majority of both the Unionist group and the Nationalist group. David Trimble, the leader of the Ulster Unionist Party (Stormont's largest party), was elected first minister, and Seamus Mallon, deputy leader of the Social Democratic and Labour Party (Stormont's second largest party), his deputy. Next came the election of the ten remaining ministers, who had to be elected in proportion to the number of seats held by each party in the assembly. As it happened, all were drawn from the four largest parties—three from the Ulster Unionists, three from the Social Democratic and Labour Party, and two each from the Democratic Unionists and Sinn Féin.

The formula applied to the election of the Executive was simple, although the results were anything but that. Power-sharing, some argued, is not power at all and carries the seeds of its own destruction. Two scholars put it another way: "Power-sharing," they wrote, "may have been the most effective and perhaps the only means of creating peace but it makes the process of 'normalising' politics in Northern Ireland very difficult." [13]

Three events that occurred soon after the Executive formed supported the claims of the two scholars. First, the Ulster Unionist Party required its leader—First Minister Trimble—to win approval for every initiative he took, however minor. This extreme form of internal party democracy, which bordered on anarchy, forced Trimble to tread carefully or risk being challenged as party leader. Second, so contemptuous of Sinn Féin was the Rev. Ian Paisley, the leader of the Democratic Unionist Party (DUP), that when Trimble called the first meeting of the Executive at the end of 1999, Paisley and his party colleagues boycotted it because the two Sinn Féin ministers were in attendance.

And third, two controversial provisions of the Good Friday Agreement threatened to cause the peace accord to implode. The first provided for the early release of IRA and Nationalist prisoners, and the second, for the IRA's decommissioning of its weapons. It was the second provision that was especially problematic, for there was no evidence that the IRA had made any progress in this area. As a result, the Northern Ireland secretary of state suspended devolved government in Stormont just weeks after the Northern Ireland's Executive first met. Three months later, the IRA announced it was prepared to put its weapons "completely and verifiably" beyond use. This announcement led to the Government's restoration of devolution and to David Trimble's reelection as first minister. But how many more times could this on-again/off-again process continue before the public lost the hope that the Good Friday Agreement had inspired?

Two thousand and one was year three of intermittent devolution for Northern Ireland and was also another year of on-again/off-again devolution. David Trimble resigned again in the summer for the same reason as before: the IRA had failed to demonstrate that it was serious about abandoning its weapons. The Executive was suspended, as was the assembly, six weeks after Trimble's resignation. This was the second time the British government had suspended devolution for Northern Ireland. In the autumn it was restored yet again after the IRA put some of its weapons out of use. Trimble was elected once again. But his party, the Ulster Unionists, was becoming increasingly impatient with the IRA as well as with Trimble for not taking a tougher stance on the IRA.

Year four of devolution for Northern Ireland, that is, 2002, was the most frustrating yet for power-sharing. There was a continuous flow of reports about IRA punishment shootings, rumors of the IRA training left-wing guerillas in Colombia, and word that it was involved in fomenting sectarian violence in unionist areas of Belfast. Trimble, in the meantime, had not given up on power-sharing, although by September, when the Ulster Unionists' Ruling Council met, he realized that he would probably be replaced as leader unless he toughened his position on the IRA. Accordingly, he gave the IRA an ultimatum: disband by early 2003 or the Ulster Unionists would no longer serve in the Executive. A month later, an IRA spy ring was uncovered at Stormont. So appalled was Trimble by this revelation that he announced that the Ulster Unionists ministers would leave the Executive unless Sinn Féin did so, and Tony Blair, realizing that the Good Friday Agreement would be dead without Sinn Féin, suspended devolution. In effect devolution was being held in abeyance until tempers cooled and talks could resume.

It was thought initially that a year would be needed before devolution could be restored. As that year was coming to an end, Trimble tried to pave the way for a return of the power-sharing arrangement by meeting with Sinn Féin's leader Gerry Adams. Heartened by the prospect that the two leaders would find a way to break the deadlock, the Blair Government announced that the already-delayed election to the Northern Ireland Assembly would be held in November 2003. As it happened, the discussions between Trimble and Adams resolved nothing, but the election was held anyway. The results produced a nightmare scenario: Rev. Ian Paisley's Democratic Unionist Party became the largest party and the largest Unionist group, and Sinn Féin became the largest Nationalist group. Predictably, the DUP would have nothing to do with Sinn Féin and demanded that the terms of the Good Friday Agreement be renegotiated. Sinn Féin, although it was willing to work with the DUP, would have nothing to do with renegotiating the Good

Friday Agreement. In the meantime, with devolution still suspended as of the end of 2006, the 108 members of the Legislative Assembly use their offices and receive their salaries, but they have no legislative responsibilities.

Power-sharing devolution for Northern Ireland has always required the triumph of hope over expectation, for power-sharing requires decision making by consensus. In the UK, however, consensual politics is not conventional politics, least of all in Northern Ireland. That, in a sentence, sums up the dilemma of devolution in Northern Ireland and suggests why, if power-sharing is restored, it will face a very uncertain future.

England

By 2000, devolution was up and running in three of the nations of the UK. But not in England. England had devolved local governments, just as the three other nations had, but it appeared paradoxical that the Blair Government did not do for England what it had done for Scotland, Wales, and Northern Ireland. This puzzled some and troubled others, especially those pressing for an answer to the so-called West Lothian Question. This was a question first raised by Tam Dalyell, a member of Parliament who had once represented the Scottish constituency of West Lothian. Why was it, he had asked, that Scottish MPs in Westminster were allowed to debate and vote on all issues pertaining to England and Wales but English and Welsh MPs were barred from voting on Scotland-only matters that fell within the province of Holyrood? This question had not been answered, and so disaffected had some become by this lack of political symmetry that they formed two pressure groups, one to campaign for an English parliament and another to champion the cause of English independence. By and large, however, the general public in England was either unaware of developments in the other three nations of the UK or, if it was aware of them, it was not bothered by them. More significantly, the English were not immediately threatened by these developments; nor did they enkindle feelings of English nationalism.

The Blair Government never seriously considered devolution for England. The closest it came to devolving power was in 1999, when it made good on its 1997 election manifesto pledge to create a regional development agency (RDA) in each of the eight regions of England outside London to stimulate economic growth. But "power" is a misnomer, for the RDAs were quangos, not elected bodies, and they have no authority to legislate. Moreover, it was never intended that they be seen as bodies comparable to the devolved parliament in Edinburgh and the assemblies in Cardiff Bay and Belfast. But a pledge Labour made in its next manifesto, in 2002, hinted at devolving a modicum of power in the form of English regional assemblies.

Under the plan, the voters of each of the eight RDA regions would decide by referendum whether to approve the creation of an elected assembly to work alongside the RDA and thus give economic planning a representational flavor. It was no secret that creating these assemblies was the brainchild of John Prescott, the deputy prime minister, for he had long been a proponent of English regional government. Creating regional government had never generated much excitement, however. Whenever the subject had been brought up in the past it had been greeted "with both yawns and derision."[14] One academic called Labour's long-standing campaign for regional government "the dog that never barked."[15]

And the dog failed to bark again in 2004. Of the eight English regions, the northeast had been judged to be the friendliest to an assembly, and thus John Prescott thought it sensible to hold the first of several referendums there. But much to the surprise of many who had been campaigning for an assembly, when the voters turned out, they rejected the proposal by a margin of nearly four to one. Reportedly, some voters were convinced that the assembly would wield little power. Perhaps other felt the same as the local government association (a professional association of local officials)—that there was a possibility of "regional assemblies 'sucking' power from town halls, rather than taking it from Whitehall."[16] This was the first—and as it turned out, the last—referendum on this subject; less than a week after the referendum results were known, Prescott announced that the Government had no plans to hold further referendums.

Conclusion

One cannot but be impressed by the number and variety of devolved governments in the UK. Local governments in England, Scotland, Wales, and Northern Ireland vary in the ways they are organized and in the powers they wield. This seemingly higgledy-piggledy arrangement did not evolve by chance, for the governments that have been in place at the local level since 1998 assumed their present forms only after a Local Government Commission had for four years systematically solicited the views of the public. Moreover, the powers devolved to the newly devolved governments headquartered in Edinburgh, Cardiff Bay, and Stormont were devised to cater to the circumstances peculiar to each.

Now that these new forms of government have been up and running for some while, what might be said about their performance? The response is necessarily provided in two parts—one for local governments and another for the governments of the three nations.

No politician is prepared to argue that there will be a return to what was described earlier in this chapter as the Golden Age of local government. That age is long gone. Trends since then, especially since the early 1980s, demonstrate that central government has steadily eroded the powers of local government by transferring some to Whitehall and others to qualgos. These changes have demoralized councilors and confused the public. So demoralized have many councilors become that they are choosing not to seek reelection. The knock-on effect is that councils increasingly are left without ample numbers of experienced decision makers having the political sophistication to pilot difficult measures through their councils and to stand up to Whitehall when circumstances warrant. So confused is the public that individuals find it difficult to know whom to praise when an activity of government lives up to expectations or to blame when it does not. That local governments have been reorganized so frequently over the decades and have had their powers reduced or withdrawn so radically since 1980 explains in large part why turnout at council elections has hovered around 40 percent—so low as to cast doubt on any grandiose claims that local governments are beacons of democracy.

The other form of devolution is not problem-free either. The Scottish parliament is not without its critics, even though its work has impressed many. It has succeeded in taking an independent course, which is what it was intended to do, and at times even at the expense of riling the Blair Government. It has done so knowing full well its actions are amply protected by the legislative powers transferred to it under the provisions of the Government of Scotland Act. This generous grant of authority could lead to demands that Westminster do for the Welsh Assembly what it did for the Scottish parliament. A small step was taken in that direction in 2004 when an all-party commission chaired by Lord Richard, a Welsh peer, proposed that the assembly be increased in size from sixty to eighty members. In addition, the commission suggested that it would be "desirable, though not essential" to assign the same powers to the assembly that had been assigned to the Scottish parliament. In the meantime, the assembly has proceeded with its responsibilities in a workmanlike manner, although the Welsh public has tired of what it sees as petty bickering in the assembly chamber. Whether Westminster will one day devolve further powers on the assembly depends on the efficiency with which the assembly processes secondary legislation and whether the Welsh accept the new status quo. Because Welsh voters had supported devolution in the referendum of 1997 by a paper-thin majority, it is unlikely Westminster will act any time soon.

In Northern Ireland, there are too few four-leaf clovers growing around Stormont to inspire much optimism about the future of devolution in Ulster. The success of this experiment is singularly dependent on the success of power-sharing, which is a fragile instrument in the toolbox of Northern Ireland's Executive. As of this writing, devolution was granted and then suspended in rather rapid succession on three occasions from 1999 through 2002 and has not yet been granted for a fourth time. One day, if devolution proves to be a success, the Executive could be in a position to recommend to No. 10 Downing Street that Ulster is prepared to proceed to the last step in the Good Friday Agreement—a referendum that would give the voters of the six counties the opportunity to choose between Ulster's remaining in the UK or being incorporated into the Republic of Ireland. If the leaders of the UK and the republic agree, the referendum will go forward. That day is a long way off. Indeed, it might never come. If it does and voters approve, there are bound to be those who will think it ironic that devolved government in Northern Ireland was so successful that it led to Ulster's exit from the United Kingdom.

12
Law, Courts, and Judges

Not long ago, students of politics paid scant attention to Britain's legal and judicial systems—its laws, courts, and judges. That was probably because most textbooks on British politics treated the topic as an afterthought, and some gave it barely a mention. Why was a topic so monumentally important given such short shrift? There are three reasons. The first was that there was nothing remotely political about British courts and judges. In their rulings, judges were barred from straying beyond what Parliament provided for in law unless there were inconsistencies in the law or the law lacked clarity. Because judges were expected to rule in scrupulous accord with what Parliament said the law was, the judiciary did not emerge as an independent force poised to engage in political struggles with Parliament and the government of the day. A second reason was that few politically charged cases came before the courts. Occasionally, legal action was initiated against ministers and officials by individuals claiming they had been wronged by their failure to do what the law required, but because judges tended to defer to the government of the day, only rarely did they find ministers and officials legally liable. A third reason was that what little judges said publicly generated hardly any interest and even less political controversy. They kept out of the limelight and saw no reason to disagree with the string of lord chancellors who admonished them to refrain from speaking out on issues of the day, even issues of justice, for fear that doing so would prompt some to question their impartiality.

So transformed were the British legal and judicial systems by the end of the twentieth century and beginning of the twenty-first that the three reasons cited above lost much of their currency. Soon after Britain joined the European Union in 1973, the courts began to hand down decisions based on European Community (EC) law as well as on law passed by Parliament. Initially, the courts found themselves on a collision course with Parliament when an EC law clashed with a British law, even though Britain in the European Communities Bill had agreed that EC law would take precedence over British law. Even today, Euro-skeptics bristle with indignation whenever an EC law or regulation strays beyond the boundaries of what they think tolerable. Another development affecting the law was the 1966 decision that allowed British citizens to seek redress for their grievances by taking their cases to the European Court of Human Rights (ECHR), as long as they first exhausted all legal remedies available to them in courts at home. When the ECHR, which based its decisions on the European Convention on Human Rights, ruled in favor of a complainant, the British government with few exceptions had to honor the decision. In 1998 Parliament incorporated the convention into British law as part of the Human Rights Act (HRA) of 1998 and empowered the courts to rule when an act of Parliament contravenes one or more rights cited in the HRA.

The number of cases brought by citizens against ministers and civil servants for failing to comply fully with the law escalated, in part because the courts tightened the standards by which the actions of ministers and civil servants could be judged. Starting in the mid-1980s judges were advised by one lord chancellor and later encouraged by a lord chief justice to speak out if they were concerned about an issue in the field of justice. Judges continued to eschew publicity, but some felt so strongly about certain issues that they did not think twice about speaking out, even though by doing so they laid themselves open to charges of judicial activism.

The law itself is the logical starting point for an examination of the law, courts, and judges in Britain's political system, in particular, the rule of law and the modifications it has undergone. Then the discussion turns to courts that patrol the law and how they too have changed. There are more of them today, with some having become highly specialized as the law has become more technically challenging, and as a consequence, administering the court system has become more complex. The judges are the third part of this triune. Their work has changed as well. Most preside in their courtrooms in wigs and gowns, as they did in the nineteenth century. However, their dockets have grown enormously, and they play a demonstrably greater role in shaping the law.

The Law

In 1726, soon after French authorities had banned him from entering Paris, the writer Voltaire left his native France to spend some time in England. When he crossed the English Channel, he "passed out of the realm of despotism to a land where . . . men were ruled by law and not by caprice." [1] These words were not Voltaire's, but rather those of the English constitutional scholar, A. V. Dicey. They might well have been Voltaire's sentiments, however, for he was far from enamoured of a law that had required him to be detained for some time in Paris' infamous Bastille nine years before for having written some satirical verses about a prominent French duke.

When Dicey penned these words in 1885, he might have been a little severe in his judgment about rule "by caprice" in Voltaire's France. Being something of a chauvinist, he left no doubt in the minds of his readers that he was proud to live in a land where the rule of law played a central role in the system of governance. Indeed, the rule of law continues to play such a role, although the meaning scholars ascribe to it today is not quite the same that Dicey ascribed to it toward the end of the nineteenth century. It is important to discuss these changes, but first it is useful to explore briefly what the functions of law in society are.

The Functions of Law in Society

What are the functions of law in society? The answer might not be immediately obvious until the question is turned around and posed in the negative: "What would society be like if there were no law?" If there were no law, there would be no *order*. Cars could course recklessly through the streets of city centers and not be required to stop when traffic lights turned red to let pedestrians cross, for there would be no traffic lights. If there were no law, there would be no individual *rights*. An innocent man who stumbled haplessly onto the scene of a crime could be confronted by a mob craving revenge and dragged to the nearest tree and hanged. If there were no law, there would be no *benefits*. A man severely injured while working at a building site could not expect to receive medical attention by licensed physicians and nurses at a state-chartered hospital because there would be no licensing or chartering authorities. If there were no law, there would be no *responsibilities*. Individuals and businesses would not be obliged to pay taxes to support such basic services as running schools, building roads, and operating fire stations. Society would be in a state of collapse. It would be a Franz Kafka novel come to life, and anarchy would reign.

Maintaining order, conferring rights and benefits, and establishing and regulating responsibilities are the functions of law. Every society recognizes the need for law, but the nature of law varies from society to society, sometimes remarkably so. The laws found in autocratic regimes differ markedly from those found in democratic ones. An autocratic regime places great emphasis on order to police and control the behavior of individuals and groups, for nothing is more important than maintaining itself in power. A democratic regime, on the other hand, balances social order with civil rights. It does not question the importance of order in society; indeed, it accepts it as a given, for without order social relations break down. But at the same time, it accepts that it is the job of the state to serve the citizen and not the other way around, and realizes the importance of establishing and ensuring individual rights. In that respect, democratic regimes face a much greater challenge than autocratic regimes, for they realize how difficult it is to strike the right balance between social order and individual rights.

In Britain, the ground rules for striking the right balance are incorporated in the doctrine of the rule of law. This term is one that politicians excitedly

313

invoke when they decry rising street crime or debate controversial legislation intended to protect citizens from terrorism, but it is more than just an attention-getting piece of rhetoric. Rather, it embodies a corpus of legal values honed by the forces of tradition that spring from one core principle: no one, not even the state, is above the law. Moreover, the rule of law serves as the reference point for different types of law.

The Rule of Law

Dicey's *Study of the Law of the Constitution,* published in 1885, was so enthusiastically received that many legal scholars predicted it would soon become a classic. They were not exaggerating. So much of an impression did it make that scholars, judges, and lawyers eagerly consulted it when searching for guidance on points of law. One of the chief contributions Dicey made was his exposition of the doctrine of the rule of law, a cogent apologia that embraced order and predictability and placed categorical limits on the authority of the state over the individual.

Dicey's work stands as a classic even today. But like many classics, it no longer commands the same authority it once did, for so much more complex has governing become that in the opinion of legal scholars, some of his theories of law, including some aspects of his doctrine of the rule of law, have had to be modified over time.[2] Despite these modifications, certain core values of this doctrine have retained much of their currency. For this reason legal scholars generally agree that these values—or principles, as Dicey called them—serve as useful points of departure for understanding how the rule of law has acquired the meaning it has today. These principles deal with arbitrariness in the law, equality under the law, and individual rights.

Arbitrariness in the Law

In Dicey's words, "no man is punishable or can be lawfully made to suffer in body or goods except for a distinct breach of the law."[3] The crucial word is "distinct," for Dicey felt that the more precise the law was, the less arbitrary politicians' decisions would be. Discretionary powers, in his view, were to be avoided at all costs, for, as he put it, "when there is discretion there is room for arbitrariness."[4] This precept presents a dilemma for modern lawmakers, for although they accept that arbitrariness is anathema to the rule of law, they are prepared to argue that a law should not be drawn up so narrowly that it stymies the efforts of public administrators to apply it to any number of different circumstances. For that reason, much of law today is couched in general language. Once a law is enacted, ministers often are empowered to devise statutory instruments (unknown in Dicey's day) that set out the details of the law and stipulate what rules must be followed when it is implemented. The law by necessity confers discretionary authority on ministers when, for example, they face having to decide whether a certain subject meets the requirements of the national school curriculum or what decibel level of noise should be considered excessive when low-flying airliners make their approaches to airports over congested areas. As the details of law are spelled out increasingly in statutory instruments, the task of modern jurists is not to claw back the discretionary authority conferred on ministers, but rather to scrutinize statutory instruments to ascertain whether they are appropriate for the tasks the law provides for.

Equality under the Law

The second of Dicey's principles is that everyone is equal under the law, or as he put it, "every official, from the Prime Minister down to a constable or a collector of taxes, is under the same responsibility for every act done without legal justification as any other citizen."[5] Those charged with breaking the law, whether public official or citizen, must be brought before what he called the "ordinary tribunals" of the land.[6] "Ordinary" is the operative word, for those familiar with Dicey's writings know how averse he was to courts of an *extra*ordinary nature. Extraordinary courts, in his mind, were administrative courts, in particular those found in France, to which citizens brought their grievances when they alleged that public officials had been culpable of unlawful conduct. In his view, cases of this nature should be dealt with by the existing courts. More important, he (mistakenly) believed that administrative courts would undermine the law by favoring government officials with special legal privileges and thus dilute the extent to which these officials were subject to it.

Today, there is an extraordinary court in Britain. The Administrative Court was established to consider the growing number of applications for judicial review. These are applications filed by citizens or groups of citizens who have been adversely affected by a minister's decisions that they believe to be illegal, procedurally improper, or unreasonable. If the court accepts an application, it reviews the minister's decision in light of what the law provides and quashes the decision should it fail to conform to the dictates of the law. Contrary to what Dicey thought about administrative courts elsewhere, in Britain they exist not to confer special legal privileges on ministers, but rather to provide speedier redress for those with legitimate grievances.

Individual Rights

When Dicey wrote about the third principle, which dealt with individual rights, he evinced an unshakeable faith in the common law. In his words, "the general principles of the constitution (as for example the right to personal liberty or the right of public meeting) are . . . the result of judicial decisions determining the rights of private persons in particular cases brought before the courts."[7] He saw no need for statutes to spell out such rights as the right to free speech and the right to a fair trial, for he maintained that individual rights—or freedoms, as he preferred to call them—were implicitly guaranteed. However, if a citizen were denied an assumed right, the aggrieved party was not without recourse, for he or she could seek redress by appealing to a court for a judgment based on the law of custom, or common law. In Dicey's day, individual rights were made explicit in only a few statutes. One example is the Habeas Corpus Act of 1679, which prohibits the state from imprisoning an individual unless it first brings charges against that individual. Apart from this and a few other exceptions, the statutes were silent about individual rights largely because statute law had not developed to the point that it did in the twentieth century.

Parliament in the meantime bowed to a body of common law derived from judges' decisions based on judgments handed down over the years, as it still does. However, with the growth of statute law, rights today have become increasingly enshrined in statutes. For example, the Equal Pay Act of 1970 gives employees the right to equal pay for the same kind of work, regardless of sex; the Access to Medical Records Act of 1988 gives patients the right to see any medical records that their doctors are asked to pass on to insurance companies and employers; and the Human Rights Act (HRA) encapsulates a myriad of individual rights, all drawn from the European Convention on Human Rights. Enshrining rights in law represents a striking departure from the past when, in contrast to continental law, British lawmakers spelled out not what one may do but what one was prohibited from doing.

Dicey's three principles have evolved to accommodate changes that have taken place, although the core values of his doctrine of the rule of law remain essentially intact. First, arbitrariness is still anathema to those who shape the law, even though conferring discretionary authority on ministers is recognized as so essential a component of the law today that it is considered commonplace. Second, ministers and public officials can still be brought before a court of law if citizens believe their actions run counter to the dictates of the law, but today the Administrative Court is entrusted to consider such grievances. And third, individual rights are still protected by the common law, but increasingly by statute law as well.

Varieties of Law

From the core values found in the rule of law, various types of law have developed over the centuries. The broadest types are statute law, common law, and equity; constitutional law and administrative law; and civil and criminal law.

Statute Law, Common Law, and Equity

Statute law, the most common type of law, is law created by an act of Parliament. Parliament typically passes between fifty and sixty laws in any given year. Ministers devise as many as 1,600 statutory instruments to accompany them, all of which have the force of law. Altogether, statutes and their associated statutory instruments fill many thousands of pages in volumes that spread across several feet of shelf space. Statute law is not a recent form of law, but neither is it the oldest. That distinction belongs to common law. This is law derived not from statutes but instead from judges' decisions that are based on custom. These have been handed down over the years, starting as early as the twelfth century. Equity, another form of law, developed about a century later. Rules of equity were used to fill in the gaps in the common law; when two parties in a dispute discovered a gap in the law, one or both would turn to the lord chancellor, the "keeper of the King's conscience," to fill in the gap as he saw fit. Rules of equity developed separately from the common law, but years later, in the Judicature Acts of 1873–1875, Parliament merged many aspects of both types of law. The doctrine of precedent, or stare decisis, requires judges to base their decisions on those handed down in previous related common law and equity cases, although they adjust their decisions to reflect new circumstances and ways of thinking.

Constitutional Law and Administrative Law

Constitutional law and administrative law are "two sides of the same legal coin," as one authority put it. [8] The constitutional law side of the coin deals with public institutions that make policy, including the way they are formed (for example, elections to Parliament), what their functions are (such as the work of the Treasury), and how they interact with each other (for example, relations between the Treasury and the Department of Trade and Industry). On the other side of the legal coin is administrative law, which is concerned with the powers, procedures, duties, and liabilities of these same institutions of government as they administer public policy. Of the two types of law, administrative law is the more recent, originating in the twentieth century as the state expanded its role and delegated a multitude of new powers to ministers.

Starting in the 1960s judges have been called upon increasingly to involve themselves in judicial review, one of the earliest examples of which was *Ridge v. Baldwin*, a landmark case that went all the way to the Law Lords in the House of Lords for a decision in 1964. The case was brought by a police constable who had been denied an opportunity to present his side of the story to the police authority before being dismissed from the force. Drawing on the common law, the Law Lords nullified his dismissal on the grounds that it ran counter to one of the basic principles of natural justice that held that no one should be condemned before being given a hearing. Since then, applications for judicial review have grown steadily, so much so that in 1987 the government of the day circulated a leaflet to ministers and senior civil servants advising them on how to make decisions that would survive judicial scrutiny. The leaflet was appropriately entitled, "The Judge over Your Shoulder."

Civil Law and Criminal Law

Civil law regulates relationships between individuals. Examples are laws on marriage, divorce, and child custody; property, including patent law and copyright law; contracts, or legally binding agreements between two or more parties; and tort, which pertains to trespass, negligence, libel, and slander. Having no direct interest in civil disputes between private parties, the state does not become involved in civil litigation. Criminal law, by contrast, is law in which the state has a definite interest. It includes crimes against the state, such as treason; against the person, such as murder; and against property, such as theft. With the expansion of the regulatory state, so too is it now a crime to drive when intoxicated, falsify tax returns, and sell cigarettes to children younger than sixteen years of age. Offences range from the less serious to the heinous. The less serious are called summary offences and include driving over the speed limit and being drunk and disorderly, and those charged are tried by a judge. The most serious acts are called indictable offences. They include murder and rape, and those accused are tried before a jury.

Statute law, common law, equity, constitutional law, administrative law, civil law, and criminal law are the major categories of British law. So much variety is there that each type has its own specialized practitioners, its own textbooks, law journals, and law reports, and in some cases even its own courts.[9] Variety does not stop there, for it is important to emphasize that the legal system is not uniform throughout the UK. The law as described to this point is English law—or to be accurate, English and Welsh law—and is separate from that of Scotland and Northern Ireland, each of which has its own body of laws and courts based on different traditions and circumstances.

When Scotland agreed to join in union with England and Wales in 1707, it insisted on keeping its legal traditions, which were strongly influenced by Roman law, that is, law that enshrined basic rights and obligations in legislative codes. It was different from the law of England and Wales, which relied instead on common, or judge-made, law. Scotland even retained certain court practices, such as the verdict "not proven" when a jury cannot decide the innocence or guilt of the accused. Northern Ireland law is not so much different from English and Welsh law as separate from it, but even here certain practices set it apart from those in the other three nations. One example is Diplock courts, which are unique to Northern Ireland. In Diplock courts, defendants accused of major criminal offences are tried without a jury. This practice, which began in 1973, brought an end to jurors being targeted for reprisals by IRA and loyalist paramilitaries for rendering verdicts of "guilty" in cases that involved one of their terrorist colleagues.

Courts

British law is highly pluralistic. Indeed, it has to be if, as intended, it applies to as many facets of British society as it does. Just as the law is pluralistic, so too is the British court system. Courts are bodies that resolve civil disputes between individuals, hand down judgments, and impose sentences in criminal proceedings. They also make rulings in cases in which citizens allege that they have been given short shrift by public officials they believe acted contrary to the dictates of the law. Before proceeding, several characteristics about British courts are worth noting. Figure 12.1, which outlines the court structure of England and Wales, shows first that there is a hierarchy of courts. The highest court is the Appellate Committee of the House of Lords (that is, until late in 2009, when a Supreme Court will serve in its place), and the lowest is the magistrates' courts. Second, the courts have a variety of specialized jurisdictions. Third, most courts deal with either civil matters or criminal matters, and some deal with both. Fourth, as the arrows in the figure suggest, cases are appealed normally from one court to another court immediately above it in the hierarchy, but on occasion appeals bypass one or more intervening higher courts. And fifth, tribunals are not courts, but they merit inclusion in the discussion because they perform an important adjudicative function.

Just as the law is categorized as either civil or criminal, so too are the courts, at least for the most part. Each court is examined separately, starting with the civil courts.

Civil Courts

The four levels of civil courts are county courts, the High Court of Justice, the Court of Appeal, and the House of Lords' Appellate Committee (Supreme Court in 2009). Below the county courts, however, are tribunals, which play a role similar to a court.

Tribunals

Most tribunals were formed in the decades following the Second World War to adjudicate disputes between individuals and between individuals and institutions, including governmental institutions. As Parliament enacted one law after another regulating such matters as safety procedures in the work place, landlord-tenant rights, and eligibility for certain tax allowances, it created a variety of tribunals to allow those claiming they had been unfairly treated to resolve their differences with others. Today, more than 2,000 tribunals meet across England and Wales to resolve more than 250,000 disputes a year that fall into more than 60 broad categories.

Tribunal hearings are presided over not by a judge but by a lawyer, who is joined by two or more lay persons who specialize in the subject matter of the hearing. Together they assess the facts in the light of the law. The parties to a case present their sides of the story usually without legal representation and in a relatively informal setting. If both parties are satisfied with the outcome, there is no reason to add yet another case to the already crowded docket of a court of law. On the other hand, if one of the parties is not satisfied, he or she may submit an application to appeal the case either to the High Court of Justice or to the Court of Appeal, thus bypassing the county court, the lowest of the civil courts.

County Courts

To give as much access as possible to those seeking redress for their grievances, 218 county courts are located all across England and Wales. These

Figure 12.1 Court Structure in England and Wales and the Appeals Process

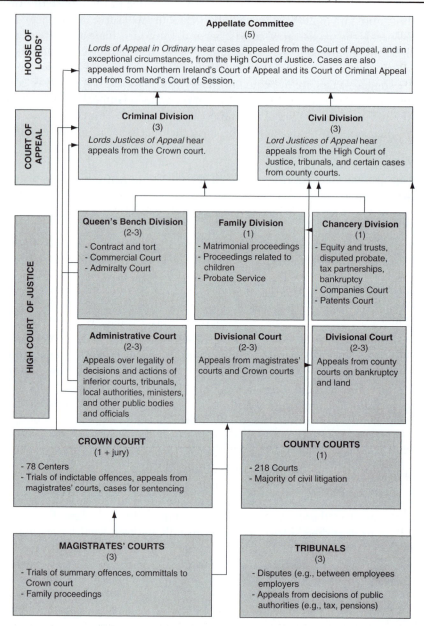

HOUSE OF LORDS*

Appellate Committee
(5)
Lords of Appeal in Ordinary hear cases appealed from the Court of Appeal, and in exceptional circumstances, from the High Court of Justice. Cases are also appealed from Northern Ireland's Court of Appeal and its Court of Criminal Appeal and from Scotland's Court of Session.

COURT OF APPEAL

Criminal Division
(3)
Lords Justices of Appeal hear appeals from the Crown court.

Civil Division
(3)
Lord Justices of Appeal hear appeals from the High Court of Justice, tribunals, and certain cases from county courts.

HIGH COURT OF JUSTICE

Queen's Bench Division
(2-3)
- Contract and tort
- Commercial Court
- Admiralty Court

Family Division
(1)
- Matrimonial proceedings
- Proceedings related to children
- Probate Service

Chancery Division
(1)
- Equity and trusts, disputed probate, tax partnerships, bankruptcy
- Companies Court
- Patents Court

Administrative Court
(2-3)
Appeals over legality of decisions and actions of inferior courts, tribunals, local authorities, ministers, and other public bodies and officials

Divisional Court
(2-3)
Appeals from magistrates' courts and Crown courts

Divisional Court
(2-3)
Appeals from county courts on bankruptcy and land

CROWN COURT
(1 + jury)
- 78 Centers
- Trials of indictable offences, appeals from magistrates' courts, cases for sentencing

COUNTY COURTS
(1)
- 218 Courts
- Majority of civil litigation

MAGISTRATES' COURTS
(3)
- Trials of summary offences, committals to Crown court
- Family proceedings

TRIBUNALS
(3)
- Disputes (e.g., between employees employers
- Appeals from decisions of public authorities (e.g., tax, pensions)

Notes: Number of judges (in parentheses) refers to the usual number of judges sitting. Not all jurisdictions and lines of appeals are shown.

*Supreme Court, not the House of Lords, effective the end of 2009. Lords of Appeal in Ordinary (or Law Lords) will be called Justices of the Supreme Court.

Source: Adapted from the Lord's Chancellor's Department, "Departmental Report 2001–2002" The Stationery Office, CM 5408, May 2002), p. 16.

courts have jurisdiction over contracts, probate, personal injury, bank-ruptcy, and insolvency matters, as well as family law as it pertains to divorce, child custody, and domestic violence. Also known as small claims courts, county courts are where claims below a prescribed maximum are lodged. Going to court can set back many financially; to keep costs to a minimum, the parties are encouraged to refrain from hiring lawyers and to resolve their differences through informal arbitration. Not all are happy with the out-come, however, and those who are not may seek to appeal their case to the next court in the hierarchy, the High Court of Justice.

The High Court of Justice

Beyond the cathedral-like main hall of the Royal Courts of Justice located in the Strand in central London are courtrooms reserved for 107 judges of the High Court of Justice. This court has three major divisions. The first is the Queen's Bench Division (QBD), which has jurisdiction over cases involving contracts and tort, as well as over claims that exceed the maximum value al-lowable for county courts. Three specialized courts also are part of the QBD. The Commercial Court deals with commercial disputes, banking, and insur-ance; the Admiralty Court with shipping matters; and the Administrative Court, which was created in 2000 to reduce the burden placed on the QBD, with the increasing number of applications that are filed for judicial review.

The second division is the Family Division, which deals with contested di-vorces, domestic violence, adoption, and probate. The third division, the Chancery Division, deals with equity. It has jurisdiction over trusts, disputed probate, bankruptcy, and tax matters. In addition, this division has two spe-cialized courts—a Companies Court and a Patents Court. If a party to a case heard in any one of these three divisions is dissatisfied with the court's ruling, it may lodge an appeal with the next court up the hierarchy, the Court of Appeal, or in rare instances, directly with the Appellate Committee of the House of Lords (or, starting in 2009, the Supreme Court).

The Court of Appeal

The Court of Appeal, which also sits in the Royal Courts of Justice, is organ-ized into the Criminal Division and the Civil Division. Once civil cases are cleared to be heard in the Court of Appeal, they are referred to the Civil Di-vision. So, too, are civil cases that originate in tribunals and county courts. The Civil Division is headed by the master of the rolls, one of the most senior judges in England and Wales, and is staffed by thirty-eight lords justices of ap-peal, any three of whom together hear one of the more than one thousand cases that come before the division every year. The Court of Appeal is the end of the line for the vast majority of cases. From time to time, however, Appeal Court judges determine that a case involves a point of law so complex that it merits consideration by the Appellate Committee of the House of Lords. If the Law Lords agree, parties to the appeal have their case settled by the highest court in the land. Otherwise, the Appeal Court's ruling stands; once it has ruled, if it has established any new precedents in this or any other case, they automatically are binding on all lower courts from that point forward.

The House of Lords

The twelve Law Lords, or Lords of Appeal in Ordinary, who constitute the Appellate Committee of the House of Lords until the Supreme Court begins to function late in 2009, sit at the apex of the UK's judicial hierarchy. These Law Lords constitute the highest court of appeal for civil cases that originate in the four nations of the UK. Not all twelve sit on a case. The process followed since 2006 involves the lord chief justice assigning usually five Law Lords to hear a case—except in the most contentious and legally complex cases, when he may assign as many as seven, and in the very rarest of occasions, nine. The only cases the Appellate Committee hears are those on appeal from the Court of Appeal or the High Court of Justice on those few occasions when cases bypass the Court of Appeal.

Before a case may proceed from either of these two courts, however, the relevant court must give the party "leave to appeal." This it will do if it agrees that the case in question raises an unresolved issue about a point of law of considerable significance. If the Law Lords agree, the appeal goes forward. If the lower court denies a petition to appeal, the Law Lords still may hear the case; if they do, it almost always means they intend to reverse the lower court's decision or bring greater clarity to the decision by restating its meaning.

Criminal Courts

Until 2009, the Appellate Committee of the House of Lords is also the highest court of appeal for criminal cases in England, Wales, and Northern Ireland. There are four levels of courts below the House of Lords. Starting at the bottom and working up, they are magistrates' courts, Crown courts, the High Court of Justice, and the Court of Appeal.

Magistrates' Courts

Approximately 95 percent of all criminal cases start and end in magistrates' courts. There are four hundred magistrates' courthouses scattered across England and Wales, more than any other type of courthouse, and there are more judges assigned to magistrates' courts than to any other—around thirty thousand. They work part-time and receive no salary. With the exception of about one hundred legally trained magistrates called district judges, the vast majority of these individuals are lay judges, although they are not called judges, but rather magistrates or justices of the peace. Aside from the one hundred, they are not even lawyers, although they receive some legal training before they begin their work on the bench, and they consult legally qualified clerks of the court for their advice whenever they need it before they reach a decision. One journalist wrote: "Foreigners find it incredible that we place . . . the criminal justice system almost entirely in the hands of these . . . amateurs." [10]

Amateurs though they are, because they are less hidebound than judges in their thinking about the law, they are seen as bringing to the bench a fresh perspective on the application of criminal justice to a wide assortment of cases. Indeed, almost all the cases that the usual panel of three magistrates hears are criminal cases. There are about 1.5 million summary, or minor, offences that magistrates hear every year, for which they are allowed to impose prison sentences of up to six months. When the law prescribes a sentence that exceeds six months, sentencing must be referred to the Crown Court. Magistrates also must commit those accused of indictable, or major, offences to the Crown court; in some instances, those charged with offences that could be tried either way also move to the higher court. Such offences are a third category for which defendants have the right to choose between being tried in the Crown court with a jury or in a magistrates' court, where there is no jury. If a defendant is tried, found guilty, and sentenced in a magistrates' court, he or she may appeal his or her case to a higher court. The 1 percent or so who do so have to appear before the Crown court.

The Crown Court

Just about every highly populated area of England and Wales has a Crown court. There are seventy-eighty Crown court centers, the best known of which is the Old Bailey, made famous by Rumpole of the Bailey, a fictional lawyer with a crotchety exterior but a warm interior who defends hopeless cases. Crown court dockets are immensely crowded, with judges hearing approximately one hundred thousand cases a year. Of these, the vast majority are committed from magistrates' courts for trial or sentencing. The rest are appeals against conviction and sentencing decisions in the magistrates' courts. Most criminal cases are settled once and for all in a Crown court, but some who are dissatisfied with the outcome seek to appeal their case to a higher court.

Appeals to Higher Courts

Cases that go from magistrates' courts, or first from a magistrates' court and then from a Crown court, follow one of two routes. One leads to the Divisional Court of the High Court of Justice, the other to the Criminal Division of the Court of Appeal. The route leading to the High Court is taken by those who argue that their case turns on a disputed point of law or that the magistrates acted without authority. First, the appellants must petition the court for "leave to appeal." If approved, the case goes forward. The other route is to the Court of Appeal. It is taken by those who wish to appeal against their conviction or the sentences they have received. Here again, the appellants must first convince the court through a petition that their case deserves further review. Whether appellants succeed in taking their case beyond either of these two courts to the House of Lords' Appellate Committee depends on what the three justices sitting on an appeal committee decide. If the committee agrees that the case raises an issue about a point of law that has an overriding degree of importance, the lord chief justice appoints five justices to the case.

Only a few who lose in a lower court are likely to convince a higher court that their case deserves to be heard again. Even if they are granted leave to appeal, there is no assurance that the court will rule in their favor. If they again lose their appeal and have the patience and wherewithal to press on, they can take their case to one of two European courts. One is in Strasbourg, the other in Luxembourg.

The Strasbourg and Luxembourg Courts

The court in Strasbourg is the European Court of Human Rights (ECHR). This court, a creation of the Council of Europe, was set up in 1959, ten years after the Council of Europe was founded to promote pan-European cooperation. The first of two of the council's most enduring contributions was a blueprint of civil and political rights called the European Convention for the Protection of Human Rights and Fundamental Freedoms, or European Convention on Human Rights for short. The second was a judicial body to enforce those rights, the ECHR, which is made up of one judge from each member state. Today, if Britons contend that their government has violated one of their convention rights, and they fail to win a judgment to their liking after exhausting every judicial recourse possible on their home soil, they are free to petition the ECHR to hear their appeal.

Just before the Human Rights Act went into effect in 2000, Britons alone were taking an average of eight hundred cases a year to the Strasbourg court, although not every application for appeal was accepted. Normally, a three-judge panel finds only a small fraction admissible, and these they refer to a chamber of seven judges for a decision. Alternatively, cases that pose especially serious or complex issues or questions are referred to the Grand Chamber, a higher chamber of seventeen judges. If, say, the court finds in a British appellant's favor, the British government is required to take corrective action and, if appropriate, compensate the complainants. Taking a case to the Strasbourg court is expensive, and appellants typically have to wait four to six years before their case is called; however, it offers Britons one last chance to seek redress of their grievances.

The second European court is the European Court of Justice. Located in Luxembourg, this is the court of the EU on which one judge from each member state sits. This court often is confused with the ECHR, but the jurisdictions of the two are different. Whereas the ECHR deals with convention rights, the European Court of Justice (ECJ) deals with EU treaties and EC law, which includes workers' rights and sex discrimination. The difference in jurisdiction can be illustrated by two cases. It was to the ECHR that convicted murderer Dennis Stafford took his case on appeal in 1998 when the secretary of state for the Home Office held him in prison beyond the terms of his sentence for fear he would commit new offenses. In 2002, the court held that because there was no evidence to support the home secretary's fears, he had wrongfully deprived Stafford of his liberty under section 5 of the convention.

Michelle Alabaster took her case of sexual discrimination to the ECJ. The case revolved around a provision in the Equal Pay Act that requires anyone claiming discrimination to demonstrate that she (or he) was denied an opportunity enjoyed by a member of the opposite sex. The denial in Alabaster's case took the form of her employer refusing to reflect as a percentage of her maternity pay the increase in salary she was earning in the period just before she went on maternity leave. The complainant took her case from her local employment tribunal all the way to the Court of Appeal in an effort to convince the courts that it would be impossible for a woman on maternity leave to find a male comparator! In 2005, nine years after she began her campaign, the ECJ ruled in Alabaster's favor, citing the sex discrimination provisions of Article 141 of the EU's first treaty, the Treaty of Rome. Because EU laws—or EC laws, as they are called—and ECJ rulings supersede the laws and rulings of the member states, Alabaster used the EC law on discrimination to trump rulings made by English courts in her case regarding equal pay. This means that on issues such as this, future Michelle Alabasters will not be required to travel to Luxembourg to procure judgments that they could more expeditiously obtain at home.

Judges

Judges have responsibilities of enormous magnitude. They have the last word on the meaning of laws, and when a case has gone as far as it can up the appeals chain, the decision of the last panel of judges is binding unless Parliament changes the law later. For many years, it was thought that no fairer form of justice could emanate from a court of law than that from England and Wales. Or could it? In recent years, some questioned whether such praise was deserved, as legal experts at home and abroad increasingly pointed to an anomaly that was alien to the norms of Western democratic legal practice—that of the fusion of the three roles performed simultaneously by the lord chancellor.

For generations, the lord chancellor served as a member of the cabinet, Speaker of the House of Lords, and head of the judiciary. Among the critics of this arrangement was the leading lawyer Baroness Helena Kennedy. In her book, *Just Law*, first written in 2004, she told about the time that she accompanied the chief justice of Russia's Supreme Court on visits to some of London's courts in Tony Blair's first Government. While on their way to meet the then lord chancellor Derry Irvine, the Russian chief justice asked Kennedy why the lord chancellor wore "three hats." He reminded her that when British lawyers had helped Russian judges make their judiciary independent from politics and the rest of government, these lawyers had recommended that Russian judges wear only one. Kennedy had on an earlier occasion urged Lord Irvine to make his mark as a reforming lord chancellor by discarding one or two of his hats, to which he responded that keeping all three "was all about tradition." Unhappy with that answer, she wondered whether he could improve on it for the Russian dignitary if, as she suggested to her guest, he were to direct the question he had asked her to Lord Irvine instead. Kennedy did not disclose how Lord Irvine replied, but as she characterized the response as "half-baked" it is not difficult to know what she thought of it. She then lamented: "How could we play a role in the development of new democracies around the world when our own practices did not bear scrutiny?" [11]

This final section on judges explores how what Lord Irvine called the "tradition" of the lord chancellor's wearing three hats was brought to an abrupt halt with passage of the Constitutional Reform Act of 2005. Other "traditions" affecting judges also generally fell away when this act of Parliament took effect; the reforms wrought are among the most radical since the judicial system was last reformed in 1875.

The Fusion of Roles

The issue of whether the lord chancellor should abandon the executive and legislative roles and carry on discharging the judicial role—or the other way around—had been a familiar topic of discussion among academics and constitutional lawyers for some years. But the pace of discussions relating to this issue began to pick up after Labour won power in 1997. Lord Steyn, one of the twelve Law Lords in the House of Lords in this period, was among many who were critical of the arrangement. He argued that it constituted a conflict of interest so serious that, as he put it, it was "no longer sustainable on either constitutional or pragmatic grounds." [12] Equally caustic was his pronouncement that it was "contrary to the public interest." [13] Two scholars in effect lent support to Lord Steyn's argument when they alleged that this fusion led to the lord chancellor's "switching between political commitment and judicial neutrality." The scholars then went on to cite disputes that had erupted in the 1990s between the lord chancellor and the lord chief justice, with the lord chancellor committed to cutting the costs of the judiciary and the lord chief justice concerned about the effects the cuts would have on the quality of justice.[14] There is no doubt what influenced the lord chief justice's stand, but one can only speculate about whether the lord chancellor's views were shaped by his role as a member of the government of the day or by his role as head of the judiciary.

As if to corroborate Lord Steyn's position, the ECHR in 2000 handed down a decision that affected Guernsey, one of several self-governing British dependencies in the English Channel off the northwest coast of France. The decision held that "any person who has a direct interest in the passage of legislation should not judge any case concerning the application of that legislation." [15] This case was a warning shot over the bow of the Blair Government's ship of state, for unless certain reforms were carried out, the lord chancellor could be found to be in breach of the European

Convention's Article 6, which guarantees the right of an independent and impartial tribunal.

Could the lord chancellor (in this case, Lord Irvine) be assured, and could he assure others, that hearing a case before the appellate committee, as he did on occasion, did not constitute a conflict of interest? He knew he had to be circumspect about choosing which cases he heard. As Speaker of the Lords, he played a role in the passage of legislation and therefore he could not hear any case based on bills over whose enactment into law he presided. What is more, he had to avoid hearing just about every case on appeal to the highest court of the land, for the vast majority of them dealt with issues on which the government of the day had invariably expressed a view. Would the casual observer be aware of these somewhat subtle norms? Probably not. That is why critics thought it imperative that the lord chancellor abandon either his judicial role or his executive and legislative roles. The reason, they argued, was that not only must justice be done; it also must be *seen* to be done.

Spring 2003 brought some inclement weather for the lord chancellor— gale-force winds in March and steady downpours in April. The March gales came in the form of a report drafted by a Dutch professor of constitutional law commissioned by the Council of Europe's Legal Affairs and Human Rights Committee. The report questioned whether Britain's judiciary was truly independent:

> Combining the function of judge with functions in other branches of government calls that independence seriously into question. The assembly therefore invites the UK to review the office of the Lord Chancellor as chairman and member of the appellate division of the House of Lords in such a way that his judicial function is no longer combined with membership of the Cabinet and with the presiding membership of a chamber of the legislative assembly.[16]

This report was followed in April by a call from the chair of the twelve-thousand-member Bar Council of England and Wales that the lord chancellor no longer serve as a judge while sitting as a minister in the cabinet. In the meantime, the Select Committee on the Lord Chancellor's Department took up the issue and, after taking testimony from the author of the report commissioned by the Council of Europe, asked Lord Irvine to appear before it.

Two months later, Tony Blair reshuffled his cabinet. Shortly after, No. 10 Downing Street issued a press release that listed those who had survived the reshuffle. Notably absent from the list was Derry Irvine, and slotted in his place was Charles Falconer. This came as a jaw-dropping surprise to most because of Irvine's close friendship with the prime minister and because he was regarded as an able lord chancellor. Jaws dropped even further when it was abruptly announced that legislation was being prepared to reform the judicial system. MPs were told to expect these reforms to be radical, which they were. First, the legislation barred the lord chancellor from sitting as a judge and terminated the lord chancellor's overlordship of the judiciary and made the lord chief justice head of it instead. Second, the lord chief justice and the eleven other Law Lords would no longer remain as members of the House of Lords but instead would serve as members of a Supreme Court that would have its own building, and the lord chief justice would serve as its president. And third, the legislation greatly weakened the lord chancellor's hold over selecting judges by creating an independent appointments body. Lord Falconer and his successors would retain the title "lord chancellor" and serve as secretary of state for the Department of Constitutional Affairs, the new name of the Lord Chancellor's Department, and although he would continue to sit in the Lords, no longer would he serve as its Speaker.

It is not known with certainty what triggered these changes. It is plausible that they were taken in response to the pressure brought by the ECHR's decision on Guernsey in 2000 and the report commissioned by the Council of Europe in 2003. Related to this conjecture is another, one articulated by a highly regarded peer when he wrote that Lord Irvine had become so powerful a lord chancellor that "his reign hastened the realisation that one person could no longer be a senior Cabinet minister and the head of the judiciary." [17] Still another possible explanation is the fallout from the increasingly rocky relations between Lord Irvine and Home Secretary David Blunkett. As judges quashed decisions made by the Home Office on various issues, asylum issues in particular, the home secretary mounted what seemed like an unremitting campaign against senior judges. On one occasion, in remarks obviously directed at the home secretary, Lord Irvine offered the following admonition: "Maturity requires that, when you get a decision that favours you, you do not clap. And when you get one that goes against you, you do not boo." [18] Because of the populist stance Blunkett took on asylumseekers and the intemperate charges he made about judges being out of touch and giving criminals lenient sentences, perhaps Tony Blair reckoned he would reap political gains by keeping Blunkett in his cabinet and removing the source of Blunkett's irritation—Lord Irvine. The prime minister also must have figured that culling Irvine from the cabinet would possibly make it easier for him to accomplish a second objective, that of reforming the judiciary in such a way as to bring it into line with the terms of the European Convention's Article 6.

Article 6 had implications for the Law Lords as well, for they too performed a fusion of roles. Not only were they Law Lords but legislators as well, and thus they might be seen as being vulnerable to conflicts of interest, although not to the same degree as the lord chancellor, as they were not part of the Government. As several sat on parliamentary committees and most no longer shied away from debating and voting on politically controversial issues (as they once did), they put themselves in the line of fire of those who argued that they could not be both judge and legislator. It did not matter that when they spoke in the chamber they did so from the cross-benches reserved for peers not affiliated with a political party. Nor did it matter that they addressed themselves only to those Government-proposed measures that dealt with administration of justice issues. What did matter was that if the lord chancellor unwittingly assigned any Law Lords to hear a case dealing with an issue on which they had established their position in debate, they had to disqualify themselves. The more that they participated in debate, the fewer would be the number available to respond to the lord chancellor's call to sit in judgment on an appeal. This is why a few Law Lords, Lord Steyn among them, never participated in House of Lords debates.

Whether there were actual conflicts of interest in the duties performed by the Law Lords cannot be known. Perhaps they themselves did not know fully. But because constitutional scholars conceive of conflicts of interest as conflicts *in appearance* as well as conflicts *in fact*, they are as concerned about the former as they are the latter. This principle was as cogent as any to justify moving the Law Lords from the House of Lords to a newly created Supreme Court.

A Court Supreme—and Independent Too?

A cardinal feature of the Constitutional Reform bill, and institutionally the most significant feature, was the creation of a Supreme Court. Like the House of Lords' appellate committee, whose place it will take in 2009, the Supreme Court will be the highest court in the UK and, with the exception of Scottish criminal cases hear cases on appeal from any of the four nations. No longer would the Law Lords, including the lord chief justice and the master of the rolls, be members of Parliament's upper house; nor would they hear cases in a room reserved for them in the House of Lords or read out their decisions in the Lords chamber. Occupying a separate building would provide more space than the relatively cramped quarters available to them in the House of Lords. More important, holding forth in a building they could call their own would give judges an opportunity to demonstrate symbolically their detachment and independence from the Lords. As one constitutional lawyer put it, "Creating a supreme court that is separate from Parliament sends a clear signal to the public and to the outside world that we have an independent judiciary."[19]

As powerful a symbol as a new name and new home was, there were some, the lord chief justice in particular, who needed assurance that the judiciary would be able to work without interference from the executive and legislative parts of government. Under the terms of the Constitutional Reform Bill, the lord chancellor headed the judiciary of England and Wales until 2006. Until then, however, he was expected to continue to serve as the judiciary's guardian by advancing and defending the views of the judiciary at the cabinet table. Such guardianship was vital, for as a leading lawyer observed,

> All recent Lord Chancellors have discovered that Cabinet colleagues resent judges pronouncing that their policies are unlawful. Lord Irvine

> battled hard in private, and occasionally in public, to educate some . . .
> Cabinet members of the virtues of the rule of law.[20]

Since 2006, lord chancellors no longer head the judiciary or sit as judges, and thus they are no longer in a position to defend the judiciary if ministers seek to undermine its independence.

What, then, can be done to safeguard the judiciary's independence? Coming up with a satisfactory answer to this question was crucial to the lord chief justice, Lord Woolf, and to the lord chancellor, Lord Falconer, who knew that without one the constitutional reform bill was unlikely to go any further in the legislative process, especially in the Lords. Woolf and Falconer therefore set about negotiating an answer. The result was a concordat that delineated the functions of the lord chief justice and the lord chancellor/secretary of state for Constitutional Affairs. So important was this agreement that it was enshrined in Clause 1 of the bill. In the words of the lord chief justice, it represented

> a comprehensive guide to the principles which will govern the future relationship between the Government and the judiciary. What was previously uncertain becomes clearly defined, so both sides know what their respective rights and obligations are.[21]

For the first time, the independence of the judiciary was set forth "explicitly by law," asserted Lord Falconer in a speech at a London think tank. He then added: "I recognize this is a break from the past. But judicial independence is too important to this country and to this Government to be any longer left unspecified, uncodified, unwritten."[22]

Among other things, the concordat bars ministers from trying to influence judicial decisions by seeking access to judges. It also empowers the lord chief justice to convey the views and concerns of the judiciary of England and Wales to Parliament and ministers, gives responsibility for administering the courts to the lord chancellor, and authorizes administrative support offices to the lord chief justice and senior judges. The concordat even revolutionized the process by which judges are selected, an issue that had to be resolved if the objective of sustaining judicial independence was to be achieved, for up to that point the lord chancellor dominated, if not controlled, the process. Moreover, how could justice be seen to be done if a cabinet minister who was no longer head of the judiciary was allowed to play a primary role in selecting judges? Could not the lord chancellor seek to advance the interests of the government of the day by promoting the selection of those most likely to do its bidding?

Before the Constitutional Reform Bill was enacted, whenever a vacancy occurred on the bench, the lord chancellor activated a search through a process its critics called "secret soundings." These were consultations the lord chancellor was thought to undertake with a coterie of senior judges and possibly even key figures from the Bar Council, a select group of civil servants, and politicians. Secret soundings—the term erroneously suggests that searches were steeped in intrigue—had by the end of the 1990s become so controversial that in 2000 the lord chancellor commissioned an inquiry into the process. Little came from it, however, apart from a recommendation that another panel be formed. This panel, the Commission for Judicial Appointments, was charged with investigating any complaints that individuals raised about the selection process. In the meantime, Lord Irvine was accused of cronyism after advancing the names of two lawyers he knew to serve on the High Court of Justice and of compromising the impartiality of his office after sending personal invitations to barristers, that is, possible future judges, to attend a party fund-raising event.[23]

When the commission unveiled its report in 2002, nothing in it gave critics of the process much hope that it would be reformed, other than that something might be done to end the "secrecy" part of the "soundings." There was even less hope that the question of whether the lord chancellor should have a role to play in selecting judges would be answered, let alone answered satisfactorily. The answer finally came when the Constitutional Reform bill was enacted in 2005. Under the terms of the concordat, the lord chancellor continued to play a role in selecting judges. But starting in 2006, his role was superseded, by an independent body called the Judicial Appointments Commission (JAC). This is a fifteen-member body drawn from various professions, the laity, and the judiciary to whom the legislation gave authority to submit the names of deserving individuals to the lord chancellor to fill vacancies on the courts as they occurred. As first proposed, the JAC would have submitted a short list of two to five names from which the lord chancellor would choose one. However, it was felt that offering him that many names would have given him too much latitude of choice, and thus the bill was amended to require that he be given one name only. Later, when the bill was enacted, it contained an even tougher provision: if the lord chancellor is not satisfied with the JAC's recommendation, he may ask it for another, but the JAC may refuse his request if it disagrees with the lord chancellor's reasons for rejecting its recommendation.

The JAC submits the names of the most qualified candidates for judgeships at every level of the court hierarchy, from tribunals to the lord chief justice (and magistrates at some indefinite point in the future). Because there is a wide range of judicial posts, it is helpful to group them into three tiers. At the bottom are tribunals. For posts that become available at this tier, the lord chancellor need not submit his choices to the monarch, for they are not crown appointments. Appointments to the bench at the next tier—the county courts, Crown courts, and the High Court of Justice—are crown appointments. The prime minister plays no part in judicial appointments at this tier, but does so at the top tier, which includes the twelve Law Lords (or justices of the Supreme Court, as they will be called when this court is scheduled to sit for the first time in 2009) and the thirty-eight lords justices of appeal of the Court of Appeal. However, the prime minister has no influence over which names are forwarded to the monarch. He or she is allowed to forward only the choices of the lord chancellor—choices, it will be remembered, that really are the choices of the JAC.

The Rise of Judicial Activism on the Bench

Judges are said to be judicially active if they make rulings that do not appear to conform to the exact wording of the law, if they appear to exercise much greater latitude of authority in their interpretation of the law, or both. In addition to being judicially active on the bench, judges are seen as being judicially active off the bench when they speak out on issues of justice that some consider political in nature. In recent years, judges have been active both on and off the bench, but especially on it.

Judges lay themselves open to criticism from strict constructionists when they stretch the meaning of the law from a narrow, literal interpretation of the language of a statute to a broad interpretation that may reflect changing events and circumstances. This stretching exercise is exemplified in some of the decisions of Lord Denning, a former master of the rolls who maintained as early as the midpoint of the last century that judges have a duty, in his words, to "fill in the gaps" when the law is silent. Although on one occasion he felt the verbal lash of an eminent Law Lord for advocating "a naked usurpation of the legislative function under the thin disguise of interpretation,"[24] Denning's propensity to fill in the empty spaces was vindicated years later, when one of his successors on the Court of Appeal summed up his contributions by saying, "Many of his decisions were ahead of his day and only years later became accepted as representing the law."[25]

Judges are left to fill in the gaps for any one of three reasons. First, there is no statute to consult. Second, the language of the statute is incomprehensible. Or third, the statute is partially or wholly out of date. As for the first reason, if no statute exists, judges search for common law decisions that relate to a case on which they might base a ruling or, in the absence of an existing common law, create a new one drawn from custom and natural law.

A second reason why judges have to fill in the gaps is that the language of a law is obtuse, a condition that afflicts all too many laws when they are enacted in great haste. In the absence of clarity, judges have no choice but to plump for one of several possible interpretations that strikes them as being the most sensible. So frustrating can it be to interpret the law that in a 1993 case, *Pepper v. Hart*, seven Law Lords forever rescinded a 223-year-old rule that barred judges from consulting *Hansard* (the record of debates in Parliament) to work out what Parliament's intentions were when it enacted a law. If a statute lacks clarity, they emphasized, judges may refer to what ministers or others promoting the bill said about it on the floor of the chamber during the debate and draw reasonable inferences from their statements. It is not a case of judges making law—although some who disagreed with the rescission thought otherwise—but rather their effort to determine what Parliament intended. So difficult is it for judges to understand Parliament's intentions when they confront the convoluted language of a statute that they have been known to ask Parliament for help in their rulings. For example, one judge in his ruling pleaded with Parliament to give "as high a priority to clarity and simplicity of expression [in the law] as to refinements to policy."[26]

A third reason why judges must be inventive in their interpretation of the law is that a statute has lost some or all of its currency. One example, a hypothetical one, deals with motorized wheelchairs. When a local authority passed a bylaw in the 1950s that banned the use of vehicles in children's play parks, "vehicles" presumably meant motor cars. Today, should that ban also apply to the motorized wheelchair, unknown in the 1950s? Banning it would seem unlikely, if not unreasonable, for a disabled parent eager to watch his or her child play presumably would not use a wheelchair recklessly. However, whether or not it should be banned would not be known unless the local authority clarifies the bylaw with an amendment. Failing that, the judges would be asked to infer whether the original proponents of the bylaw would object to allowing motorized wheelchairs in the park.

When judges are forced to make a ruling when there are no relevant statutes to consult, the language of the statute is impenetrable, or the statute is out of date, some are bound to criticize them for being judicially active. The same charge is heard from time to time when judges hand down decisions involving the laws of the EU, human rights law, and judicial review.

Since 1973, when Britain joined the EU, British judges have been required to apply European Union treaties, EC law, and European Court of Justice case law to their rulings when British law has been in conflict with them. In applying any one of these three, British judges have had to favor a continental European approach to interpreting law over the time-honored English approach. The difference in the two is illustrated in a case brought by an employer to the Court of Appeal in 1979 after an industrial tribunal ruled that the employer had discriminated against a woman by paying her less than her male predecessor for the same kind of work. The employer's lawyer argued that even though the Equal Pay Act of 1970 required that women and men receive the same pay for the same work, a woman was not entitled to receive the same pay if she took on the same job just after a man had left it. The court disagreed. The principle of equal pay as enshrined in Article 119 of the European Community's Treaty of Rome, the court held, applied to situations in which men and women were employed both simultaneously and successively by the same employer. The court then reflected on the differences in the ways EC law and English law are interpreted:

Article 119 is framed in European fashion. It enunciates a *broad general principle* and leaves the judges to work out the details. In contrast the Equal Pay Act is framed in English fashion. It states no general principle but lays down *detailed specific rules* for the courts to apply . . . without resort to considerations of policy or principle.[27]

Because many EC laws have been incorporated into English law, British judges are today expected to interpret these laws in the same manner as their continental colleagues do. In doing so, however, they run the risk of being criticized for going beyond their remit. Ironically, the criticism directed at them is probably less a criticism of judicial activism than it is a thinly veiled attack on EC law and perhaps even on the EU itself.

The Human Rights Act (HRA) can be singled out as a further reason why judges are sometimes accused of overstepping their bounds. Ever since it came into effect in 2000, judges have been empowered to decide whether a law on which a case is brought before them is compatible with the HRA. Judges are powerless to overturn a law if they declare that it is not compatible; however, if it is incompatible, the effect of their judgment is that it puts substantial pressure on the government of the day to bring the law into line with the appropriate provisions of the HRA. Powerless though the courts are, they are put in a vulnerable position when they make such declarations, as the celebrated *Belmarsh* case of 2004 illustrates.

The case, *A and Others v. Secretary of State for the Home Department,* was brought by nine held in Belmarsh and in another high-security British prison who argued that a section of the Anti-terrorism, Crime and Security Act of 2001 was incompatible with a section of the HRA. Specifically, the plaintiffs, who were foreign nationals under suspicion of engaging in international terrorist activity, claimed they would not have been held for three years and without charge or a trial had they been British nationals. Unlike some nonnationals, the nine could not be deported to the countries from which they came, for returning them would have put them at risk of being tortured. This would have made Britain complicit in violating the HRA's Article 3, which prohibits torture. Therefore, instead of removing them, the Home Secretary had decided to incarcerate them indefinitely. So contentious—and significant—was the case, that it was only the second time since the Second World War that a total of nine Law Lords were assigned to the Appellate Committee to hear arguments. Eight of the nine ultimately found in favor of the prisoners. In the words of the ruling, the appellants were "treated differently both from suspected international terrorists who were not UK nationals but could be removed and from those who were UK nationals and could not be removed," and being treated differently was discriminatory.

In the appellate committee's ruling, Lord Bingham, the senior Law Lord who summarized the thinking of his seven colleagues, responded to several points used by the attorney general in oral argument that Bingham correctly anticipated also would be used by countless others who would find fault with this decision. The attorney general had made the point that the democratic organs of Parliament and the executive, not the courts, were capable of assessing the threat to protect the public. Bingham did not dispute that the courts were not prepared to undertake a threat analysis. In effect, he took issue with the implication that the courts were not democratic:

It was true that judges were not elected and not answerable to Parliament. It was also true that Parliament, the executive and the courts had different functions; but the function of independent judges charged to interpret and apply the law was universally recognized as a cardinal feature of the modern democratic state, a cornerstone of the rule of law itself.[28]

It can be irritating to ministers when court decisions turn on interpretations of the law that run counter to their own, especially when such decisions have the effect of curbing their powers. Curbing ministerial powers can result from judicial review, the review by a court of complaints leveled by citizens adversely affected by ministerial decisions that they believe to be unlawful. The court examines these decisions in the light of what the law provides for and quashes them if they fail to conform to its dictates. Not all applications for judicial review result in a review, for not all complaints are deemed legitimate. Nevertheless, the number of applications has risen sharply over the years—from more than five hundred a year in 1980 to more than four thousand a year in the early years of the twenty-first century.

A little more than 60 percent of the applications for judicial review do not progress to the review stage; of those that do, roughly 25 percent result in findings against a minister or an official. Rulings against ministers once were much less common, for unless a minister abused his or her power with obvious blatancy, the courts were inclined to take the side of the minister. Then things started to change. Judges appeared to become more sympathetic to complainants and demanded higher standards of performance from ministers. At one time, rulings could go against ministers if they exceeded their legal powers (ultra vires) or failed to do what the law required them to do (intra vires). But starting in the late 1970s, the courts also ruled against ministers if their decisions were unreasonable, illogical, or nonsensical, or if they failed to observe proper procedures, such as consulting those who would be affected by their decisions.

Beset with an increasing number of reversals in the courts of law, ministers and other politicians became more combative. In one nineteen-month period in the mid-1990s the courts ruled against the home secretary on eight occasions; most of these rulings arose from judicial review proceedings. Among them was a decision by the High Court that the home secretary's denial of a visa to the controversial Rev. Sun Myung Moon was "unlawful by reason of procedural unfairness." So incensed were some Conservative back-bench MPs with this ruling that they let out a loud cheer in the Commons chamber for a party colleague when he denounced the decision as "yet another, further example of the contempt with which some members of the judiciary seem to treat the views both of this House and of the general public."[29]

Speaking of . . .

KNOCKING JUDGES

Although retired as lord chief justice, Lord Woolf has not retired from defending the independence of the judiciary. The legal editor of *The Times* reports on how, on one occasion, he took ministers to task for knocking judges for their rulings—including one poorly understood ruling (which is not alluded to in this article) that precipitated calls to dilute the Human Rights Act:

> "However exemplary a government's behaviour is normally, there will be occasions when, consciously or unconsciously, it will do things unlawfully."

"A former Lord Chief Justice has called on politicians to stop attacking judges and making 'spur of the moment remarks' that damage public confidence.

"In his first public comments since stepping down last October [2005] as Britain's most senior judge, Lord Woolf said that it was counterproductive for ministers to make 'ill-informed comments' about individual rulings. . . .

"Lord Woolf said: 'However exemplary a government's behaviour is normally, there will be occasions when, consciously or unconsciously, it will do things unlawfully. It is the job of the judges to ensure that if it does step out of line, and acts unlawfully, then somebody puts them right.'

"Tension between the judiciary and government was healthy, and he recognised the right of ministers to be critical when the criminal justice system went wrong. But he did not support 'ill-informed comments on individual decisions in individual cases'.

"Judges, he said, could not answer back. 'The Government has an open goal, a free hit, because there is no response.' But the Government had an interest, as did judges, in the public having confidence in judicial independence.

" 'Anyone is capable of making remarks on the spur of the moment but they have got to try to exercise self-control and realise the damage that this is going to have on the independence of the judiciary.'

"The danger, he said, was that judges who were not of a 'hardy calibre' might be deterred from making the right decision. . . .

"Lord Woolf also issued a staunch defence of the Human Rights Act, at a time when the Prime Minister has suggested that it might need to be reviewed. He said: 'Notwithstanding the recent clamour [critical of the Act], which I think is not based on sound foundations, the reality is that the Act has—day in, day out—been applied by the courts with no one being at all disturbed by the results.' He emphasised the importance of the public being properly informed about how measures such as the Human Rights Act worked."

Source: Reprinted with permission of *The Times* and NI Syndication Ltd.

The Rise of Judicial Activism off the Bench

Judges are tagged as being judicially active not only when they are accused of overstepping their bounds in their rulings, but also when they speak out publicly on issues of justice that some claim have unmistakable political overtones. At one time, judges held their tongues. Lord Kilmuir issued a rule to his colleagues soon after he became lord chancellor in 1954 to remind them that when they kept silent, their reputation for impartiality could not be challenged. This ban remained in effect for three decades and five lord chancellors, until Lord Mackay became lord chancellor in 1987 and declared that judges themselves should decide whether to keep silent. Moreover, he saw nothing wrong with their either agreeing or disagreeing publicly with issues generated by the government of the day as long as they did not compromise their impartiality in cases that came before them. Not long after Mackay's rescission of the ban, some senior judges, as if on cue, began to emerge from the shadows.

Lord Taylor was the first to be appointed lord chief justice after Lord Mackay lifted the Kilmuir ban. In 1992 he made judicial history when he appeared on BBC television to give a lecture on the judiciary. Introducing his guest, the host of the program remarked it would have been "unthinkable" for any of Taylor's predecessors to have accepted such an invitation. Nearly as unthinkable were some of the points the lord chief justice made in his lecture. He went beyond Lord Mackay's guidance of allowing judges to speak out by insisting that they speak out "when our justice system is debated," and that it was right for them "to answer criticism." Later in his lecture, he was among the first of the senior judges to call upon John Major's Government to incorporate the European Convention on Human Rights into British law, and he urged the Treasury to allocate more funds to the justice system to safeguard the rule of law.[30]

After Taylor's death those who followed in his footsteps also followed his advice, Lord Woolf in particular. In the 1990s, Woolf, who then sat on the Court of Appeal, chaired an inquiry into factors that had fueled riots that broke out in one of Britain's major prisons. The report that followed severely criticized prison overcrowding; Woolf later took issue with the home secretary for favoring punishment over rehabilitation. In 2000, he attacked the shortcomings in Britain's prison policy again, this time several months after he had become lord chief justice. He acknowledged that his message was politically unpopular. Just as unpopular were some of his later pronouncements. In an address to the Institute of Legal Executives at a time when crime figures were on the rise in the spring of 2002, Woolf warned that a series of measures proposed by the Government to curb lawlessness would have little effect.[31] He then went on to identify another issue that concerned him, one that the master of the rolls had addressed only a few weeks before—the Treasury's failure to fund reforms of the civil justice system that the Government had instituted two years earlier.

A few months later, Woolf spoke out yet again, this time on the politically sensitive issue of sentencing policy. The home secretary was still smarting from a ruling of the ECHR that denied him the authority to set minimum jail sentences for two juveniles who had murdered a toddler. The court had held that the European Convention allowed only a judge, not a politician, to set minimum terms for juveniles who had committed serious offences. It was only a matter of time, Woolf predicted, before the courts in Britain or the ECHR would overturn the home secretary's authority to set minimum jail sentences for serious offences committed by adults as well. The home secretary did not take too kindly to this prediction. But as it happened, it proved correct; at the end of 2002, seven Law Lords sitting as members of the appellate committee of the House of Lords unanimously stripped the home secretary of this authority—along with a bit of his political pride.

In the nearly three years remaining before his retirement in 2005, Woolf continued to speak out on a variety of issues. Among other things, he claimed that the huge rise in the prison population was the fault of politicians intent on demonstrating their determination to be tough on criminals. He insisted that he—not politicians—decide whether judges should chair important public inquiries on issues that might cast doubt on their judicial impartiality. Others in the judiciary spoke out as well. For example, in 2005 when the Government decided to allow pubs to choose to remain open until the early morning hours, a council representing Crown court judges criticized the decision, arguing that it would contribute to a rise in alcohol-fueled violence.

Very shortly after Lord Phillips succeeded Lord Woolf as lord chief justice in 2005, Tony Blair in his monthly press conference complained that the courts were too slow and the justice system too ineffective to protect the public from drug dealers and thugs. On that same day, as it happened, Lord Phillips too was before the press for the first time as Britain's most senior judge. As if in response to the prime minister, he said: "Occasionally one feels that a politician is trying to browbeat the judiciary, and that is wholly inappropriate." And then he added: "I am taking up this office when it is said in various quarters that judges are in conflict with the Government. Judges are in conflict with no one. [32] It looked like judges, the lord chief justice in particular, would continue to speak out.

Conclusion

Until the 1970s, judges and their work were little known outside their courtrooms. Except for the occasional incautious remark made by a judge within earshot of an alert reporter that made its way into the next morning's edition, these custodians of the law were rarely heard. The reason for this was simple. Their work was important, but it was unspectacular. Certainly, there was nothing spectacular about presiding over bankruptcy proceedings, listening to opposing sides in contested divorce cases, or even sentencing murderers and rapists to jail. In most cases judges could do no more than declare that the law was what Parliament said it was, for Parliament held sovereign sway over lawmaking. Judges could shape the law only when the language of a statute was so garbled that they had to come up with their own interpretation of its meaning; when there was no statute, they could search through the common law for a precedent or even create a brand new one. Apart from these exceptions, judges had no impact on public policy.

Starting in the 1970s, things began to change. Many of those appointed to the bench had a far different mind-set from that breed of judges of a generation before who deferred to ministers. That they were more open-minded became evident when, at the invitation of various governments, several took on extrajudicial responsibilities chairing high-profile commissions and tribunals of inquiry. As the judges probed such thorny issues as race riots, standards of conduct in government, the criminal justice system, problems generated by mad cow disease (BSE), and the prison system, they were found to be ideally suited to the task. They could be counted on to scrutinize facts impartially and in their reports to criticize constructively. This was one way in which they were having an impact on public policy.

It was on the bench, however, that judges had a greater impact, especially in judicial review cases starting in the 1980s. Judges began to tighten the standard by which they scrutinized ministers' decisions; as they did so, the courts became more formidable. So much of an impact did judicial review have on ministerial decisions that some started to question whether anything more than a fine line could be drawn between the work of parliamentarians and judges; parliamentarians had the power to make the law, but judges had the power to interpret it. So far-reaching were their interpretive powers that they could at times make a substantial difference in the way the law was actually implemented.

That fine line grew even finer after Parliament incorporated the European Convention into UK law in the Human Rights Act of 1998. With every bill the Government has introduced since the law went into effect in 2000, ministers are required to certify that its provisions are compatible with the European Convention. If one or more judges find that they contravene provisions of the HRA, they are empowered to communicate their position to Parliament by issuing a declaration of incompatibility. In this way parliamentary sovereignty is in no way threatened, for Parliament has the right either to amend the bill in line with the judges' findings or to ignore the declaration altogether. In addition, judges have expanded the scope of judicial review from issues of legality, reasonableness, and procedural fairness to matters of substantive rights. Judges may do this whenever any one of the various convention rights incorporated into domestic law trumps a law enacted before the HRA took effect. A court may not strike down a statute, but the moral force of its pronouncements can be so momentous that after only a year's experience with the act, one of Britain's foremost authorities on public law asserted it was "already altering the balance of powers in our constitution between unelected judges and elected politicians."[33]

New judges with a new outlook, a new Supreme Court, the 1998 Human Rights Act, and a reinvigorated approach to judicial review have all brought judges from just beyond the wings of the political stage onto the stage itself. They will never occupy center stage, for center stage is reserved for elected politicians. But that they will play an increasingly important role in the unfolding drama of making policy for the nation, there can be little doubt.

13

Britain and the European Union

The British political system has undergone numerous changes in recent decades, all rising from a variety of sources and circumstances and some having far-reaching effects on the business of politics. None, however, has had more impact than Britain's entry into the European Union in 1973 and its membership in it in the years since. The bill that authorized its entry was the European Communities Bill, and when the division bells summoned MPs to the chamber to vote one autumn afternoon in 1972 they reckoned that this bill, on which debate had just concluded, was one of the most momentous and contentious they would ever vote on. It was indeed momentous, because when Parliament agreed to it later that day, Britain was just weeks away from becoming a member of Europe's three "communities"— the European Coal and Steel Community, the European Atomic Energy Community, and most important of all, the European Economic Community.

When Britain was formally inducted on January 1, 1973, it joined the communities' six founding members—France, Italy, and West Germany, along with Belgium, the Netherlands, and Luxembourg (the BENELUX nations)—plus two others that entered with Britain: Ireland and Denmark. In time this legislation would prove to be as contentious as it was momentous. The telltale signs were there from the beginning, for although Britain's entry touched off eleven days of celebration across Britain called Fanfare for Europe, not all were in a celebratory mood. As the embers from the fireworks wafted to the ground, some questioned the wisdom of Britain's entry, fearing it would transform its public policies and its political system in ways few could then possibly imagine.

Ever since the Fanfare for Europe celebrations, Britons have blown hot and cold on the European Union (EU), but rarely hot. More often, they have blown warm and cool, but mostly cool. Many have been ambivalent. If they have blown hot at all, it is from gains they have reaped from trading in a common market, but they have blown cold from the thought of adopting a common currency to use in that market. They have warmed to receiving EU funds for projects in economically depressed areas but cool to contributing more funds to support the EU's infrastructure. Britain is a key player, so why has it been ambivalent about being part of an internal market that, with a population approaching half a billion, is the largest in the world?

Britain's Relationship with the Rest of Europe

Britain and the rest of Europe have never embraced each other with whole-hearted affection. Following the Second World War Britain distanced itself from most pan-European master plans and remains at arm's length even today. For example, in 2002, when twelve of the then fifteen EU member nations replaced their national currencies with the euro, the EU's new currency, Britain decided not to do so until it could be certain that it would be in its economic interest. To get a sense of Britain's relationship with the EU today, it helps to trace Britain's hesitancy about linking its destiny to continental Europe's in general and to the EU's in particular and, after joining the EU, its opposition to some of the EU's major policies.

Councils, Conferences, and Communities

In just a few short years, from 1914 to 1945, Europe had experienced more than ten years of unimaginable devastation from two world wars. With the founding of the United Nations in 1945, Europe's elder statesmen, who were determined to prevent a repetition of the horrors of war, were heartened by the prospect of swords being turned into plowshares. In the meantime, they faced the immediate challenge of rebuilding their war-torn economies. Starting in 1948, the United States came to their aid by making millions of dollars in grants and loans available through the Marshall Plan for distribution by the Organization for European Economic Cooperation. As helpful as this foreign aid was, however, many of Europe's leaders realized that Europeans and Europeans only could prevent a repetition of the grim years of 1914–1918 and 1939–1945.

As European governments got on with rebuilding their economies, more than eight hundred delegates from sixteen European nations gathered in The Hague, the Netherlands, in the spring of 1948 to search for ways of building an integrated Europe. Calling their gathering the Congress of Europe, delegates engaged in intense discussions and produced several resolutions. The most prominent of these called for creation of a political and economic union made up of the nations of Europe, one that included a common currency and the abolition of all trade barriers among its members.

Twelve months later, in 1949, Congress of Europe delegates met again, this time in Strasbourg, France. Britain in the meantime had been in the vanguard of those opposed to moving in such a radical direction. As it happened, there was little evidence of support among delegates for a European-wide political and economic union, and the delegates of ten nations agreed instead to form an intergovernmental body to which representatives would come when they felt the need to discuss issues of mutual concern. Thus was born the Council of Europe.

It was in this period that Britain's reluctance to participate fully in European-wide endeavors became manifest. On the one hand, it became a founding member of the Organization for European Economic Cooperation in 1948, and in 1949 it was among the first twelve to join the North Atlantic Treaty Organization (NATO). On the other hand, it disagreed with its neighbors to the east about the need to create a system of supranational government for Europe. Britain took its seat on the Council of Europe in 1949 after contributing probably more than any other member to writing the council's European Convention for the Protection of Human Rights and Fundamental Freedoms. For many years after that, however, it refused to adopt two changes the other members had embraced from the beginning. The first of these allowed citizens of the member nations to challenge judicial decisions in cases they lost in their home jurisdictions by appealing to the European Court of Human Rights, the court set up to enforce the European Convention. The second change was incorporation by the member governments of the European Convention into their own laws.

The Council of Europe was born from compromise, primarily because of Britain's opposition to a political and economic union. Because the compromise produced little more than talk, it failed to satisfy those who had turned up at the Congress of Europe in 1948 and 1949 to rally support for their plans to create closer political and economic ties among the nations of Western Europe. Their turn would come when Robert Schuman, France's Foreign Minister, seized upon an idea proposed to him by Jean Monnet, a French high civil servant who was engrossed in rebuilding the French economy. In 1950, two years after Congress of Europe delegates first assembled and on the eve of an important conference that brought the French and British together in London, Schuman made a dramatic announcement in which he called for creation of the European Coal and Steel Community. Under the plan, known initially as the Schuman Declaration, all French and West German coal and steel production would be placed under a single authority, an arrangement that would, in the words of the declaration, "make any war between France and Germany ... not merely unthinkable, but materially impossible."

Regardless of the high-minded purpose of the plan, Britain would have nothing to do with it. The Attlee Government had just brought coal and steel under public ownership through its much vaunted nationalization program and was not about to relinquish control to an authority that would be predominantly foreign. Moreover, the Attlee Government was disturbed by eight words from the Schuman Declaration that cited the European Coal and Steel Community (ECSC) as being "a first step in the federation of

Europe." These words were reminiscent of the rhetoric heard in The Hague two years before, and in 1950 British politicians disliked "federation" even more than they had in 1948. Britain would have been welcomed into this proposed community, but its membership was not essential for it to be launched; in 1951 the ECSC became a reality when France, Italy, West Germany, and the BENELUX nations signed the Treaty of Paris.

"The Moment Has Arrived"

It was only a matter of time before a federal Europe, or something approaching it, would become a reality. So thought many who had gathered at The Hague conference in 1948 and who later applauded the creation of the ECSC. In 1955, just three years after the ECSC started its work, its six foreign ministers invited the foreign ministers of several non-ECSC states, Britain's among them, to a conference in Messina, Italy, to think further about what could be done to strengthen ties among the countries of Western Europe. A resolution issued at the end of the conference announced: "The moment has arrived" for "the development of common institutions, the merging of national economies, the creation of a common market, and the gradual harmonization of social policies." Britain sent a senior civil servant to Messina to observe but chose not to endorse the resolution or the conclusions that flowed from the intergovernmental negotiations that got under way a year later. Before that year was out, Britain withdrew from the negotiations, convinced that nothing would come of them and mindful too, no doubt, of the view Winston Churchill had articulated two years before about Britain's relationship with the continent when he asserted "we are with them but not of them." [1] Britain thus lost an opportunity to shape an organization it later joined—the European Economic Community (EEC).

Nineteen fifty-seven was the year of two treaties, both of which were called the Treaty of Rome. The first and more important one established the EEC; the second created the European Atomic Energy Community (EURATOM). The preamble of the treaty establishing the EEC spoke of the determination of the six to "lay the foundations of an ever closer union among the peoples of Europe." The union that was envisioned took the form of a united trading bloc. The six would gradually remove all tariff and non-tariff barriers among them and impose a uniform tariff on all imported non-EEC goods and services. No longer would there be impediments to the free movement of goods, persons, capital, and services among the six nations. The six would have a common market, and "Common Market" is what the EEC was frequently called in this period.

The EEC had its own institutions, including an assembly and a court. They functioned as institutions of the ECSC, and starting in 1958 became the assembly and the court of the EEC and EURATOM as well. A commission and the Council of Ministers were then added. The nine-person commission, the executive arm of the EEC, consisted of two commissioners each from France, Italy, and West Germany plus one from each of the BENELUX nations. The Council of Ministers was the legislative arm and was made up of one minister from each nation, with each minister drawn from the home government's department that was responsible for whatever issue the council was then considering.

Of these two major features of the treaty—the Common Market and the EEC's institutions—it was the Common Market that concerned Britain more. As one observer put it:

> When the Treaty was actually signed and soon afterwards ratified by all of its six members, alarm bells started ringing in Westminster. If the Common Market of the Six was becoming a reality, Britain faced economic isolation from the Continent and had to rethink its strategy.[2]

Some in Britain started to wonder: Could the country afford not to join the EEC?

A Second Chance

The economic gains achieved by the EEC in its first three years were impressive. Its rate of economic growth outstripped that of Britain, as did its industrial output. Moreover, it was beginning to attract a greater share of inward investment from the United States than Britain. Britain's immediate response to the creation of the EEC had been to organize a tariff barrier-free zone in 1960 called the European Free Trade Association (EFTA) with six other non-EEC members—Austria, Denmark, Norway, Portugal, Sweden, and Switzerland. But the economic benefits of EFTA did not even come close to those achieved by the EEC. Convinced now that Britain could no longer afford to remain outside the EEC, Prime Minister Harold Macmillan in 1961 announced that Britain would apply for membership.

Britain's application was submitted not once, not twice, but three times. Britain was turned down in 1961 after Macmillan applied and again in 1967 after Prime Minister Harold Wilson applied. Membership was denied in each instance by French president Charles de Gaulle, who was concerned that Britain would challenge French hegemony in the EEC and serve as a Trojan horse for the United States. The governments of the five remaining states disagreed with de Gaulle's veto, yet many on the Continent nevertheless suspected that Britain was less than enthusiastic about joining. When Britain was finally invited into the EEC in 1971 under Prime Minister Edward Heath (two years after de Gaulle had resigned), the British appeared so divided about entering that many on the Continent were now convinced that Britain's heart was not in it. By then, the Euro-skeptics who swelled the ranks of both the Conservative and Labour Parties in Westminster had become a force to be reckoned with; when Parliament approved the European Communities Bill in 1972, it did so by a margin of only seventeen votes.

Having entered the EEC, would Britain remain in it? This was not an idle question, emerging as it did just after Wilson's Labour Party wrested power from Heath's Conservative Party in 1974. Wilson was less than satisfied with the terms of membership the Heath Government had agreed to, and thus during the campaign he made two pledges to the voters: if the Government failed to convince the other EEC members to agree to the new terms a Wilson Government would insist on, Britain would leave the EEC; and if it got what it wanted, the electorate would be given a chance in a referendum to say whether it wished Britain to remain a member. After winning the election, Wilson kept his word. His Government negotiated agreeable new terms and the referendum that followed in 1975 attracted 64 percent of registered voters, 67 percent of whom affirmed their wish to stay in. Four days later Wilson declared an end to the debate.

But the debate did not end with the referendum, despite the fact that two out of every three who voted favored staying in the EEC. Before long, support for Britain's membership started to flag. The economy continued to languish—membership in the EU had produced no quick fixes—and public opinion polls once again showed a majority opposing Britain's membership. The Labour MPs who had argued against entry once again aimed their broadsides at the EEC.

The Awkward Partner

As Britain settled into its new role as a member of the EEC, its relations with the other members were relatively harmonious. But the harmony was not to last. Shortly after the Conservatives came to power in 1979, Prime Minister Margaret Thatcher, never a shrinking violet, shocked her European colleagues and even her advisers by insisting that Britain's annual contribution to the EEC budget was far more than it should be in relation to its wealth. Moreover, because there was a large gap between what it contributed and what it received in return, Thatcher argued that Britain's overpayments entitled it to a refund. Thatcher's campaign for a rebate dragged on for nearly five years, and although in the end she settled for two thirds of what she had struggled for, she did so at great cost. As one scholar put it, "Her domineering and insulting style in dealing with her supposed partners had at times turned Britain into an outsider, almost a pariah, in European circles."[3] So prickly had she been on one occasion that Jacques Chirac, then France's prime minister, called for Britain's expulsion from the EEC.

In 1986, the heads of government of the member states were presented with the Single European Act (SEA) for their signatures. This was a new treaty for the EEC, the product of nearly two years of planning. It was called a *single* European act because it collected together in one instrument the founding treaties of each of the three communities along with their revisions. Its principal purpose was to remove all barriers to trade that remained so that a single market could at last become a reality. Once it was in place, people, goods, services, and capital could move freely from Edinburgh to Athens, Lisbon to Bonn, and to all points in between. By the time the SEA was signed, the EEC had grown to twelve members, as Greece had joined in 1981 and Spain and Portugal in 1986; the governments of each of the twelve had until the end of 1992 to eliminate nearly three hundred trade barriers. These barriers included everything from frontier controls to variable laws on competition and mergers.

Thatcher had no hesitation about signing the SEA, for it embraced one of her ideals—the deregulation of markets. There were references in the SEA to an Economic and Monetary Union (EMU), but nothing in the instrument committed the signatories to it. Nevertheless, interpretations differed. Thatcher held to the view that references to EMU were references to what the SEA had achieved—economic and monetary *cooperation*—and nothing more. Most of her fellow heads of government saw EMU as that which the EEC had yet to achieve—a central bank and a single currency. For most of what remained of Thatcher's premiership her interpretation irritated her European partners—as did theirs hers. In time, however, she came to accept that the EEC was moving inexorably toward a central bank and a single currency, although she opposed both. By the end of 1990, however, her opposition did not matter, for she was no longer prime minister.

Trouble at Home

Over the years, the two major parties in Parliament retreated from and then reversed their original positions on the EEC. There were Euro-skeptics and Euro-philes in both parties all along. A majority of Conservatives in the 1960s and 1970s were Euro-philes, largely because of the EEC's commitment to free trade. One Conservative prime minister—Edward Heath—had brought Britain into the EEC; another—Margaret Thatcher—had signed legislation to complete the single market. Starting in the mid-1980s, however, Conservative parliamentarians took an increasingly hard line against the EEC—not against Britain's membership, but against ceding greater authority to the EEC and, above all, adopting the single European currency. Labour parliamentarians, in the meantime, began to warm to the EEC, primarily because of the social legislation the EEC was promoting and in particular legislation that enhanced workers' rights.

By the end of the 1980s and early 1990s, Conservative leaders became increasingly concerned that the party was seriously divided on the EEC and that this division was alienating the electorate. Probably none was more concerned than John Major, Thatcher's successor. Shortly after he became prime minister in late 1990 he made no secret of his wish that Britain be "right at the heart of the community," as he put it. Because a number in his party disagreed, after Major met with the EEC's other leaders in Maastricht, the Netherlands, in 1991 to negotiate the Treaty on European Union, he had to go to great lengths to convince his party that he had successfully defended Britain's position on three sticking points. Each one brought to mind that emotive term, "federal Europe."

The first was over a combination of foreign and defense issues, criminal justice issues, and issues involving judicial cooperation. Major's position was that these responsibilities, if made subject to EEC-wide decision, would usurp the sovereign right of each member nation to decide such things for itself. He argued that there was nothing to prevent the member nations from gathering to discuss these matters on an intergovernmental basis, however, and if they wished they could coordinate their policies and even adopt them as policies of the European Union (the EEC's new name under the proposed treaty). The prime minister's position, agreed to by other heads of government at Maastricht, was consistent with the principle of subsidiarity. The principle that Britain had long advocated, subsidiarity meant that decisions should be made at the supranational level only if they could not be made effectively at the national level. Apart from effectiveness, he argued, certain matters, such as defense and foreign affairs, had to be left to each government as a sovereign right.

On that sticking point, subsidiarity won out—not federalism, or centralized decision making, which is what most meant when they used the term federalism. Federalism, however, won out on the two remaining sticking points. In each case Major's fellow EEC leaders threw him a lifeline, one he happily caught. They were called opt-outs. Until Parliament agreed otherwise, Britain was excused first from adopting the Social Chapter, which dealt with such workers' rights as on-the-job safety standards, vacation entitlements, and the participation of employees in workplace decision making; and second, from adopting the European single currency.

The Maastricht Treaty was approved by Parliament in 1993, although majorities in the Commons were difficult to muster on some votes leading to final passage. Conservative opposition to further European integration had hardened, and it hardened even more in 1994, when MPs were asked to support an increase in Britain's contributions to the EU budget. So enraged with this proposal were eight Conservative MPs that they defied their party's three-line whip and voted against the increase. By then, Major's governing majority had dropped to eleven. Despite the shrinking numbers, the party leadership decided to withdraw the whip from the eight rebels, that is, suspend them not as members of Parliament but as members of the parliamentary party. Withdrawing the whip surprised few, for Major was infuriated with the recalcitrance of the eight. Jaws did drop seven months later, however, when, still hounded by the Euro-skeptics in his party, Major announced his resignation as party leader. In the next breath, he asked his party colleagues in the Commons to back him or sack him when he stood for reelection twelve days later. As if on cue, John Redwood, a leading Euro-skeptic, resigned from the cabinet to challenge him, and even though Major defeated Redwood 219 to 89, nearly half the party's backbenchers supported Redwood. Major spent the rest of that parliament treading carefully with his party on European issues, and when the parliament came to an end in the spring of 1997, so too did his premiership.

A New Beginning?

John Major was not the only leader who wanted Britain at the heart of Europe. Labour's leader, Tony Blair, wanted Britain there as well. Following Labour's return to power in 1997, would Blair receive better treatment at home over European issues than Major? One factor in Blair's favor was that since the mid-1980s Labour had become more Euro-friendly than the Conservatives, and with Labour's landslide there were bound to be more Euro-friendly MPs than before. But would this Euro-friendliness last?

Blair was faced with the challenge of addressing two audiences whose members in effect had been at odds with each other over a number of issues in the past. He had to assure his European partners that his premiership signaled a new beginning and that he would engage more constructively with the rest of Europe than had Thatcher and Major. He then had to convince his party that he would steadfastly oppose a European, federal superstate. Signing up to the Social Chapter and doing so soon after Labour came to power pleased the members of both audiences. The Government's decision in 1997 not to adopt the euro at the first possible opportunity in 1999 disappointed most of Blair's European partners, however. At the same time, it took the pressure off many in the parliamentary party whose constituencies opposed the single currency. Adoption would hinge on two factors, the Government announced. First, five economic tests would have to be satisfied; second, once these tests were satisfied, the voters would have to agree to adopt the single currency in a referendum. Halfway through Blair's second term, in 2003, the Government delivered a progress report: Britain was on the way to meeting the five criteria, but it had not satisfied them all and was unlikely to do so before the next general election. In 2005, one month after the general election, the Blair Government announced without explanation that it would rule out adoption of the euro at any point in the parliament that had just gotten under way.

Blair's relations with his European partners were relatively harmonious during his first term, but less so in his second and (as of this writing) his third. Blair's initial opposition in 2003 to a plan to develop a European defense force outside NATO's command structure irritated France, Germany, Belgium, and Luxembourg, the nations which had proposed it. Another decision he made that same year on a non-EU matter, the decision to join the United States in a massive attack on Iraq, came close to rupturing his relations with the leaders of the governments of several Western European nations, in particular those of France and Germany.

In 2005, just as the ice in Blair's relationship with some of his EU partners was beginning to thaw, another issue emerged that slowed the thaw: the EU's budget for 2007–2013. The year before, ten nations from central and eastern Europe and the Mediterranean had been inducted into the EU, raising the number of its members from fifteen to twenty-five. Also raised were its members' expectations that an enlarged EU would require an enlarged EU budget.

As EU leaders gathered in the spring of 2005 to discuss its future and its budget, France's president Jacques Chirac blurted out the demand that Britain demonstrate its "solidarity toward Europe" by relinquishing most of the budget rebate Margaret Thatcher had negotiated twenty-one years before. Under the terms Thatcher had negotiated, every year Britain was owed a rebate of 66 percent of the difference between what Britain contributed to the EU and what it received from it the year before. Nearly one half of the overall EU budget is earmarked for the Common Agricultural Policy (CAP), and most of the CAP budget is spent on agricultural subsidies. Massive amounts of Britain's contributions are spent on subsidies, but it receives few subsidies in return because its farming sector is small. France's farming sector, on the other hand, is considerable; because of that it had been receiving about a quarter of the EU's entire subsidies budget. Britain had long argued that there was a need to reform the CAP, and thus it was natural for Blair to respond to Chirac's demand with a quid pro quo: Britain would put its rebate on the table for discussion if France would do the same with the CAP.

Two weeks after Blair's encounter with Chirac, it was Britain's turn to assume the six-month rotating presidency of the European Council. Many thought Britain's presidency during the second half of 2005 would give Blair the leverage he needed to resolve the rebate versus CAP issue and then go on to broker negotiations on the EU's seven-year budget, approval of which was required by early 2006. However, Britain was no closer to resolving the EU's budget issues by the end of its presidency in December than it had been when its presidency began in July. All the while, Blair's critics reminded him that the strength of Britain's economy made it difficult to justify the size of Britain's rebate, especially when the poorer eastern European nations that had recently joined the EU were contributing to the EU budget but temporarily foregoing any subsidies in return. The effect of Blair's stance was to give the impression that Britain was pursuing narrowly nationalistic aims at a time when the EU's members needed to close ranks.

Shared Governance

What role does Britain play as it works alongside others in the governance of the EU? "Alongside others" is the key phrase here: the "others" are the governments of the other twenty-six member states of the EU, including Bulgaria and Romania, whose citizens rang in the New Year by celebrating the entry of their countries into the EU in January 2007. "Alongside" implies sharing, which is what all twenty-seven governments do when they assume responsibility for governing the EU. To understand how Britain works alongside others, it is helpful to focus on the institutions in which they all work. It is first necessary to get a sense of the overall organizational structure of the EU, as ordained by the Maastricht Treaty.

The Treaty on European Union is the formal name given to the treaty agreed to in Maastricht, the Netherlands, that came into force in 1993. Usually referred to as the Maastricht Treaty, this agreement gave the EEC both a new "architecture" (Euro-speak for organization) and a new name. Out went the "European Economic Community" and in came the slimmed-down designation, "European Community" (EC). As for its new architecture, the EC would henceforth be one part of a larger whole, although the architects preferred "pillars" to parts. All together, the three pillars would be called by another new name, "European Union."

The EC pillar includes the ECSC and the EURATOM. Including both in this pillar did not mean there would be a change in the work of what was once called the EEC and is now called the EC. Political executives, lawmakers, and judges drawn from the member states continue to make decisions—supranational decisions—about agriculture, trade, transportation, the environment, and several other policy areas. The laws that arise from these decisions are technically EC laws, not EU laws, for the second and third pillars have no lawmaking authority. What, then, do the second and third pillars do?

The second pillar is the Common Foreign and Security Policy pillar, and the third, the Police and Judicial Cooperation in Criminal Matters pillar. Decisions made by these two pillars are not supranational decisions, but rather intergovernmental decisions, that is, they are made on a government-by-government basis. The British government or any other member government is free to negotiate with and formally agree or not agree with other member governments on any issue not addressed in EC law, for example, participating in a European defense force, coordinating efforts to reduce unlawful drug trafficking, or enforcing border controls. If a government wishes not to enter into an agreement with other governments, there is no requirement that it do so. Yet it became clear during the negotiations at Maastricht that there was a desire to cooperate on some matters that cross national borders.

European Council

The British prime minister is one of twenty-five heads of government, plus heads of state in the case of France and Finland who, together with their foreign ministers and the president of the European Commission, serve as members of the European Council. This body, which has been likened to "the board of directors of a company,"[4] is the highest political authority of the EU. It decides, sometimes in broad outline and sometimes in specific detail, what direction the EU should take and asks the European Commission to frame proposals that reflect its decisions. Each member nation holds forth as president of the European Council for six months (member states are presidents, not their heads of government), giving that nation's head of government, ministers, and officials the authority to address and attempt to resolve the most pressing issues facing the EU. Near the end of the six months, the president's head of government hosts a summit to report what progress has been made and to identify any unresolved issues facing the EU that need to be addressed during the tenure of the next president of the European Council.

The last two times Britain held the presidency of the European Council were in the first half of 1998 and the second half of 2005, in both cases when Tony Blair was prime minister. Three major actions were taken during Britain's presidency in 1998. The first was getting accession negotiations under way with the governments of the ten nations that joined the EU six years later. The second was deciding that eleven of the then fifteen member states had satisfied the necessary conditions for adopting the euro. The third was ratifying the Europol Convention that authorized ground rules for the exchange of information by police forces in the member states to aid in the pursuit of criminal investigations or the prevention of crime in various parts of the EU.

All three actions were taken during the British presidency but not because they were British initiatives, for they had been on the EU's agenda for some while. Britain's initiatives, announced at the summit towards the end of its presidency, took the form of entreating member states to develop strategies to deal with rising unemployment, combat social exclusion, foster lifelong learning, and promote small and middle-size businesses. These were objectives that the member states worked on as one and then another assumed the presidency of the European Council. Britain's presidency was seen as undistinguished undoubtedly because Labour had not been in power long enough to produce a more eye-catching, if not reformist, agenda.

Britain's presidency in 2005 was regarded by most as not so much undistinguished as disappointing. When its presidency began on July 1 a new constitution for the EU that had been three years in the making had just been rejected by the voters in referendums held in France and the Netherlands. In view of the demise of the proposed constitution, Blair announced that it would be important in the months ahead to pause to reflect on the EU's future. Important though that was, most member governments were convinced that nothing was more important to the EU's future than putting many of the final touches on the EU's budget for 2007–2113. Blair appeared to agree but insisted that planning the EU's budget could not proceed until the dispute over the British rebate and reform of the CAP was settled. Nearly halfway through the British presidency, European Commission president José Manuel Borroso lamented: "We're in this pause for reflection, but there has not been much reflection so far." [5]

A month later, in October, Blair followed through on the promise he had made at the beginning of Britain's presidency to hold a special summit on the EU's future. At the summit he announced that task forces would carry out work on several areas of reform, among them creation of a European-wide energy grid and control of the flow of migration. Also that month, Britain had overcome great odds in meetings in Luxembourg to convince certain member states, Austria in particular, that the EU should begin talks with Turkey on its eventually joining the EU. In November, at a summit on antiterrorism that Britain organized in Barcelona for EU member nations and ten nations bordering the Mediterranean, leaders condemned terrorism and promised to fight it, but made little progress on how to fight it when they were unable to agree on how to define it. In December, having failed to break the deadlock with France and other members over the rebate and CAP issues, and having failed to convince the ten new members to accept reduced contributions from the EU's budget, Britain's presidency came to an unsatisfactory and disappointing end.

European Commission

The European Commission is the EU's executive. At the top of its hierarchy are twenty-seven commissioners, one from Britain and one each from the other member states. All are nominated by their governments, including the president of the commission, who must be acceptable to the governments of all the member states. The British prime minister nominates Britain's commissioner, and if Britain's nominee and the nominees from the other member states are acceptable to the president-designate, the president-designate assigns portfolios to each of the other commissioners. All commissioners are then subject to confirmation by the European Parliament. The parliament votes first on whether to approve the nominee for president, and then, if he or she is approved, on whether to approve all the nominees en bloc.

Although commissioners are nominated by their national governments for renewable five-year terms, when they are formally inducted they are mindful of the oath they take to promote the interests of the EU, even if these clash with those of their home governments. When Britain's commissioner-designate for Trade, Peter Mandelson, a close friend of Tony Blair and former Labour cabinet minister, was questioned by members of the European Parliament in a confirmation hearing in 2004, he emphasized that his friendship with the prime minister would continue, but he had "moved on." In other words, his allegiance was no longer to the British government but to the European Commission. As he put it, "I am not a British Labour Government man, I am a European Commission man. I know where my interests, loyalties, allegiances and energies will be devoted."[6] Had Mandelson been required to demonstrate his loyalty, he could not have done it more dramatically than he did a year later, when he warned British ministers that Britain's influence in the EU was certain to diminish during Britain's presidency of the European Council if it failed to resolve the impasse over the EU's budget for 2007–2013. As Mandelson's warning suggested, British prime ministers would be making a serious miscalculation were they to presume that Britain's commissioner was their mouthpiece in Brussels.

The British commissioner takes no instructions from London on any of the roles that commissioners perform. What roles are these? There are four, and initiating EC policy is the most important one. Not only is Mandelson responsible for the most important policy area in the EU—trade—he also sits on four of the commission's five most powerful committees—Communications,

Competitiveness, External Relations, and Economic Strategy. These committees are powerful because they often take the first step in determining the EC's policies. Once Mandelson and his fellow commissioners are of one mind on which policies to pursue, they submit them to the Council of Ministers to consider, but usually only after they have consulted informally with the European Parliament, the governments of the member nations, and any pressure groups from the member nations that wish to be heard.

A second role the commissioners play is that of devising statutory instruments authorized by the Council of Ministers. The bulk of statutory instruments are regulations pertaining to price levels for various agricultural commodities. A third role is overseeing the treaties of the EU and EC law, which is based on the treaties. So massive is this job that investigating whether member governments are in compliance cannot be much more than a hit-and-miss effort. Should an instance of noncompliance come to light from a review the commission initiates or from complaints one or more member governments bring to the commission's attention, commissioners serve notice on the errant government. If that government fails to correct its ways, the commissioners may take it to the European Court of Justice to ensure enforcement. A fourth role the commissioners fulfill is managing the EC's finances. Every year, they prepare the budget, submit it to the Council of Ministers for its preliminary approval, and send it next to the European Parliament. After the parliament has approved it, the commissioners make disbursements and later account for how funds were spent.

None of these roles could be performed without the help of others. Mandelson and his colleagues draw upon the skills of approximately twenty-thousand civil servants—administrators, researchers, translators, interpreters, and secretaries—all of whom are from Britain and the other member states. These civil servants work in Brussels in the commission's twenty-three directorates general (DGs). DGs are the basic building blocks of the commission's organization, and each is headed by a director general answerable to a commissioner. Directors general are similar to permanent secretaries in Whitehall; commissioners are like ministers; and DGs are equivalent to departments, with each DG assigned a different remit. For example, seventeen deal with matters that are primarily internal to the EU, such as agriculture and rural development and transport and energy, and the remaining six address external matters, including trade and overseas aid.

Council of Ministers

Because commissioners are supposed to leave their nationality at the commission door, British prime ministers accept that they cannot count on their "man or woman in Brussels" to serve as their Government's mouthpiece in that forum. But they know they can bank on their ministers to fly to Brussels to defend the Government's position in the Council of Ministers, and it is crucial that they do so because that is where final decisions are made on EC legislation.[7]

Council of Ministers meetings are called by a minister of the government of the state whose turn it is to serve as president of the European Council. "Council" is something of a misnomer, for there are nine councils, all of which are subject-based. Three of the busiest are the Agricultural and Fisheries Council, the Economic and Financial Affairs Council, and the Transport, Telecommunications and Energy Council. Which minister flies to Brussels depends on the subject. For example, if an issue or legislative proposal dealing with agriculture arises, it is Britain's secretary of state for Environment, Food and Rural Affairs who flies to Brussels to meet with agriculture ministers from the other member states on the Agricultural and Fisheries Council.

The member states agreed from the beginning that their interests and those of the community should be kept in reasonable balance; however, controversy erupts every now and again over which system of voting best gives effect to this principle. Early in the EU's history, there was a "population question" (should every nation be accorded the same voting strength, regardless of size?) and an "issues question" (should all issues be resolved by the same voting method?). The member states agreed that the answer to both was "no." As for the population question, each state was assigned a weighted vote, with high-population states receiving more votes than low-population states. The total number of votes assigned to the 27 member states since Bulgaria and Romania joined the EU in January 2007 is 345, which includes 10 votes to Bulgaria and 14 votes to Romania, the most recent entrants to the EU. As one of the most populated countries, Britain has 29 out of these 345 votes, as have France, Germany, and Italy. The least populated, Malta, has 3.

As for the issues question, it was thought that if every state were allowed a veto, the dissenting nation's interests would be protected, but the community's would be held back. On the other hand, adopting a system of simple-majority voting would have the opposite effect: the EU's interests would be advanced, but states in the minority could allege they had been given short shrift. This dilemma was resolved (probably as much as it could be) when the member states agreed to adopt three forms of voting, with each form determined by a measure's importance, as established in EU treaties and subject to the European Commission's interpretation.

Measures of major importance, such as inviting new members to join the EU, require the agreement of the minister from each member nation (345 votes); proposals of much less importance, such as introducing minor procedures, are settled by a simple majority vote of 173 or more votes. Measures of mid-level importance, however, are settled by a third form of voting that is literally an extraordinary majority but called a qualified majority. Britain has balked when EU treaties have stipulated that certain measures be approved by qualified majority voting (QMV) rather than unanimous consent. In addition, it has challenged the European Commission's interpretation of some of the language in the treaties that, in the commission's view, requires the Council of Ministers to approve measures such as health and safety by QMV. At the heart of Britain's concern is that not only could it lose a vote taken by QMV but also, depending on the issue, it could lose one of its basic rights as a nation-state.

Allaying Britain's concern to some extent, however, are the obstacles a measure requiring QMV must surmount. To begin with, the measure must attract a minimum of 255 out of 345 votes, that is, nearly 80 percent of the total. Second, it requires the support of a majority of member nations. And third, it must win the backing of member nations representing 62 percent or more of the EU's population. What is more, the Council of Ministers is reluctant to force a vote on a measure by QMV when it arouses controversy. The norm is for ministers to settle their differences by consensus so that they can eventually unite behind a common position. As a result, QMV is used in only approximately 20 percent of the cases in which it could be used.

Estimates vary, but between 60 percent and 65 percent of Britain's new laws today originate in Brussels. When ministers meet in Council of Ministers sessions, which they do about ninety times a year, they debate and ultimately vote on one of two forms of EC law. One is called regulations and the other directives. An example of a regulation is the requirement that tachographs, which record driving speeds and the duration of driving periods, be installed in and used by all vehicles registered in member nations employed to transport goods. Once the Council of Ministers agrees to a regulation, it is sent to the government of every member nation together with a deadline for implementation.

Regulations have the force of law and are binding on all member nations; directives too have the force of law and are binding, but not necessarily on all member states. An example is the requirement issued to, say, eighteen member nations to raise the quality of drinking water to a prescribed standard. (The quality in the rest of the member nations is at or above the standard and therefore the directive does not apply to them.) In addition to applying to some member nations but not others, directives differ from regulations in yet another important way: they outline the objectives that the governments of the member nations must achieve and the date by which they must achieve them, but without telling them how to do it. What happens if a government fails to implement a regulation or directive? It risks being cited by the European Commission and possibly taken to the European Court of Justice.

Meeting the administrative needs of the Council of Ministers is the Council Secretariat, which has a staff of more than 2,500. Apart from the secretariat staff and the many ministers who fly in and out of Brussels for meetings of the Council of Ministers, the most familiar figures passing through the corridors of the Council of Ministers building are diplomats and civil servants posted to Brussels by Whitehall and by other member governments. All are attached to their home governments' embassies to the EU, which are officially referred to as permanent representations. Britain's contingent is called United Kingdom Permanent Representation (UKREP for short). Like the other permanent representations, UKREP is headed by an ambassador (formally, a permanent representative). Both the ambassador and his or her deputy are senior officials in the Foreign and Commonwealth Office (FCO); the remaining fifty or so UKREP officials are drawn not only from the FCO, but also from other departments that deal with EC issues such as agriculture, trade, and the environment.

Most of the work of UKREP officials is undertaken below the ambassadorial level. Officials maintain contact with their Whitehall departments to learn of any changes in policy that might be evolving, develop position papers, and take soundings of what other delegations are thinking by conferring with those in the other permanent representations. UKREP is as committed to promoting its government's position as any other delegation is in advancing its own government's, but UKREP officials are not always successful in their efforts to convince. When that happens they turn to their ambassador to try his or her hand at doing so in the ambassadors' group, which is called the Committee of Permanent Representatives (COREPER). At both levels, UKREP tries to resolve any differences that other delegations might have with the British government's position even before ministers enter the building to make their way to a Council of Ministers meeting. So demanding is UKREP and COREPER's work that if ministers were left to do it on their own, they would not begin to scratch the surface of what has to be done, let alone carry on with their usual ministerial duties in London.

European Parliament

Were the British government intent on pressing the EU to enact an EC law, that is, a directive, it would concentrate most of its efforts on the European Commission and then the Council of Ministers—not the European Parliament. That is not to suggest that the European Parliament plays no role in lawmaking, for it does. Its powers actually have grown since 1979, when its members were elected for the first time. But not only has it not yet acquired the powers that one would expect a parliament to possess, it is not the only lawmaking body of the EU.

The European Parliament is the only body of the EU whose members are directly elected. To accommodate the 54 members of the European Parliament (MEPs) from Bulgaria and Romania, starting in January 2007, the total number of MEPs was increased to 786. (The number will revert to the pre-2007 total of 732 when Euro-elections are held in June 2009.) Every nation has a set number, based on its population. Britain has seventy-eight MEPs, as have France and Italy. Only Germany's delegation is larger, with ninety-nine. Malta's is the smallest, with five. All MEPs are elected by proportional representation, and all simultaneously, for fixed five-year terms that run parallel to the European commissioners' five-year terms. Once elected, MEPs sit not as members of national delegations, but rather as members of seven rather broadly based political party groups. MEPs from

Britain's two major parties sit on the largest two, Labour with the Party of European Socialists and the Conservatives with the European People's Party and European Democrats. Britain's Liberal Democrats sit with the European Liberal Democratic Reform Party.

The European Parliament has no authority to make laws on its own. It may neither initiate legislation nor be assured of having its way when it amends it. Only the European Commission may initiate measures, although it usually informally seeks the advice of key MEPs in the drafting process. The commission and the Council of Ministers have as much impact on a measure's progress as the parliament does. Parliament does not decide; rather, it co-decides along with the Council in what is formally referred to as the co-decision procedure.

The essence of what happens is as follows. Once the European Commission has finished drafting a measure, it refers it to the council and the parliament for a vote. The parliament normally amends the measure, and if the council accepts the amendments the measure is passed. If the council amends parliament's amendments and an absolute majority of 394 or more MEPs is mustered to vote against the council's amendments, the commission steps in. Any of parliament's amendments that the commission accepts are incorporated in an amended version of the proposal and referred to the council. If the council persists in opposing parliament's amendments, it must do so unanimously. A unanimous vote kills the amendments unless an equal number of representatives from both institutions sit on a conciliation committee and work out their differences. They have up to six weeks to do so. If they cannot agree on an identical version, or if parliament, the council, or both later rejects an identical version agreed to by the conciliation committee, the measure dies.

In addition to what minimal legislative powers it possesses, the European Parliament exercises control over the EU's budget and has certain oversight responsibilities. As for the budget, the parliament has the power to approve, amend, or reject the annual budget the commission proposes. How much will be spent and for what purposes, however, are decisions that parliament must share with the Council of Ministers. Oversight, however, is not a shared responsibility. In addition to confirming the appointment of all commissioners, parliament may by a two-thirds vote require the commissioners to resign en bloc if it takes strong exception to something one, some, or all have done. However, it is not possible to fire just one or some, and dismissing them all at once is not practicable, so this power has never been used, although the threat of it can have a moderating effect on the commissioners' actions. Finally, there are two other ways by which parliament engages in oversight. One is by empowering temporary commissions of inquiry; the other is by MEPs putting questions to commissioners and council ministers when they appear before them in parliament.

European Court of Justice

EC law is an all-embracing term that includes EC regulations and directives and the EEC and EU treaties on which they are based. The member nations, as a condition of their entry into the EU, agree to abide by all such laws—past, present, and future. If the government of a member nation chooses to ignore an EC law, the errant government could be taken to the European Court of Justice (ECJ).

Located in Luxembourg, the ECJ was established to ensure that the member nations and the EU's governing institutions would uphold the laws of the community. It fulfills that responsibility when it hears direct actions cases and preliminary rulings cases. As for direct actions cases, there are two subtypes: infringement proceedings and judicial review proceedings. Infringement proceedings occur when a member nation is accused by the commission or by another member nation of failing to comply with the law. If the court rules that the member nation has failed to comply, the nation must fall into line without delay or run the risk of incurring a heavy fine. Judicial review proceedings represent the second subtype of direct actions cases. These proceedings come into play when a member state, the Council of Ministers, the commission, and, in limited circumstances, the parliament or individuals decide to challenge the legality of an action taken by one of the EU's governing bodies or when one of these governing bodies fails to act. If the court finds in favor of the complainant, the errant body in question is obliged to comply fully with the law.

In addition to direct actions cases, there are preliminary rulings cases. These are rulings the court makes in response to requests put to it by judges from the member states who are searching for the appropriate interpretation of EC law to apply to cases before their courts. Once the ECJ has provided its interpretation, the case returns to the national court, where the interpretation is applied. The interpretation is binding in the case in which the ruling was sought and represents one more way by which the ECJ enforces the application of community law.

One ECJ judge is British, and the remaining judges are drawn from each of the other member nations. Their stature as jurists is such that they would be worthy of appointment to high judicial office in their home countries, and although their terms are limited to six years they may be re-appointed for a further six years. One of the judges is elected by secret ballot by his or her fellow judges to serve three years as president of the court.

The president of the court directs its work, which includes, among other things, assigning cases to chambers made up of three or five judges. If a case deals with a particularly complex or controversial point of law, the president will assign it to a grand chamber of thirteen judges. With the growth of EC law, another court was created in 1989 and given jurisdiction over the more routine cases to lighten the judges' expanding workload. Called the Court of First Instance, it too is made up of twenty-seven judges, one of whom is British. Its president, who is elected in the same manner as the president of the ECJ, also usually assigns cases to chambers of three or five judges. As the phrase "first instance" in the court's name implies, cases may be appealed to the ECJ, but only if they turn on a point of law of considerable significance.

Because most cases are not appealed, judges who sit on the higher court are free to concentrate on cases of greater significance.

The EU's Impact on the British Political System

Inveterate Euro-philes and Euro-skeptics in Britain disagree on just about everything having to do with the EU. But they agree on two points. The first is that membership in the EU has produced profound changes in the British political system; the second is that more changes are yet to come. What they do not know is what those changes will be and what their effects will be. Perhaps their thinking has been influenced by that of their elders, who have told them how most Britons in the 1960s and 1970s never thought that a six-nation trading bloc called the Common Market would be transformed into the supranational organization it is today that boasts its own governing institutions and laws, its own central bank and currency, and, some venture to say, one day even its own foreign policy and military.

With a few notable exceptions, the changes that have been introduced since Britain joined the EU have been ushered in without fanfare. Some have been too controversial to single out, others too complex to explain, and still others too trivial to mention. As a result many changes have escaped the attention of most. Among them are changes in the ways in which Britain's institutions of government have been linked up to deal with EU affairs. These institutions include the cabinet, the Foreign and Commonwealth Office (FCO), and several of the other departments of state and Parliament.

As for the cabinet, included in its committee system are two committees, one called European Policy (which deals with European issues in general), and the other, European Union Strategy. In the Cabinet Office there is the European Secretariat. This unit has responsibility for confirming that the departments of state fully comprehend those EU policies that pertain to them, which helps to ensure that the Government speaks with one voice when responding to developments in the EU. It also checks to see that EU policies are being faithfully executed. The European Secretariat is assisted in its coordinating role by the FCO, which also has a coordinating role.

It is to the FCO that the other departments refer important policy proposals and issues; those that are especially important the FCO refers to the European Secretariat. In the meantime, the FCO is in frequent contact with UKREP and exchanges information with officials there as they interact with other delegations and with the EU's major governing institutions on matters ranging from fisheries policy to foreign policy. In addition, most of the rest of the departments have civil servants whose job is to offer policy advice to ministers on any EU issues that touch on their departmental jurisdictions. Parliament, too, has reorganized itself to deal with EU matters. The House of Commons' European Scrutiny Committee and the House of Lords' Select Committee on the European Union stand out, as do three standing committees on Europe in the Commons. All five committees have been charged with scrutinizing the positions taken by governments of the day on proposed EC laws and assessing what impact these proposals are likely to have on Britain.

In addition to these institutional and procedural changes, there are several other changes brought about by Britain's membership in the EU. Three are particularly significant. The first deals with Britain's sovereignty, the second with political representation, and the third with parliamentary oversight and ministerial accountability.

Sovereignty

"The day that Britain joined the European Union is the day that Britain surrendered its sovereignty." So claim the Euro-skeptics, who speak in unison when they say that no issue that involves Britain in its relations with the rest of Europe troubles them more. Euro-philes see it differently. Most are prepared to argue that Britain's legal sovereignty has remained intact, although Euro-philes inclined to think otherwise are quick to say that a loss of sovereignty was not too high a price to pay for the benefits Britain has received in return. Has Britain in fact lost its sovereignty? If so, can it be reclaimed? If it can be reclaimed, could it be said that it lost it in the first place?

The classical notion of sovereignty holds that a nation is sovereign if it is free to function without interference from or dependence on other nations. Most no longer accept this rendition as an accurate picture of a world in which there is a high degree of interdependence among nation-states. That is why some argue that there is no such thing as sovereignty today, and others assert that sovereignty merely needs to be updated with a twenty-first-century definition. Those who take the latter view argue that nations are sovereign as long as they are capable of maintaining the form of government they prefer and are able to administer the laws they enact. What is more, if they join such multinational organizations as the World Trade Organization and NATO, they do so freely and for the purpose of advancing their economic and security interests.

When a nation joins the EU, it is usually said that it pools its sovereignty with that of the other member nations. Yet pooling sovereignty is a contradiction in terms, for a nation cannot both pool its sovereignty and retain it at the same time. It can, however, join with others in delegating certain of its powers to the EU's governing institutions without the risk of its losing its sovereignty, for to delegate power is not to surrender it. Indeed, implicit in a nation's decision to delegate is its right to withdraw that which it has delegated. If it wishes, a nation can go one step further and secede from the EU altogether.

One can conclude from this that when Euro-skeptics lament the loss of British sovereignty, perhaps without thinking of it in these terms, they are expressing their discontent with Parliament for having delegated certain powers to the EC when it enacted the European Communities Bill. Before Britain joined the EU, no individual or body of individuals except Parliament itself could overturn an act of Parliament. Not even judges could declare a law null and void.

When Parliament enacted the European Communities Bill, it agreed to accept as its own all EC laws that were already on the books of the six original member nations and all future EC laws. As mentioned earlier, an estimated 60 percent to 65 percent of all laws put into effect in Britain originate not in Westminster but the EU. In addition, more than 80 percent of regulations pertaining to the production, distribution, and exchange of goods, services, and capital in Britain were devised not by British ministers, but by EU decision makers.[8]

What applied to Parliament applied equally to the courts. Just as Parliament was required to enact legislation to implement an EC directive even if it clashed with an existing British law, so too were the courts obliged to honor an EC law in their rulings even if it was at variance with British law. Contrary though it was to British jurisprudence, the courts were forced to face up to this change starting with a series of related cases that got under way in 1989.

These are the *Factortame* cases (*Factortame* being shorthand for *R. v. Secretary of State for Transport, ex parte Factortame Ltd.*). By way of background, under EC fisheries policy each member nation is assigned a quota on its catches. Starting in the mid-1980s, British fishermen and politicians became concerned that Spanish fishermen who had registered their ninety-five trawlers as British under a law enacted in 1894 were drawing down Britain's quota. To ensure that British fishermen could fish for 100 percent of their quota, Parliament in 1988 enacted a law that stipulated that fishing boats could be registered as British only if they were owned by Britons. This law, called the Merchant Shipping Act, alarmed Factortame, a Spanish-owned company registered as British under the earlier law but suddenly barred from doing so under the new law. Convinced that the 1988 law violated EC law, Factortame set in motion a series of cases, starting in the High Court in London.

After hearing the case, the court requested a preliminary ruling from the ECJ as to whether the law was contrary to EC law. Because the Spanish fishermen would be prevented from earning a living in the two years it would take before the ECJ would rule, the High Court ordered the secretary of state to refrain from enforcing the 1988 law until a final judgment could be handed down. But could a court set aside an act of Parliament, even temporarily? Convinced that it could not, the Government appealed the case to the Court of Appeal, which overruled the High Court's decision to grant such relief, and gave the master of the rolls the opportunity to assert that "Any attempt to interfere with primary legislation would be wholly unconstitutional."[9]

The case then went from the Court of Appeal to the House of Lords. The Law Lords agreed with the Court of Appeal, arguing that providing interim relief was "directly contrary to Parliament's sovereign will."[10] Nevertheless, they decided to seek a preliminary ruling from the ECJ on whether EC law gave the fishermen an inherent right to interim relief. The question of granting interim relief was the second of two issues that emerged in this case. The first and most pressing one was whether the requirement of being British as found in the Merchant Shipping Act contravened EC law.

On this issue the European Commission intervened and took the British government to the European Court. Until it could hear the case, the ECJ declared, the British government was to refrain from imposing the British nationality requirement. Soon after this, the ECJ issued its preliminary ruling to the House of Lords on the question of interim relief, declaring in effect that the High Court's decision had been consistent with EC law: the fishermen were entitled to relief. All that remained was the ECJ's preliminary ruling on the provision of the 1988 law pertaining to the nationality requirement. That ruling, handed down in 1992, held that the provisions governing nationality were incompatible with EC law; shortly after this, the Government brought British law into line with the court's judgment.

Several conclusions can be drawn from all of this. First, no longer does Parliament have sole authority to make all of Britain's laws; in certain policy realms the EU has the last word. Second, the EU's lawmakers—the European Commission, the Council of Ministers, and the European Parliament—constrain Parliament's freedom to legislate. So, too, in effect does the European Court of Justice, which expects the national courts of the member states to hand down decisions that comply with EC law and ECJ case law, including the ECJ's preliminary rulings. That means that British courts are empowered to set aside any British laws that clash with EC laws.

Third, the loss of parliamentary sovereignty has led to Britain's loss of sovereignty, or so some believe. Technically, however, Britain has not lost its sovereignty, because that which Parliament enacts it may later repeal. Notwithstanding that, repeal—which would result in Britain's leaving the EU—is a prospect that even many Euro-skeptics are unwilling to contemplate. As the decades pass and the benefits of membership multiply, so entrenched could Britain's membership become that pulling out would be impracticable. For all practical purposes, then, Britain would have indeed lost its sovereignty.

Representation

The British parliament's diminished authority to legislate has had an unmistakable knock-on effect on constituency representation. As a succession of treaties since the mid-1980s have made increasing numbers of public policy areas the preserve of the EU, decisions dealing with agriculture, the environment, international trade, transportation, public health, consumer affairs, and several other policy fields are forged not in London but in Brussels. With this shift in responsibilities, some question whether ministers and backbench members of Parliament have been left with enough areas of responsibility to act on what is in Britain's best interests.

In the meantime, British voters must live with EC regulations that Parliament is not allowed to amend and with laws based on EC directives that

Parliament might well oppose were it allowed to do so. As a result the electorate faces a democratic deficit: they continue to exercise their right to vote, but their vote carries little weight. No longer can they look to their members of Parliament to legislate on matters that have become the responsibility of the EU. Ironically, neither can they look to their MEPs to legislate on issues that are before EU decision-making bodies. There are three reasons why British MEPs cannot make up for this deficit. The first has to do with the size of their constituencies, the second with their numbers in the European Parliament, and the third with the powers of the European Parliament.

Since 1999, Britain's MEPs have been elected by proportional representation, as mandated by the EU. Northern Ireland's three MEPs are elected by the single transferable vote variant of proportional representation (as they always have been), and the remaining seventy-five of the UK's parliamentarians by another variant of proportional representation, the multimember list system. To accommodate the multimember list system, England, Scotland, and Wales in the 2004 Euro-election were divided into eleven regions. These vast multimember constituencies are each represented by between three and ten MEPs. This was a radical departure from the single-member constituency arrangements that have long existed for Westminster parliamentarians and the single-member constituencies represented by mainland Britain's Euro-parliamentarians before the 1999 Euro-election.

Whereas the average number of electors per constituency in the UK in 2005 was not much more than 68,400 and the average number per Euro-constituency before 1999 was more than 506,000, for the 2004 Euro-election the number per Euro-constituency was anywhere from a low of nearly two million (represented by three MEPs) to a high of a little more than six million (represented by ten MEPs). This meant that the two largest of the new Euro-constituencies were ten to twelve times greater in electoral population than the old Euro-constituencies, and nearly seventy-five to ninety times greater than the average Westminster constituency. With constituencies that size, MEPs find themselves frustrated in their efforts to sound out the opinions of those they purport to represent. Constituents too can be frustrated in their efforts to contact an MEP to request help or register a point of view. Much of their frustration is the result of their not knowing the names of any of the three to ten MEPs elected to represent them, let alone the names of those who are members of the party they support. Once they do find out who represents them, the next challenge they face is tracking them down by finding the addresses of their offices in Brussels or any that they maintain in their far-flung constituency. A second reason why there is a deficit in representation is that even if all Britain's seventy-eight MEPs were united on an issue before the European Parliament, they make up only 10 percent of that body's MEPs. A majority from some or all of the twenty-six other delegations could easily outvote the seventy-eight.

The third and probably most serious deficit in representation is traceable to the legislative impotence of the European Parliament. Its powers have increased over the years, but it still has no authority to initiate legislation. That is the prerogative of the European Commission. Moreover, it may not amend proposals unless the commission agrees. The only power it may wield on its own is the power to veto a measure approved by the Council of Ministers, but so too can the council veto a measure approved by the European Parliament. EU treaties have granted more power to the European Parliament in recent years, and future treaties may grant it further powers. Were that to happen, however, the Westminster Parliament would almost certainly lose powers that correspond with any the European Parliament would gain. Given the size of Britain's Euro-constituencies and the number of British MEPs relative to the number of MEPs from the twenty-six other member nations, conferring additional power on the European Parliament might well diminish the voting strength of the British electorate all the more.

Parliamentary Oversight and Ministerial Accountability

The term "democratic deficit" has been used thus far to focus on deficiencies in representation. It can apply equally to deficiencies in Parliament's efforts to oversee government decision making and hold ministers to account when they are involved in EU decision making. These deficiencies have evolved for two reasons. One is that backbenchers take little interest in most EU issues. The other is that despite the best efforts of Parliament's scrutiny committees to monitor lawmaking in the EU, the legislative process there is so impermeable that it is difficult for these committees to hold British ministers to account.

As for backbenchers being drawn to issues emerging in Brussels, usually only a sensational news story or provocative editorial piques their interest. Most have neither the time nor the inclination to sift systematically through the many EC draft laws, policy initiatives, and other documents that are in continuous flow from the European Commission. Experience has convinced them that the vast majority are not particularly salient, some are too complex to understand, and hardly any are relevant to their constituents' interests. For these reasons, most MPs are content to rely on the work of the European Scrutiny Committee.

The European Scrutiny Committee sifts through an estimated 1,300 or so EU documents a year. Of these, they report on about six hundred. Draft regulations and directives are among the documents the committee receives. The FCO receives them first, and soon after that they arrive at the committee, each accompanied by an explanation memorandum (EM). Which department is responsible for the subject covered by the draft? Will it have any impact on British law? What does the government of the day think of it? These among other questions are raised and answered in EMs, each of which is signed by the responsible minister.[11]

About thirty documents are then referred to three standing committees on European legislation, each of which deals with different policy realms. There, any draft regulations, directives, and other initiatives that raise political or legal issues that concern their members are studied. Despite their hard work, these committees are seen as operating "outside the political mainstream," as one political journalist wrote, and as a result, he continued, "their public meetings and frequent reports are largely ignored by fellow MPs."[12] Moreover, so low is EC draft legislation on backbenchers' lists of concerns that usually no amount of lobbying by interested backbenchers and the European Scrutiny Committee can convince the Government to schedule a debate on the floor of the Commons, even on the most important issues. All too often, their entreaties are shrugged off with impunity.

EC draft legislation passes *through* Parliament but it is not passed *by* Parliament. Passing EC legislation is the job of ministers from the twenty-seven member nations when they meet in formal session in the Council of Ministers. How can the Commons exert any influence over what British ministers decide in these sessions? Here, the four European committees—the three standing committees in particular—play a key role. These committees call on ministers to appear before them to divide their time between responding to questions put to them by any backbenchers who wish to attend the session and participating in debates on issues that committee members raise.

Because there are so many draft regulations and directives, committee members often find themselves locked in a race with the clock as they try to say everything they wish about a measure before the minister leaves for Brussels to vote on it. All too often in the past, parliamentarians lost the race. However, a provision in the Amsterdam Treaty of 1997 gave them more time when it forbade the Council of Ministers from considering a draft proposal any sooner than six weeks from the date the commission distributed all documents dealing with the proposal to the council and the European Parliament. In addition, MPs have benefited from a resolution passed by the British parliament called the scrutiny reserve. According to its provisions, British ministers may not agree to any proposal in the Council of Ministers that has not been cleared by one of the three standing committees on Europe. Despite that prohibition, there are times when ministers cannot comply with it, for example, when the council has to rush ahead with a vote on a measure before the committee has had a chance to take it up. Whatever the reason, when that happens ministers are required to return to the committee to explain why.

The principal raison d'être of the scrutiny committees is to influence ministers' decisions before they begin to debate and vote on EC legislation in the Council of Ministers. If parliamentarians register any interest in a measure, it tends to peak at this stage. Soon after the measure has been agreed to, interest subsides and eventually disappears. Generating enthusiasm for investigating the recent actions of ministers under these circumstances is difficult enough. The co-decision process in Brussels makes it even more difficult as this process involves not only the Council of Ministers, but the commission and European Parliament as well. The commission may decide to reject amendments the European Parliament proposes, and if the council and European Parliament cannot agree on the same version of a measure, they have a limited period to resolve their differences before the measure dies. At some juncture in this process, a British minister might have to retreat from the position he or she agreed to abide by with the standing committee on European legislation.

Parliamentarians do not usually regard a retreat as breaking faith with the committee, for they realize the minister needs room to maneuver, within reasonable limits, while negotiating with other ministers to advance Britain's position. These negotiations are almost always complex as twenty-seven ministers from twenty-seven states cut deals with each other, consult key staff from their permanent representations, and engage in bargaining with key European parliamentarians. Complexity breeds confusion: after ministers who attend the same council meeting, which almost always proceeds behind closed doors, return to their home capitals, they often report widely different versions of what took place. Most agree that negotiations proceed more efficiently behind closed doors, away from the glare of publicity. But there is a price to pay, and it is paid by those in the British Parliament who attach greater importance to transparency of decision making so that ministers can be made all the more accountable to Parliament for their actions in Brussels.

Conclusion

Apart from two brief periods, the British public has demonstrated little support for Britain's membership in the EU and even less enthusiasm. The exceptions were the several days of countrywide celebrations that took place when Britain went into the EEC in 1973, and the second was the 1975 referendum held when the electorate voted two-to-one to remain in. Coming forward in time, one is struck by the high incidence of public ambivalence toward the EU. One might think such ambivalence would have abated by now. Instead it has persisted and has even increased. When pollsters have asked respondents over the years whether membership is "good," "bad," or "neither good nor bad for Britain," what is revealing is the slightly upward trend in the percentage of those saying "neither good nor bad." Even more revealing is that the number replying "neither good nor bad" is as high as nearly a third of all respondents. If the "don't knows" are added, more than a third of the public is ambivalent about Britain's being a member of the EU.[13]

What explains such widespread ambivalence, and why has it persisted? One might be tempted to say that Britain's island status offers the answer to both parts of this question. Like others who live on islands, Britons tend to see themselves as separate and different and, therefore, special. They are often suspicious of outlanders, sometimes to the point of being xenophobic. And Britain is an island in more than a geographical sense; as its history reveals, although the Continent is a mere channel away, Britons have successfully fended off invasions from the east for a thousand years, nourished a separate language and literature, practiced a different religion, and developed distinctive political and legal institutions and values.

Imbued as Britain's occupants are with an identity that is separate and different from their neighbors on the Continent, it is not surprising that many of them find it difficult to call themselves "European," let alone *feel* "European." Until the 1990s, many of their leading politicians did little to try to dispel these feelings. For example, Winston Churchill, one leader whose influence was felt over several decades of the last century, spoke in the 1930s of "having our own dreams and our own tasks," after which he quickly added: "We are with Europe but not of it." [14] During the war years, however, he seemed to envision a much closer relationship between Britain and the Continent; at the conclusion of the Second World War he even called for a "United States of Europe." In reality, although he thought it important that Britain support an integrated Europe, he thought it equally important that Britain not be part of it.

But Britain is part of it, even though between approximately 25 and 35 percent of the public in recent years have regarded membership as "bad" for Britain.[15] Any effort to win more support for EU membership must appeal not only to the "neither good nor bad" respondents, but the "bad" respondents as well. That is a task Britain's government, its leading politicians, and such pressure groups as Britain in Europe cannot begin to complete until they embark on an imaginative, long-term public education campaign that includes providing answers to the following questions:

- What powers are vested in the EU and how does it use these powers?

- What benefits do Britons derive from the EU?

- How is the EU governed and how does Britain participate in its governance?

If Britain is serious about its commitment to the EU, such a campaign is vital. Without it, many Britons will wonder, quite justifiably, whether Edward Heath did the right thing by taking Britain into this union of European nations all those many years ago and whether the five prime ministers who have succeeded him have done the right thing by keeping the country in.

Notes

Chapter 1 Notes

1. Quoted in Michael Lynch, *Scotland: A New History* (London: Century, 1991), p. 310.
2. Linda Colley, *Britons: Forging the Nation, 1707–1837* (London: Vintage, 1996), pp. 27–29; and *The Oxford Companion to English Literature*, 5th ed., ed. Margaret Drabble (Oxford: Oxford University Press, 1985), pp. 765–766 (John Bunyan) and p. 4 (John Foxe).
3. G.M. Trevelyan, *The English Revolution, 1688–1689* (Oxford: Home University Library, 1938), p. 120.
4. Quoted in Colley, Op. cit., p. 50.
5. Quoted in E.N. Williams, *The Eighteenth Century Constitution* (Cambridge: Cambridge University Press, 1960), p. 56.
6. Colley, Op. cit., p. 58.
7. Quoted in Norman Longmate, *Island Fortress: The Defence of Great Britain, 1603–1945* (London: Hutchinson, 1991), p. 121.
8. Quoted in Longmate, Op. cit., p. 131.
9. Quoted in Ibid., p. 260.
10. Frank O'Gorman, *The Long Eighteenth Century: British Political and Social History, 1688–1832* (London: Arnold, 1997), p. 311.
11. R.F. Foster, *Modern Ireland, 1600–1972* (London: Allen Lane, 1988), p. 280.
12. Quoted in Colley, Op. cit., p. 111.
13. O'Gorman, Op. cit., p. 348, footnote 3.
14. Colley, Op. cit. p. 331.
15. Ibid., p. 325.

16. Sir Wilfred Lawson, "Learn to Think Imperially," in C.C. Eldridge, *The Imperial Experience: From Carlyle to Forster* (London: Macmillan, 1996), p. 3.

17. Colley, Op. cit., p. 61.

18. P.J. Cain and A.G. Hopkins, *British Imperialism: Innovation and Expansion, 1688–1914* (London: Longman Group UK, 1993), p. 89.

19. Colley, Op. cit., p. 69.

20. Keith Robbins, "British Culture versus British Industry," in *British Culture and Economic Decline: Debates in Modern History*, ed. Bruce Collins and Keith Robbins (London: Weidenfeld and Nicolson, 1990), p. 21.

21. Jonathan C.D. Clark, *English Society, 1688–1832: Ideology, Social Structure and Political Practice during the Ancient Regime* (Cambridge: Cambridge University Press, 1985), p. 65.

22. Trevor May, *An Economic and Social History of Britain, 1760–1970* (Harlow: Longman Group UK, 1987) pp. 34, 151.

23. Ibid., p. 34.

24. Ibid., p. 150.

25. Quoted in Keith Robbins, *Nineteenth-Century Britain: Integration and Diversity* (Oxford: Clarendon Press, 1988), p. 18.

26. Robbins, *Nineteenth-Century Britain*, Op. cit., p. 27.

27. Ibid., p. 156.

28. Colley, Op. cit. pp. 42, 233–234.

29. Ibid., p. 43.

30. David Cannadine, "The Context, Performance and Meaning of Ritual: The British Monarchy and the 'Invention of Tradition', c. 1820–1977," in *The Invention of Tradition*, ed. by Eric Hobsbawm and Terence Ranger (Cambridge: Cambridge University Press, 1984), p. 10.

31. Walter Bagehot, *The English Constitution* (London: Fontana/Collins, 1963), p. 94.

32. Robbins, *Nineteenth-Century Britain*, Op. cit., pp. 171–172.

33. O'Gorman, Op. cit., p. 313.

34. Quoted in Cannadine, Op. cit. p. 119.

35. Ibid. p. 123.

36. Ibid. p. 121.

37. Sydney D. Bailey, *British Parliamentary Democracy* (Westport, Conn.: Greenwood Press, 1978), p. 130.

38. Colley, Op. cit., p. 383.

39. Glyn Williams and John Ramsden, *Ruling Britannia: A Political History of Britain, 1688–1988* (Harlow: Longman Group UK, 1990), p. 194.

40. Ibid., p. 254.

41. Martin Pugh, *The Making of Modern British Politics, 1867–1939* (Oxford: Blackwell, 1982), p. 6.

42. W.D. Rubinstein, *Britain's Century: A Political and Social History, 1815–1905* (London: Arnold Publishers, 1998), p. 198.
43. Quoted in D.G. Boyce, " 'The Marginal Britons': The Irish," in *Englishness: Politics and Culture, 1880–1920,* ed. Robert Colls and Philip Dodd (Beckenham: Croom Helm, 1986), p. 236.
44. Ibid., pp. 230–253.
45. Quoted in Magnus Linklater, "Doom Wasn't Nigh at All," *The Times,* December 30, 1999, p. 20.
46. Quoted in Ibid.

Chapter 2 Notes

1. Paul Theroux, *The Kingdom by the Sea* (Harmondsworth: Penguin, 1989).
2. Raphael Samuel, *Island Stories: Unravelling Britain: Theatres of Memory,* Volume II, ed. Alison Light with Sally Alexander and Gareth Jones (London: Verso, 1998), p. 50.
3. Education supplement, *The Guardian,* January 29, 1991, p. 5.
4. Ben Hoyle and Devika Bhat, "A Grieving World in One City as Many Nations Suffer Loss," *The Times,* July 11, 2005, p. 8.
5. Richard Ford, "One in 12 of Population Born in Other Lands," *The Times,* June 15, 2004, p. 15.
6. *Mandla v. Dowell Lee* (1983).
7. Stephen Bevan and Nicholas Rufford, "Is Britain Really a Nation of Racists?" *Sunday Times,* February 28, 1999, p. 15.
8. Ibid.
9. Richard Ford and Stewart Tendler, "Police to Have Ethnic Quota System," *The Times,* February 10, 1999, p. 1.
10. Richard Ford, "Whitehall Urged to Show True Colours," *The Times,* February 8, 1999, p. 6.
11. Frances Gibb, "The Queue for Judges Is Here..." Law supplement, *The Times,* June 29, 2004, p. 10.
12. Laura Smith, "Too Few Black and Asian Faces at the Top," *The Guardian,* November 17, 2005, p. 29.
13. *Election 2005: Turnout: How Many, Who and Why?* (London: The Electoral Commission, 2005), p. 18.
14. Jonathan Petre, "Christianity 'in Crisis' as Pews Empty," *Sunday Telegraph,* November 28, 1999, p. 15.
15. Daniel Snowman, *Kissing Cousins: An Interpretation of British and American Culture, 1945–1975* (London: Maurice Temple Smith, 1977), p. 118.
16. Peter G.J. Pulzer, *Political Representation and Elections in Britain* (London: George Allen & Unwin, 1975), p. 102.
17. Arthur Marwick, *Class: Image and Reality in Britain, France and the USA since 1930* (London: Fontana/Collins, 1981), p. 19.

18. Eric Jacobs and Robert Worcester, *We British: Britain under the MORIscope* (London: Weidenfeld and Nicolson, 1990), p. 140.

19. Ivor Crewe, "The Electorate: Partisan Dealignment Ten Years On," in *Change in British Politics*, ed. Hugh Berrington (London: Frank Cass, 1984).

20. Erik Wright, *Classes* (London: Verso, 1985), p. 43.

21. Ferdinand Mount, "Uppers and Downers," *The Sunday Times*, August 29, 2004, News Review section, p. 2.

22. Alexandra Frean, "Middle Classes Say They Are the Workers Now," *The Times*, August 21, 2002, p. 9.

23. J. Goldthorpe, *Social Mobility and Class Structure in Modern Britain*, 2nd ed. (Oxford: Clarendon Press, 1987).

24. Andrew Adonis and Stephen Pollard, *A Class Act: The Myths of Britain's Classless Society* (London: Penguin, 1997), p. 57.

25. Alexandra Frean, "A Third of Britain's Young Live in Poverty," *The Times*, September 22, 1999, p. 8.

26. "Fighting Child Poverty: A Long Way to Go," *The Economist*, June 17, 2006, p. 31.

27. Polly Toynbee, "We Will Never Abolish Child Poverty in a Society Shaped Like This One," *The Guardian*, July 7, 2006, p. 31.

28. Adonis and Pollard, Op. cit., p. 6.

29. *Disaffected Democracies*, ed. Susan J. Pharr and Robert D. Putnam (Princeton: Princeton University Press, 2000).

Chapter 3 Notes

1. Quoted in Peter Hennessy, *The Hidden Wiring: Unearthing the British Constitution* (London: Indigo, 1996), p. 29

2. Ibid.

3. Walter Bagehot, *The English Constitution* (London: Fontana/Collins, 1963), p. 111.

4. Op cit., p. 65.

5. Quoted in Ibid., p. 65.

6. Stein Rokkan and Derek Urwin, "Introduction: Centres and Peripheries in Western Europe," in *The Politics of Territorial Identity: Studies in European Regionalism*, ed. Stein Rokkan and Derek Urwin (London: Sage, 1982), p. 11.

7. Vernon Bogdanor, *Devolution in the United Kingdom* (Oxford: Oxford University Press, 1999), p. 293.

8. O. Hood Phillips, *Constitutional and Administrative Law*, 6th ed. (London: Sweet & Maxwell, 1978), p. 46.

9. A. V. Dicey, *An Introduction to the Study of the Law of the Constitution*, 10th ed. (London: Macmillan, 1959), pp. 39–40.

10. Philip Norton, *The Constitution in Flux* (Oxford: Martin Robertson, 1982), p. 11.

11. Ferdinand Mount, *The British Constitution Now: Recovery or Decline?* (London: William Heinemann, 1992), p. 193.
12. Ibid., p. 197.
13. Ibid., p. 82.
14. Lord Radcliffe, as quoted in Mount, Op. cit., p. 25.
15. Bagehot, Op. cit., p. 65.
16. Leo Amery, *Thoughts on the Constitution* 2nd ed. (Oxford: Oxford University Press, 1953), p. 28.
17. Bagehot, Op. cit., p. 66.
18. *Judges on Judging*, a Channel 4 British television documentary, February 10, 1989.
19. "Rape of a Wife is Unlawful," *The Guardian*, October 30, 1991, p. 23.
20. *Judges on Judging*, Op. cit.
21. John P. Mackintosh, *The British Cabinet* (London: Stevens & Sons, 1977), p. 13.
22. Geoffrey Marshall and Graeme C. Moodie, *Some Problems of the Constitution*, 5th ed. (London: Hutchinson, 1971), pp. 22–23.
23. Bradley and Ewing, Op. cit. p. 31.
24. *The Changing Constitution*, 4th ed., ed. Jeffrey Jowell and Dawn Oliver (Oxford: Oxford University Press, 2000), p. v.
25. Kenneth C. Wheare, "Walter Bagehot: Lecture on a Master Mind," *Proceedings of the British Academy*, vol. 60 (Oxford: Oxford University Press, 1974), p. 25.
26. Bradley and Ewing, Op. cit.
27. Peter Clarke, "The Edwardians and the Constitution," in *Edwardian England*, ed. Donald Read (Croon Helm: the Historical Association, 1985), p. 46.
28. William Gladstone, *Gleanings of Past Years, 1844–1878*, vol. I (London: John Murray, 1879), p. 245.
29. A. V. Dicey, Op. cit.

Chapter 4 Notes

1. Sydney D. Bailey, *British Parliamentary Democracy*, 3rd ed. (Westport, Conn.: Greenwood Press, 1978), p. 12.
2. Maurice Ashley, *England in the Seventeenth Century: 1603–1714* (Harmondsworth: Penguin, 1961), pp. 145 and 148.
3. Stephen Ingle, *The British Party System*, 2nd ed. (Oxford: Basil Blackwell, 1989), p. 5.
4. E. J. Evans, *Political Parties in Britain, 1783–1867* (London: Methuen, 1985), p. 8.
5. B. W. Hill, "Executive Monarchy and the Challenge of Parties, 1689–1832," *The Historical Journal*, vol. 13, no. 3: p. 396.

6. David Judge, *The Parliamentary State* (London: Sage, 1993), p. 74.
7. Philip Norton, "Opposition to Government," in *The Commons Under Scrutiny,* ed. Michael Ryle and Peter G. Richards (London: Routledge, 1988), p. 100.
8. David Dutton, *British Politics since 1945* (Oxford: Blackwell, 1997), p. 9.
9. Peter Hennessy, *The Prime Minister: The Office and Its Holders since 1945* (London: Lane/Penguin, 2000), p. 356.
10. Quoted in Dennis Kavanagh and Peter Morris, *Consensus Politics: From Attlee to Major,* 2nd ed. (Oxford: Blackwell, 1994), p. 9.
11. Quoted in Steven Fielding, "A New Politics?," in *Developments in British Politics 6,* Patrick Dunleavy et al. (London: Macmillan, 2000), p. 10.
12. Tony Blair, "The Third Way: New Politics for the New Century," Fabian Society Pamphlet No. 588 (London: Fabian Society, 1998).
13. Quoted in Fielding, *Op. cit.,* p. 20.
14. Blair drew from Anthony Giddens, *The Third Way: The Renewal of Social Democracy* (Cambridge: Polity, 1998).
15. Blair, *Op. cit.*
16. Daniel Collings and Anthony Seldon, "Conservatives in Opposition," *Parliamentary Affairs,* vol. 54, no. 4 (October 2001): p. 628.
17. Philip Cowley and Mark Stuart, "More Bleak House Than Great Expectations," *Parliamentary Affairs,* vol. 57, no. 2 (April 2004): p. 311.
18. Ibid., p. 301.
19. Philip Cowley and Mark Stuart, "Hunting for Votes," *Parliamentary Affairs,* vol. 58, no. 2 (April 2005): p. 264.

Chapter 5 Notes

1. *Yes Prime Minister: The Diaries of the Right Hon. James Hacker*, ed. Jonathan Lynn and Antony Jay (London: BBC Publications, 1986), vol. 1, p. 175.
2. Quoted in Peter Madgwick, *A New Introduction to British Politics* (Cheltenham: Stanley Thornes, 1994), p. 41.
3. *Westminster's Secret Service*, BBC2 Television, May 21, 1995.
4. Ibid.
5. Donald D. Searing, *Westminster's World: Understanding Political Roles* (Cambridge, Mass.: Harvard University Press, 1994), pp. 247–249.
6. *Westminster's Secret Service,*" Op. cit.
7. Quoted in Philip Goodhart, *The 1922* (London: Macmillan, 1973), p. 15.
8. Margaret Thatcher, *The Downing Street Years* (London: Harper-Collins, 1995), pp. 185–186.

9. David Cowling, "Keeping Up Appearances," *The House Magazine,* September 30, 1996, p. 34.
10. Stephen Ingle, *The British Party System,* 2nd ed. (Oxford: Blackwell, 1989), p. 5.
11. James Landale and Alice Thomson, "New Model Army Marches in Step to Blair's Tune," *The Times,* September 30, 1996, p. 8.
12. Harold Wilson, *The Governance of Britain* (London: Sphere Books, 1977), p. 200.
13. Patrick Seyd, "Why the Red Rose Must Tend Its Grassroots and Branches," *The Guardian,* June 16, 1992, p. 16. See also Patrick Seyd and Paul Whiteley, *Labour's Grass Roots: The Politics of Party Membership* (Oxford: Oxford University Press, 1992).
14. Julian Critchley, *Westminster Blues* (London: Futura, 1985), p. 92.
15. Quoted in Richard Kelly, "Power and Leadership in the Major Parties," in *Britain's Changing Party System,* ed. Lynton Robins, Hilary Blackmore and Robert Pyper (London: Leicester University Press, 1994), p. 45.
16. Robert Garner and Richard Kelly, *British Political Parties Today* (Manchester: Manchester University Press, 1993), p. 114.

Chapter 6 Notes

1. Arend Lijphart, *Patterns of Democracy: Government Forms and Performance in Thirty-Six Countries* (New Haven: Yale University Press, 1999), p. 177.
2. Samuel E. Finer, *Anonymous Empire* (London: Pall Mall Press, 1958).
3. Harry Eckstein, "The British Political System," in *Patterns of Government,* 2nd ed., Samuel H. Beer and Adam B. Ulam (New York: Random House, 1962), pp. 170–171.
4. G. Jordan and W. Maloney, *The Protest Business? Mobilizing Campaign Groups* (Manchester: Manchester University Press, 1997), p. 192.
5. Geraint Parry, George Moyser, and Neil Day, *Political Participation and Democracy in Britain* (Cambridge: Cambridge University Press, 1992), pp. 286–295.
6. Wyn Grant, *Pressure Groups and British Politics* (New York: St. Martin's Press, 2000), p. 2.
7. Bill Coxall, *Pressure Groups in British Politics* (Harlow: Pearson, 2001), p. 17.
8. Ibid., p. 27.
9. Ibid., p. 98.
10. Andrew Marr, *Ruling Britannia: The Failure and Future of British Democracy* (London: Michael Joseph, 1995), p. 281.
11. *The British Political Process: An Introduction,* ed. Tony Wright (London: Routledge, 2000), p. 290.

Chapter 7 Notes

1. Polly Toynbee and David Walker, *Did Things Get Better? An Audit of Labour's Successes and Failures* (London: Penguin, 2001), p. 6.
2. David Butler and Dennis Kavanagh, *The British General Election of 1997* (Basingstoke: Macmillan, 1997), p. 98.
3. David Butler, *British General Elections since 1945* (Oxford: Blackwell, 1995), p. 96.
4. David Butler and Dennis Kavanagh, *The British General Election of 2001* (Basingstoke: Palgrave, 2001), p. 225.
5. Ibid., pp. 225–226.
6. Dennis Kavanagh, "The United Kingdom," in *Electioneering: A Comparative Study of Continuity and Change,* ed. David Butler and Austin Ranney (Oxford: Clarendon Press, 1992), p. 81.
7. Committee on Standards in Public Life, Fifth Report: The Funding of Political Parties in the United Kingdom, Cmnd. 4057, October 1998, p. 43.
8. Stuart Weir and David Beetham, *Political Power and Democratic Control in Britain: The Democratic Audit of the United Kingdom* (London: Routledge, 1999), p. 88.
9. Electoral Commission, *Election 2001: The Official Results* (London: Politico's, 2001), p. 66.
10. Arend Lijphart, *Electoral Systems and Party Systems* (Oxford: Oxford University Press, 1994).
11. Michael Meadowcroft, "The Politics of Electoral Reform" (London: Electoral Reform Society, November 1991), pp. 14–15.
12. David Butler and Dennis Kavanagh, *The British General Election of 1992* (Basingstoke: Macmillan, 1992), p. 353.
13. Richard Kelly, Oonagh Gay and Isobel White, "The Constitution: Into the Sidings," *Parliamentary Affairs,* vol. 58, no. 2 (April 2005): p. 222.
14. The Electoral Commission, *Election 2005: Turnout: How Many, Who and Why?* (London: The Electoral Commission, 2005), p. 36.
15. John Curtice, "Turnout: Electors Stay Home—Again," *Parliamentary Affairs,* vol. 58, no. 4 (October 2005): p. 778.
16. Ibid., pp. 778–79.
17. The Electoral Commission, *Election 2005*, Op, cit.
18. Curtice, Op. cit., pp. 779–80.
19. The Electoral Commission, *Election 2005*, Op. cit., pp. 29–32.
20. Curtice, Op. cit., pp. 784–85.
21. David Sanders, Harold Clarke, Marianne Stewart, and Paul Whiteley, "The 2005 General Election in Great Britain," a report for the Electoral Commission, August 2005, p. 21.
22. David Butler and Donald Stokes, *Political Change in Britain,* 2nd ed. (Basingstoke: Palgrave Macmillan, 1974), p. 77.

23. David Denver, *Elections and Voters in Britain* (Basingstoke: Palgrave Macmillan, 2003), p. 124.
24. The Electoral Commission, "Election 2005," Op. cit., pp. 40, 46.

Chapter 8 Notes

1. Julian Critchley, *The Palace of Varieties* (London: Faber and Faber, 1990).
2. Philip Norton, *The Commons in Perspective* (Oxford: Basil Blackwell, 1985), p. 13.
3. A. Lawrence Lowell, *The Government of England,* vol. II (London: Macmillan, 1924), pp. 76–78.
4. Leo S. Amery, *Thoughts on the Constitution* (Oxford: Oxford University Press, 1947), p. 12.
5. J.A.G. Griffith and Michael Ryle, *Parliament: Functions, Practice and Procedures* (London: Sweet and Maxwell, 1989), p. 10.
6. Edmund Burke, *Works,* vol. II (Oxford: Oxford University Press, 1906–1907), pp. 164–165.
7. Philip Norton, Op. cit., p. 59.
8. Quoted in Donald D. Searing, *Westminster's World: Understanding Political Roles* (Cambridge, Mass.: Harvard University Press, 1994), p. 155.
9. Quoted in *Westminster and Beyond*, ed. Anthony King and Anne Sloman (London: Macmillan, 1973), pp. 26–27.
10. Searing, Op. cit., pp. 146–147.
11. Quoted in Ibid., p. 155.
12. Ibid., p. 124.
13. Donald Shell, *The House of Lords,* 2nd ed. (London: Harvester Wheatsheaf, 1992), p. 63.
14. Robert Rogers and Rhodri Walters, *How Parliament Works,* 5th ed. (London: Pearson, 2004), p. 280.
15. Lord Hailsham, *The Elective Dictatorship*, the Dimbleby Lecture, BBC1 Television, October 19, 1976.
16. First Report from the Select Committee on Procedure (1977–1978) HC 588, para. 1.5.
17. Stuart Weir and David Beetham, *Political Power and Democratic Control in Britain* (London: Routledge, 1999), p. 373.
18. Austin Mitchell, *The House Magazine,* May 23, 1994, p. 17.
19. Rogers and Walters, Op. cit., p. 219.
20. Donald Shell, "The House of Lords: Time for a Change?" in *British Government and Politics since 1945: Changes in Perspective*, ed. F.F. Ridley and Michael Rush (Oxford: Oxford University Press, 1995), p. 235.
21. Rogers and Walters, Op. cit., p. 219.
22. Ibid., p. 218.

23. Scott Birnbaum, "Could Parliament Be More?," essay submitted for course, British Politics and the European Union, American University London Semester Program, September 1997.
24. Rogers and Walters, Op. cit., p. 335.
25. Robin Cook, *The Point of Departure* (London: Simon & Schuster 2003), p. 153.
26. Rogers and Walters, Op. cit., p. 229.
27. Ibid., p. 231.
28. Ibid., pp. 362–363.
29. Griffith and Ryle, Op. cit., p. 10.

Chapter 9 Notes

1. Michael Foley, *The Rise of the British Presidency* (Manchester: Manchester University Press, 1993), p. 2. [Emphasis this author's.]
2. Margaret Thatcher, *Margaret Thatcher: The Downing Street Years* (London: HarperCollins Publishers, 1993), p. 855.
3. Winston Churchill, *My Early Life: A Roving Commission* (London: Odhams, 1947), p. 22.
4. G.W. Jones, "The Prime Minister's Power," in *The British Prime Minister,* ed. Anthony King (Basingstoke: Macmillan Publishers, 1985), p. 199.
5. Quoted in Dennis Kavanagh, *British Politics: Continuities and Change,* 3rd ed. (Oxford: Oxford University Press, 1996), p. 271.
6. Simon James, *British Cabinet Government* (London: Routledge, 1992), p. 129.
7. Quoted in P.M. Punnett, *British Government and Politics*, 2nd ed. (Aldershot: Dartmouth Publishing 1994), p. 195.
8. James, Op. cit., p. 14.
9. Martin Gilbert, *Never Despair: Winston S. Churchill, 1945–1965* (London: Heinemann, 1988), p. 1118.
10. Peter Riddell, "President Blair and the Commons Denominator," *The Times,* November 26, 2003, p. 24.
11. Quoted in Peter Riddell, *Parliament under Blair* (London: Politico's, 2000), p. 245.
12. Peter Hennessy, Second Gresham College Lecture, November 8, 1994.
13. Thatcher, Op. cit., p. 167.
14. Peter Hennessy, *The Prime Minister: The Office and Its Holders since 1945* (London: Penguin, 2000), p. 80.
15. Ibid., p. 476.
16. Ibid., p. 523.
17. Peter Riddell, "Tories Should Focus on What Really Matters," *The Times,* August 1, 1997, p. 8.
18. Roland Watson, "Mandelson Says Party 'Inflated Claims'," *The Times,* November 2, 2000, p. 15.

19. James Barber, *The Prime Minister since 1945* (Oxford: Blackwell, 1991), p. 71.
20. Quoted in John P. Mackintosh, *The British Cabinet,* 3rd ed. (London: Stevens & Sons, 1977), p. 504–505.
21. Hennessy, Op. cit., p. 482.
22. Stuart Weir and David Beetham, *Political Power and Democratic Control in Britain* (London: Routledge, 1999), p. 132.
23. James, Op. cit., p. 181.
24. Lord Lawson and Lord Armstrong of Ilminster, "Cabinet Government in the Thatcher Years," *Contemporary Record,* vol. 8, no. 3 (winter 1994): p. 443.
25. James Naughtie, *The Rivals: The Intimate Story of a Political Marriage* (London: Fourth Estate, 2001), p. 104.
26. Jack Cunningham, in "The Top Job," BBC Radio 4, October 23, 2000.
27. "The Butler Report," supplement to *The Independent,* July 15, 2004, p. VII.
28. Anthony Sampson, *Who Runs This Place? An Anatomy of Britain in the 21st Century* (London: John Murray, 2005), p. 107.
29. "The Butler Report," Op. cit.
30. Lord Butler, as interviewed by Boris Johnson, "How Not to Run a Country," *The Spectator,* December 11, 2004, p. 13.
31. Naughtie, Op. cit., p. 105.
32. Peter Riddell, *The Unfulfilled Prime Minister: Tony Blair's Quest for a Legacy* (London: Politico's, 2005), p. 44; and Naughtie, Op cit., p. 111.
33. Naughtie, Op. cit., pp. 69–75; Riddell, Op. cit., p. 18.
34. Gerald Kaufman, *How To Be a Minister* (London: Faber and Faber, 1997), p. 34.
35. Colin Thain and Maurice Wright, *The Treasury and Whitehall* (Oxford: Clarendon Press, 1995), p. 104.
36. George Jones, "Mrs Thatcher and the Power of the PM," *Contemporary Record,* vol. 3, no. 4 (April 1990), pp. 2, 5, and 6; and George Jones, "Prime Minister and Cabinet," in *Wroxton Papers in Politics* (Oxfordshire: Wroxton College, 1990), p. 13.
37. Foley, Op. cit., pp. 282 and 283.
38. Quoted in Hennessy, Op. cit., p. 48.
39. Weir and Beetham, Op. cit., p. 148.
40. The Earl of Oxford and Asquith, *Fifty Years of Parliament,* vol. 2 (London: Cassell, 1926), p. 185.
41. Jones, "The Prime Minister's Power," Op. cit., p. 216.

Chapter 10 Notes

1. Lynn Barber, "Harriet Harman: Will She Jump?" *Observer Life,* May 31, 1998, p. 4.

2. Robert Armstrong, "The Duties and Responsibilities of Civil Servants in Relation to Ministers," in *Ministerial Responsibility*, ed. Geoffrey Marshall (Oxford: Oxford University Press, 1989), p. 141.

3. Quoted in Geoffrey Marshall, "Introduction," in *Ministerial Responsibility,* Ibid., p. 7.

4. Quoted in Diana Woodhouse, *Ministers and Parliament: Accountability in Theory and Practice* (Oxford: Oxford University Press, 1994), p. 154.

5. "Taking Forward Continuity and Change" (London: Her Majesty's Stationery Office), Cmnd. 2748 (January 1995), p. 28.

6. Public Service Committee, "Ministerial Accountability and Responsibility" (London: Her Majesty's Stationery Office), Session 1995–1996, HC 313, vol. 1, paragraph 21.

7. Stuart Weir and David Beetham, *Political Power and Democratic Control in Britain* (London: Routledge, 1999), p. 339.

8. Woodhouse, Op. cit., p. 157.

9. "Public War of Words over Private Sector Policy," *The Times,* July 8, 1999, p. 6.

10. Gerald Kaufman, *How To Be a Minister* (London: Faber and Faber, 1997), p. 41.

11. Ibid., p. 14.

12. Quoted in Dennis Kavanagh and David Richards, "Departmentalism and Joined-up Government: Back to the Future?" *Parliamentary Affairs,* vol. 54, no. 1 (January 2001): p. 10.

13. Colin Pilkington, *The Civil Service in Britain Today* (Manchester: Manchester University Press, 1999), p. 72.

14. Ibid., p. 81.

15. Quoted in Gavin Drewry, "The New Public Management," in *The Changing Constitution,* 4th ed, ed. Jeffrey Jowell and Dawn Oliver (Oxford: Oxford University Press, 2000), p. 185.

16. Quoted in Robert Pyper, *The British Civil Service* (Hemel Hempstead: Prentice Hall/Harvester Wheatsheaf, 1995), p. 183.

17. Quoted in Peter Riddell, *Parliament under Blair* (London: Politico's, 2000), p. 84.

18. Margaret Thatcher, *The Downing Street Years* (London: Harper-Collins, 1993), p. 677.

19. Peter Riddell, "Where Do We Point the Finger?" *The Times,* January 16, 1995, p. 18.

20. Camilla Cavendish, "I've Just Found That Hole They're Pouring Our Taxes Into," *The Times,* December 20, 2003, p. 22.

21. Weir and Beetham, Op. cit., pp. 201 and 221.

22. Ibid, pp. 220 and 223.

23. Lewis Smith, "Public Misled over Danger of Crop Spraying," *The Times,* September 23, 2005, p. 33.

Chapter 11 Notes

1. John Stewart, *The Nature of British Local Government* (London: Macmillan, 2000), p. 95.
2. Malcolm Grant, "Central-Local Relations: The Balance of Power," in *The Changing Constitution,* 2nd ed., ed. Jeffrey Jowell and Dawn Oliver (Oxford: Clarendon Press, 1989), p. 272.
3. Martin Loughlin, "The Restructuring of Central-Local Government Relations," in *The Changing Constitution,* 4th ed., ed. Jeffrey Jowell and Dawn Oliver (Oxford: Oxford University Press, 2000), p. 141.
4. Stuart Weir and David Beetham, *Political Power and Democratic Control in Britain* (London: Routledge, 1999), p. 247.
5. Tony Byrne, *Local Government in Britain,* 7th ed. (London: Penguin, 2000), p. 463.
6. Quoted in David Wilson, "Local Government: Diversity and Uniformity," *Parliamentary Affairs,* vol. 54, no. 2 (April 2001): p. 295.
7. *The Economist,* May 18, 2002, p. 14.
8. Byrne, Op. cit., p. 190.
9. Ibid., pp. 322 and 690–691 (footnote 59).
10. Vernon Bogdanor, *Devolution in the United Kingdom* (Oxford: Oxford University Press, 1999), p. 1.
11. Robert McCreadie, "Scottish Identity and the Constitution," in *National Identities: The Constitution of the United Kingdom,* ed. Bernard Crick (Oxford: Blackwell Publishers, 1991), p. 43.
12. Dafydd Elis Thomas, "The Constitution of Wales," in *National Identities,* Ibid., p. 57.
13. Jonathan Bradbury and James Mitchell, "Devolution: New Politics for Old?" *Parliamentary Affairs,* vol. 54, no. 2 (April 2001): p. 267.
14. *The Economist,* Op. cit.
15. Christopher Harvie, "English Regionalism: The Dog That Never Barked," in Crick, Op. cit., pp. 105–118.
16. Peter Hetherington, "Soundings on Devolution in England," *The Guardian,* December 3, 2002, p. 12.

Chapter 12 Notes

1. A.V. Dicey, *An Introduction to the Study of the Law of the Constitution,* 10th ed. (London: Macmillan, 1959), p. 189.
2. A.W. Bradley and K.D. Ewing, *Constitutional and Administrative Law,* 11th ed. (London: Longman, 1993), p. 102.
3. Dicey, Op. cit., p. 188.
4. Ibid.
5. Ibid., p. 193.
6. Ibid.
7. Ibid., p. 195.

8. Paul Denham, *Law: A Modern Introduction* (London: Hodder and Stoughton, 1994), p. 135.

9. Gavin Drewry, *Law, Justice and Politics* (London: Longman, 1981), p. 31.

10. Trevor Grove, *The Magistrates' Tale* (London: Bloomsbury, 1998), p. 207.

11. Helena Kennedy, *Just Law* (London: Vintage, 2005), pp. 133–135.

12. Quoted in Colin Turpin, *British Government and the Constitution: Text, Cases and Materials,* 4th ed. (London: Butterworths, 1999), p. 51.

13. Quoted in David Pannick, "Lord Chancellors Should Leave the Judiciary to the Pros," Law supplement, *The Times,* March 12, 2002, p. 8.

14. Peter Madgwick and Diana Woodhouse, *The Law and Politics of the Constitution of the United Kingdom* (London: Harvester Wheatsheaf, 1995), p. 101.

15. Daniel Lightman, "Lord Chancellor and Master of the Multifarious Roles," Law supplement, *The Times,* February 27, 2001, p. 3.

16. Frances Gibb, "Irvine Can't Be a Judge, Says Human Rights Report," *The Times,* March 3, 2003, p. 1.

17. Lord Alexander of Weedon, "Is This a Ruthless Grab for Power?" Law supplement, *The Times,* July 1, 2003, p. 3.

18. Quoted in Richard Ford, "Blunkett and Irvine Scrap over Bad Behaviour Bill," *The Times,* April 21, 2003, p. 8.

19. Rabinder Singh, "Modest Steps to Entrench Judicial Independence," Law supplement, *The Times,* September 14, 2004, p. 7.

20. David Pannick, "Why Judicial Independence Must Be Preserved," Law supplement, *The Times,* June 24, 2003, p. 4.

21. Speech by the Lord Chief Justice of England and Wales at the Lord Mayor's Dinner for HM Judges, July 21, 2004.

22. Quoted in Frances Gibb, "Falconer Pledge on Freedom of Judges," *The Times,* December 4, 2003, p. 2.

23. Frances Gibb, "Honest and Able but Undone by Hint of Cronyism," *The Times,* February 20, 2001, p. 4; and James Landale, "Lords to Question Irvine Role in 'Cash for Wigs'," *The Times,* February 20, 2001, p. 4.

24. J.A.G. Griffiths, *The Politics of the Judiciary* (London: Fontana, 1977), pp. 272–273.

25. Frances Gibb, "The People's Judge: Lord Denning Celebrates His Centenary," *The Times,* January 26, 1999, p. 43.

26. Quoted in Turpin, Op. cit., p. 371.

27. Quoted in Ibid., p. 346. [Emphasis this author's.]

28. "Law Report: 'Detention of Foreign Suspects is Incompatible'," *The Times,* December 17, 2004, p. 78.

29. Frances Gibb and Richard Ford, "Judges Angry over Attacks by Ministers," *The Times,* November 3, 1995, p. 1.

30. Lord Taylor, *The Judiciary in the Nineties,* the Dimbleby Lecture, BBC 1 Television, November 30, 1992.
31. Frances Gibb and Richard Ford, "Blair's Crime Crackdown Won't Work, Says Law Chief," *The Times,* May 17, 2002, p. 1.
32. Philip Webster and Frances Gibb, "Blair Baits Judges over Slow Justice," *The Times,* October 12, 2005, p. 33.
33. Michael Beloff, "The Human Rights Act: One Year On," Law supplement, *The Times,* October 2, 2001, p. 9.

Chapter 13 Notes

1. Quoted in Sir William Nicoll and Trevor C. Salmon, *Understanding the European Union* (London: Longman, 2001), p. 452.
2. Ernest Wistrich, *The United States of Europe* (London: Routledge, 1994), p. 33.
3. Colin Pilkington, *Britain in the European Union Today* (Manchester: Manchester University Press, 1995), p. 40.
4. Stephen George, *Politics and Policy in the European Union,* 3rd ed. (Oxford: Oxford University Press, 1996), p. 12.
5. Anthony Browne and Charles Bremner, "Blair Invisible on Europe, Say Critics," *The Times,* September 22, 2005, p. 41.
6. Anthony Browne, "'I Have Moved on from New Labour,'" *The Times,* October 5, 2004, p. 14.
7. Although "Council of the European Union" is the new name of the Council of Ministers, it is commonly called by its old name, probably to differentiate it from the European Council and possibly to underscore who its members are—the ministers of the various governments.
8. Simon Hix, "Britain, the EU and the Euro," in *Developments in British Politics 6,* Patrick Dunleavy et al. (London: Macmillan, 2000), p. 48.
9. Colin Turpin, *British Government and the Constitution: Text, Cases and Materials,* 4th ed. (London: Butterworths, 1999), p. 353.
10. Ibid.
11. Robert Rogers and Rhodri Walters, *How Parliament Works,* 5th ed. (London: Pearson, 2004), p. 357–358.
12. Peter Riddell, *Parliament under Blair* (London: Politico's, 2000), p. 21.
13. *British Political Opinion 1937–2000: The Gallup Polls,* ed. Anthony King (London: Politico's, 2001), pp. 301–302.
14. Quoted in Pilkington, Op. cit., p. 8.
15. King, Op. cit.

Index

Figures and tables are denoted by "f" and "t."